New Sudans

Over a million southern Sudanese people fled to Sudan's capital Khartoum during the wars and famines of the 1980s, 1990s, and 2000s. This book is an intellectual history of these war-displaced working people's political organising and critical theory during a long conflict. It explores how these people thought through their circumstances, tried to build potential political communities, and imagined possible futures. Based on ten years of research in South Sudan, using personal stories, private archives, songs, poetry, photograph albums, self-written histories, jokes, and new handmade textbooks, *New Sudans* follows its idealists' and pragmatists' variously radical, conservative, and creative projects across two decades on the peripheries of a hostile city. Through everyday theories of Blackness, freedom, and education in a long civil war, Nicki Kindersley opens up new possibilities in postcolonial intellectual histories of the working class in Africa.

NICKI KINDERSLEY is Senior Lecturer in African History in the School of History, Archaeology and Religion at Cardiff University. She was previously a Harry F. Guggenheim Research Fellow at Pembroke College, University of Cambridge, and holds a PhD from Durham University.

African Studies Series

The African Studies series, founded in 1968, is a prestigious series of monographs, general surveys, and textbooks on Africa covering history, political science, anthropology, economics, and ecological and environmental issues. The series seeks to publish work by senior scholars as well as the best new research.

Editorial Board

David Anderson, *The University of Warwick*
Carolyn Brown, *Rutgers University, New Jersey*
Christopher Clapham, *University of Cambridge*
Richard L. Roberts, *Stanford University, California*
Leonardo A. Villalón, *University of Florida*

Other titles in the series are listed at the back of the book.

New Sudans

Wartime Intellectual Histories in Khartoum

NICKI KINDERSLEY
Cardiff University

CAMBRIDGE
UNIVERSITY PRESS

CAMBRIDGE
UNIVERSITY PRESS

Shaftesbury Road, Cambridge CB2 8EA, United Kingdom

One Liberty Plaza, 20th Floor, New York, NY 10006, USA

477 Williamstown Road, Port Melbourne, VIC 3207, Australia

314–321, 3rd Floor, Plot 3, Splendor Forum, Jasola District Centre, New Delhi – 110025, India

103 Penang Road, #05-06/07, Visioncrest Commercial, Singapore 238467

Cambridge University Press is part of Cambridge University Press & Assessment, a department of the University of Cambridge.

We share the University's mission to contribute to society through the pursuit of education, learning and research at the highest international levels of excellence.

www.cambridge.org
Information on this title: www.cambridge.org/9781009422376

DOI: 10.1017/9781009422383

© Nicki Kindersley 2024

This publication is in copyright. Subject to statutory exception and to the provisions of relevant collective licensing agreements, no reproduction of any part may take place without the written permission of Cambridge University Press & Assessment.

When citing this work, please include a reference to the DOI 10.1017/9781009422383

First published 2024

A catalogue record for this publication is available from the British Library.

A Cataloging-in-Publication data record for this book is available from the Library of Congress

ISBN 978-1-009-42237-6 Hardback

Cambridge University Press & Assessment has no responsibility for the persistence or accuracy of URLs for external or third-party internet websites referred to in this publication and does not guarantee that any content on such websites is, or will remain, accurate or appropriate.

For my father Peter Torin Kindersley

Contents

List of Figures	page x
Acknowledgements	xi
List of Abbreviations	xiii

	Introduction	1
	I.1 Intellectual Life in Khartoum: Displaced Workers' Political Thought	2
	I.2 Fragmented Political Possibilities, 1983–2005	6
	I.3 Race, and Ideas of a Black Future	9
	I.4 Teaching and Learning New Sudans	13
	I.5 Histories of Urban Refuge	15
	I.6 Methodology and Positionality	20
	I.7 Structure of the Book	26
1	Dar es Salaam: Flight and the Fight for Space in Khartoum, 1988–1992	29
	1.1 The War Reaches Khartoum	34
	1.2 Emergency Reconstruction	36
	1.3 Old Black Khartoum	40
	1.4 The Golden Age of Migrant Khartoum	44
	1.5 Social Life and Mutual Aid in the Early 1980s	51
	1.6 Claiming Space after Disaster	53
2	Building Marginalisation in the Displaced City	58
	2.1 Challenging the Heartland	59
	2.2 Fighting for Space	66
	2.3 Alienation, Removal, Subjugation, and Performance: The Civilising Project in Practice	73
	2.4 Policing Public Space	78
	2.5 The Utility of the Underclass	82
	2.6 Economic Pacification	84
	2.7 The Limits of Acculturation: Direct Violence	89
	2.8 On the Peripheries	92

3	**Community Space and Self-Defence**	95
	3.1 Risks and Mutual Self-Help	98
	3.2 Asserting Authority: Chiefs, Neighbourhood Committees, and Intermediaries	101
	3.3 New Neighbourhoods and Making Community	108
	3.4 The Space Available	110
	3.5 Black Khartoum	115
	3.6 New Ideas and Free Women	121
	3.7 Women's Black Skin	129
	3.8 Managing Change and Controlling Behaviour	134
	3.9 Cultural Organising and Reasserted Patriarchy	137
	3.10 Conclusion	140
4	**Alternative Education**	142
	4.1 A Critical Education	145
	4.2 Educational Associational Life	150
	4.3 Displaced Schools	157
	4.4 The Teachers	164
	4.5 Rewriting the Curriculum and Making History	171
	4.6 Linguistic Competition and Collaboration	173
	4.7 Conclusion: Education and New Knowledge	176
5	**Intellectual Work and Political Thought on the Peripheries**	178
	5.1 Texts and Translation	183
	5.2 Discursive Worlds	185
	5.3 Brave Writing	189
	5.4 Painful Histories	192
	5.5 A Political Education	197
	5.6 Building Political Community	209
	5.7 Fighting for What?	214
	5.8 The Limits to Solidarity	220
	5.9 On Sell-Outs and New Societies	223
	5.10 Conclusion	227
6	**Akut Kuei and Wartime Mobilisation**	230
	6.1 Underground Politics	232
	6.2 Talking Shop	237
	6.3 Class Privilege, Social Divides, and Separate Political Spaces	246
	6.4 The Working-Class Underground	250
	6.5 Akut Kuei	251
	6.6 Jongo	256
	6.7 Conclusion	260

7	Military Independence and Khartoum's Warlord Communities	263
	7.1 Everyday Self-Defence and Government Employment	265
	7.2 Ashara Wilayat	268
	7.3 Southern Militias: Independence on Other Terms	270
	7.4 Abdel Bagi Ayii Akol	272
	7.5 Militias and Economic Organisation	277
	7.6 Military Work	281
	7.7 Conclusion	284
8	Return to the South, 2005–2011	288
	8.1 Black Monday	289
	8.2 Return and Reconstruction in the South	293
	8.3 South Sudan's Trajectories	298
	8.4 The Hard Questions of the Future	302
	Conclusion: Intellectual Histories for Other Possibilities	305
	C.1 Reflections on South Sudan's Political Path	308
Bibliography		310
Index		336

Figures

I.1 Map of Sudan, 2010	*page* xiv
1.1 Map of Khartoum, 1987	37
2.1 Displaced people's settlements in the Greater Khartoum area, c. 2009	65
3.1 Angelina and friend, dancing in Comboni dormitory, late 1990s	128
3.2 Angelina and friend, posing in African wax print tailoring, at home in Khartoum, mid-1990s	133
5.1 Friends of Angelina selling their books of writing and poetry on a stall in Haj Yousif, c. 2000	182

Acknowledgements

So many people across South Sudan have shared their time, knowledge, and work for this project, and I hope that I have represented this knowledge and work with some justice here. I owe this book to my friends and advisors Joseph 'Gai Thok' Tong Ngor, his wife Ahok and kind cousin Abuk Deng, and to Joseph Malual, Ayak, and your wonderful family. I have relied on the good advice of the late Lazarus 'Makom' Lual Bol Ker, Deng Daniel, Dau Maduok, Dominic Chol Autiak Malek, Angelina Majok Juac, Diing Chen Diing, Marco Mathiang Deng, and Lual Lual Aguer Ayam. Thank you also to the Maper Akot chess club, and to Josephine, Awen, Raja, Susan, and Bakhita for your coffee and kindness. Dr Richard Tongu Loboka has been a guide and friend throughout. Paulino Dhieu Tem and the late, lamented Santino Garang Akot have been patient and generous with their expertise, and I am extremely grateful to Parek Madut Jok, Ngor Santino Akech Chol, and Wol Aluk Chol for their energy and thoughtfulness working on translations of songs and poetry.

I am grateful to be part of Juba's archive community: Youssef Onyalla, Becu Thomas Alex, Opoka Musa Obalim, Nyarek Youannes Reik, James Lujang Marino, Aluel Isaiah Kulang, Peter Tako Angelo, Susan Keji Richard, and Paska Kejji Massimo, and the late, great Edward Jubara. It has been an immense privilege to work with Douglas H. Johnson in the archives and after, and I am always grateful for his patience with me. My much-missed late teacher Wafa'a Housseini is still an inspiration. At the University of Juba, Leben Moro, Yosa Wawa, Rebecca Lorins, Elfatih Atem, Christopher Oringa, Chaplain Kenyi, and the late Edward Yakobo Momo have all provided invaluable advice, reassurance, and friendship over the too-many years of this project.

This book rests on a doctoral project that relied on the patience, encouragement, attention, and trust of my long-suffering doctoral supervisors Justin Willis and Cherry Leonardi. I have been extremely lucky to have their time and knowledge. Work for this project depended on the support, experience, and guidance of Jok Madut Jok, John Ryle, Paul Lane, Wendy James, and Jane Hogan, Derek Peterson and Sharath Srinivasan, and the friendship and kindness of a wide and wonderful research community: Zoe Cormack, Feri Dávid Marko, Mohamed A. G. Bakhit, Naomi Pendle, Harriet Kuyang Logo, Eddie Thomas, Øystein Rolandsen, Laura Mann, Martina Santschi, Peter Hakim Justin, Diana Felix da Costa, Sebabatso Manoeli, Jane Hogan, Joshua Craze, Angela Impey, Dan Large, Christopher Tounsel, Willow Berridge, Chris Vaughan, Matthew Benson, Tamador Khalid-Abdalla, Brendan Tuttle, Loes Ljinders, Poppy Cullen, Reetta Humalajoki, Ade Browne, Sarah Marriott, and many others. At the University of Cambridge, I am grateful for the kindness and patience of Tim Harper, Sertaç Sehlikoglu, and Surer Mohamed.

The Rift Valley Institute in Juba has provided invaluable support and a warm home over the lifetime of this project, and I am incredibly grateful for the energy, care, and creativity of Anna Rowett, Mawa Musa, Alex Miskin Simple, Machot Amuom Malou, Elizabeth Nyibol Malou, Mawal Marko Gatkuoth, Ohide Johnson, Mimi Bior, and Magnus Taylor. Joseph Diing Majok is a patient advisor and a brilliant research partner.

The Economic and Social Research Council UK made this project financially possible, and I am grateful also for the financial support of the Royal Historical Society; Durham University's Hatfield College, History Department, and the Institute for Hazard, Risk and Resilience; the Department of Law and Anthropology at the Max Planck Institute for Social Anthropology; and the Harry F. Guggenheim Foundation through their Research Fellowship at Pembroke College, Cambridge. The work would not have been possible without the logistical support of AECOM, the United Methodist Committee on Relief (UMCOR), and the Rift Valley Institute.

Finally, I am always grateful for the worried but constant support of my late father Peter Kindersley and my mother Linda Kindersley. In Cardiff, the book found final form among my small radical family: thank you to Rebecca Wilks, Adam Watkins, Ella Wilkinson, Nora, and all my union friends, and thank you forever to Rob Doherty for your humour and patience.

Abbreviations

ANF	African National Front
AYU	Aweil Youth Union
CPA	Comprehensive Peace Agreement
IDP	internally displaced persons
JIU	Joint Integrated Units
NAM	National Action Movement
NCP	National Congress Party
NDA	National Democratic Alliance
NIF	National Islamic Front
NSF	National Salvation Front
OLS	Operation Lifeline Sudan
PDF	Popular Defence Forces
RRC	Relief and Rehabilitation Commission
SAF	Sudan Armed Forces
SANU	Sudan African National Union
SCC	Sudan Council of Churches
SOLO	Sudan Open Learning Organisation
SPLM/A	Sudan People's Liberation Movement/Army
SSDF	Southern Sudan Defence Forces
USAP	Union of Southern African Parties

Figure I.1 Map of Sudan, 2010.
By Kate Kirkwood for the Rift Valley Institute.

Introduction

Sudan is our country, our country
Sudan is the land of the Black people
We shall struggle for it.
             Akut Kuei, 'Thudän ee Panda' (Sudan our country)[1]

In August 2013, I was sat drinking sweet black tea with Dhieu, who was then a history teacher and the headmaster of Mayen Ulem village school in now-independent South Sudan, while we watched his young daughters play on their family farm. Dhieu had grown up in refugee camps in Darfur, after his mother Abuk had fled north with him and his siblings to escape armed raids on their village just outside the railway town of Wadweil in about 1987. He then moved to a neighbourhood on the edge of Haj Yousif in Khartoum North to pursue secondary school education in the late 1990s. Dhieu had been telling me about selling cigarettes to get cash for school supplies. I asked Dhieu what he remembered wanting to happen in Sudan, back in around 2000, when he finally graduated from secondary school:

We didn't think of secession ... at that moment, in Khartoum, we were thinking of the total liberation of the country, so that the Islamists will be smashed out of the country and the country will stay united – and people will practice democracy.... But in 1999, because that principle of self-determination was granted in peace negotiations which were held in Nairobi ... they [Sudan People's Liberation Movement/Army (SPLM/A)

---

[1] Lyrics in Dinka in a pamphlet of Akut Kuei songs in November 2003, typed by the teacher Lino Alëu Anic Dut for the Dinka Cultural Society Committee as a 'trial edition' of the Khartoum Workshop Programme. There were a small number of photocopied and stapled pamphlets with thin cardboard covers produced, with cartoons by a now-unknown artist. The Akut Kuei songwriter James Akec Nhial provided initial English-language translation notes, and the pamphlet was collaboratively translated with Parek Madut Jok, Ngor Santino Akech Chol, and Wol Aluk Chol in 2014.

supporters] said that it is better for southerners to get away from Sudan, because the country isn't going to be entirely liberated, and Arab ideology won't end in the country, unless we go – so that we can make our own state.... And people began to discuss this. And we felt worried about such a thing. We thought that if the SPLA was able to liberate the whole country, this would be a success. But if not, then this idea of separation will fail.

... and the change which is going on now, in our new [South Sudan] government, it is what? It is a false change. It is not an *environmental* change.[2]

This book explores the intellectual histories of southern Sudanese people displaced to Sudan's capital Khartoum over the second Sudanese war in the 1980s to 2000s. It addresses how people were trying to think through their circumstances and possible ways out of them, and trying to organise potential political communities towards these futures. It aims to incorporate the political thought of displaced people surviving a long war and impoverished urban working lives into intellectual history. This is also a history of Khartoum neighbourhoods that have since dispersed and (mostly) returned south since the end of this war in 2005, and of their ideas, projects, and hopes that have now been lost, or rendered impossible.

This book contains fragments of just a few of the (variously radical and defensive) projects of people trying to take some kind of action within about two decades of fast personal and political change and sustained violence, on the displaced peripheries of a hostile capital. This includes histories of idealist, radical, inclusive imagined futures, as well as more limited and supposedly pragmatic projects of ethnic self-defence. It tries to detail how people worked to convince themselves and each other about what was possible, and about the limits of potential change and better futures.

I.1 Intellectual Life in Khartoum: Displaced Workers' Political Thought

This book is part of a growing field of African intellectual history, which is often focused on predominantly written cultures of modern

---

[2] Dhieu Kuel, in Mayen Ulem, 21 August 2013, speaking in English.

I.1 Intellectual Life in Khartoum

political thought.[3] This book moves away from print media and university spaces, towards only partially written intellectual projects that circulated via evening study groups, courts, and 'multi-purpose' meeting shelters; privately-funded primary and secondary schools; church yards; and dance groups within the heavily surveilled peripheries of wartime Khartoum. These are the creative spaces of this book's over-stretched and stressed southern Sudanese thinkers, who made up (and still partly make up) the working poor of the city.

For this field, and for studies of South Sudan especially, a focus on the intellectual life of working-class people within wars is important. Often histories of wartime political thought focus on the war's political protagonists – its military intelligentsia, religious and political organisers, and commentators – and their next generation of university students and ambitious graduates.[4] In South Sudan in particular, this approach risks supporting a common simplification: that the region's

---

[3] Emma Hunter and Leslie James, 'Introduction: Colonial Public Spheres and the Worlds of Print', *Itinerario* 44, no. 2 (2020): 227–42; Emma Hunter et al., 'Another World? East Africa, Decolonisation, and the Global History of the Mid-Twentieth Century', *Journal of African History* 62, no. 3 (2021): 394–410; Nate Plageman, 'Recomposing the Colonial City: Music, Space, and Middle-Class City Building in Sekondi, Gold Coast c. 1900–1920', *Interventions* 22, no. 8 (2019): 1013–31; Adom Getachew, *Worldmaking after Empire: The Rise and Fall of Self-Determination* (Princeton University Press, 2019); Emma Hunter, *Political Thought and the Public Sphere in Tanzania* (Cambridge University Press, 2015); *African Print Cultures: Newspapers and Their Publics in the Twentieth Century* (University of Michigan Press, 2016); Derek R. Peterson, *Creative Writing: Translation, Bookkeeping, and the Work of Imagination in Colonial Kenya*, Social History of Africa (Heinemann, 2004); Derek R. Peterson and Giacomo Macola, eds., *Recasting the Past: History Writing and Political Work in Modern Africa* (Ohio University Press, 2009); Jonathon Glassman, *War of Words, War of Stones: Racial Thought and Violence in Colonial Zanzibar* (Indiana University Press, 2011); James R. Brennan, 'Blood Enemies: Exploitation and Urban Citizenship in the Nationalist Political Thought of Tanzania, 1958–75', *Journal of African History* 47, no. 3 (2006): 389–413; Stephanie Newell, 'Articulating Empire: Newspaper Readerships in Colonial West Africa', *New Formations* 73 (2011): 26–42.

[4] For example, Hodgkinson and Melchiorre, 'Introduction: Student Activism in an Era of Decolonization', *Africa* 89, no. S1 (2019): S1–S14; Elleni Centime Zeleke, *Ethiopia in Theory: Revolution and Knowledge Production, 1964–2016* (Brill, 2019); Mélanie Lindbjerg Guichon, '(Black) Neo-colonialism and Rootless African Elites: Tracing Conceptions of Global Inequality in the Writings of George Ayittey and Kwesi Kwaa Prah, 1980s–1990s', *Intellectual History Review* 32, no. 4 (2022): 737–60; Gideon Boadu, 'Change and Continuity in Ghana's Intellectual History: From Late 19th Century to the Eras of Decolonisation and Independence', *African Studies* 78, no. 4 (2019): 457–76.

collective future was only really discussed by a tiny political and military leadership who mobilised the 'ordinary' masses.[5] In this reading, everyday South Sudanese people become subject to these often-violent national political projects, because they were instead focused either – viewed ungenerously – on their own ethnic and local priorities, or – more realistically – on community protection and moral order in the face of extractive and violent national regimes. Either way, this view underestimates or ignores the intellectual agency of most South Sudanese people. It drastically narrows our view of the field of political action, and misses a sprawling history of the intellectual life of people working through wars.

This book challenges materialist and instrumentalist analyses that dominate studies of civil wars and violent authoritarian states in Africa. It abandons patrons and their clients, and does not itemise drivers of conflict or conflict actors. The book instead challenges the marginalisation of African histories of ideas in dominant political theory by demonstrating how working people's thinking and discussions shaped action and set – or challenged – the boundaries of what was considered possible. An intellectual historical approach allows us to explore the terms, assumptions, and principles that evolved over time within the web of conflicts, brutalities, and often-grim work that made up the civil war. It challenges neat post-hoc determinations of what the war was over and for, who it was fought by, and who gets to explain it. Intellectual histories of conflict allow us to escape the determinism of neopatrimonial analysis by exploring paths not taken, half-finished projects, and disputed terms, which destabilise assumptions about where power lies.[6] This rich intellectual terrain might also offer some ideas about the often-depressing fields of postcolonial conflict and state collapse: even in the most inauspicious times for political imagination, working people have been building ideas that sit in exercise books, suitcases, cupboards, photo albums, cassette tapes, and MP3s on mobile phones, and these are live projects.

This book is therefore an effort to emphasise the intellectual creativity of displaced people working at the deeply stressful edges of a

---

[5] This is a common characterisation. Jok Madut Jok, *Sudan: Race, Religion and Violence* (Oneworld, 2005), 35–36.

[6] See also Emma Hunter, 'Dialogues between Past and Present in Intellectual Histories of Mid-Twentieth-Century Africa', *Modern Intellectual History*, 22 June 2022, 1–9.

I.1 Intellectual Life in Khartoum

wartime political economy. It focuses on majority southern Sudanese displaced neighbourhoods in Khartoum, where in the humanitarian literature these residents were apparently entirely 'politically passive' in the wars of the 1990s and 2000s.[7] This was of course not true: these neighbourhoods' political work was publicly quiet because it mostly did not involve direct confrontation with the Sudanese state on its doorstep, and focused more on creating safe spaces for projects of different types of liberation. Drawing on songs, poetry, photograph albums, jokes, self-made textbooks, and history pamphlets, and wide discussions with tea ladies, porters, builders, farm labourers, bricklayers, bakers, primary teachers, civil servants, office clerks, and cleaners, this book works to set their intellectual histories within the cardboard-constructed homes, shacks on building sites, precariously rented houses, bakeries, and brick-laying sites on the Nile, and in the dusty displaced camps on the edges of Khartoum, which offered some personal freedoms at the expense of some economic security. It traces people on pathways through Darfur and Kordofan that let people go to fight, to work, to old and new homes, and to paths beyond Sudan.

These people have been variously called 'popular urbanists', 'peasant intellectuals', and so on in recent academic work on everyday political thought.[8] Here, however, I avoid a collective label, as there is no real collective class to describe. These residents move widely, across the city and beyond, and do a range of types of work and thinking. Their projects draw on rural and urban terms, languages, and references. Different people whose work is presented here explain personal categorisations and class structures in various different ways, which I do not want to try to contain within an academic phrase. The book tries instead to incorporate this wide range of people's work, including many women's extensive funding of educational projects, their songs and stories, and their investments in radios and cassettes of political speeches and poetry. Students are the most fluid category

---

[7] John Rogge, 'Relocation and Repatriation of Displaced Persons in Sudan: A Report to the Minister of Relief and Displaced Persons Affairs', Disaster Research Unit, University of Manitoba (1990), 31.

[8] Emily Callaci, *Street Archives and City Life: Popular Intellectuals in Postcolonial Tanzania* (Duke University Press, 2017), 8; Steven Feierman, *Peasant Intellectuals: Anthropology and History in Tanzania* (University of Wisconsin Press, 1990); Derek Peterson, *Ethnic Patriotism and the East African Revival: A History of Dissent, c. 1935–1972* (Cambridge University Press, 2012).

here, including full-time students (mostly men) fighting for a university education but (more commonly) also people seeking out and organising study groups and self-made evening schools across the city.

This is a wide net, and so this book gratefully contains fragments of a wide circuit of projects: groups formed and re-formed, songs written and rewritten, poems half-remembered and re-translated, what remains of theatre and study groups, albums of composed studio photographs and disposable camera shots of parties, portraits and self-portraits of high points of clothes and hair and skin care, cassette tapes that travelled through the city and back to the south, handwritten marriage agreements and outcomes of court cases, stamps and certificates of various kinds. This book tries to trace ideas, not organisations, because this more realistically portrays these patchworks of projects started over time.

I.2 Fragmented Political Possibilities, 1983–2005

The world of African intellectual history is often hopeful. Its global turn from the early 2000s has explored travelling political ideas and mobile organisers across the continent and oceans, reconstructing Black political connections and questions about radical change and decolonial futures.[9] Most of this work has focused primarily on the 1900s to the 1960s, when new worlds seem possible and fragile connections are being built by Black and African thinkers moving across borders and oceans.[10]

---

[9] Brandon R. Byrd, 'The Rise of African American Intellectual History', *Modern Intellectual History* 18, no. 3 (2021): 833–64; Getachew, *Worldmaking after Empire*; 'Response to Forum on Worldmaking after Empire', *Millennium* 48, no. 3 (2020): 382–92; Omnia El Shakry, 'Rethinking Arab Intellectual History: Epistemology, Historicism, Secularism', *Modern Intellectual History* 18, no. 2 (2021): 547–72; Rita Abrahamsen, 'Internationalists, Sovereigntists, Nativists: Contending Visions of World Order in Pan-Africanism', *Review of International Studies* 46, no. 1 (2020): 56–74; Samuel Moyn and Andrew Sartori, *Global Intellectual History* (Columbia University Press, 2013); Steffi Marung, 'Out of Empire into Socialist Modernity: Soviet-African (Dis)Connections and Global Intellectual Geographies', *Comparative Studies* 41, no. 1 (2021): 56–70; Ismay Milford, 'Federation, Partnership, and the Chronologies of Space in 1950s East and Central Africa', *Historical Journal* 63, no. 5 (2020): 1325–48; Hunter et al., 'Another World?'.

[10] Ashley D. Farmer, 'Black Women's Internationalism: A New Frontier in Intellectual History', *Modern Intellectual History* 19, no. 2 (2021): 625–37; Leslie Alexander, Brandon R. Byrd, and Russell Rickford, *Ideas in Unexpected*

I.2 Fragmented Political Possibilities, 1983–2005

This book, unfortunately, is situated in the aftermath of these mid-century possibilities. It starts at the beginning of the 1980s with structural adjustment and debt, Soviet collapse, and the rise of a global capitalist liberal consensus. In Sudan, this included the re-ignition of internal war over political and economic power and inequality, the quick return of a Sudanese military autocracy, and a new, economically liberalising Islamist order that became partly internationally sanctioned. Displaced southern residents found limited possibilities for either external escape or connection, beyond the scope of fax machines, cheap radios, expensive international phone calls, messages carried by hand or cassette tape, or risky flight to Cairo or Addis Ababa.

In this way, this book is a kind of anti-view of the new intellectual histories of the 1960s and 1970s. It looks at ordinary working people's visions of worlds to be made within the 'lost decades' of the 1980s and 1990s, and takes a view from below.[11] It demonstrates how imaginations and alternative possibilities continued to be argued, even within the triumph of neoliberalism, and under violent military surveillance, among a refugee community.

The book also demonstrates the methodological and conceptual possibilities of building modern intellectual histories beyond the literary classes or elite political actors. This includes rethinking ideas of international intellectual connections. This book details the fragments, partial views, misinterpretations, and reworkings of what displaced residents could see, hear, and reconstruct of global economic and political discourse, thinkers, and theories, through what bits people could access.[12] The new wave of world intellectual history pursues threads and conversations across languages, spaces, times, and forms,

---

Places: Reimagining Black Intellectual History (Northwestern University Press, 2022); Guichon, '(Black) Neo-colonialism and Rootless African Elites'; Christopher Cameron, 'Haiti and the Black Intellectual Tradition, 1829–1934', *Modern Intellectual History* 18, no. 4 (2021): 1190–99; Reiland Rabaka, *The Routledge Handbook of Pan-Africanism* (Routledge, 2020).

[11] Alden Young, 'The Intellectual Origins of Sudan's "Decades of Solitude", 1989–2019', *Capitalism* 2, no. 1 (2021): 204.

[12] Following the use of Jürgen Müller's idea of semiohistory by Duncan Omanga and Kipkosgei Arap Buigutt, 'Marx in Campus: Print Cultures, Nationalism and Student Activism in the Late 1970s Kenya', *Journal of Eastern African Studies* 11, no. 4 (2017): 571–89.

but this book also highlights the importance of mis- or re-readings, and re-ascriptions of ideas and terms. A variety of 'bits' of political philosophies were interpreted, made accessible, and critiqued themselves, through discussion but also via place names, slurs, and caricatures. A broad array of political ideas were worked into common languages, older vernacular stories and local histories, and new jokes and satire.[13] Signifiers – for example, the neighbourhood renamed Mandela – could mean many things to different people at different times. This book therefore draws on ideas of the conditionality of knowledge, and encourages us (as readers) to also see our knowledge as conditional and partial, intermingled with our own circumstances and conversations.

This leads to a second step this book takes in intellectual history. This project does not hunt concepts; it does not seek out specific discussions around big questions of democracy, citizenship, or liberation, but picks them up where they are found. This allows the book to survey a wider field of African epistemologies, giving space for multiple definitions and discussions across languages, spaces, and times, and avoiding being trapped into an English-language conceptual frame.[14] These debates were part of this intellectual terrain anyway, well beyond definitional questions. Khartoum's wartime displaced residents were confident discussing the specifics of (in the words of Robert Fletcher) 'what freedom is freedom from: "inequality", "exploitation" and "oppression," variously defined. But what does freedom realise? How does one know when one has achieved it?'[15] These were common questions among southern Sudanese residents in Khartoum,

---

[13] For similar approaches, see Brennan, 'Blood Enemies', 390; Barbara Trudell, 'When "Prof" Speaks, Who Listens? The African Elite and the Use of African Languages for Education and Development in African Communities', *Language and Education* 24, no. 4 (2010): 248; Jane Sugarman, 'Imagining the Homeland: Poetry, Songs, and the Discourses of Albanian Nationalism', *Ethnomusicology* 43, no. 3 (1999): 429; Marissa Moorman, *Intonations: A Social History of Music and Nation in Luanda, Angola, from 1945 to Recent Times* (Ohio University Press, 2008).

[14] See also Alden Young and Keren Weitzberg, 'Globalizing Racism and De-provincializing Muslim Africa', *Modern Intellectual History* 19, no. 3 (2022): 933.

[15] Robert Fletcher, *Beyond Resistance: The Future of Freedom* (Nova, 2007), xvii.

summarised by the teacher and writer Santino Garang in one of his pamphlets: 'How shall we *give* freedom?'[16]

I.3 Race, and Ideas of a Black Future

Across people's accounts, questions about building a free political community were most commonly framed within languages of race and Blackness. Histories of race and being Black are fundamental to Sudan: race was used by colonising powers as the organising logic for economic predation and the emerging Sudanese state over the nineteenth and early twentieth centuries.[17] The state was built on a violent racial hierarchy, emerging from histories of slave raiding, slave armies, and slave labour.[18] Residents of Sudan's peripheries have had long experience of these racist systems of slavery and exploitation. Impoverished and coercively displaced people continue to be the core labour pool for successive colonial and postcolonial Sudanese states and armies today. By the 1960s many people – particularly from the

---

[16] Santino Garang, 'The Dinka Customology of Marriage', pamphlet (Khartoum, 2001), 12. Similar questions are posed by Achirin Nuoi Mou in the 'Reading Magazine of Dinka Culture' (SOLO, 2004), 9–10. For the histories and contents of these projects, see Chapters 4 and 5.

[17] Hale, 'Nationalism, "Race", and Class: Sudan's Gender and Culture Agenda in the Twenty-First Century', in Carolyn Fluehr-Lobban and kharyssa rhodes eds., *Race and Identity in the Nile Valley: Ancient and Modern Perspectives* (Red Sea Press, 2003), 174, 181; Al-Baqir al-Afif Mukhtar, 'The Crisis of Identity in Northern Sudan: A Dilemma of a Black People with a White Culture', CODESRIA African Humanities Institute (2004); Edward Thomas, *South Sudan: A Slow Liberation* (Zed Books, 2015), 17; Eve M. Troutt Powell, *A Different Shade of Colonialism: Egypt, Great Britain, and the Mastery of the Sudan* (University of California Press, 2003); *Tell This in My Memory: Stories of Enslavement from Egypt, Sudan, and the Ottoman Empire* (Stanford University Press, 2012).

[18] Jok Madut Jok, *War and Slavery in Sudan* (University of Pennsylvania Press, 2001); Ahmed Alawad Sikainga, *Slaves into Workers: Emancipation and Labor in Colonial Sudan* (University of Texas Press, 1996); 'Slavery, Labour, and Ethnicity in Khartoum: 1898–1956', draft article, Sudan Archives Durham SAD.307/6/1-65 (1980); Douglas H. Johnson, 'The Structure of a Legacy: Military Slavery in Northeast Africa' *Ethnohistory* 36, no. 1 (1989): 72–88; 'Recruitment and Entrapment in Private Slave Armies: The Structure of the zarā'ib in the Southern Sudan', *Slavery & Abolition* 13, no. 1 (1992): 162–73; Wendy James, 'Perceptions from an African Slaving Frontier', in Léonie Archer, ed., *Slavery and Other Forms of Unfree Labour* (Routledge, 1988).

southern regions – were claiming a specifically African and Black identity, as an explanatory shorthand for the deep inequalities, marginalisations, exploitations, and abuses they were subject to.[19]

Talking about Blackness and racial structures is a way of discussing this historical, political, and economic position, part of a flow of African and global Black discourse in the twentieth century but also as part of a local commentary on Sudanese systems of power and exploitation.[20] But Black political discourse is still a generally undervalued part of South Sudanese political thought, despite critical interventions by Scopas Poggo, Francis Deng, Eve Troutt Powell, and Jok Madut Jok, among others.[21] In one of the few specific discussions of race in the Nile valley, Carolyn Fluehr-Lobban and kharyssa rhodes have commented that in scholarly discussion 'race has been underrepresented, submerged, or ignored'.[22] This is particularly true of the literature that has emerged about independent South Sudan written by non-Sudanese researchers, which (like wider academic scholarship on Africa) has often focused on

---

[19] Jok Madut Jok, 'Post-Independence Racial Realities', in Fluehr-Lobban and rhodes, *Race and Identity*, 193; James, 'Perceptions from an African Slaving Frontier', 130; Heather Sharkey, 'Arab Identity and Ideology in Sudan: The Politics of Language, Ethnicity, and Race', *African Affairs* 107, no. 426 (2008): 29; Alex de Waal, 'Who Are the Darfurians? Arab and African Identities, Violence and External Engagement', *African Affairs* 104, no. 415 (2005): 197, 199; Rebecca Lorins, 'Inheritance: Kinship and the performance of Sudanese identities', PhD thesis, University of Texas (2007), 30.

[20] See also James R. Brennan, *Taifa: Making Nation and Race in Urban Tanzania* (Ohio University Press, 2012); Harry Garuba, 'Race in Africa: Four Epigraphs and a Commentary', *PMLA* 123, no. 5 (2008): 1640–48; Achille Mbembe, *Critique of Black Reason* (Duke University Press, 2017), 38.

[21] Francis Mading Deng, *War of Visions: Conflict of Identities in the Sudan* (Brookings Institution, 1995); Jok, *Sudan*; Scopas Poggo, *The First Sudanese Civil War: Africans, Arabs, and Israelis in the Southern Sudan, 1955–1972* (Palgrave Macmillan, 2009); Peter Adwok Nyaba, *The Politics of Liberation in South Sudan: An Insider's View* (Fountain Publishers, 1997); Troutt Powell, *A Different Shade of Colonialism*.

[22] Introduction, in Fluehr-Lobban and Rhodes, eds., *Race and Identity in the Nile Valley*, xiii–xiv. Eddie Thomas notes the continued 'accidental constructivism' of most accounts of 'African' and 'Arab' racial issues: Thomas, *South Sudan*, 31. More broadly, Africanist academia has only recently re-engaged with race and Blackness within African communities themselves, outside of southern Africa and colonial histories: see Jemima Pierre, 'Race in Africa Today: A Commentary', *Cultural Anthropology* 28, no. 3 (2013): 547–51, and *The Predicament of Blackness: Postcolonial Ghana and the Politics of Race* (University of Chicago Press, 2012).

the politics of ethnic identification at the expense of a deeper and wider language and history of race and identity.[23] It is only in the last few years that a reinvigorated academic conversation about race in Africa, and Blackness in the Sudans, has emerged.[24]

In contributing to this renewed conversation in the Sudans, this project follows Rogers Brubaker in exploring ethnic, national, and racial identities as a 'family of forms' of understanding and action; this is partly why this book does not use a national 'South' or a specific ethnic collective as its focus.[25] But it also draws on critiques of this wider lack of local and global histories of race in Africa as a force of capitalist modernity that shapes geographies and relations.[26] Histories of political thought on race and Blackness are fundamental to any modern history of global and local discriminations, capitalist violence, and societal marginalisation, and the production of knowledge itself (see below); this is why it was central in my conversations with people across Aweil, Kuajok, Wau, and Juba, and as such is a thread through this book.

By centring on the political and intellectual lives of Black displaced people from southern Sudan, this book tries to avoid labelling people

---

[23] See Michelle Christian, 'A Global Critical Race and Racism Framework: Racial Entanglements and Deep and Malleable Whiteness', *Sociology of Race and Ethnicity* 5, no. 2 (2019): 170.

[24] Christopher Tounsel, *Chosen Peoples: Christianity and Political Imagination in South Sudan* (Duke University Press, 2021), 13, and 'Race, Religion and Resistance: Revelations from the Juba Archive', *Journal of Eastern African Studies* (2017): 249–65; Sebabatso Manoeli, 'Narrative Battles: Competing Discourses and Diplomacies of Sudan's "Southern Problem", 1961–1991', PhD dissertation, University of Oxford (2017); Elena Vezzadini, 'Setting the Scene of the Crime: The Colonial Archive, History, and Racialisation of the 1924 Revolution in Anglo-Egyptian Sudan', *Canadian Journal of African Studies* 49, no. 1 (2015): 67–93; Zachary Mondesire, 'The Worldliness of South Sudan: Space, Home and Racial Meaning Making in Post Independence Juba', PhD dissertation, UCLA (2018); see also Young and Weitzberg, 'Globalizing Racism', 912.

[25] Rogers Brubaker, 'Ethnicity, Race, and Nationalism', *Annual Review of Sociology* 35, no. 1 (2009): 21–42.

[26] Pierre, 'Race in Africa Today', 548; Sedef Arat-Koç, 'New Whiteness(es), Beyond the Colour Line? Assessing the Contradictions and Complexities of "Whiteness" in the (Geo)Political Economy of Capitalist Globalism', in Thobani Razack Smith, ed., *States of Race: Critical Race Feminism for the 21st Century* (Between the Lines, 2010), 148; Jemima Pierre, 'Slavery, Anthropological Knowledge, and the Racialization of Africans', *Current Anthropology* 61, no. S22 (2020): 220–31.

as specifically southern Sudanese, or according to their ethnic identifications. These names and categories have colonial baggage and political histories, and this book attempts to carefully unpick their deployment. 'Junubi' (southerner) was in this period a political-geographic potentiality with an uncertain shape, and only one identifier for people who were also categorised, and categorised themselves, by locality, ethnicity, Blackness, and various economic categories and heritages including histories of slavery.[27]

Similarly, ethnicity here is not a political system or a neat alternative to a supra-ethnic or regional nation. Like other historically rooted communities, ethnicities are parcels of linguistic and cultural tools and histories, and systems of social and personal security, that provide people with core mutual understandings of responsibility, society, and mutual futures. Ethnicity has become part of Sudanese modern politics as people have used reductionist, essentialised 'ethnic groups' to set out political and economic relationships, but this specific use of ethnic categorisation is still neither total nor accepted by everyone as part of their personal identification. People are inherently pluralistic; they can maintain (often several) ethnic community and ethno-political affiliations while also, sometimes, believing in other political projects for the future. This study tries to incorporate the creativity, rebellious courage, and radical imaginations of people, as well as their xenophobia and parochial, defensive prejudices.

The practical projects that people were engaged in were also not necessarily articulated clearly and arrayed neatly against each other as 'visions'. As ever, people held multiple, and sometimes paradoxical, ideas of the present and future, through a long but also fast-shifting war. In this period, the most well-known attempt to spell out a liberatory Black and pan-Sudanese political philosophy is the idea of a New

---

[27] This book focuses on the 1970s onwards, when the label 'junubi' was increasingly used across Sudan, including to make claims on Southern Regional Administration resources as 'fellow southerners'. Mukhtar, 'The Crisis of Identity in Northern Sudan', 207–8; Elena Vezzadini, *Lost Nationalism: Revolution, Memory and Anti-colonial Resistance in Sudan* (Boydell & Brewer, 2015), 33. For wider discussions about post-slave trade racialised pejoratives, see Felicitas Becker et al., 'Researching the Aftermath of Slavery in Mainland East Africa: Methodological, Ethical, and Practical Challenges', *Slavery & Abolition*, 44, no. 1 (2022): 131–56.

Sudan, a Sudan that would be supportive and representative of everyone within and beyond its multiple Black communities. This idea was initially articulated across leftist Sudanese politics, and was the phrase coined by Sudanese Communist Party leader Abdel Khaliq Mahgoub, during the first civil war period in the mid- to late 1960s; the idea of a New Sudan was then most famously articulated by the late SPLM/A leader John Garang de Mabior.[28] This potential for a wider and liberated political community across Sudan is a continued question at the time of writing: in South Sudan, as the state's military-security apparatus silences popular discussion and continues grinding economic exploitation, and in Sudan, particularly since the fall of Sudan's twenty-year president Omar al-Bashir in 2019, whose rule forms a backdrop to this book.

I.4 Teaching and Learning New Sudans

The second framing of this book is the idea of education. This is unsurprising: southern Sudanese people have frequently rebelled over generations of educational exclusion, over the language and detail of what is taught, and over how education takes children, wealth, and futures into (and out of) the hands of communities. The denial of education was a key grievance in the founding manifesto of the SPLM/A. Education as 'secondary resistance' was a well-understood concept within southern communities in Khartoum.[29] A displaced school administrator emphasised that 'In Khartoum people don't fight with guns. People fight with minds. Teaching is another way of fighting.'[30]

For Khartoum residents, access to education was a key reason in seeking out refuge in the city. Khartoum had always been an educational hothouse: even in the 1970s, southern labourers in Khartoum were understood to be engaged in intense projects of political

---

[28] Young, 'Intellectual Origins', 203.
[29] As observed by Anders Breidlid, 'Sudanese Migrants in the Khartoum Area: Fighting for Educational Space', *International Journal of Education* 25, no. 3 (2005): 568; Marc Sommers, *Islands of Education: Schooling, Civil War and the Southern Sudanese (1983–2004)* (UNESCO, 2005).
[30] Quoted in Sommers, *Islands of Education*, 243–44.

thought.[31] Education also transformed displaced communities over the 1980s to 2000s: in 1976 about 90 per cent of southerners had not been to school, but by 2005, southern literacy in Khartoum was on a par with that of their northern neighbours.[32]

This book does not specifically document the histories of either formal or informal schools, but instead looks at what people tried to use a vast array of educational possibilities and projects to achieve. Aside from a handful of mostly Christian-run formal primary and secondary schools, displaced people organised a plethora of educational projects within intensely practical constraints, including financial, family, social, and psychological pressures and a general lack of time. These educational projects often specifically addressed these practical circumstances (about practical needs, social and well-being issues, children's mental and physical health and futures, everyday security, and anger).

Often this educational work used only chalk or paper and pencil, or the specifically late twentieth-century technology of cassette players and tape recorders, photocopiers, printers and staplers, and fax machines. But through these often-borrowed means, in church and workplace offices, people created magazines, poem and history pamphlets, textbooks, self-recorded song cassettes, and art projects, using fragments of information from international news, history textbooks, gossip, and radio shows, multiply translated and often unreliably shared – this book includes pamphlets with probably a few dozen photocopies made on a church photocopier after hours.

The political ideas and organising detailed here were not necessarily instrumental in wider politics. Much of this book might not be called 'resistance' work, or insurrectionary, or liberatory. Many of the discussions and work here are reactionary and patriarchal. The theme of 'self-defence' runs through modern southern Sudanese politics, including (entirely normally) resistance to a variety of forms of

---

[31] John Philips to James Callaghan, 'About the Status of the Addis Ababa Agreement', 30 September 1975, National Archives UK (NAUK) FCO932.720, 7.

[32] Andrew Epstein, 'Maps of Desire: Refugee Children, Schooling, and Contemporary Dinka Pastoralism in South Sudan', PhD dissertation, University of Wisconsin (2012), 93; Sommers, *Islands of Education*, 218.

change. People emphasised how hard it was and is to tell, in the moment, what is a 'good' action, and people of course act in contradictory ways, moved by ideas and economic priorities to think contrary to what they do, or don't then do. Even people who wanted to be active insurrectionaries could not tell whether work like passing on information on troop movements or political rumours in Khartoum, for example, was actually rebellious, or had any real consequences other than heightened personal risk. In the discussions for this book, we spent a lot of time talking about bravery and bravado, and accounts here are suffused with a range of self-aggrandisement and embarrassment, laughter and comedic stories, (quiet?) pride, and self-depreciation.

All of this does not necessarily fit into a neat account of a national liberation struggle, but it made up the texture of both everyday wartime life and thought. This book is about people living and thinking in an everyday war, and building their own political and intellectual worlds. As Paul Kuel, a part-time student and bricklayer in Khartoum since the mid-70s, explained:

You know, in 1976, my opinion was not clear, but my opinion became clearer in 1985.... Because I was born in war – and I've grown up in war – and I thought, it's an unsolvable war. Which means that people have to think of something alternative. Change minds – find a way out – for making something new.[33]

I.5 Histories of Urban Refuge

All the sons of the Black people, they do not sleep
The women, also, they do not sleep
The sons of Black people everywhere, even in the land of Beja,
They don't sleep, their wives don't sleep
The land of Darfur is also crying, their women do not sleep
...
The order would come and say, take the Dinkas to the desert,
Take them to Jabarona, take them to Soba,

---

[33] Paul Kuel, in Maper Two, 9 August 2013, his emphasis.

Take them to Machar Col, take them to the desert[34]
They have no land, they sleep in the open air.

Andrew Bol Deng, song of lament, written during displacement to Khartoum in the mid-1980s and sung at a community meeting at Maper Akot Aru on 23 August 2017[35]

This book focuses on Khartoum, because the city itself can be seen as Sudan in microcosm.[36] Khartoum is a symbol and site of repression, often used as a synecdoche for describing the central government of Sudan and its elite local power base around the junction of the two Niles. It is also a place of opportunity, refuge, and education for those subject to this repression. Southern Sudanese people have shaped the capital since its inception, as soldiers, slaves, and workers of various kinds. Since Sudan's independence in 1956 the city has been reshaped by the consequences of the Sudanese state's violence, as people displaced by war and famine, and escaping impoverished and exploitative peripheries, built new neighbourhoods at the centre of the Sudanese state.

From about 1980 to 2005, Sudan's sustained wars and famines saw about one and a half million people move into Khartoum. To successive Sudanese governments these new residents were deeply politically suspect. From 1983, southern newcomers in particular were potential 'fifth columnists' for the rebel group the Sudan People's Liberation Army (SPLA).[37] But these new residents were also a very

---

[34] These are names of neighbourhoods in Khartoum; Jabarona and Machar Col are local nicknames. For further discussion of names in the city, see Chapters 2 and 3.

[35] I am very grateful to the Rift Valley Institute's South Sudan Customary Authorities Project, funded by the Swiss Government, for the opportunity to commission Andrew to perform these historic songs at this meeting. For Andrew's work and the context of this song, see Chapter 1.

[36] Observed by Sara Pantuliano et al., 'City Limits: Urbanisation and Vulnerability in Sudan: Synthesis Report', Humanitarian Policy Group (2011), 1; and by African Rights, *Sudan's Invisible Citizens: The Policy of Abuse against Displaced People in the North* (1995), 14.

[37] Mark Duffield, 'Aid and Complicity: The Case of War-Displaced Southerners in the Northern Sudan', *Journal of Modern African Studies* 40, no. 1 (2002): 87. Also see Archbishop Gabriel Zubeir to Caritas Germany, 4 July 1986, Comboni Archives Rome (CAR) 6734.21.1, 8159–8166. This was an experience reported by several interviewees during research: for instance, Paul was suspected or accused of being an SPLA member when working as a cook for a petroleum company: interview in Aweil town, 17 October 2013. In 1988, Tom Masland

I.5 Histories of Urban Refuge

useful source of extremely cheap and nearly rights-free migrant labour in the city and its agricultural heartlands to the south-east. To most humanitarian agencies in the same period, this group of displaced people were generally unreachable: in 1995, an international aid worker noted that 'the Khartoum displaced must be the least consulted group in the history of humanitarian aid'.[38]

This book is focused on this very specific history of Khartoum's displaced neighbourhoods because intellectual histories cannot be extracted from the context of their production.[39] The projects here are shaped by practical, material constraints and the moral and emotional pressures of living in this wartime capital. These pressures included daily drains on time – to manage a variety of jobs, to take endless buses and wait for them, to maintain homes, find romance, and navigate paperwork and local politics – and the strange atemporality of a long war, which often felt both unending and also too quick-changing and complex to keep up with.

The people in this book used some of their time to stay linked with networks of friends, relatives, and information across an explosion of displaced camps, regional cities, and distant resettled refugee communities.[40] All of these places, from Melbourne to Cairo, had different discursive currents due to different forms of access to civil war news and local contexts for fermenting political ideas. Because of its particular political position, Khartoum (like many other places) stood somewhat at a distance from the mainstream Sudan People's Liberation

---

reported that 'some officials warn that the teeming shantytowns could breed a "third column" in support of the Dinka-based guerrilla movement of John Garang, a former army colonel leading the rebels in the south. "Every southerner is considered a Garang supporter," said Martin Kiir Majote [sic], an official of the Aweil Youth Union.' Martin was interviewed during research for this book; see Chapter 1. Masland, 'Khartoum Bursting with Refugee Slums', *Chicago Tribune*, 30 September 1988.

[38] African Rights, 'Food and Power in Sudan: A Critique of Humanitarianism' (1997), 160, quoting an Operation Lifeline Sudan staff member.

[39] See Christian Christiansen, Mélanie Lindbjerg Guichon, and Sofía Mercader, 'Towards a Global Intellectual History of an Unequal World', *Global Intellectual History* (2022), 1–17.

[40] Across Egypt, Ethiopia, Uganda, Kenya, Canada, the United States, Israel, the United Kingdom, Australia, and the key refugee camps of Arua, Adjumani, Itang (until 1991), Gambella, and Kakuma.

Movement and Army (SPLM/A) news pipeline, unlike (for example) Kakuma refugee camp in northern Kenya from the early 1990s, which was plugged much more directly into conflicts across the border.[41] News about the local and international direction of the war moved through Khartoum's suburbs via gossip, quiet political discussions, fragmentary international news, and inconsistent formal channels like Sudanese newspapers and (briefly) SPLM/A radio. The Sudanese capital thus developed its own distinctive political discourse about the war, and about marginalisation, exploitation, self-determination, and independence.

This book is part of wider histories of migrants and workers in modern African cities, part of a wave of new work following Abdoumaliq Simone's path that explores organisation and community-building among workers in post-1970s urban settlements and 'informal' economies.[42] These urban migrant studies are one of the richest parts of Sudan's historiography.[43] This book, though, is not a history of these

---

[41] See Bram Jansen, *Kakuma Refugee Camp: Humanitarian Urbanism in Kenya's Accidental City* (Zed Books, 2018); 'The Refugee Camp as Warscape: Violent Cosmologies, "Rebelization," and Humanitarian Governance in Kakuma, Kenya', *Humanity* 7, no. 3 (2016): 429–41.

[42] Abdoumaliq Simone, 'People as Infrastructure: Intersecting Fragments in Johannesburg', *Public Culture* 16, no. 3 (2004): 407–29; Frederick Cooper, *On the African Waterfront: Urban Disorder and the Transformation of Work in Colonial Mombasa* (ACLS, 2014); Jesper Bjarnesen and Mats Utas, 'Introduction: Urban Kinship: The Micro-Politics of Proximity and Relatedness in African Cities', *Africa* 88, no. S1 (2018): 1–11; Stefano Bellucci and Bill Freund, 'Introduction: Work across Africa: Labour Exploitation and Mobility in Southern, Eastern and Western Africa', *Africa* 87, no. 1 (2017): 27–35; Miles Larmer, 'Permanent Precarity: Capital and Labour in the Central African Copperbelt', *Labor History* 58, no. 2 (2017): 170–84.

[43] See, for example, Muna A. Abdalla, 'Poverty and Inequality in Urban Sudan: Policies, Institutions and Governance', PhD dissertation, Leiden University (2008); Ahmed Alawad Sikainga, *'City of Steel and Fire': A Social History of Atbara, Sudan's Railway Town, 1906–1984* (Heinemann, 2002); Vezzadini, *Lost Nationalism*; Abdel Ghaffar M. Ahmed and Mustafa Abdel Rahman, 'Small Urban Centres: Vanguards of Exploitation: Two Cases from Sudan', *Africa* 49, no. S3 (1979): 258–71; Valdo Pons, 'Urbanization and Urban Life in the Sudan', PhD dissertation, University of Hull (1980); Sondra Hale, 'The Changing Ethnic Identity of Nubians in an Urban Milieu', PhD dissertation, University of Michigan (1979); Adil Mustafa Ahmad, 'The Neighbourhoods of Khartoum: Reflections on Their Functions, Forms and Future', *Habitat International* 16, no. 4 (1992): 27–45; Naseem Badiey, *The State of Post-conflict Reconstruction: Land, Urban Development and State-Building in Juba, Southern Sudan* (Boydell & Brewer, 2014); Willow Berridge, '"Nests of

I.5 Histories of Urban Refuge

people's relationships to the city or to state agencies as specifically 'displaced' people or as citizens negotiating rights and aid.[44] Instead, this study seeks to contribute to new histories of Sudan's economic transition over the long twentieth century to present, a tradition that underpins both Sudan and now South Sudan's formalised 'wars' and its wider conflicts, including the moving frontiers of private property and waged labour, and shifting ideas of land, race, and rights to power.[45] This book is a small part of these wider histories, and people's projects here are part of these changing theories and practices of economic power and wealth-building. In Khartoum this included the rise of militia-running businessmen from across Darfur and the south in the late 1980s, taking advantage of new Islamic state possibilities for private investments, commercial agricultural production, and militia financing. These men and their networks and investments are part of the history of displaced southern life in the city especially by the late 1990s, and detailed in later chapters here, as their power grows in the city.

---

criminals"': Policing in the Peri-urban Regions of Northern Sudan, 1964–1989', *Journal of North African Studies* 17, no. 2 (2012): 239–55; Léonie Newhouse, 'Urban Attractions: Returnee Youth, Mobility and the Search for a Future in South Sudan's Regional Towns', United Nations High Commissioner for Refugees (UNHCR) (2012); Alice Franck, Barbara Casciarri, and Idris Salim El-Hassan, eds., *In-Betweenness in Greater Khartoum: Spaces, Temporalities, and Identities from Separation to Revolution. Space and Place* (Berghahn Books, 2021). This book takes up Cherry Leonardi's research on the productivity of urban margins for articulating personal identifications and political community. Leonardi, *Dealing with Government in South Sudan: Histories of Chiefship, Community & State* (Boydell & Brewer, 2013).

[44] For this vein of research, see Laurent Fourchard, 'Undocumented Citizens and the Making of ID Documents in Nigeria: An Ethnography of the Politics of Suspicion in Jos', *African Affairs* 120, no. 481 (2021): 511–41; Enrico Ille, 'Brothers, Arrivals, Refugees: South Sudanese as Subjects of Naming and Reporting Practices in Sudan's Humanitarian Sector', *Diaspora* 22, no. 1 (2022), 11–32.

[45] Edward Thomas, 'Patterns of Growth and Inequality in Sudan, 1977–2017', Durham Middle East Papers (2017); 'Moving towards Markets: Cash, Commodification and Conflict in South Sudan', Rift Valley Institute (2019); Alden Young, *Transforming Sudan* (Cambridge University Press, 2018); following studies including Ali Bhagat, 'Governing Refugee Disposability: Neoliberalism and Survival in Nairobi', *New Political Economy* 25, no. 3 (2020): 440; Mike Davis, *Planet of Slums* (Verso, 2007).

I.6 Methodology and Positionality

You cannot spend all your life studying, just staying like that, because we are Africans. If we were like white people or other nations whose lives are stable, you can study your whole life without any problem.

> Luciano, interviewed in Khartoum by Samuel Nicola Cornelio, 25 September 2019[46]

This is not my history; my own political interests drew me into archiving work and research into ideas of political and economic world-building in southern Sudan, and towards the intellectual projects of people I did not hear in the historical record. I am only able to attempt to sketch this history here because of the global inequalities of university infrastructure, educational access, and colonial academic entitlement that have produced this project, and structured the education and work of the people within it. I have been privileged to learn from people living in South Sudan on the sharp edges of a colonial capitalist world system within which I have had the luxury of studying.

This study therefore has fundamental limitations of language, access, insight, and time. It is originally based on a doctoral project undertaken between 2011 and 2016, and draws very gratefully on work with the Rift Valley Institute and the British Council in South Sudan over 2015 to 2019. I initially set out to record a history of displaced communities in Khartoum that had already mostly disappeared by 2011, as around two million displaced people returned from Sudan and rebuilt their lives in the south, often making new villages and suburbs called New Khartoum.[47]

The main problem (and obvious charge against) this book is that it does not rest on work in Khartoum. In 2011, when I began this project, I was very briefly detained in Khartoum and then blacklisted for visas. This – combined with the fact that by 2011 the majority of southern residents of Khartoum had returned, or were busy with the intensely time- and energy-consuming process of packing up their lives – meant

---

[46] Reprinted with the permission of Samuel Nicola and the Rift Valley Institute's X-Border Local Research Network project.
[47] IOM, 'Village Assessment Survey Report' (2013); IOM, 'Sustainable Reintegration of South Sudanese: Final Draft Strategy' (March 2012).

I.6 Methodology and Positionality

that my research became a project of retrospectives from research in South Sudan. This book combines people's own accounts with pieced-together archival marginalia in Durham, Birmingham, London, Amsterdam, Rome, Juba, and Nairobi.[48] This archival documentation spans the field of texts: from missionaries' personal letters to old students, Sudan government local security files, British colonial notes, rebel news sheets and transcript broadcasts, and a wide array of aid agency paperwork and other wartime ephemera including petitions, open letters, and transcribed songs. The majority of this documentation was in English, with some Arabic and South Sudanese–language documents, with which I have tried my own translations for the former and sought help for the latter. I am particularly grateful for my year's education as a Rift Valley Institute intern at the South Sudan National Archives, working with the dedicated archive staff on reconstructing the archive.[49]

Since 2011, I have been able to slowly build a collection of photographs, self-written histories, satirical plays and political pamphlets, school textbooks, poetry and song collections, and hundreds of conversations, cross-referenced insofar as possible to fragmentary archival records. These records reflect Khartoum intellectual life, where people worked with what they had, including some books, photocopied pamphlets, church texts, curriculum and vernacular self-written and published texts, poetry, and music of all kinds, and national, (briefly) rebel, and international media and radio. Everything was cross-referenced, repeated, creatively edited, copied, memorised, and rewritten. During research interviews, people cited everything from Dickens's *Tale of Two Cities* to Holt and Daly's core academic history *A History*

---

[48] The Sudan Archive (SAD) and the Middle East Documentation Unit (MEDU), Durham University; the South Sudan National Archives, Juba (SSNA); the Save the Children Fund (SCF) and Church Missionary Society (CMS) Archives, Special Collections, University of Birmingham; the National Archives, London (NAUK); the Comboni Mission Archives, Rome (CAR); the National Archives of Kenya, Nairobi (NAK); Amnesty International Archives, International Institute for Social History in Amsterdam (IISH); the Royal Geographical Society, London (RGS).

[49] For more on this project, see 'National Archive of South Sudan', Rift Valley Institute website, accessed 2 May 2023; Dominic Nahr, 'Can Archivists Save the World's Newest Nation?', *National Geographic News*, 3 November 2016; 'Boxing the Past', JubaintheMaking.com (2018).

of Sudan from the Coming of Islam to the Present Day, and – more commonly – songs, texts, curriculum books, quotations and political speeches, personal libraries, notes, photograph albums, and music catalogues.[50] I tried to pursue the genealogies of this Khartoum organisational life, hunting graduation certificates, posters, music tapes, MP3s, photographs, textbooks, and pamphlets, both in people's personal collections and in markets across South Sudan and Uganda. Many people had lost their physical archives or had been forced to edit their most important belongings into a curated travelling collection. Throughout research, people told me what they'd lost, and sometimes gave me lists or notes, or sang me songs and poems, for the record.

Even outside the South Sudan National Archives, I was surrounded by archival spaces, including battered tea stalls and vans driven down from the north, house painted colours that matched homes left behind, furniture, clothes, and piles of suitcases that were all archival material from Khartoum. I became interested in archival sounds, and what people listened to. Khartoum (like all urban spaces) is a palimpsest of noises, and making music (and noise) can be an assertion in the city, both in public – to claim, remake, make familiar city space – and in private, through headphones or in homes.[51] I also became interested in images, partly because photos were treasured memories and aide-mémoires during discussions, but also because of Sudan's wide traditions of portraiture in photography studios, which are both a fun activity and a commemorative and compositional project. Because these are not my own images, and their owners did not know how to contact all the people in these photos for permissions for their copying and discussion, I am drawing on only a limited selection here for which I have permission, but they all colour my thinking.

---

[50] P. M. Holt and M. W. Daly, *A History of the Sudan from the Coming of Islam to the Present Day*, 6th ed. (Longman Pearson, 2011). For similar methods, see David Zeitlyn, 'Anthropology in and of the Archives: Possible Futures and Contingent Pasts. Archives as Anthropological Surrogates', *Annual Review of Anthropology* 41, no. 1 (2012): 461; Callaci, *Street Archives*, 10–11.

[51] Following Plageman, 'Recomposing the Colonial City', 1–4; Juliet Gilbert, 'Mobile Identities: Photography, Smartphones and Aspirations in Urban Nigeria', *Africa* 89, no. 2 (2019): 246–49.

I.6 Methodology and Positionality

Intellectual history is rooted in languages, and this book is built on translations and re-translations of what I will also call the vernacular, and these translations are not (and will not be) settled.[52] The way that all these texts and songs were reproduced and reused over time and through different circumstances challenges the idea of an 'original'. For instance, in group-translating several well-known songs from Khartoum, my four interpreters argued that they knew better versions of the lyrics – despite the fact that the lyrics had been provided, in written form, by their actual composer.[53] Songs and texts gathered during research were discussed and translated with their authors, singers, teachers, and students, depending on who had them and whom I was able to share them with. I also paid groups of students and teachers (with Sudanese Arabic, Dinka, and English language skills) to work with me on translating books of songs. Disputed translations of racial, southern, ethnic, clan, and regional identifiers and descriptives were scattered throughout texts and interviews, layering these weighted terms to try to describe life in neighbourhoods that included other poor people from Darfur, the Nuba Mountains, and from the far north and east of Sudan.[54] But this is not a linguistic history, because I do not have mastery of these languages, and because these questions of translation are alive and unsettled to everyone I asked for help. Tackling even a corner of the tangled multilingual conceptual history of southern Sudan's conflicts and human experience is well beyond me and this book.

This book therefore cannot be a history of Khartoum, or of southern communities in Khartoum. I started research in Northern Bahr el Ghazal, the region bordering southern Darfur in the north-west of what is now South Sudan, because around half a million people had

---

[52] See also Nile Green, 'The Waves of Heterotopia: Toward a Vernacular Intellectual History of the Indian Ocean', *American Historical Review* 123, no. 3 (2018): 848; Derek Peterson, 'Vernacular Language and Political Imagination', in Ericka Albaugh and Kathryn Luna, eds., *Tracing Language Movement in Africa* (Oxford University Press, 2018).

[53] For further discussion of this debate, see Chapter 5.

[54] As explored by Wendy James, 'War and "Ethnic Visibility": The Uduk on the Sudan-Ethiopia Border', in Katsuyoshi Fukui, ed., *Ethnicity & Conflict in the Horn of Africa* (James Currey, 1994); Laura Hammond, *This Place Will Become Home: Refugee Repatriation to Ethiopia* (Cornell University Press, 2004); Bascom, *Losing Place: Refugee Populations and Rural Transformations in East Africa* (Berghahn Books, 1998).

recently returned to the area, mostly from Khartoum and Darfur.[55] An estimated quarter of the displaced southern population in Khartoum were Dinka people, mostly from this region, because of its particular history of devastating famines and raids through the 1980s.[56] Around Aweil I met with Nuba, Zaghawa, Shilluk, and Luo people living in the region, and I tried to redress my imbalances (and challenge dominant narratives from Aweil) through meetings in Juba in autumn 2013 with Nuer, Bari, Kuku, Kakwa, Lotuho, and Zande residents. Further research in Yambio and Torit in the West and East Equatoria was stopped by renewed war in December 2013. This means that of the roughly 130 interviews from 2012–13, the slight majority are with Dinka Malual people. The book also draws on nearly 100 meetings with other ex-Khartoum residents from Kakwa, Zande, Bari, and Pari communities over 2015–17, and a further roughly 120 interviews in Aweil over 2017–19, as I tried to track down authors, poets, and songwriters of texts and cassettes that I found in markets in Juba and Kampala, whose work had been cited in previous conversations. It is in no way exhaustive or reflective of all experiences of displaced Khartoum life.

This project is also based on two different moments of retrospection. The first was from early 2012 to the beginning of December 2013, a period of reconstruction, some hope, and the continued reframing of wartime experiences in a new social and political context. During this research, people were busy trying to stay connected to old friends and

---

[55] Some 476,143 returnees were registered by IOM from 2007 to 2013 in Northern Bahr el Ghazal alone, 100,000 more than in the whole of the three Equatorian states: IOM, 'Village Assessment Survey Report' (2013); Larissa Meier, 'Returning to Northern Bahr El Ghazal, South Sudan', MSc. thesis, Lund University (2013), 2.

[56] Sommers, *Islands of Education*, 210; nearly half of these displaced people were understood to be either Dinka or Nuba (25.4% and 20.6%, respectively). 'The Dinka' – or in Dinka, *monyjiang*, or *jieng* – have, however inaccurately, long been considered as a broad ethno-political collective, although united more by common language and mutual cultural practice than as a coherent 'tribal' entity. See Simon Harragin and Chol Changath Chol, 'The Southern Sudan Vulnerability Study', Save the Children Fund (1999); for a more recent discussion of the collective 'Dinka' people, see Zoe Cormack, 'The Making and Re-making of Gogrial: Landscape, History and Memory in South Sudan', PhD dissertation, Durham University (2014).

I.6 Methodology and Positionality

reflecting on their often reluctant and generally underwhelming resettlement to the south. This work was explicit in photo albums. For instance, Josephine spent her last year in Khartoum buying photo albums and organising studio photo shoots with friends from Darfur, the Nuba Mountains, and other Sudanese communities in her neighbourhood 'for memory': 'We knew that, in future, we are going to scatter to different places and we need to remember ourselves.'[57] The second period of research, during 2015 to 2017, was within South Sudan's internal war that horrifically instrumentalised reductionist tribal labels and smashed a lot of trust. The narrative trajectory of this book also reflects these dashed political hopes, including my own very naive ones.

This is therefore not a definitive history but a history of remembrance and reflection. Here I follow Elleni Centime Zeleke and seek to trace shared memories in the aftermath.[58] This book's centring of memory is probably best demonstrated through how I tried to learn about Khartoum's geography. I copied, printed, and stuck together sixteen A4 pages of a basic line-drawn Google map of greater Khartoum, including unlabelled roads with sudden ends and both Arabic- and English-language neighbourhood names. I pulled this out at (I hope) appropriate quiet social moments for everyone's amusement in working out where they lived, worked, studied, and travelled to. During discussions at tea shops, bus stops, and homes on quiet Sundays, people renamed roads and neighbourhoods, added streets and homes, drew bus routes, and disputed Google's interpretation of road layouts. As such this book is a happy non-resolution of the historical narrative. As Dhieu noted during one of our often-methodological discussions in 2013, 'you will get very many histories'.[59]

This project relied so heavily on people's advice and patient guidance over many years that these people deserve to be credited within this book itself and not only in a separate acknowledgements section. This book tries to balance requests for anonymity and pseudonyms with recognition of the intellectual work of its contributors. It rests on the work and advice of Joseph 'Gai Thok' Tong Ngor, Youssef Onyalla, the late great Wafa'a Housseini Onyalla, Marko Mabior Bol, the late Lazarus Makom Bol, Angelina Majok Juac,

---

[57] Josephine, in Maper Two, 26 June 2013.   [58] Zeleke, *Ethiopia in Theory*, 27.
[59] Dhieu Kuel, in Mayen Ulem, 4 July 2013, speaking in English.

Abuk Deng, Dr Jimmy Wongo, Professor Leben Moro, Joseph Diing Majok, Dr Douglas H. Johnson, Professor Wendy James, Professor Cherry Leonardi, Professor Jok Madut Jok, Professor Justin Willis, the late much-missed Santino Garang Akot, Dr Zoe Cormack, Professor Yosa Wawa, and all my other advisors who always knew much more about what I was asking than I did. Ideally, this book would not be a sole production but a work of collective writing and thinking.

Decolonising intellectual history requires radically shifting current structures of educational access and time, the power dynamics and practicalities of funding and co-working, and the racialised ethics and risks of research, including systems of care for each other. We need a sea change in not just who individually writes these histories, but how all our histories are researched, understood, and discussed.[60] I know that this book is not doing this, but I hope in my wider work I am contributing to attempts to chip away at making as many structural changes for emancipatory forms of study and intellectual production as I learn how. For now, though, the people I write about here should have their work in history, and this book is a place marker.

I.7 Structure of the Book

The book's structure reflects the narrative arc of protagonists' lives in Khartoum. Chapters 1–3 trace and locate the people we follow from their displacement to the city in the late 1980s, and focus on the urgent societal reconstruction that was undertaken by displaced new residents to lay claim to safe space, in the face of local authorities' efforts to exclude, deport, exploit, and silence them. As shown in Chapter 3, in the early 1990s, Khartoum's displaced residents were investing their energies in rebuilding personal futures and securing spaces 'to keep people safe', creating community-governed spaces at a distance from state power, that could give room for 'real work'.[61]

The work done in these spaces is the focus of Chapters 4–6, starting with fast-growing education projects. Chapter 4 is based on private archives of teaching resources, school records, aid agency archival

---

[60] In this I am learning from Saidiya Hartman, 'Intimate History, Radical Narrative', *Journal of African American History* 106, no. 1 (2021): 127–35.
[61] Lual Lual Aguer, in Apada, 15 August 2013.

1.7 Structure of the Book

marginalia, and personal accounts, detailing how residents of all socioeconomic and ethnic backgrounds organised adult night schools, and taught their own syllabuses of critical political and social education, often using self-written alternative history textbooks.

These educational projects contained a confusion of ideas and arguments about the form and future of political community, within and after the war. These contents are the subject of Chapter 5, spanning the 1990s to 2000s and highlighting competing critiques of economic, political, and social circumstances, conflicts, and ideas of the future. Looking at the political theory within self-produced works, cassettes, photocopied pamphlets, song sheets, and lyric books, the chapter highlights discussions over the possible shape and extent of a political community rooted in common Black experiences of exploitation and marginalisation, versus a political community drawing on more specific ethnic parameters. It also highlights common critiques of the civic and moral failings of the wealthy, apathetic, culturally promiscuous, and politically ignorant.

Chapter 6 explores some of what this work inspired, including mobilising songs, propaganda-sharing, fundraising and rebel military recruitment, and other (disputed, uncertain) attempts at resistance. Not all of this rebellious work was specifically 'southern' or pro-SPLA. Some young men were inspired to go back to their family's villages to fight in local ethnically organised militias against predation from the Sudan government and SPLA forces alike. Others (men and women) joined the SPLA's New Sudan Brigade, or the pan-Sudanese and pan-Africanist underground organisations of the African National Front and the National Democratic Alliance, among other small political parties and 'spying' work.

But there were practical limits to what was possible within Khartoum as the fragmented wars in the south evolved in the late 1990s and 2000s. People needed to work, and the war was a source of employment for many displaced people who worked within the Sudanese state and military forces. A growing number of southern militia leaders built their networks and diversified their investments in Khartoum over the 1990s, and their interventions in displaced community spaces increasingly constrained both practical and imaginative possibilities. Chapter 7 explores the parallel systems of governance in Khartoum that southern militia-running businessmen (including Kerubino Kuanyin Bol, Paulino Matip, Abdel Bagi Ayii Akol, and others) organised in Khartoum, including their own prisons, barracks, and offices. These systems secured spaces for some people to work, live, and learn, but also propagated their own ideas of future structures of political community based on regional zones of ethno-political authority.

The book closes with the year 2005, not because of the Comprehensive Peace Agreement, but because of the sudden death of the SPLA's leader John Garang de Mabior, which sparked riots and racially motivated murder across Khartoum, and which for this book's interviewees marked a fundamental shift in relationships in the city. Chapter 8 briefly discusses how displaced spaces were closed down after 2005 during mass movements southwards, where ex-Khartoum residents built new settlements that were often called New Khartoum. As political possibilities collapsed into a path to independence for South Sudan in 2011, secession was still not a panacea or end goal for most of these returnees, and this final chapter and the Conclusion reflect returning residents' discussions of the lost possibilities of past projects.

1 Dar es Salaam
Flight and the Fight for Space in Khartoum, 1988–1992

At the beginning of April 1988, a woman and six children starved to death at the train station in south Khartoum, after arriving on a train loaded with about 6,000 desperate people fleeing from the south.[1] Their deaths echoed those of previous arrivals a year earlier in April 1987, when a reported 10,000 people had tried to board one train heading north from the government-controlled town of Aweil. Around 7,000 people were left at Meiram, where thousands starved to death; only 2,000 reached Khartoum, and many died in the train station before they could reach family.[2]

For these displaced Dinka families, this violence, famine, and flight north was *makurup*, the term for a disaster that came and covered everything, and spared no one. From 1982 onwards, violence, armed raids, and famines served to depopulate large areas of southern Sudan, the Nuba Mountains, Blue Nile, and Greater Upper Nile. Increasing violence and disruption of food supplies and agriculture forced about 2 million people to leave southern Sudan over 1986 to 1988, with most people from the northern regions of Upper Nile and Bahr el Ghazal heading northwards into central Sudan.[3] These specifically local,

---

[1] Over April–June 1988 it was estimated that 60,000 people headed north from Northern Bahr el Ghazal alone specifically due to militia raids; 40,000 were estimated to be heading east to Ethiopian refugee camps and rebel groups. Scott Kraft, 'Refugees from Sudan Civil War: Starving Boys Walk for Months to Relief Camps', *Los Angeles Times*, 3 June 1988.

[2] Roberta Cohen and Francis Mading Deng, *The Forsaken People: Case Studies of the Internally Displaced* (Brookings Institution, 1998) 145; Hearing before the Select Committee on Hunger, House of Representatives, 100th Congress, Washington, DC, 14 July 1988, 104; African Rights, 'Food and Power in Sudan: A Critique of Humanitarianism' (July 1997), 104.

[3] John Ryle and Kwaja Yai Kuol, 'Displaced Southern Sudanese in Northern Sudan with Special Reference to Southern Darfur and Kordofan', Save the Children Fund UK (February 1989), 7; Kraft, 'Refugees from Sudan Civil War'. Equatorian community histories of Khartoum follow somewhat different timelines and trajectories.

personal disasters made up most people's experience of the first years of civil war.[4]

The largest number of those displaced northwards came from the Dinka sections and clans, particularly from northern Bahr el Ghazal.[5] In late 1985, Rizeigat and Humr Messiria militias from southern Darfur intensified horrifically violent raids into northern Bahr el Ghazal and Abyei, assisted by Sudan government army helicopters and supplies in the growing war against the rebel SPLA.[6] These militiamen – themselves seeking to cope with environmental crisis, drought, and disenfranchisement as large agricultural firms bought Darfur and Kordofan land from under them – worked to depopulate the area in their hunt for herds and spoils, defecating in household cooking pots and bags of grain during raids.[7] By early 1987 they had exhausted the cattle populations of Bahr el Ghazal and Abyei, but still benefitted from an impoverished labour supply, as destitute men, women, and children fled northwards on foot.[8]

Families knew these seasonal labour migration routes, but from 1986 these paths were one-way.[9] They walked – as a court member from Aweil, the now-elderly Aguer Agor, recalls, 'as a community, as a family' – along the railway to El Meiram, Muglad, Babanousa, and

---

[4] This is why this chapter does not formally introduce Sudan's civil wars with a narrativised history of events and key actors, or follow the standardised chronology of the c. 1955–1972 and 1983–2005 civil wars. This book comes across the war's main parties – government, militia, and rebel armies and leaderships – as and when they appeared in the lives and histories of the working-class people at the heart of this study. This is a conscious effort to complicate understandings of how civil wars work, 'from below' and from the everyday. For introductory surveys of Sudan's political history, see Douglas H. Johnson, *South Sudan: A New History for a New Nation* (Ohio University Press, 2016); Jok, *Sudan*.

[5] Tekle Woldemikael, 'Southern Migrants in a Northern Sudanese City', *Horn of Africa* 8, no. 1 (1985): 26.

[6] Ryle and Yai Kuol, 'Displaced Southern Sudanese', 10; Andrew Mawson, 'Il Murahaleen Raids on the Dinka, 1985–89', *Disasters* 15, no. 2 (1991): 141.

[7] Santino Ayak, in Maper chiefs' court, 13 April 2013.

[8] Ryle and Yai Kuol, 'Displaced Southern Sudanese', 19–20; Ahmed Mahmud and Ali Baldo, 'The Dhein Massacre: Slavery in the Sudan', Sudan Relief and Rehabilitation Association (1987), 25, 32; Mawson, 'Il Murahaleen Raids', 142. For wider histories of slavery in Sudan, see Sikainga, *Slaves into Workers*; Janet Ewald, *Soldiers, Traders, and Slaves: State Formation and Economic Transformation in the Greater Nile Valley, 1700–1885* (University of Wisconsin Press, 1990).

[9] Ryle and Yai Kuol, 'Displaced Southern Sudanese', 12.

Dar es Salaam: Flight and the Fight for Space in Khartoum

onwards, through Misseriya territory, or to the north-west through Safaha to Ed-Daein in South Darfur's Rizeigat lands.[10] Many younger men and boys, aware that they would be seen as SPLA rebels, took paths towards Ethiopia instead, and into SPLA training camps.[11] Exhausted and starving, travellers were easy prey for local residents who wanted free workers for their fields and homes. Deng Nhial, a displaced farmer from Nyamlel, was forced with eighteen members of his family and village into digging a militiaman's fields in exchange for food and water, at gunpoint.[12] Arou Piol, later a volunteer teacher in Khartoum and then militia recruit, related how he was sold by his family as a boy to a chief in Meriam for his safekeeping, while his parents took the dangerous roads on to Khartoum.[13] Like Deng, many people remained in these areas throughout the war, indentured for their survival or abducted during raids or from refugee camps or the roadside into slave labour.[14] But there was little in the way of choice for those who were not enslaved. Arou's father was not the only man who made desperate bargains for his survival, and the survival of his children. On the way north, parents were asked if they would sell their children into indentured labour:

But you don't know where he is coming from, and he doesn't know where are you going to. In this case, if you refuse, he will turn to kill you, and still take the child. In that case, we have to give them children, for – for us to survive. And hoping, like, you may even get your child [back], or you may not get – but still, it remains the same, because [if] people refuse, they still kill you and take your children.[15]

Those who could continue northwards into the towns and refugee camps of Darfur and Kordofan were subject to one of the worst famines ever recorded. By late 1987, there were well over 8,000 emaciated and dying men, women, and children around Meiram town alone.[16] Relief workers were rarely allowed access but estimated that

---

[10] Aguer Agor, in Maper chiefs' court, 13 April 2013; Mawson, 'Il Murahaleen Raids', 141–43.
[11] Ryle and Yai Kuol, 'Displaced Southern Sudanese', 14.
[12] Deng Nhial Ayak, in Maper chiefs' court, 13 April 2013.
[13] Arou Piol Adam, in Apada village, 21 July 2013.
[14] Ryle and Yai Kuol, 'Displaced Southern Sudanese', 28; Raymond Bonner, 'A Reporter at Large: Famine', *The New Yorker*, 13 March 1989, 69.
[15] Aguer Agor, in Maper chiefs' court, 13 April 2013.
[16] Mawson, 'Il Murahaleen Raids', 141–43.

at least 3,000 people had been buried around the town over July to September, and bodies were scavenged by hyenas and vultures.[17] Local authorities did not allow a registry of deaths, or any surveys, in Meiram or elsewhere.[18]

Many people can remember this flight, and the organisation and solidarity that survived even during this disaster. Malou Tong, a family elder from Marial Bai, remembers how those who found some paid work would share the dividends in an effort to keep everyone in his extended family of travellers alive, 'until we reached Khartoum'. Family elders and community leaders called on old standards of mutual assistance in crisis, collecting what food or money family members had left and distributing it more widely.[19] Some can tell stories of escaping indentured or servile labour as children and finding protection and new opportunities through linking up with other Dinka or southern groups in camps or on routes northwards.[20]

Across Sudan, throughout the civil war, people fleeing their homes could not rely on (or even access) irregular food aid. People had to rely on each other. Abuk Deng remembers the long walk towards Khartoum as a young girl, and the relief she felt when her father met distant relatives in a market in Muglad. Her relatives offered them help settling in the neighbourhood of Shajjara in Khartoum, living in cardboard shelters at the back of a northern Sudanese domestic compound, along with Nuer and Ngok Dinka displaced families.[21] Wei Moya, a Nuer man who arrived on a truck with his wife and two children from Malakal, found shelter with a cousin on the fast-growing peripheries of Haj Yousif.[22] Lazarus Lual, about twelve years old at the time he arrived in the city, hunted bakeries – he only knew his brother worked in a bakery – and was directed on to the next bakery by Nuer, Dinka

---

[17] Bonner, 'A Reporter at Large', 61, 66.
[18] Roland Sewell, 'Report on Visit of Oxfam and SCF Representatives to El Meiram – South Kordofan 4–8 September 1988', Oxfam, MEDU 17/3/REF/22. There were no surveys or records in Kosti, Malakal, or Renk at the same time: Janny Kosters, 'Medical Programme for Displaced People in Renk, Upper Nile Province, Three Monthly Report', MSF Holland, August 1989, MEDU 17/3/REF/15, 6.
[19] Malou Tong Tong, in Juba, 16 August 2017.
[20] Lazarus Lual, in Juba, 19 October 2013; Abuk Deng, in Apada, 5 June 2013.
[21] Abuk Deng, in Apada, 5 June 2013.
[22] Masland, 'Khartoum Bursting with Refugee Slums'.

Bor, and then Dinka Malual workers until he found someone who recognised a family resemblance and could help him find his brother.[23]

From 1986, as increasing numbers of destitute and starving people arrived in the city, southern residents tried to organise their arrival and support. They built on established systems. Way-stations, reception teams at bus and train stations, and mutual funds for transport had been organized since the 1960s by residents in Khartoum.[24] With the disaster, new arrivals were 'directed towards "their people"' by organisations such as the Aweil Youth Union (AYU), which was established in 1985 and grew in 1986 with the primary agenda of assisting people 'pouring in' to Khartoum, using branches in the northern cities of Nyala, Wad Medani, Kosti, and Babanusa; some members were working with Oxfam in El Obeid.[25] Michael Thiop Lang, a manual labourer from Gok Machar who fled back to Hilla Fouk in Haq Yousif in 1985 (where he had been a jobbing bricklayer before the war), was assisted by the AYU on his way – 'they heard [about family coming to Khartoum], even sometimes they came to meet people at the border and they take them ... they just meet in Daein or Babanusa [and Nyala].'[26] As well as information, these organisations collected clothes, food, and money in Khartoum for new arrivals, funded partly by tithing from members.[27] For AYU, as organiser Martin Kiir Majok explained, this was made easier once the association gained a rare

---

[23] Lazarus Lual, interview in Juba, 19 October 2013.

[24] Bona Malwal, 'Report of the Secretariat to the General Meeting of the Southern Front on 6 February 1965', CAR A/90/8/10; Hasan Makki Mohammed Ahmed, 'Christian Missionary Activity in the Three Towns', December 1983, CAR 674.20.4, 12.

[25] Fouad N. Ibrahim, 'The Conditions of the Southern Sudanese Women Migrants in Abu Siid Shanty Town, Omdurman, Sudan: A Case Study of Cultural Change', *Geojournal* 20, no. 3 (1990): 251; Masland, 'Khartoum Bursting with Refugee Slums'; Paul Kuel, in Maper Two, 9 August 2013; Martin Kiir, in Apada, 14 August 2013; Diing Chen Diing, in Aweil, 15 July 2013; Ayii Bol, in Aweil, 16 August 2013; all talked about the founding of AYU. The work in El Obeid was noted by Albino Madhan, in Aweil, 9 August 2013; Diing Chen Diing, in Aweil, 12 August 2013; and Ayii Bol, in Aweil, 16 August 2013.

[26] Michael Thiop Lang, in Aweil, 10 July 2013.

[27] SudanAid successfully petitioned the World Food Programme (WFP) for an initial feeding programme of two months' food rations for those who needed it on arrival, organised by local area committees who knew the applicants. Edward Jubara and Tamrat Tawolde, 'Displaced Southerners in the Three Towns: A Survey Summary', SudanAid National Relief Section, 4 September 1986, CAR 7634.21.1.

government permit to operate, organised by civil servants from Aweil still working in the government in the mid-1980s.[28] This transit network included Cairo, where AYU worked with the Irish aid agency CONCERN, giving details of new people, their health conditions, and their time of arrival to help them get NGO assistance.[29]

At the railway station in Shajjara, as at bus and train stations across the city and in towns on routes northwards, AYU and other Nuer, Shilluk, and Bari community groups and church workers collaborated to sort, aid, and organise these thousands of traumatised and starving arrivals, and helped to direct sporadic aid distributions by Christian and other NGO agencies.[30] In re-establishing community connections and family links, this first desperate organisation articulated complex identifications that are a theme of this book. As Catherine Miller notes, people looked for other people with whom they could communicate.[31] AYU members would divide new arrivals by the names of their local executive chiefs in their villages and areas in the south, and would call contacts and other associations for those of other clans, regions, and ethnicities, and direct people to areas of Khartoum where they knew people from the same communities lived.[32] As Ngor Jonkor (a labourer, and later Dinka Malual court member in Khartoum) emphasised, though, 'even if you find a [Black man] that you've never seen in your life, you have to contact him and greet him to come and drink water, in the north'.[33]

1.1 The War Reaches Khartoum

For these new residents of Khartoum, this was the start of the civil war. Over 1987 to 1992, the city was the destination for well over a million

---

[28] Elizabeth Bassan, 'Background Information and Program Recommendation on Displaced People in Khartoum', SudanAid, 30 April 1987, MEDU 17/4/AID; Diing Chen Diing, in Aweil, 12 August 2013; Paul Kuel Kuel, in Aweil, 9 August 2013; Albino Madhan, in Aweil, 9 August 2013.

[29] Ayii Bol, in Aweil, 16 August 2013.

[30] Albino Madhan, in Aweil, 9 August 2013; CONCERN, 'Emergency Programme: Sudan 1988', MEDU 17/4/AID, 2.

[31] Catherine Miller, *Language Change and National Integration: Rural Migrants in Khartoum* (Khartoum University Press, 1992), 50.

[32] Albino Madhan, in Aweil, 9 August 2013.

[33] Ngor Jonkor used the Dinka word 'jieng', which was translated by the group listening to his history variously as Black man or as Dinka. Ngor Jonkor, in Apada, 8 June 2013; Abaker Thelatheen, in Apada, 8 June 2013.

displaced people from the south, joining over 100,000 people displaced from Darfur and South Kordofan by the famines of 1983–85. Khartoum boomed from around 1.8 million residents in 1983 to an estimated 4 million people by 1990.[34] By the end of 1986, the rate of arrivals peaked: the church-run humanitarian organisation SudanAid registered 48,474 people from October 1986 to February 1987, which 'indicates a startling influx of more than 12,000 people per month or 3,000 per week'.[35]

This was utterly overwhelming for the small number of organisations with aid funds to spend in Khartoum.

> The size of the problem is daunting ... basic information about the social composition of the shantytowns is lacking. Generally they are described as being composed of 'Southerners', 'Dinka', 'Westerners', or 'Mixed.'... Aweil Dinka form a majority in at least three Khartoum shantytowns (Col Macar in Omdurman, Kalakala and the Bentiu section of Bagiar).[36]

A basic lack of information undermined efforts to assist, even after major flooding in August 1987 brought international journalists to report on the washed-away clay and cardboard homes of hundreds of thousands of recently displaced people.[37] By 1990, estimates of the number of displaced people in Khartoum spanned from 600,000 to 3 million. Continued waves of displacement that year overwhelmed these estimates: throughout the 1990s and 2000s, displacement totals were recorded as a rounded 2 to 3 million.[38]

In these years of famine and mass movement between 1986 and 1992, there were almost no social or basic services; newcomers were unaware of official processes and held no documentation; overcrowded housing put family life under huge strain; labour markets

---

[34] Miller, *Language Change and National Integration*, 16–17.

[35] Brian Stockwell, Edward Jubara, Tamrat Tawolde, and Felix Lupai, 'Displaced Persons in the Khartoum Archdiocese: A Survey of Population and Basic Needs, September 15th to October 15th 1986', Khartoum Diocese, Catholic Church, October 1986, MEDU 17/3/REF/8, 1.

[36] Ryle and Yai Kuol, 'Displaced Southern Sudanese', 39. The first two place names in Khartoum noted here are transliterated in this book as, respectively, Machar Col and Kalakla, based on the pronunciation and written versions provided by people in Aweil and Juba during research.

[37] 'Minutes: Record of a Donors Emergency Meeting Held at the RRC on Thursday 13 August 1987', MEDU 17/4/AID; Bonner, 'A Reporter at Large'.

[38] Millard Burr, 'Sudan 1990–1992: Food Aid, Famine, and Failure', US Committee for Refugees, May 1993, MEDUC 17/3/REF/19, 11.

were over-saturated, while labourers attempted to support usually dozens of relatives and friends, often while coming to terms with the loss of their old homes, possessions, farms, and cattle. People built 'huts from cardboard, twigs, scrap cloth, metal and plastic on any waste ground, unused land or rubbish dump'.[39] They were joined by thousands of individuals and families from the fortified military towns of Wau and Juba who had managed to get flights to Khartoum.[40]

Many people who remember this period note a collective feeling of paralysis and breakdown.[41] Arou Piol, arriving from barely paid labour in northern Darfur in 1990, emphasised that 'some people felt shock, and died of feeling shock'.[42] In a 1990 research project about survival in the new shantytowns, 'two of the 60 interviewed women reported that their husbands [had] become insane in Khartoum'.[43] Abaker Thelatheen, a trader from Ariath who later became a chief in the city, remembers 'that time they sat down and they just discussed about the destruction of the south. For us, even some people felt shocked until they died, about the destruction of the south.'[44]

1.2 Emergency Reconstruction

These new residents made fundamental changes to Khartoum's social and political geography between 1988 and around 1991, marking out and protecting new political space in a period many people called the 'establishment' of Khartoum. This was a time of massive organisation within new neighbourhoods.

Trauma, starvation, family deaths, and personal impoverishment placed immense strain on comparatively small family and community

---

[39] Amnesty International, 'Sudan's Secret Slaughter: Recent Human Rights Violations in the Civil War', 15 April 1988, SAD 985/6/26-50; 'Testimony of Roger P. Winter, Director, US Committee for Refugees, before the Senate Committee on Foreign Relations Subcommittee on Africa', 23 February 1989, SAD 945/8/17-24, 21; Inger Andersen, 'Situation Report Sudan July–September 1986', SudanAid Relief Section, 16 September 1986, CAR 6734.21.1.
[40] Jimmy Wongo, in Juba, 18 October 2013.
[41] Also noted by Amnesty International, 'Sudan's Secret Slaughter'.
[42] Arou Piol Adam, in Apada village, 22 July 2013. See Chapter 4 for Arou's projects.
[43] Ibrahim, 'Southern Sudanese Women Migrants', 253–54.
[44] Abaker Thelatheen, in Apada, 8 June 2013; see Chapter 3 for Abaker's organisational work.

1.2 Emergency Reconstruction

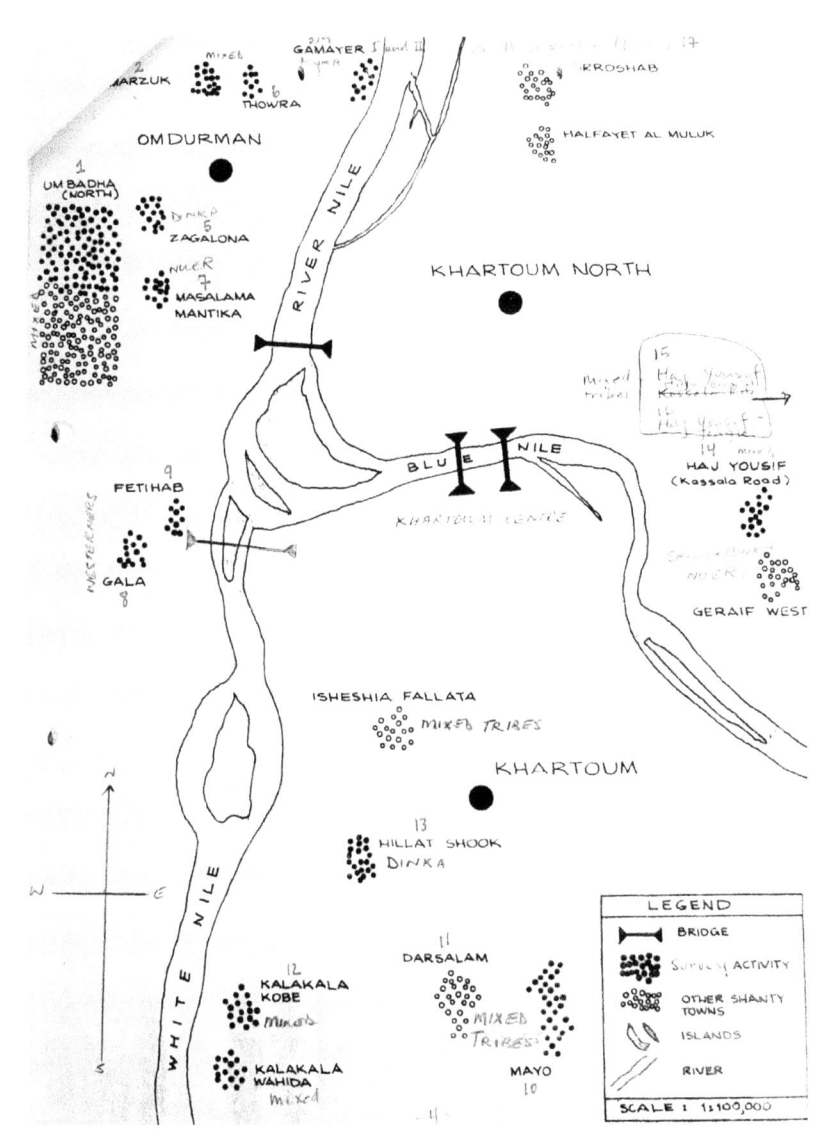

Figure 1.1 Hand-drawn map of Khartoum displaced settlements by Betsy Bassan prepared for the report 'Background Information and Program Recommendation on Displaced People in Khartoum', 30 April 1987.

Durham University Middle East Documentation Unit 17/4/AID/125. Reproduced with permission of Betsy Bassan, Panagora Group.

networks in Khartoum.[45] The emergency needed management. In marginalia and footnotes, the few aid reports now available note self-arranged systems of intermediaries that organised the local logistics of relief projects and aid distributions.[46] These individuals, associations, and other ad hoc groups of people were summarised as 'chiefs' or 'traditional authority' in aid notes from the time. But relief agencies' 'lists' of chiefs disguise the heterogeneous systems and individuals who emerged to manage this initial societal reorganisation and reconstruction, and to work with emergency assistance.[47]

Some of these individuals and groups picked up both northern and southern Sudanese terminologies for community authorities, appointing themselves (and being collectively nominated) as sultans or chiefs, running courts, and asserting a kind of social and moral clout beyond the straightforwardly political or administrative.[48] Many people noted the establishment in around 1989 of common courts and pan-ethnic groups of chiefs, who would (in theory) work together to solve inter-ethnic and local issues in their suburbs.[49] These (mostly) men also worked to organise and administrate exploded family networks across Sudan, as one clan, village, or local area spread across multiple suburbs and refugee camps across the country. Members of established chiefly families from Bahr el Ghazal, Warrap, and Upper Nile, such as paramount chief Riing Thiik's family in Aweil North, were encouraged by friends and relatives – or chose themselves – to act as chiefly proxies and community middlemen. For instance, William Deng Aken, who had gone to work in Khartoum's Pepsi factory in the 1970s, became a *gol* leader in the city when members of his extended family and community arrived in the late 1980s: 'so I've been working there before

---

[45] SudanAid noted this near-collapse in a survey conducted in July and August 1986 in Khartoum and extended to other northern towns by September. Andersen, 'Displaced Southerners in Khartoum', SudanAid, 1987, MEDU 17/4/AID/129; Stockwell et al., 'Displaced Persons in the Khartoum Archdiocese'; Sudan Council of Churches and UNICEF, 'Report of MCH Survey among the Displaced Populations, Khartoum Area', MEDU 17/4/AID/127; Jubara and Tawolde, 'Displaced Southerners in the Three Towns'.

[46] Wijnroks, 'The Displaced People of Khartoum: Report of an Exploratory Mission', MSF Holland, March 1988, MEDU 17/3/REF/7, 8.

[47] Abaker Thelatheen, in Apada, 15 August 2013. Many men interviewed for this study were part of this confusion, made 'sub-chiefs' in various places in Khartoum, or became executive chiefs for parallel displaced communities in Khartoum.

[48] See Leonardi, *Dealing with Government*. [49] See Chapter 3.

1.2 Emergency Reconstruction

the war, and after the war that was when I set permanently in Khartoum'.[50] In doing this, these men extended networks of family and clan authority that stretched across Darfur and Kordofan back into the south.[51] As Joseph Ukel, a politician resident in Khartoum in this period, recalled,

> whenever food is [found], or whatever is given to them, their own people will be responsible for distribution, instead of [agencies] bringing these items and putting it down and people have not organised themselves. So that was the beginning of making [the] so called now 'chiefs'. They were called chiefs, but – the problem was that, customarily, the chief is somebody who selected by the tribe, to head in the area, but how do you have a chief, in Juba or in Wau – and another chief in Khartoum? Or El Obeid? So this was the question. But we said – you, these chiefs who are selected in these displaced areas, as soon as we get peace, the moment you return to the south, you don't go as a chief, because it will bring problems with your original chief.[52]

The limits of this authority were blurred and disputed, and made competitive because of people's desperation for food, assistance, and opportunity. As some frustrated British-appointed paramount chiefs who had relocated from northern Bahr el Ghazal complained, 'the gate [was] open to everybody' – 'there were so many [chiefs], because every time, when there is food distribution, and a group feels that they were not properly provided, then they can break away and form another, [with] their own chief. It was something for them to get food.'[53] But these new organisers and arbitrators were not only opportunists; they often brought the social, linguistic, and political knowledge required to negotiate food and relief distribution, and to manage local disputes and agreements with Darfuri and northern Sudanese neighbours and authorities. This included Luol Dut, who found himself 'caught' by this volunteer organisation work since he had been working as a trader in Haj Yousif since his mid-twenties.[54] Many men who gained importance in Khartoum in 1989 (the common date given for the coordinated 'organisation' of southern-origin community authorities in Khartoum) had arrived in the city from 1981 to 1985, and had already established

---

[50] William Deng Aken, in Apada, 18 July 2013.
[51] Lists of chiefs and their nominated point people across different displaced camps in Kordofan and Darfur can be found in Ryle and Yai Kuol, 'Displaced Southern Sudanese'.
[52] Joseph Ukel Abango, in Juba, 29 October 2013.   [53] Ibid.
[54] Luol Dut Tong, in Maper chiefs' court, 13 April 2013.

themselves as traders or workers in low levels of the civil service, police, or army.[55]

To the surprise of many contemporary humanitarian reports, the emergency settlement, organisation, and social reconstruction of displaced communities across Khartoum – which created entirely new suburbs in the process (see Chapter 2) – happened relatively quickly during this period.[56] This was because this reconstruction was not from scratch.

1.3 Old Black Khartoum

This emergency management was rooted in a long history of neighbourhood and community associations for the city's migrant residents and visiting workers. Ethnic associations and migrant organisations are fundamental to colonial and postcolonial urban spaces around the world, even if their activists, organisers, and fundraisers are often working on the geographical and social margins of cities and towns, and subject to racial and political abuses and violence.[57]

In Khartoum, the people trying to deal with the disasters of the late 1980s built their work on long histories of organisational and associational life in the city. This organisation was developed over at least three previous generations of migration from Sudan's peripheries, and tied regional migrants into a network of social security and opportunity within Sudan's low-pay, manual, and grey economies that were the preserve of racially marginalised residents since at least the time of slave trading and military recruitments under the Ottoman empire.

---

[55] As explained by Acien Acien Yor, in Aweil town, 11 July 2013; Abaker Thelatheen, in Apada, 15 August 2013; Ngor Jonkor, in Apada, 8 June 2013; Joseph Ukel Abango, in Juba, 29 October 2013. 'Non Athway Escapes Slavery', c. 1987, SAD 307/6/1-5; Ibrahim, 'Southern Sudanese Women Migrants', 251.

[56] Joseph Ukel Abango, in Juba, 29 October 2013; Miller, *Language Change and National Integration*, 23; Sudan Council of Churches and UNICEF, 'MCH Survey'. Corroborated by Michael Thiop Lang, in Aweil, 10 July 2013; William Deng Aken, in Apada, 18 July 2013.

[57] Abdoumalik Simone, *City Life from Jakarta to Dakar: Movements at the Crossroads* (Routledge, 2010); Callaci, *Street Archives*; David Pratten, *Return to the Roots? Migration, Local Institutions and Development in Sudan* (Edinburgh University Press, 2000); Sikainga, *City of Steel and Fire*; Cooper, *On the African Waterfront*; Badiey, *The State of Post-Conflict Reconstruction*; Brennan, *Taifa*; Bjarnesen and Utas, 'Introduction: Urban Kinship'; Thompson, Mohamoud, and Mahamed, 'Geopolitical Boundaries and Urban Borderlands'.

These associational cultures were not necessarily ethnically demarcated or specifically 'southern', but they used common knowledge of regional and village life and language to create travelling systems of reciprocity and trust across Sudan's urban and rural labour routes.

These systems were built on the networks and knowledge established by these great-grandparents and their families who had attempted to evade, work within, or had been captured by successive armed venture-capitalists – from slave-raiding traders to Ottoman and British imperial elites – who since at least the 1700s had mined Sudan's southern reaches for slaves and ivory.[58] Khartoum's new residents in the 1980s came from this old 'frontier of enslaveable people', who had long been the human resources for imperial and capitalist projects.[59] These were the lands of the Nubians, an ambiguous descriptor that had little geographic or ethnic definition but incorporated ideas of ancient Black Sudanese kingdoms of Nubia and Cush, primitive martial Black races, and regions beyond state control.[60] Generations of predation brought slaves, slave soldiers, and their wives and children northwards. They were joined by migrant workers, escapees, and other wanderers from Sudan's borderlands and the wider horn of Africa and West Africa throughout the nineteenth century.[61]

This violent history shaped the heartland of the emergent state at Khartoum. Slave armies were the foundation for twentieth-century Sudanese cities. Following the abolition of the slave trade in 1899, many slaves stayed in Khartoum; by the end of the First World War there were an estimated 20,000 slaves in the city.[62] They were joined by a fast-growing population of rural migrants to feed new agricultural

---

[58] Douglas H. Johnson, 'Sudanese Military Slavery from the Eighteenth to the Twentieth Century', in Léonie Archer, ed., *Slavery and Other Forms of Unfree Labour* (Routledge, 1988), 151; for further discussion of the term 'Nubian', see Johnson, 'The Structure of a Legacy'.
[59] James, 'Perceptions from an African Slaving Frontier', 133.
[60] It references the Nubian Christian kingdom in northern Sudan, which dominated the Nile valley in the eighth century CE and which was subsumed within Arab territorial and political expansions by the fourteenth century. Al-Afif Mukhtar, 'The Crisis of Identity in Northern Sudan', 14.
[61] Sikainga, 'Military Slavery', 23; Sikainga, *Slaves into Workers*; Ewald, *Soldiers, Traders, and Slaves*.
[62] Mohamed El Awad Galal al-Din, 'The Nature and Causes of Labour Migration to the Khartoum Conurbation', in Valdo Pons, ed., *Urbanization and Urban Life in the Sudan* (University of Hull Press, 1980), 426; Sikainga, 'Slavery, Labour, and Ethnicity in Khartoum: 1898–1956', 8.

labour markets, soldier recruits, and low-level government service workers, including drivers and personal servants, and their wives and children. The political landscape, labour markets, and racial hierarchies of opportunity and exploitability set out by successive regimes in Khartoum since the late 1800s structured possibilities for these Black travellers from across Sudan. Ex-slaves congregated in the al-Diyum slums with other migrants, with Hayy al-Dubbat (the Officers' Quarter) in Omdurman housing West African migrants, ex-slaves, and others not claiming Arab ancestry; ex-slave soldiers and their descendants founded suburbs known as *malakiyas* in towns across Sudan.[63] While migration from the three southern provinces was heavily restricted by the closed district regulations such as the Passport and Permits Ordinance of 1922, many people – including wives and children of traders, and staff of civil servants posted to the south – moved or were moved to Khartoum, particularly during the late 1940s.[64]

The three towns of Khartoum grew massively through the 1930s to 1950s. Agany Macham, who arrived in Khartoum in 1988, and became a bricklayer and chief's court representative for the Dinka Malual of the Pariath clan in Haj Yousif, remembers his father talking about going to Khartoum with his friends as young men in the 1920s and 30s.

> By that time Dinka don't even enter inside the house, they just stay outside, just laying the bricks until it finished, then they go back.... You know they were footing from southern Darfur up to Khartoum, they spent three months on the road. This is a long way.[65]

The Second World War prompted, as one hostile contemporary observer put it, the 'enrolment of children of the backwards areas into the

---

[63] Sikainga, 'Military Slavery', 29; Leonardi, *Dealing with Government*, 83. Although there is no formal data before the 1955/6 census, a 1921 population count of Omdurman found in Khartoum University Library by Farnham Rehfisch in 1965 showed a southern Sudanese population of 3.2 per cent, and a western Sudanese population of 2.4 per cent. Rehfisch, 'An Unrecorded Population Count of Omdurman', *Sudan Notes and Records* 46 (1965): 34–35, 38.

[64] Farnham Rehfisch, 'A Study of Some Southern Migrants in Omdurman', *Sudan Notes and Records* 43 (1962): 50–104.

[65] Agany Macham, in Apada chiefs' court, 8 June 2013.

army and their pouring into Khartoum'.⁶⁶ It also brought real financial incentives to move to agricultural schemes and towns at the centre of Sudan, particularly after a 1950 ordinance increased wages.⁶⁷ By the 1955/6 census, Omdurman had grown by 260 per cent, although southerners still made up 3.9 per cent of the population (outpaced by the western Sudanese population at 5.5 per cent).⁶⁸

This urban growth re-patterned the city, and in doing so forced people to articulate a complex array of historical-geographical, politicised, and racial descriptors and demarcations to define their neighbours and neighbourhoods. Harold Barclay's study of the peri-urban village Burri al Lamaab in 1964 provides a good example.⁶⁹ In the late 1950s to early 1960s, during Barclay's study, about half of the village considered themselves to be of 'slave descent', mostly from the Nuba regions of Kordofan, with some Dinka and Fertit from western Bahr el Ghazal; half of these were descendants of slaves owned by other village residents.⁷⁰ These people were colloquially called *muwaaliid* (slave descendants) or *abiid*, slaves. People from the broad southern regions of Sudan were noted by geographical origin as *junubiin* (southerners), or by major ethnic groups such as the majority Dinka and Nuer residents. These Dinka and Nuer residents were divided between slave and non-slave descent, but being *abiid* was sometimes extended 'to include anyone from the southern pagan tribes whether he has been a slave or not', because for other longer-term residents or newcomers from other 'un-enslaved' areas of Sudan, the southern region was a historical source of slaves, and entirely Black.⁷¹ 'The term [*abiid*] may also be applied to anyone who is particularly black in colour, but this is often done in jest.'⁷² Barclay noted the social visibility of Nuer, Nuba,

---

⁶⁶ Mohammed Ahmed, 'Christian Missionary Activity', 2.
⁶⁷ Al-Din, 'Labour Migration', 428–29.
⁶⁸ Rehfisch, 'An Unrecorded Population Count of Omdurman', 34–35, 38.
⁶⁹ Harold Barclay, *Buurri al Lamaab: A Suburban Village in the Sudan* (Cornell University Press, 1964); K. D. D. Henderson, *Sudan Republic* (Benn, 1965); Peter McLoughlin, 'The Sudan's Three Towns: A Demographic and Economic Profile of an African Urban Complex. Part I. Introduction and Demography', *Economic Development and Cultural Change* 12, no. 1 (1963): 70–83; Sondra Hale, 'Nubians in the Urban Milieu: Greater Khartoum', paper presented at the 17th annual conference of the Philosophical Society of Sudan, 'Urbanization in the Sudan', 1972.
⁷⁰ Barclay, *Buurri al Lamaab*, 95.   ⁷¹ Ibid., 95–96.
⁷² Ibid., 129–30. This echoes Mukhtar and Boddy's works on skin colour in northern Sudan. 'The understanding was that the lighter the colour of the skin,

western Sudanese, and Dinka residents in Burri al Lamaab through their physiognomy, employment, and lifestyle, not necessarily only identified by their specific regions of origin.[73] Slave descendants, in Barclay's study, exclusively married other descendants; 'according to the dominant group, "slaves" do not have as good "morals"', because of their beer-brewing and sexual activity.[74] Class, social standing, moral character, and economic success could all temper or override colour; but Barclay also noted that people sometimes self-referenced as *abiid*.[75]

1.4 The Golden Age of Migrant Khartoum

By the 1950s, migrant networks and paths across Sudan's changing rural-urban landscape were established, and people were commonly taking up seasonal labour or paths to Khartoum for opportunity and escape.[76] After Sudan's independence in 1956, and the removal of travel restrictions for southern residents, there was a widely recorded exponential increase in southern populations across Khartoum, particularly in 1962 due to flooding and famine in Upper Nile and Bahr el Ghazal; this growth not only was from Nilotic regions, but included significant numbers of Equatorian migrants.[77] In Rehfisch's

---

the closer the person is to the centre, and the more authentic his or her claim to Arab ancestry': Mukhtar, 'The Crisis of Identity in Northern Sudan', 215; Boddy, *Wombs and Alien Spirits: Women, Men, and the Zar Cult in Northern Sudan* (University of Wisconsin Press, 1989).

[73] Barclay, *Buurri al Lamaab*, 96.   [74] Ibid., 128.
[75] Hale, 'Nationalism, "Race", and Class', 181; Barclay, *Buurri al Lamaab*, 129, 126–27. The appropriation and deployment of slurs and derogative terms has a wider literature than can be dealt with here; see Claudia Bianchi, 'Slurs and Appropriation: An Echoic Account', *Journal of Pragmatics* 66 (2014): 35–44; Cassie Herbert, 'Precarious Projects: The Performative Structure of Reclamation', *Language Sciences* 52 (2015): 131–38; Tom W. Smith, 'Changing Racial Labels: From "Colored" to "Negro" to "Black" to "African American"', *Public Opinion Quarterly* 56, no. 4 (1992): 496–514.
[76] El-Wathig Kameir, 'Nuer Migrants in the Building Industry in Khartoum: A Case of the Concentration and Circulation of Labour', in Pons, ed., *Urbanization and Urban Life*, 457; Hale, 'Nubians in the Urban Milieu'.
[77] This Equatorian presence was demonstrated in Farnham Rehfisch's self-described 'unrepresentative' survey of Omdurman in 1960, using mostly Equatorian-origin students as surveyors; 'A Study of Some Southern Migrants in Omdurman', 51. In the survey conducted by his southern Sudanese students, 73 per cent of informants in Omdurman came from Equatoria; 57. Jimmy

1962 survey of southern migrants to Khartoum, only six people out of 252 had nobody in the city to receive them and help them, even though fifty people had travelled north alone.[78] By 1960, the city was already heterogeneous: a survey in 1960 found 13,000 West Africans, 73,000 Nubiyin migrants, 10,000 West Darfurians, 12,000 Nuba Mountains migrants, 28,000 Beja residents, 11,000 southerners, and 33,000 'miscellaneous' residents in Khartoum, making up just over a third of Khartoum Province's total estimated population.[79] In Rehfisch's 1962 survey, 30 per cent of those claiming to have been born in the southern region were women; these included young runaways, wives, and former slaves.[80]

Throughout the 1960s, Khartoum's migrant population boomed.[81] Mass migration to the city was encouraged also by the escalating violence of the civil war in the southern region from 1963, encouraging those who could leave to seek opportunities – particularly for formal education – in the north.[82] This was an option particularly for

---

Wongo also noted extensive Equatorian migration in this period in conversation in Juba, 18 October 2013.

[78] Rehfisch, 'A Study of Some Southern Migrants in Omdurman', 76.
[79] R. A. Henin, *Economic Development and Internal Migration in the Sudan* (University of Khartoum, 1960).
[80] Rehfisch, 'A Study of Some Southern Migrants in Omdurman', 54.
[81] Fouad N. Ibrahim, 'Migration and Identity Change in the Sudan', *GeoJournal* 25, no. 1 (1991): 5–6; 'Southern Sudanese Women Migrants'; Siri Lamoureaux, 'Message in a Mobile Risālah fī jawāl = Risaala fi jawaal: Mixed-Messages, Tales of Missing and Mobile Communities at the University of Khartoum', PhD dissertation, Leiden University (2011), 215; Bedri Omer Elias and Hassan Yassin Bedawi, 'The Squatters Housing Problem: A Review of Government Policy and Solutions', in El-Sayed Bushra, ed., *Urbanization in the Sudan: Proceedings of the Seventeenth Annual Conference, Khartoum, 2nd–4th August, 1972* (Philosophical Society of the Sudan, 1972), 213–21; al-Din, 'Labour Migration', 428–29, quoting the Khartoum annual provincial report for 1950. Many people in Aweil and Juba gave examples of familial migration experience: Abaker's father and grandfather had been travelling north since the 1910s (Abaker Thelatheen, in Apada, 8 June 2013). This movement was reflected in the few population statistics available: Khartoum town at independence in 1956 had 93,000 inhabitants, and expanded to around 350,000 by 1973; Omdurman had similar levels of expansion, from 113,000 people in 1956 to about 300,000 in 1973. El-Sayed Bushra, *An Atlas of Khartoum Conurbation* (Khartoum University Press, 1976); also see Bushra, ed., *Urbanization in the Sudan*.
[82] Øystein H. Rolandsen, 'The Making of the Anya-Nya Insurgency in the Southern Sudan, 1961–64', *Journal of Eastern African Studies* 5, no. 2 (2011): 211–32.

Equatorian residents, many of whom had better access to missionary school education and so saw better employment and living opportunities in Khartoum.[83] Thousands of southern women sought opportunities in Khartoum through nurse and teacher training from the 1950s onwards.[84] While most civil war refugees fled from Equatoria to East and Central African countries, the expulsion of Christian missionaries and collapse of the southern regional school system and civil service brought large numbers of aspiring students and low-grade wage labourers to towns across Sudan. From 1964 the main secondary schools in the southern region (including Rumbek and Juba Commercial) were moved to Khartoum, where they stayed for eight years, taking in migrant southern students.[85] The civil war amnesties declared repeatedly from 1966 onwards called on refugees and ex-combatants to return to Sudan, and many people responded from around 1968 onwards, particularly wage labourers, students, and those wanting access to towns and jobs in Sudan after working elsewhere in East Africa – a worker on two shillings per day in Juba would earn seven shillings four pence per day in Khartoum in 1971.[86] Files from the 1960s and 1970s of Juba's regional ministries in the South Sudan National Archives are full of transport and job requests for Khartoum.[87] Although most accounts emphasise that these migrants were overwhelmingly young men, contemporary small surveys show a significant number of women also moving to Khartoum from the peripheries; there was one woman for every two men from Bahr el Ghazal in Abdelrahman's 1979 survey, and twenty years earlier, Rehfisch noted the oddity that 1956 census figures implied large numbers of self-described 'southern' single women in

---

[83] Alfred Taban, in Juba, 16 October 2013.
[84] 'Gordon Memorial Sudan Mission Minutes of Mission Conference Held at Yei', 14–20 January 1956, KNA MSS 61/712 (A).
[85] John Howell, 'Political Leadership and Organisation in the Southern Sudan', PhD dissertation, University of Reading (1978), 185.
[86] Foreign Office internal correspondence, 13 October 1966, NAUK FO 371.190465 VS1821.6; John Rogge, *Too Many, Too Long: Sudan's Twenty-Year Refugee Dilemma* (Rowman & Allanheld, 1985), 30, 127; Foreign Office margin notes, 13 October 1966, NAUK FO 371.190465 VS1821.6; Marvine Howe, 'Promise of Regional Autonomy for Sudan Separatists Brings Mass Return to Southern Towns', *The Times*, 1 January 1971.
[87] For example, the South Sudan National Archives (SSNA) file Equatoria Province 65.B.5; and the Ministry of Southern Affairs 'Flimsy File' for 1971.

1.4 The Golden Age of Migrant Khartoum

Omdurman – 33 per cent of women claimed to be born in the south.[88] Poor arrivals congregated in old migrant areas, around Deim, Ishash Fellata, Burri, and Haj Yousif, taking up railways and labourer jobs.[89] Other poorer residents walked there, including Lual Lual Aguer, who first went to Khartoum in 1979 seeking education as a young boy. There he lived behind a factory with a group of southern youth from all over the region, and worked as a manual labourer with them, pooling salaries to 'feed each other'.[90]

The idea of separate rural and urban spheres was breaking down in practice by the 1970s. Chain and cyclical migration from the south increased with the extension of the railway line to Bahr el Ghazal in the 1960s.[91] Of migrants surveyed by Abdelrahman in 1979, 83 per cent knew something about Khartoum life before they arrived, half of them because of previous visits, and the others from returned migrants.[92] Popular reasons for migration from the south, as recorded by Abdelrahman in a 1979 social survey, included 'life in the rural areas is often restricted by traditions', 'one is freer in Khartoum to do what one wants', and 'to be more important and civilised'.[93] As Garang Mayuen, about twelve years old in 1979, explained:

---

[88] Sharon Hutchinson, *Nuer Dilemmas: Coping with Money, War, and the State* (University of California Press, 1996); Babiker Abdalla Abdelrahman, 'Internal Migration in the Sudan: A Study of the Socio-economic Characteristics of Migrants in Khartoum', PhD dissertation, University of Glasgow (1979), 114; Rehfisch, 'A Study of Some Southern Migrants in Omdurman', 54.

[89] Edward Jubara, in Juba, 14 March 2013.

[90] Lual Lual Aguer, in Apada chiefs' court, 3 June 2013.

[91] Abdelrahman, 'Internal Migration in the Sudan', 123. This route was taken by two men interviewed in Aweil: Diing Chen Diing, in Aweil, 15 July 2013; William Manyang Tong, in Apada, 17 August 2013.

[92] Rehfisch, 'A Study of Some Southern Migrants in Omdurman', 71. By 1979, most migrants were making one visit home per year on average, and most Khartoum residents from southern Sudan had visitors at least once a year: Abdelrahman, 'Internal Migration in the Sudan', 155, 189, 192.

[93] Abdelrahman, 'Internal Migration in the Sudan', 157. By 1980, al-Din noted that 'there are more and more migrants whose attitudes and aspirations are increasingly out of keeping with the opportunities available in an essentially rural economy'; al-Din, 'Labour Migration', 433. This was also noted by members of the Dinka Cultural Society, in Apada, 11 August 2013, and by Hassaballa Omer Hassaballa, 'Displacement and Migration as a Consequence of Development Policies in Sudan', in Eltigani El Tahir Eltigani and Hatim Ameer Mahran, eds., *The Displacement Problem in the Sudan: Essays on the Crisis*, draft manuscript (1991), SAD.940/5/2, 46.

You know, we wanted to escape from the cattle.... some of my age, you know, we planned to escape from the house; and then we travelled farther north. [It] was '79 ... Then we escaped our family, we went to the nearest station where the train passed, and climb[ed] on, and went up to Khartoum.[94]

By the early 1970s, many wealthier and longer-established residents in Khartoum felt like the city was being overwhelmed. A 1971 survey estimated that about 270,000 of the 650,000 residents of Greater Khartoum were migrants, and about half of the children in the conurbation were theirs.[95] Urban organisations were struggling to cope with the demands of these poor new residents, particularly those displaced by the civil war in the south. The Sudan African National Union (SANU) office – a southern political organisation – worried in 1968 that 'many Southern young men and girls are today thrown to extreme poverty, especially those deprived of parents ... more than 200 of these children have approached SANU Office for recommendation, help, and many of them are still roaming about in the Northern towns without jobs'.[96] The few southern MPs living in Khartoum were struggling to cope, their houses full of relatives and friends.[97] The marginalisation of, and prejudice against, southern and other Black peripheral migrants by the city and national government offices put more pressure on regional institutions, associations, and individuals, as supplicants were passed on. An employee of the Ministry of Southern Affairs, established in 1969, wrote in frustration that

since the inception of this Ministry, it has been our daily experience to witness endless streams of unemployed citizens from the Southern Provinces calling at this Office seeking employment. While a few admittedly came here out of desperation, the majority of those who invaded these premises, are usually directed here by other Governmental Ministries, Corporations and institutions. I have particularly noted that EVEN the Labour Exchange Bureau Regional Offices are playing a leading roll [sic]

---

[94] Garang Mayuen Mayuen, in Apada, 11 August 2013; William Manyang Tong, in Apada, 17 August 2013.
[95] Al-Din, 'Labour Migration', 431.
[96] L.D. Logoye, in SANU Youth Organ, *Monthly Bulletin*, no. 2, November 1967, CAR A/86/28, 5–7.
[97] Toby Maduot, 'Resume of a Talk by Dr Tobi Maduot, MP for Thiet North (Sudan)', 1968, CAR A/90/13/21.

1.4 The Golden Age of Migrant Khartoum

in this unfortunate game.... this very Office which is being invaded has not the means to cater for those craving for work.[98]

The Addis Ababa Agreement, which ended the first civil war in 1972 with arrangements for southern regional administration, did not end this migration into the city. Numbers of arrivals continued to rise in the 1970s, including Nubian communities displaced by further dam-building along the Nile to the north of Khartoum; poor arrivals made cardboard villages on the outskirts of Khartoum and other major northern cities.[99] According to contemporary scholar Ali Mazrui, 'some calculations of Dinka in the north put them at nearly half-a-million'.[100]

The pressures of this massive immigration to Khartoum shaped everyday experiences of local, ethnic, and historical frustrations and violent oppressions over the 1970s. As southern, western, and Nuba Mountains migrants filled (and continue to fill) the low-status menial labour sector in Khartoum, combinations of moral, social, and economic marginalisation, niche labour markets, and historical racial stereotyping resulted in particular forms of group identification.[101] Collectively, these low-status jobs were 'considered inferior and only for "lower" social groups', and these Sudanese Black and peripheral populations 'were still regarded as culturally inferior and descendants of slaves'.[102] But more specifically, for example, Nubian workers dominated septic tank cleaning through the 1970s, and as such anyone else working in the same sector was automatically called a Nubian; the idea of 'becoming Nubi' was still in use as descriptor for urbanised rural people in the 1980s, much like the term *malakiyan*.[103] The label *junubi*, southerner, was just one of several common personal short-hands from the 1960s and 1970s onwards.

---

[98] Philip Obang to Abdalla Abdelkarim, 'Employment of Southerners', 12 March 1970, SSNA MSA 11.B.1.
[99] Bushra, *Urbanization in the Sudan*, 9, iii; Hale, *Nubians in the Urban Milieu*.
[100] Ali Mazrui, 'The Black Arabs in Comparative Perspective: The Political Sociology of Race Mixture', in Dunstan M. Wai, ed., *The Southern Sudan: The Problem of National Integration* (Routledge, 1972), 72.
[101] Pratten, *Return to the Roots?*.
[102] Sikainga, 'Slavery, Labour, and Ethnicity in Khartoum: 1898–1956', 8.
[103] Hale, 'Nationalism, "Race", and Class', 172; Johnson, 'The Structure of a Legacy', 83–84.

The development of a 'southern' identification cannot be abstracted from these histories of urban terminologies and collectives – the Nubians, *malakiyans*, *abiid*, and *junubiin*, among many other more local and ethnic specificities – and their economic, political, and moral weightings. These markers underpinned the politics of migration to Khartoum by the mid-century. Their history is ambiguous partly due to the various attempts at appropriation and re-ascription made by their constituents: being *junubi* was increasingly preferential to the pejorative *abiid*, and self-referencing as Nubian or *malakiyan* was a form of appropriation and reconditioning of older imposed identifications. The same period saw the re-appropriation of being Sudani – being Sudanese, and being Black, with the term's Arabic roots in the colour. Claiming to be truly Sudani could be done both to avoid more derogatory terms and to assert claims to equal national status, as Rehfisch observed:

There is a growing tendency in the Three Towns to refuse to associate oneself with a tribe, since there is a feeling that tribalism is a factor leading to national disunity. Many educated and non-educated alike insist that they are not members of any tribe, being purely and simply Sudanese. Some of those classed as 'Miscellaneous' [in the 1956 Census] are probably Southerners who were either born in the North or have lived there for a long time and do not wish to proclaim their origin, since Southerners in the North suffer from some prejudice and social disability.[104]

These complex and cross-cutting socioeconomic, racial, and cultural identifications evolved in the city through this period. Social and cultural associations, built out of ethno-linguistic and regional ties, sharpened ethno-regional identifications, but these regional, ethnic, village, and clan identifications were used as much for broad practical organisation and routes for mutual social support as they were held up as clear moral and political collectivities (see Chapter 3). These identifications were both asserted and blurred by the realities of Khartoum life and the proximities of racial and social experience, and by families just living, intermarrying, and growing up together. Mazrui commented in 1973 that 'if the country survives, the Sudan may be the first modern nation in Africa to have creatively used a combination of socialism and sex for national integration'.[105]

[104] Rehfisch, 'A Study of Some Southern Migrants in Omdurman', 53.
[105] Mazrui, 'The Black Arabs in Comparative Perspective', 79.

1.5 Social Life and Mutual Aid in the Early 1980s

By the 1980s, then, there was an established society and economy for Black peripheral migrant communities in Khartoum, and many of those fleeing northwards from 1986 had previous experience of pathways to the city. Michael Thiop had picked up skills as a bricklayer in Khartoum when he went north in 1980 for a few years, and had a good time:

> there was a club in which people played dominoes, and others playing cards. In the night also you can go for cinema. It was the whole of Sudan including South of Sudan, because some people board the train here from South Sudan to Khartoum. There were also Ethiopians, the Arab girls, it was mixed. If you find that I'm from Aweil, you have to stay with me. And those of Upper Nile also interact with Bahr el Ghazal, they have to come also and join you.... And for that we organise the social and cultural activities, like on Friday we used to [dance;] the Luo can dance, the Dinka Malwal, they dance alone, and the rest of the tribes, they also practice their traditional dance, in a very large yard, people come and they stay there then they see the different dances from different tribes. So there were Dinka in Khartoum since the beginning, I think.[106]

Diing Chen also went to Khartoum when he left school in Aweil aged fifteen:

> For work, looking for clothes, seeking some money, if you are not a student you can go there and work to get some money, so that here you can come and buy a cow [to pay for a marriage settlement]. For myself, I went there for work, since 1982. I didn't return back, I stayed there, and there I joined the Comboni school.[107]

New arrivals from Bahr el Ghazal, Abyei, the Nuba Mountains, and Upper Nile fitted into this racial history, economy, and geography of Khartoum. In this immediate disaster, discussions of whom to assist involved layers of obligation and negotiations about group

---

[106] Michael Thiop Lang, in Aweil, 10 July 2013.
[107] Diing Chen Diing, in Aweil, 15 July 2013. James Garang Ngor's paternal uncle was already in Khartoum when his family fled north in 1988, and his grandparents had also visited Khartoum for work; interviewed in Aweil, 30 June 2013. Emmanuel was already a student at Comboni college when the war started; he was on his own, with no family in Khartoum, but he knew his cousin: she moved there in the 1960s, living in Wad el Bashir with a southern husband; Emmanuel Deng Anei, in Apada, 3 June 2013.

responsibility. For AYU member Albino Madhan, his fellow Dinka clans of Northern Bahr el Ghazal were the priority, followed by all Dinka, then all southerners, then all Black people – 'that's the order we do'.[108] Despite the ethno-regional names of community organisations, assistance was part of a scale of commonality, under which 'they helped whoever came from the South to the North'.[109] As Albino explained:

We talk to our people ... so when we see people from [the] south coming, we don't care whether he's Dinka, Shilluk, Nuer, whatever; he's [a] southerner ... we have to take care of him; we cannot leave him to die and take our own people.[110]

People extended this mutual obligation partly in reaction to homogenising and uncivilised stereotypes of Black (and) southern people in Khartoum, and to the political and personal shame of ignoring the immediate poverty and desperation of fellow southerners. Diing Chen emphasised:

We don't need our own people ... to come across the city walking naked, and we are wearing so smart, because they [northerners] would laugh at us, say look – these are their families walking naked and they're wearing smart![111]

This local organisation was part of Khartoum life for all of its residents – particularly its poor labourers and rural migrants – as, with economic constraints and political stagnation by the late 1980s, city government broke down and organisation at the neighbourhood level became crucial.[112] Emergency organisation from 1986 onwards built on older cultures of urban association and mutual assistance. Increasing numbers made space for clan-level associational cultures that centred on immediate family and local ethnicity, but also created a wider organisational culture within Black, marginalised, exploited, and economically stressed neighbourhoods. The ideas of political community, Sudanese society, and Black self-organisation that this history produced are the focus of this book.

[108] Albino Madhan, in Aweil, 9 August 2013.
[109] Santino Akak Kuon, in Aweil, 3 July 2013.
[110] Albino Madhan, in Aweil, 9 August 2013.
[111] Paul Kuel Kuel, in Aweil, 9 August 2013.
[112] Ahmad, 'The Neighbourhoods of Khartoum', 41–42.

1.6 Claiming Space after Disaster

When harvests failed across Darfur in 1983 and 1984, and war escalated in southern Sudan in 1986, people moved to Khartoum in far greater numbers and with significant emotional, economic, and political baggage. Their arrival again reshaped Khartoum, but their settlement and self-organisation in this emergency built on the city's long history of peri-urban poor Black settlement. This is also the period when literature on southern communities in Khartoum dries up, and where this book begins.[113]

By January 1988, SudanAid estimated that 1.5 to 1.8 million southern and Nuba Mountains migrants were now in Khartoum, amounting to over half of the total urban population.[114] The size of this in-migration created new neighbourhoods around Khartoum, including Takamul, Wehda, Barona, and Shigla.[115] These places were often termed 'villages' in vernacular and English-language interviews, as opposed to idea of the government-owned 'town'.[116] These were for – as Paulino Dhieu, who arrived in this period, explained – 'the Black only': 'you can find Darfurians, you can find southerners like Nuba, and the other tribes of southern Sudan'.[117] These spaces allowed these new communities to establish their own grey economies and financial solidarities. Washing work and bricklaying were popular, for instance, as a means to be self-employed or employed by fellow southern or western Sudanese residents.[118] Entire areas of the

---

[113] Literature after 1978 is mostly on urban geography and survival needs, for example, Ibrahim, 'Southern Sudanese Women Migrants'; Abdel Hamid Bakhit, 'Availability, Affordability and Accessibility of Food in Khartoum', GeoJournal 34, no. 3 (1994): 253–55; Abdel Hamid Bakhit and A. Johayna, 'Mubrooka: A Study in the Food System of a Squatter Settlement in Omdurman, Sudan', GeoJournal 34, no. 3 (1994): 263–68; Fouad Ibrahim, 'The Southern Sudanese Migration to Khartoum and the Resultant Conflicts', GeoJournal 25, no. 1 (1991): 13–18.
[114] Miller, Language Change and National Integration, 18. The city government's Commission for the Displaced was using a figure of 1,621,200 people by 1989. Mohad E. Abu Sin and H. Davies, The Future of Sudan's Capital Region: A Study in Development and Change (Khartoum University Press, 1991), 24.
[115] 'Displaced Mothers and Homeless Children Society Project Document' (October 1986), MEDU 17/4/AID.
[116] Many Aweil informants used the Dinka term 'baai'. For a discussion of this term, see Cormack, 'The Making and Re-making of Gogrial', 173.
[117] Peter Deng Akok, in Maper, 29 June 2013.
[118] Rehfisch, 'A Study of Some Southern Migrants in Omdurman', 79.

city – for example, Haj Yousif and Umbadda – were urban spaces dominated by darker-skinned residents originating from Sudan's peripheries, with their own markets, industries, and centres. This new geography of Khartoum was not solely 'ethnic' (as Fouad Ibrahim argues) or 'a small-scale copy of the South', but by the 1990s the city had become a complex mental map of plural, politicised affiliations and sites of aggregate strength and experience for its peripheral residents.[119] As Michael Thiop, the bricklayer, observed:

There are some places that you will not visit if you don't have reason of going there ... even if it is near, like this mango tree, you cannot reach it.... We used to move from the place where Dinka are, to another place where there are Dinka, like Comboni ground.[120]

This occupation of Khartoum is best demonstrated through the changing place names of city suburbs, particularly over 1986 to 1992.[121] Local, darkly humorous names developed fast from 1988 to 1990: Hillat Kusha, 'the settlement of garbage', Hillat Alkawaja Dagas in Mayo ('the foreigner who was fooled'), Karor ('rubbish'), and Ras Satan ('head of Satan') in western Jabarona were all names that amused informants in Aweil.[122] Hillat Shook in Mayo meant 'the village of barricades', but was also called Bentiu (a border area of southern Sudan) and, in 2004, 'Abu Ghraib' by some of its inhabitants.[123] Similarly, Khartoum North had a settlement called Jonglei, a reference to the southern Jonglei region, by 1986.[124] Names and self-descriptions were, simultaneously, expressions of situational anger and sadness, snide political jokes, and self-aware references to common slurs against the 'IDPs' (internally displaced persons). The words *nazihiin* – internally displaced, or internal refugees – and *al-ashwai* – informal – were

[119] Ibrahim, 'Southern Sudanese Women Migrants', 251.
[120] Michael Thiop Lang, in Aweil, 11 July 2013.
[121] As noted briefly by Ahmad, 'The Neighbourhoods of Khartoum', 44; Sikainga, *City of Steel and Fire*, 68; Hanaa Motasim, 'Deeply Divided Societies: Charting Strategies of Resistance', *Respect* 8 (2008): 13.
[122] Members of the Dinka Cultural Society, in Apada, 11 August 2013; anonymous women in Apada, 21 July 2013.
[123] Rogge, 'Relocation and Repatriation', 28; Members of the Dinka Cultural Society, in Apada, 11 August 2013. Abu Ghraib is the Iraqi prison used by US military forces in the 2003 war, and references the systematic abuse and torture of its inmates.
[124] Jubara and Tawolde, 'Displaced Southerners in the Three Towns: A Survey Summary'.

1.6 Claiming Space after Disaster

self-employed pejoratives.[125] The central Catholic Comboni school and grounds were commonly called Comboni Majaneen, meaning 'just people who are staying without work ... the drunkard people stay there, and people who are just conversing and what, they just overcrowd [*sic*]'.[126]

And they have [the suburb of] Mandela. This Mandela means they are suffering, they are in prison like Mandela, who had been imprisoned by the British government in South Africa so that he can give up the country, the rebel leader. So all these names ... they name the place according to their grief for the situation that they were [in].[127]

These names were used with a full awareness of their emotional baggage.[128] The multiplicity of names, one man explained, 'came as a result of sadness ... each one would call it according to his own atmosphere ... that could satisfy his sadness [laughs]'.[129]

Despite ongoing government attempts to rename these sites after their own nationalist symbols, such as Hai Mayo (in memory of the May revolution) and Hai el Baraka (Blessings Quarter, known to most people instead as Karton Kassala), these alternative names persisted. Popular place names, used instead of 'official' ones, have been a means of political and class commentary in Sudan for decades. Wealthy areas of Khartoum have borne sarcastic names since the 1960s, like Hai Al-Mazahir ('Appearances' or 'Exteriors' Quarter), a comment on the pretentiousness and exhibitionism of its resident elites. Ar-Riyad, At-Ta'iff, and Al-Mamoura are all satirically named after richer Middle Eastern city regions.[130] Takamul ('Integration'), allegedly named in the late 1970s, 'meant to symbolise, by analogy and with irony, the integration of all Sudanese people'.[131] In Atbara, Ishash was named after the straw huts 'associated with former slaves, West African

---

[125] These terms were used across interviews in Aweil and Juba; Miller, *Language Change and National Integration*, 18.
[126] Deng Atak Abuk, in Apada, 13 July 2013.
[127] Dhieu Kuel, in Mayen Ulem, 21 August 2013; also explained by Arou Piol Adam, in Apada village, 22 July 2013.
[128] Arou Piol Adam, in Apada village, 22 July 2013. [129] Ibid.
[130] Ahmad, 'The Neighbourhoods of Khartoum', 44; in Juba, the new capital of South Sudan, the area where the South Sudanese president, vice president, and many ministers live, was also named Riyadh sarcastically by locals in the early 2000s.
[131] Miller, *Language Change and National Integration*, 27.

immigrants, and marginal groups, and [which] were considered dens of social deviance'.[132] Competing place names as such demonstrate similarly competing powers and agency in Khartoum: the urban poor are displaced, but also move themselves; new suburbs gain official names, but unofficial ones often prove more powerful.

These place names also connected new residents to longer histories of displacement, slavery, and economic exploitation across Sudan. The village names Jabarona ('we were forced'), Zagalona ('we were thrown/forced out'), and Taradona ('they expelled us') have long histories and can be found all over Sudan since at least the 1910s.[133] One Zagalona was established before 1920 to the north-west of El Obeid, the capital of Northern Kordofan and a major post on the route to Khartoum, and remained on the maps I could find in 1933 and 1964.[134] Another Zagalona was recorded west of Aba Island and north of Kosti, among the sugar plantations on the White Nile in 1927; a further Zagalona was recorded between 1929 and 1937 nearby at Abu Rukka, and another east of the railway line near Atbara town, north-east of Khartoum, in the 1930s;[135] another Zagalona appears west of Al Fashir in North Darfur in 1961.[136] The Jabarona squatter settlement in Yei town in southern Sudan that developed during the first civil wars was translated phonetically as 'Jah ba rau', 'they come alone' in Juba Arabic, in 1969.[137] Such village names were often communally used, but some places like Abu Adam and Zagalona also developed vernacular names, such as Kowic, meaning 'thorns' in Dinka.[138] Zagalona was called Machar Col by many Dinka, although the origin of the name is disputed – some women believed it to stem from a founder's cattle, and others believed it to refer literally to 'Black People'.[139] Either way, these names were assertions of

---

[132] Sikainga, *City of Steel and Fire*, 68.
[133] Ahmad, 'The Neighbourhoods of Khartoum', 44.
[134] Map of El Obeid 55.1, War Office, 1920, Royal Geographical Society UK (RGS) 551787; map of El Obeid 55.1, Survey Office Khartoum, 1933, SAD.PF 4/2; Kordofan land and water use survey map S/D.9, 1964, RGS 551919.
[135] Map of Aba Island 55.J, Survey Office Khartoum, 1927, RGS Sudan Gen 46.
[136] Map of El Fasher, Survey Office Khartoum, 1961, RGS Sudan Gen 46.
[137] *Voice of the Nile Republic*, 15 November 1969, CAR A/86/21/3.
[138] Dhieu Kuel, in Mayen Ulem, 21 August 2013; anonymous women in Apada, 21 July 2013.
[139] Anonymous women in Apada, 21 July 2013.

1.6 Claiming Space after Disaster 57

spatial control.[140] When Machar Col was forcibly removed to a barren area outside Khartoum, to create the government-named Dar es Salaam ('Peace Village'), it became known as Jabarona, specifically named in colloquial Arabic 'so that the government can hear'.[141]

By naming the city, new residents demonstrated their knowledge of divided and abusive histories, mocked the slurs and stereotypes they suffered under, and challenged the government's sterilisation of their neighbourhoods (as 'Peace Village' or 'Blessings Quarter') with overt political statements that asserted their control of city space. The most essential claiming of the city through suburban names was the common assertion of historical ownership of Khartoum itself, now a popular refrain among returned residents in the South. For many Dinka people, Khar Tuom meant, in Dinka dialect, the meeting of two rivers; Omdurman was similarly reinterpreted as meaning 'boy calling for his mother'.[142] Tuti Island was named after the Nuer name Tut, and the name of Bahri came from the Dinka *bahr*, 'come here'. Shendi apparently developed from the Dinka name Chendit, and Burri from Burrij, a fisherman.[143] These roots are often disputed – there are many options and interpretations for Equatorian and Nuer residents – but fundamentally claim that 'even in the far north is our land. ... When we talk about the Sudan, we don't mean the southern part. No. The whole Sudan.'[144] As Madut Tong, disabled in the war and barely surviving the long journey to Zagalona in 1988, emphasised: 'Khartoum – old Khartoum – is our land, and we were the ones who named it.'[145] This fight for control of the city is the subject of the next chapter.

---

[140] For similar discussions of names and ownership, see Brendan Tuttle, 'Life Is Prickly: Narrating History, Belonging, and Common Place in Bor, South Sudan', PhD dissertation, Temple University (2013), 39.
[141] Arou Piol Adam, in Apada village, 22 July 2013.
[142] Arou Piol Adam and small group discussing the handmade map of Khartoum, in Apada village, 22 July 2013.
[143] Members of the Dinka Cultural Society, in Apada, 11 August 2013; Acien Acien Yor, in Aweil town, 11 July 2013; Arou Piol Adam, in Apada village, 22 July 2013; Manoa Aligo, in Koboko, 10 March 2017; and many others.
[144] Members of the Dinka Cultural Society, in Apada, 11 August 2013.
[145] Madut Tong, in Khartoum Gedid, Kuajok, 28 August 2013.

2 | Building Marginalisation in the Displaced City

While hundreds of thousands of starving and homeless rural people moved to Khartoum over (roughly) 1985 to 1993, this was also – not coincidentally – a period of massive change to Sudan's ruling elite. Gaffar Nimeiri was overthrown in a coup in 1985, replaced by a fragile democratic coalition government led by Sadig al-Mahdi, including the National Islamic Front (NIF), founded by Hassan al-Turabi in 1985. A military coup brought down the divided government in June 1989, led by Omar al-Bashir and with the support of the NIF. The new National Salvation Front rule (الإنقاذ الوطني, abbreviated to al-Ingaz), with Turabi as intellectual architect, claimed they would lead a national revival of Sudanese Arabic-Islamic civilisation. Al-Bashir, chair of the Revolutionary Command Council, became president in 1993.

These fundamental political shifts, underpinned by growing economic crises and rapidly escalating war in the south, all played out across Khartoum. The war, the collapsing economy, and the apparent crisis of Sudanese culture were made visible to the city's comparatively affluent and insulated central Sudani residents by the arrival of large numbers of impoverished and desperate Black people.[1] In response, local and national authorities attempted to exert often violent control. As coups and popular revolutions changed the central government, state policy on these displaced remained consistent: their physical dispersal, removal, and containment, and their use as cheap and silenced labour.[2]

In the tradition of colonial and postcolonial governments alike, the post-1989 regime framed this as a benevolent civilising project, *mashru al-hadari*, promoting a common national culture and modernisation

---

[1] Amnesty International, 'Sudan's Secret Slaughter', 21.
[2] Duffield, 'Aid and Complicity', 88.

for the benefit of those from otherwise 'primitive' regions. This chapter notes that, in practice, this was not a project of acculturation (through policies summarised as Arabization [*t'arib*] and Islamisation [*hidayah*]); for those subject to government authority in this period, this was a project of exclusion, silencing, and exploitation, using impoverishment, fear, and direct violence. The Sudanese government, local authorities, and neighbourhood committees exerted themselves to create physical and social distance between those who could perform as 'legitimate' residents, and dangerous Black immigrants. They excluded those who could not or would not look, speak, behave, or silence themselves from humanitarian aid, urban employment, and central space, and forcibly removed neighbourhoods to Khartoum's peripheries or deported people to agricultural schemes. This alienation was economically useful, creating a population dependent on exploitative or marginal employment in Sudan's fields and factories. This is how this project was understood by new southern residents of Khartoum: as a stripping and silencing, as cultural, economic, and physical violence, rather than as acculturation and absorption. The people attempting to re-establish their fragmented lives in the city in these years remember this as physical and psychological pacification.

By about 1991, Khartoum's urban and social space had been restructured by these state and neighbourhood authorities' efforts, setting out the space available for displaced communities (see Figure 2.1). This period was a battle over where and how people were allowed to establish public lives. In fighting for forms of residence and safety, new residents carved out a geography of their own, and created defensive neighbourhoods on the outskirts of the city.

2.1 Challenging the Heartland

Khartoum's population exploded at the same time as the coup in 1985.[3] The arrival of nearly a million new residents by 1988 made the conflict and impoverishment in Sudan visible to Khartoum's

---

[3] Ann Mosely Lesch, *The Sudan: Contested National Identities* (James Currey, 1998), 61; Ibrahim Elnur, *Contested Sudan: The Political Economy of War and Reconstruction* (Routledge, 2008); Willow Berridge, *Civil Uprisings in Modern Sudan: The 'Khartoum Springs' of 1964 and 1985* (Bloomsbury, 2015).

residents. These generally darker-skinned rural poor were a direct challenge to the assumed 'Arab-Islamic' integrity of three central Sudanese identities: of Khartoum city, of the Sudanese state centre, and of local elites who felt they had ownership of both.[4] At the same time, over 1983–88, the SPLA were seizing ground and significant victories in the south. By 1989, the southern war was spreading towards northern territories, with the SPLA operational in some areas of Darfur, Southern Kordofan, and Blue Nile, finding broader appeal outside southern Sudan in part thanks to John Garang's explicit declarations of a pan-Sudanese uprising for a 'New Sudan'. In mid-1988 Amnesty International noted that

> as the savagery of the southern conflict increases, it is being matched and encouraged by a hardening of northern attitudes, with the economic, political and military crises fomenting a search for scapegoats to blame, be they refugees, displaced southerners, foreign aid workers or street children.[5]

The displaced were a fundamental security threat, 'a "fifth column" of the SPLA'.[6] Martin Kiir Majok, the volunteer organiser with the Aweil Youth Union from Chapter 1 – who is now resident back in Aweil – was interviewed by a *Chicago Tribune* reporter at the railway station in September 1988, at the height of the crisis: 'Every southerner is considered a Garang supporter.'[7] The administrative director of Khartoum District Council, Ali El Tayeb, emphasised to the press that 'the influx of the displaced southerns [*sic*] is part of an overall plan to create disturbance, insecurity, and to deepen racial conflicts'.[8] The non-'displaced' populace of Khartoum felt increasingly threatened by the southern and Darfur influx, particularly within their own suburbs.[9] These attitudes were encouraged by the Sudanese press and northern political parties – 'with headlines such as "Squatters intrude into capital and cause danger" and "Increase of displaced people is part

---

[4] For an example of this idea, see Abdelrahman, 'Internal Migration in the Sudan', 37.
[5] Amnesty International, 'Sudan's Secret Slaughter', 10.
[6] African Rights, 'Food and Power in Sudan', 103.
[7] Masland, 'Khartoum Bursting with Refugee Slums'.
[8] Press report, quoted in Amnesty International, 'Sudan's Secret Slaughter', 23.
[9] Richard Greenfield, 'Two Months That Shook Sudan', *Horn of Africa* 8, no. 1 (1985): 9; Wijnroks, 'The Displaced People of Khartoum', 6; Amnesty International, 'Sudan's Secret Slaughter'.

2.1 Challenging the Heartland

of a whole plan to bring about insecurity"'.[10] Oxfam noted that the Khartoum press frequently referred to the displaced as 'infidels'.[11] This was not necessarily media hyperbole; in this period, academics and politicians both wrote of the fear of the 'politically dangerous', 'destructive physical force' of the displaced communities, specifically on two bases: 'the threat of superior power' through their numbers, and 'a possible fifth column in the capital'.[12] Amnesty International reported:

> A group of the most educated people in Khartoum, such as the doctors, lawyers and others living in Riyad, have even set up the 'Riyad Residents Self Defence Group' to stockpile food, fuel and weapons in anticipation of violence and insecurity involving southerners. They are believed to have requested the Commissioner for Khartoum Province and the police to remove the displaced.[13]

These fears built on older attitudes about poor urban migrants.[14] The contemporary Sudanese anthropologist Fouad Ibrahim noted that many residents originating from the riverain centre of Sudan or who had been resident in the city for generations saw new arrivals (from famines or local conflicts, or just fortune-seekers) as 'a threat to health, security, and social order', as well as a drain on goods and services.[15] Since Khartoum's three towns started their boom in the late colonial period, residents stressed over Black regional migrants' morality, crime, sexual violence, and political ideas – a continuation of older fears over slaves, ex-slaves, and other migrants in the city, as the social and political risk of slaves and ex-slaves preoccupied state authorities

---

[10] Amnesty International, 'Sudan's Secret Slaughter', 48; Wijnroks, 'The Displaced People of Khartoum', 48–49, 35.
[11] Oxfam, 'Confidential Report by Oxfam on the Humanitarian Situation in Sudan', SAD.93/2/1-7, 3.
[12] Jane Perlez, 'Sudanese Troops Burn Refugee Camp', *New York Times*, 4 November 1990; Salah El-Din El-Shazali Ibrahim, 'War Displacement: The Socio-cultural Dimension', in Eltigani, ed., *The Displacement Problem in the Sudan*, 65–66; Rogge, 'Relocation and Repatriation', 27.
[13] Amnesty International, 'Sudan's Secret Slaughter', 23.
[14] Racialised fears of criminality and disorder are common to the middle and upper classes across many urban centres across the world; see, for example, David Pratten, 'The Politics of Protection: Perspectives on Vigilantism in Nigeria', *Africa*, 78, no. S1 (2008): 1–15.
[15] Ibrahim, 'War Displacement', 60.

from the 1900s.[16] Government agents worried about freed slaves 'inundating towns and forming "parasitic communities"'.[17] The poor and racially Black immigrant – 'the stereotypical slave' – would create 'vagrancy, prostitution, crime, and drunkenness'.[18] By the 1960s, specifically southern newcomers were 'commonly referred to as having come "straight from the bush" to earn money in order to buy cattle and to enable them to pay bridewealth'.[19] These new residents, particularly those from such apparently backwards areas, were seen as overwhelmed socially and morally by the civilisation of the city.[20] Panic grew among local elites, state bureaucrats, and suburban residents from the early 1960s, with calls for surveys of the new urban populations, and a growing field of urban studies at universities in Khartoum focusing on health problems and overcrowding.[21] Residents were worried about the 'ruralisation' of their neighbourhoods by cardboard villages of migrant families.[22] Barclay's 1964 study of the peripheral urban village of Burri al-Lamaab notes how sexual anxiety and drunken disorder led to 'a group of young Lamaab men appoint[ing] themselves the task of ordering each landlord to evict all southern tenants'.[23]

By the mid-1960s, these poor Black workers appeared to be, in the words of an urban planner, 'ready-made material for organised political recidivism'.[24] As the civil war with the Anya Nya escalated in the south, there were reports of violence against Black residents in

---

[16] Jok, 'Post-Independence Racial Realities', 193.
[17] Sikainga, 'Slavery, Labour, and Ethnicity in Khartoum: 1898–1956', 7.
[18] Fluehr-Lobban and rhodes, 'Introduction', in *Race and Identity in the Nile Valley*, xvi; Sikainga, *Slaves into Workers*, 7.
[19] Kameir, 'Nuer Migrants in the Building Industry', 456.
[20] Abdullahi Mohammed Abdel Hadi, 'The Impact of Urbanization on Crime and Delinquency', in Bushra, ed., *Urbanization in the Sudan*, 188.
[21] 'Social Survey of Citizens from Southern Provinces Resident in the Three Towns', c. 1972, SSNA EP 1.A.7; for example, see Umar Muhammad Abd al-Rahman Aqra' et al., *Housing Rentals in the Sudanese Capital: Popular Settlements, Phase II, 1986–1988*, Sudanese Group for Assessment of Human Settlements (1988), 96.
[22] Abu Sin and Davies, *The Future of Sudan's Capital Region*, 26; Bushra, *Urbanization in the Sudan*, iii.
[23] Barclay, *Buurri al Lamaab*, 100.
[24] 'Social Survey of Citizens from Southern Provinces Resident in the Three Towns'.

2.1 Challenging the Heartland

Khartoum, and (as a contemporary southern writer put it) 'fear of the "junuby" (Southerner) has developed a psychosis'.[25] On 6 December 1964, when rumours spread that Clement Mboro, a prominent politician from Western Bahr el Ghazal, might have been killed on his way back from a fact-finding tour of the civil war in the south, thousands of southern labourers rioted in the centre of Khartoum, and were themselves attacked at the Coliseum cinema and football stadium by other residents. At least fourteen people died.[26] The demonstrations over the death of the Dinka politician William Deng Nhial on 12 May 1968 were similarly violent: a large group gathered at the Sudan African National Union (SANU) club throwing stones at police, who used tear gas. Twenty people were injured and six killed, including one police officer, and over 100 were arrested.[27] Black Sudanese workers from across Sudan's peripheries, employed in the growing agricultural and manufacturing sectors around and inside Khartoum through the 1970s, were an ominous political potentiality, including in the 1981 strike (although violently suppressed).[28]

On 30 June 1989, a military coup deposed the civilian government of Sadig al-Mahdi and brought Omar al-Bashir and the National Islamic Front (NIF)-backed National Salvation Revolutionary Command Council to power. With the Council came a purge of military and security forces, the judiciary, and universities, of women from government positions, and the closing down of labour, trade, political, and professional organisations.[29] By the end of the year the Council reorganised the Relief and Rehabilitation Commission (RRC), and forced NGOs into new restrictions or out of Sudan. RRC officials visiting Washington in December 1989 said that the government

---

[25] Abraha Dengel, 'Negro Fear Fills Arab Townsmen with Panic', 8 September 1964, CAR A/94 Busta 1/21.
[26] Henderson, *Sudan Republic*, 211–12; Norman Nunn, 'When the Mob Takes Over', 8 December 1964, SAD.642/10/27-28.
[27] '100 Arrested in Sudan Demonstrations', *The Times*, 13 May 1968, TNA FCO 39.181.
[28] Ahmad Alawad Sikainga, 'Organized Labor and Social Change in Contemporary Sudan', Durham Middle East Papers 74 (2003), 16.
[29] Willow Berridge, 'Under the Shadow of the Regime: The Contradictions of Policing in Sudan, c. 1924–1989', PhD dissertation, Durham University (2011), 18.

'would not allow any humanitarian program in the southern Sudan that does not support our [the government's] military objectives'.[30]

The NIF and the Council continued incoherent but brutal efforts to manage the Khartoum displaced. This took two main forms: spatial control and sociocultural subjugation. As Fouad Ibrahim observed:

> The revolutionary potential of proletarianization may turn to its antithesis – a destructive physical force. It seems not unwarranted to assume that the authorities seem to have a clear understanding of this destructive potential, and accordingly seek to evacuate the displaced from the large cities.[31]

In the neighbourhoods of Khartoum's three towns, the NIF's popular committees (*lejna shaabiya*, generally NIF members) and police, military patrols, civilian informants, and security services worked to remove impoverished displaced Black populations from the line of sight of Khartoum residents, through forced removals and resettlement, the policing of 'civil' spaces and public services, and the organisation of checkpoints.[32] When these undesirably displaced people had to be visible, they could at least be made unthreatening through cultural and social markers of formal Arabic, Islamic names, dress, and public practice. This public performance of assimilation was made necessary for displaced residents in order to access basic services and formal job opportunities, but otherwise usefully minimised access to resources, public space, and markets. For some this might have been good social work, aiming to convert lost people to urban Islamic ways; but for the city and national authorities, this work also kept these new displaced populations at arm's length from their publics and from resources and opportunities, maintaining a usefully poor workforce, limiting their ability to act socially or politically in Khartoum, and working to counteract what both former civilian governments and the post-coup regime saw as a potentially politically dangerous force within the capital.

---

[30] Norwegian Refugee Council, 'Profile of Internal Displacement: Sudan' (2005) 18.

[31] Ibrahim, 'War Displacement: The Socio-cultural Dimension', 66.

[32] Agnès de Geoffroy, 'Fleeing War and Relocating to the Urban Fringe – Issues and Actors: The Cases of Khartoum and Bogotá', *International Review of the Red Cross* 91, no. 875 (2009): 523.

2.1 Challenging the Heartland

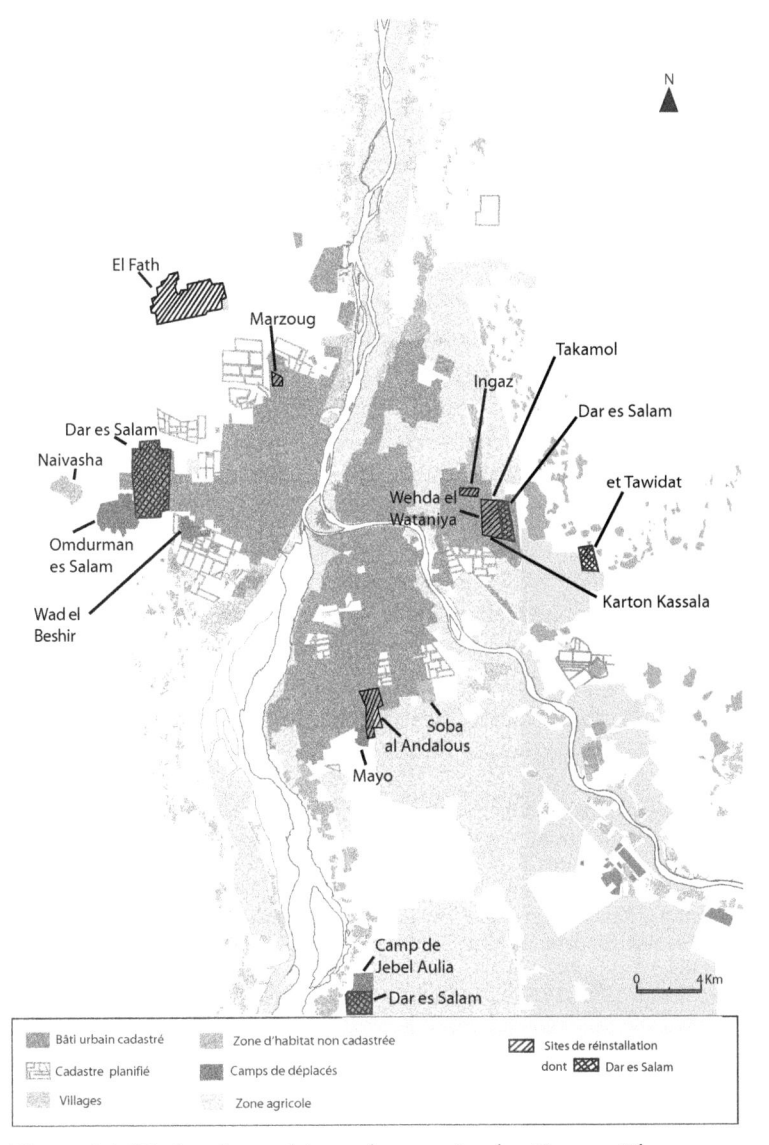

Figure 2.1 Displaced people's settlements in the Greater Khartoum area, c. 2009.

Reproduced with permission from Agnès de Geoffroy, 'Fleeing War and Relocating to the Urban Fringe – Issues and Actors: The Cases of Khartoum and Bogotá', *International Review of the Red Cross* 91, no. 875 (September 2009): 509.

2.2 Fighting for Space

Especially between 1988 and 1992, new residents were engaged in a physical fight for space in Khartoum. Old colonial and postcolonial practices of violent urban planning (detailed below), using forced displacement and bulldozing of neighbourhoods, were intensified under the al-Mahdi government and then the NIF regime. Forced relocations were relatively uncoordinated and determined by combinations of local gentrification and political pressure from residents, demands for the land, and social cleansing.[33]

The 1989 coup and National Islamic Front regime hardened rather than changed this general establishment approach to both Khartoum urban control and the state narrative of the war. The regime avoided defining a 'southern' population in Khartoum, increasingly using the homogenising, a-politicising and generalising term 'displaced', whose plight was explicitly due to 'natural causes', officially designating those arriving in the city after 1984 as squatters and thus also justifying their forcible relocation.[34] Machar Col (sometimes known as Zagalona) and Mawela, both in relatively central Omdurman, were demolished in 1988, and their populations created Jabarona, Mandela, and further parts of Haj Yousif. Demolitions stepped up in 1990.[35] Other people

---

[33] The dynamics described here were echoed in other urban sites of refuge for Sudanese people in Cairo in these decades. See Carla Daughtry, 'Conflict and Community in Church-Based Refugee Havens in Cairo: The Quest for Space to Be Dinka', *Arab Studies Journal* 14, no. 2 (2006): 39–59; Leben Nelson Moro, 'Interethnic Relations in Exile: The Politics of Ethnicity among Sudanese Refugees in Uganda and Egypt', *Journal of Refugee Studies* 17, no. 4 (2004): 420–36.

[34] Burr, 'Sudan 1990–1992', 24; Saadia Izzeldin Malik, 'Displacement as Discourse', *Ìrìnkèrindò: A Journal of African Migration* (2005); Norwegian Refugee Council, 'Profile of Internal Displacement: Sudan', 87; for an example of this official narrative, see Sharaf Eldin Ibrahim Bannaga, *Peace and the Displaced in Sudan: The Khartoum Experience* (Swiss Federal Institute of Technology, 2002).

[35] Miller, *Language Change and National Integration*, 19; Sharif Harir, 'Recycling the Pin the Sudan: An Overview of Political Decay', in Terje Tevdt and Sharif Harir, eds., *Short-Cut to Decay: The Case of the Sudan* (Nordiska Afrikainstitutet, 1994), 16–17; 'Sudan: Refugees in Their Own Country: The Forced Relocation of Squatters and Displaced People from Khartoum', *Africa Watch* 4, no. 8 (1992); Burr, 'Sudan 1990–1992', 24. For the legal background to this displacement, see Jemera Rone, *Behind the Red Line: Political Repression in Sudan* (Human Rights Watch, 1996), 15–16.

2.2 Fighting for Space

arrived in Jabarona from Souk Manthaga and Izzba, which was created after the destruction of Kilo, and some 30,000 residents of Hillat Shook were forcibly relocated to Jebel Aulia, 25 miles south of Khartoum centre, in October 1990.[36] James Wala Kot (*sic*, likely Wol Akot), a township resident, described the start of the operation: 'The army said they would come on Saturday, but they came at 6 A.M. on Sunday. They turned off the water outlets. They told people they had to pack up their things or they would be burned. We escaped going to Jebel Aulia because we know there is no water there.' The twenty-eight-year-old and sixteen members of his extended family dismantled their canvas home and lugged it and two beds and cooking pots to a dusty back alley in the city.[37]

Policies centred on forced or coercive removal to outside Khartoum or back to the south, rather than any substantial and more realistic urban planning.[38] New camps – called *dar es salaams*, peace villages – were formally created by 1989, and established firmly in 1991 as people arrested during mass police and army actions in poor urban areas scheduled for redevelopment were dumped in these new sites.[39] Ibrahim Abu Ouf, Deputy Minister for Relief and Displaced Persons, told aid agencies in 1990 that all of the displaced in Khartoum would be 'out of the city within a year'.[40] Alongside demolitions, there were a few 'returns programmes': in early 1990, the government began a Voluntary Returns Programme aimed at moving 50,000 displaced people to the south, aided by military intimidation and promises of assistance from some aid agencies and the Sudan Council of Churches.[41] In mid-1992, the UN conceded on the principle of

---

[36] James Garang, in Maper, 30 June 2013; Rogge, 'Relocation and Repatriation', 28; African Rights, 'Food and Power in Sudan', 142.
[37] Perlez, 'Sudanese Troops Burn Refugee Camp'.
[38] Amnesty International, 'Sudan's Secret Slaughter', 45.
[39] For discussion of *dar es salaams* in Sudan from the 1960s onwards, see Nicki Kindersley, 'Subject(s) to Control: Post-war Return Migration and State-Building in 1970s South Sudan', *Journal of Eastern African Studies* 11, no. 2 (2018): 7–8; de Geoffroy, 'Fleeing War', 514; Archdiocese of Khartoum, '"To Save the Saveable": An Attempt at Providing Education for Displaced Children and Youth in Khartoum', 1986, CAR 6734.21.1.
[40] Perlez, 'Sudanese Troops Burn Refugee Camp', 63; Bonner, 'A Reporter at Large'.
[41] Bannaga, *Peace and the Displaced in Sudan*, 50–51; for government statistics on repatriation convoys from 1992 to 1996, see pp. 91–92 and appendices; Burr, 'Sudan 1990–1992', 7.

relocations, and encouraged communities to participate.[42] From 1992 to 1995, these efforts moved about 32,000 people back to the south.[43] Forced relocation efforts peaked in mid-1992.[44] By May, over 600,000 people had been relocated within Khartoum. By the end of 1992, there were five official *dar es salaam* camps, made partly from the demolition of relatively settled areas, such as Kermuta around the Islamic University in December 1991, which had a considerable Ethiopian refugee community.[45] Resettlements slowed, but continued since this period, including the forced relocation of 10,000 people from the Angola squatter settlement in December 1995.[46]

Relocations were not un-resisted, particularly if they were violent or done without prior warning and negotiation.[47] Dozens of people died during demolitions in the early 1990s, including three people killed during the burning of Hilla Shook in October 1990, and at least twenty-one people dead after Kordofani and Darfuri residents resisted the demolition of Kurmuta in December 1991, which turned into three days of fighting. Amnesty International reported six people killed when state forces opened fire on protesting displaced people in a neighbourhood of Haj Yousif in late 1990. Again, on 22 December 1991, forces shot at residents trying to stop the demolition of an area of Dar es Salaam near Jebel Aulia, with at least twenty-one people killed. Three people were shot dead in evictions in Kober on 15 January 1992, and fourteen people died in Kadier suburb in Omdurman in October 1994, when police shot into a protesting crowd.[48]

Most stories of raids and demolitions included points of negotiation or resistance.[49] Shelters were built with flexibility and ease of transportation in mind, and people hedged their bets by building cheap *rakubas* (wooden shacks, often open-sided) and spreading family

---

[42] African Rights, 'Food and Power in Sudan', 175.   [43] Ibid., 165.
[44] Ibid., 151.
[45] Burr, 'Sudan 1990–1992', 25; 'Unclassified AIDAC American Embassy Telegram: Sudan Emergency Operations – Khartoum Displaced Relocation Sites', 16 March 1992, SAD.947/6/9-11; 'Unclassified Agency for International Development Telecommunications Centre: Sudan Emergency Operations – Khartoum Displaced Camps Destruction Continues', May 1992, SAD.947/6/12.
[46] African Rights, 'Food and Power in Sudan', 180.
[47] Rone, *Behind the Red Line*, 9; also see Chapter 3.
[48] Amnesty International Index 1992, IISH AFR 54/06/92; African Rights, 'Food and Power in Sudan', 166–67.
[49] See Rone, *Behind the Red Line*, 188–92, 254–64, for an account of the violent demolition of Khoder on 15 October 1994.

members between sites. In 1990, Rogge recorded, 'the fear of relocation to Jebel Awlia or elsewhere is currently causing considerable movements within Khartoum as people seek out locations where they perceive themselves not at risk from relocation programmes'.[50] As in previous forced relocations in the 1970s and '80s, the evicted transported old beams and building materials to new sites.[51] People also physically resisted unannounced demolitions, generally aiming for either a delay or a warning period before eviction.[52] For example, in 1988, police and members of Khartoum District Council were stoned and threatened with knives for attempting to burn down squatters' houses in central Khartoum.[53] A news report recorded the relocation of Zagalona in 1988: '"We are prepared to die here," said John Jok, who serves as chief of the camp, advised by traditional tribal elders.'[54] In Machar Col, a major settlement particularly for Dinka Malwal from Aweil, residents also initially resisted demolitions: 'the following day the bulldozer came. We all, men and women, gathered before the bulldozer and said "you first crush us before you destroy our houses." Thus twice we frightened them.'[55] After later clashes with police resulted in deaths, locals then successfully negotiated, partly through the advocacy of George Kongor Arop (a career police officer, Dinka ex-governor of Bahr el Ghazal State, and at the time vice president of Sudan), for the installation of water points at the new site in Jabarona, and for a guarantee that their relocation to a new site would be permanent and that they would be undisturbed there.[56]

The rapid growth of suburbs to accommodate these huge new communities between 1986 and 1990 created community heartlands around Khartoum, particularly in older-established migrant neighbourhoods of Haj Yousif, Eshash, Arkawit, Mayo, Umbadda, and Thawra.[57] By 2000, the four *dar es salaam* camps around

---

[50] Rogge, 'Relocation and Repatriation', 30.
[51] Sa'ad Ed Din Fawzi, 'Old and New Deims in Khartoum', in Pons, ed., *Urbanization and Urban Life*, 519; Peter Deng Akok, in Maper, 21 June 2013.
[52] George Dhieu, in Maper, 4 June 2013.
[53] Amnesty International, 'Sudan's Secret Slaughter', 48; Masland, 'Khartoum Bursting with Refugee Slums'.
[54] Masland, 'Khartoum Bursting with Refugee Slums'.
[55] Quoted in Miller, *Language Change and National Integration*, 26.
[56] Mathok Diing Wol, in Ariath, 21 August 2013.
[57] See SudanAid, 'Maternal Child Health Activities among the Displaced Populations in the Khartoum Region', MEDU 17/4/AID, 124.

Khartoum – in Wad al-Bashir, Mayo Farms, Jebel Aulia, and Omdurman – held a combined population of 400,000, with a total of about 1.5 million displaced people spread across the city.[58] These people were not considered residents. The Ministry of Housing classified these 'displaced' residential lands as 'fifth class', which officially allowed only houses built of non-permanent materials like wood, grasses, and cardboard.[59]

This often-violent removal and demolition strategy was part of a long struggle to control Khartoum's geography since the 1910s. Particular groups – slaves, soldiers, and those of specific trades and ethnicities – have long been associated with particular areas of Khartoum's Three Towns, such as Hay al-Dubbat, 'the officers' quarter', in Omdurman in the early 1900s, and in regional Sudanese settlements in Omdurman, Bahri, and the *deims*, 'native lodging areas', of Khartoum from 1912 onwards.[60] The systems of first- to third-class land designations, which were ordered on racial and class lines, were maintained throughout colonial and postcolonial periods.[61] By 1956, Khartoum was 'perhaps the most over-planned city in the world', with several 'master plans' and endless re-planning schemes.[62] With the rapid growth of new unauthorised *deims* in the 1960s, copying the layout of their more central counterparts, the over-ambitious and often contradictory master plans were constantly outpaced.[63] Khartoum authorities, already struggling to design the ideal capital city, dealt with this apparent social and spatial threat through forcible removal – ideally to areas of origin but, when this failed, to new (and often remote and un-serviced) suburbs.[64]

Although demolitions and forcible relocations gained international attention in the 1990s, they were a popular method of re-planning in Khartoum since the 1930s, particularly in areas of brothels and beer

---

[58] Davis, *Planet of Slums*, 48.   [59] Malik, 'Displacement as Discourse', 3.
[60] Pantuliano et al., 'City Limits', 3; Sikainga, 'Military Slavery', 23; Bushra, *An Atlas of Khartoum Conurbation*, 36.
[61] Aqra' et al., *Housing Rentals in the Sudanese Capital*, 89; Fawzi, 'Old and New Deims', 516.
[62] Bushra El Tayed Babiker, 'Khartoum: Past, Present and the Prospects for the Future', Durham Middle East Papers (2003), 16. For a contemporary summary of these urban studies, see Abdelrahman, 'Internal Migration in the Sudan', 24.
[63] Aqra' et al., *Housing Rentals in the Sudanese Capital*, 90–91; Pantuliano et al., 'City Limits', 7.
[64] El-Sayed Bushra, *Development Planning in the Sudan (1985)*, 59.

2.2 Fighting for Space

houses.[65] Demolitions were usually conducted at times of heightened stress on Khartoum's urban and state image; there were evictions in July 1978 as a form of landscaping in preparation for a prestigious meeting of the Organisation of African Unity in the city.[66] These interventions, though, were sporadic. By the 1970s, some technically illegal settlements were already decades old, such as Kalakla, opposite Soba, and the 'Fellata village', named after the collective name for Hausa, Fulɓe, Borno, and other migrant communities from western Africa, a term with a derogatory association with menial and low-status labour and questionable citizenship.[67] Umbadda (sometimes called 'New Omdurman') grew from a small village into clusters of illegal settlements during the 1950s and 1960s; attempts at re-planning and legalising parts of it in the late 1960s only encouraged further squatting.[68] This overcrowding was compounded by the massive dislocation of people from northern Sudan by the Aswan dam, creating new ethnic enclaves.[69] Governments and local authorities were deeply inconsistent in their negotiations with these settlements and associations – for instance, under Nimeiri's government there were increasing collaborations between locally organised neighbourhood authorities and city officials, but the central state used false promises of assistance to coerce relocations, and blocked United Nations High Commissioner for Refugees (UNHCR) water holes.[70] Over the 1970s and early 1980s, moments of particular stress prompted renewed depopulation campaigns, for instance, after (as the southern Anya Nya leader and then politician Joseph Lagu records)

the attempt to change the government through what appeared as an invasion in 1976, and most of the people involved in the attempt being from those other regions. Subsequently, as it was difficult to identify them from each other, they were lumped together to be thinned out of the capital.[71]

---

[65] Fawzi, 'Old and New Deims', 518; Sikainga, *City of Steel and Fire*, 68; African Rights, *Sudan's Invisible Citizens*, 26.
[66] Bascom, *Losing Place*, 39.
[67] G. Hamdan, 'The Growth and Functional Structure of Khartoum', *Geographical Review* 50, no. 1 (1960): 21; Sikainga, 'Slavery, Labour, and Ethnicity in Khartoum: 1898–1956'. Also see the map of Khartoum G.23, Sudan Survey Department 1940, RGS 551847.
[68] Aqra' et al., *Housing Rentals in the Sudanese Capital*, 177, 13.
[69] Hale, *Nubians*, 9.   [70] Greenfield, 'Two Months That Shook Sudan', 20.
[71] Joseph Lagu, 'In Quest of Lasting Peace', 6 June 1989, SAD 945/7/1-8. Similarly, there was a mass expulsion of labourers and refugees from drought in

These demolitions were, for their victims, a core part of the long Sudanese state history of slavery and racism. Demolitions and removals were based significantly on racial profiling.[72] They were explicitly intended to maintain a ruralised and poor Black working population distinct from (and useful to) the state's urban heartland and, as Sudanese geographer El-Sayed El-Bushra put it, to avoid 'a mere transplantation of poverty from the rural areas into the door-steps of our modern centres'.[73] Joseph Lagu noted in 1989 that these purges 'actually provided Southerners and those others for the first time with some common formula that they were all not wanted in the developed areas'.[74] In Khartoum Arabic, police sweeps were called *kasha*, colloquially meaning 'search', and this term was also increasingly used for large-scale relocations.[75] But this term was often reinterpreted in a variety of languages and linguistic fashions, linked fundamentally to Sudanese racial discourses. In 1985, Matthew Obur, a prominent southern politician, explained the term *kasha* as coming 'from [the] Amharic "Kushasha" which means dirt or filth or garbage'.[76] The term was also translated to me in Aweil as a corruption from English:

In 1983 there is what is called kasha, for the Blacks.... Nimeiri, he said – why are gathering all these people, they will make you problems, they will

---

1981–82: African Rights, 'Food and Power in Sudan', 32; Amnesty International, 'Sudan's Secret Slaughter', 20.

[72] Jok, *Sudan*, 9.

[73] Bushra, *Urbanization in the Sudan*, iii; Mohamed A. G. Bakhit, 'Negotiations of Power and Responsibilities in Khartoum Shantytowns', in Elke Grawert, ed., *Forging Two Nations: Insights on Sudan and South Sudan* (OSSREA, 2014), 129; PaanLuel Wël, *The Genius of Dr John Garang: Speeches on the War of Liberation* (CreateSpace, 2015), 41: Garang's speech on 22 March 1985 emphasised 'the apartheid-like "Kacha", a policy under which many poor and unemployed have been forcibly driven en masse to their regions of origin, mainly Western and Southern parts of the country, for the simple reason that they do not "belong" to Khartoum'.

[74] Lagu, 'In Quest of Lasting Peace', 4.

[75] The term *kasha* is used for sweeps and raids more widely; for example, Mathew Haumann describes how the SPLA 'had a kasha to get new recruits' by rounding up older boys in local schools in Nimule in the early 1990s: *Travelling with Soldiers and Bishops: Stories of Struggling People in Sudan* (Paulines Publications Africa, 2004), 70–71; Human Rights Watch also documented street *kasha* by the public order police: Rone, *Behind the Red Line*, 130.

[76] Matthew Obur Ayang, 'National Action Movement on Racism and Religious Persecution in the Sudan', National Action Movement, 18 January 1985, SAD.93/1/1-26, 8.

2.3 The Civilising Project

give you a lot of problems! Why don't you catch them, and take them back to their homes. So ... that was called *kasha* in Arabic, catching Black people! And taking them to their areas.... Nimeiri is telling people that you go to the bush! Don't stay here! It's just where this [idea of] separation happened. It's Nimeiri who introduced it! Who introduced it to the southerners, to the Blacks![77]

Many people I met who had experienced *kasha* themselves asserted a further reading of the purpose of this 'catching'. This 'blasting out of the southerners' from central Khartoum, in the words of office worker and schoolteacher Dhieu Lual, was also the expropriation of the residents' hard work and co-ordination in 'cleaning' the original area: a defiant inversion of government rhetoric.[78] The residents had done what the government was apparently incapable of doing, in physically and communally urbanising barren or polluted tracts of the city. Bricklayer and migrant worker Peter Deng explained that 'when [the government] saw that you have created the land well, and the land is well organised, then they can allocate you forcefully to another dirty place for you to go and clean it'; then – William Deng explained –

after we clean it ... the Arabs come and demolish that area. They don't like the Dinka, Blacks, to stay in a clean place.... If you have been there in Khartoum, the camps you have been passing – there's Mandela, Jebel Aulia, Jabarona, Machar Col, Haj Yousif, Gereif Akaba; all these were established by Dinka, and they were just pushed away by Arabs.[79]

2.3 Alienation, Removal, Subjugation, and Performance: The Civilising Project in Practice

They don't want to southerners to [be] inside the city, they want them to go outside ... because if the number of southerners increased [too much, then] they are going to change society.[80]

Dhieu Lual, former office worker and teacher in Khartoum, speaking in
Mayen Ulem, 4 July 2013

---

[77] Members of the Dinka Cultural Society, in Apada, 11 August 2013.
[78] Dhieu Kuel, in Mayen Ulem, 21 August 2013.
[79] Peter Deng Akok, in Maper, 29 June 2013; William Deng Aken, in Apada, 18 July 2013. Also noted by chiefs' court members in Maper, 29 June 2013; and by Mathok Diing Wol, in Ariath, 21 August 2013.
[80] Dhieu Kuel, in Mayen Ulem, 4 July 2013.

The physical purging of the city was a primary aspect of the Khartoum government's response to the urban detritus of the civil war. As the then-Minister of Construction, Housing and Public Utilities for Khartoum State (and according to Human Rights Watch in 1996 the 'government czar of slum clearance') Sharif Bannaga happily stated in November 1994, 'we started... with a struggle with the squatters and we even had some casualties. Now we don't have any resistance [and] we don't expect any criticism.'[81] Once physical distance and control were established over these risky Black residents, government offices then endeavoured to make them passive and powerless, to limit their ability to act culturally and socially as well as politically. If impoverished Black residents had to be visible within the capital, they could at least be visibly 'civilised' and unthreatening, and be useful to the city. In the words of John Gau Riak, who arrived from Darfur in 1989 to pursue his education, 'they were treating the southerners, and the Black people, as inhuman. They don't want them to appear to the world, this country.'[82] Hanaa Motasim elaborated: 'with time, the southerners are forced to camouflage themselves within the city. To dissolve into the fabric, to become unseen, unrecognised, forgotten in a sense.'[83]

This government work was what many academics describe as projects of acculturation, aiming to organise a population in the approximate image of the Islamic, Arab-heritage cultured centre, 'a bounded homogeneity that reflects Northern interests and dominance'.[84] A summary of how Sudan's national image narrowed to that of its Khartoum provincial residents is not possible in the space here, and other authors explain these forces better.[85] But by the early 1970s, President Nimeiri's ideas of a 'melting pot' of Sudanese culture really assumed assimilation to this central political-cultural imaginary rather than any two-way process. This was a 'lopsided... Sudanese nationalism', a product of what the Darfur intellectual and politician Sharif

---

[81] Rone, *Behind the Red Line*, 254; Amnesty International Index video transcript, 22 November 1994, IISH AFR 54/55/94.
[82] John Gau Riak, in Aweil, 28 June 2013.
[83] Motasim, 'Deeply Divided Societies', 8.
[84] Duffield, 'Aid and Complicity', 92.
[85] Harir, 'Recycling the Past', 20; Sharif Harir, *Racism in Islamic Disguise? Retreating Nationalism and Upsurging Ethnicity in Dar Fur, Sudan* (University of Bergen Press, 1993), 293, 295; de Geoffroy, 'Fleeing War', 518.

2.3 The Civilising Project

Harir later described as the 'centrifugal tendencies' of central Sudanese sociopolitical elites – with central Sudanese and Islamic character set out in a national image, posited against comparatively 'embarrassingly primitive and outdated' local customs.[86]

Through the 1960s and 1970s, successive government projects endeavoured to extend this Sudanese character to its peripheries, through the promotion of Arabic as a national language, and the declaration of Friday rather than Sunday as the collective day of rest, for instance. These efforts were theoretically consolidated as part of the NIF regime's 'civilisation project' (*mashru al-hadari*). According to Amir Idris, this project expanded established state ideology 'about the historical right of Arabized Islamized peoples to rule over non-Muslim and non-Arab groups'.[87] For the NIF regime, this was an explicitly proactive agenda for 'defence and cultural salvation' against international and internal threats to the integrity of this nationalist vision for Sudan.[88]

In these terms, the new impoverished displaced population was, according to government rhetoric, an urgent humanitarian issue, framed as a crisis of culture, poverty, and integration, not of the outcomes of political violence. Sharif Bannaga explained: 'it is a fact that the displaced are from the poor layers of the community, unable to administer life affairs ... the most immediate impact of the misconduct, malpractice and ill behaviour of the displaced was on public health'.[89] Abdelaziz Shiddo, then Minister of Justice and Attorney-General, responded to criticism of *kasha* and the civilisation project in 1994 by complaining of the 'alarming numbers of conversions to Christianity ... [and] the vices wildly [sic] spread among children including addiction, pornography, prostitution and sale of organs'.[90]

---

[86] Malik, 'Displacement as Discourse'; Harir, *Racism in Islamic Disguise?*, 293, 295.
[87] Amir Idris, *Conflict and Politics of Identity in Sudan* (Palgrave Macmillan, 2005), 17.
[88] Malik, 'Displacement as Discourse'; Rone, *Behind the Red Line*, 2.
[89] Bannaga, *Peace and the Displaced in Sudan*, 36–37, 41.
[90] 'Statement by HE Mr Abdelaziz Shiddo, Minister of Justice and Attorney-General of the Republic of the Sudan and Leader of Sudan Delegation to the 50th Session of the Commission of Human Rights, Commenting on the Report of Dr Gaspar Biro, Special Rapporteur on Human Rights Situation in the Sudan under Agenda Item 12', 25 December 1994, SAD 306/7/36-46.

For Sudanese intellectuals and external observers, these assumptions, practices, and projects are generally summarised as a 'systematic [program] of Arabization and Islamization', a 'cultural front' in the civil war that was most aggressively pursued in the heartland of Khartoum's elite urban space.[91] The binaries behind the terms 'Arabization' and 'Islamization' have been broadly challenged; many authors have pointed out the complexity of the Arab and Islamic in Sudanese history, and the insecure foundation of an 'Arab' identity in Sudan.[92] But these instances of shorthand have survived as common descriptors for the content and impact of these supposedly assimilatory projects, particularly in much of the human rights, migration, and development studies literature and reporting. Under al-Bashir, in these reports, 'African traditions clash with the strict application of Islamic law', and 'processes of both Arabicization [sic] and Islamization [among] Southern Sudanese displaced in the North' create 'alienation, ... extraction and abstraction from all ... cultural roots'.[93] The very limited research among the mostly southern urban poor and displaced from 1986 to 2003 primarily focuses on humanitarian or sociological issues and generally sets out stories of southern migrant social survival under a violent and assimilatory Arab Islamic state, which consistently targets these Black peripheral migrant populations through clear policies of Arabization (*t'arib*) and Islamization (*hidayah*).[94]

---

[91] Lesch, *The Sudan*, 213; Jok, *Sudan*, 288. See also Sharkey, 'Arab Identity and Ideology in Sudan', 25. Many others argue for this sharpening of Arabism as racial ideology, for example, Idris, *Conflict and Politics of Identity*; de Waal, 'Who Are the Darfurians?'; Gérard Prunier, *Darfur: The Ambiguous Genocide* (Hurst, 2005); Harir, *Racism in Islamic Disguise?*; Rex O'Fahey, 'Islam and Ethnicity in the Sudan', *Journal of Religion in Africa* 26, no. 3 (1996): 258–67.

[92] James Copnall, *A Poisonous Thorn in Our Hearts: Sudan and South Sudan's Bitter and Incomplete Divorce* (Oxford University Press, 2014), 14; Hale, *Nubians*, 15–16; Sharkey, 'Arab Identity and Ideology in Sudan'; Elwathig Kameir, 'Operationalizing the New Sudan Concept', in Francis Mading Deng, ed., *New Sudan in the Making? Essays on a Nation in Search of Itself* (Red Sea Press, 2010), 24. On marginality, see Idris, *Conflict and Politics of Identity*, 207, 214; Lesch, *The Sudan*, ix, 212; Deng, *War of Visions*; Francis Mading Deng, *Dynamics of Identification: A Basis for National Integration in the Sudan* (Khartoum University Press, 1973), 11; J. Spaulding, 'The Concept of "Afro-Arab"' (1986), SAD 987/7/44-47.

[93] Human Rights Watch Africa, 'Children in Sudan: Slaves, Street Children and Child Soldiers' (September 1995), 1.

[94] Sharkey, 'Arab Identity and Ideology in Sudan', 21; African Rights, 'Food and Power in Sudan', 187.

2.3 The Civilising Project

The terms 'Arabization' and 'Islamization' continue as a common political and academic shorthand for a mix of policies, attitudes, and violence, although few studies actually set out what was entailed in this project in the wider context of Khartoum in this period, or ask whether these impositions were intended to assimilate in the first place.[95] Rogaia Abusharaf emphasises that 'an ethnographic analysis of El-Mashru El-Hadari is ultimately an account of domination'.[96] For displaced residents of Khartoum it was not, however, an account of assimilation. Rather than being an incorporative project, Arabization and Islamization were in effect a set of practices and assumptions that enforced and legitimated difference rather than seeking to erase it, marking and policing a marginal space for a subordinate population, and demanding that people 'camouflage themselves into the existing cultural fabric' when in view.[97] In practice, the direct efforts most cited as government 'civilising' projects by the early 1990s were explicitly exclusionary and violent; they were not intended to build a homogenous nation.[98]

The following section details the fundamentally exclusionary and intimidatory policies and abuses that the various parts of the Khartoum state apparatus took against displaced residents, often referred to in the local press as 'infidels'.[99] As Rogaia Abusharaf says, 'this program was designed not to assimilate non-Arab, non-Muslim groups but to dominate them', but it was also to hold them at arm's

---

[95] Rogaia Mustafa Abusharaf, *Transforming Displaced Women in Sudan: Politics and the Body in a Squatter Settlement* (University of Chicago Press, 2009), 33. See, for example, Philip Abbas Ghaboush to Prime Minister Heath, 'Arabization and Islamization', 27 December 1971, TNA FCO 39.901; and the Archdiocese of Khartoum report 'To Save the Saveable': 'We must also point to the fact that some powerful Northern Muslim groups welcome the present crisis as an opportunity to Arabize and Islamize as many southerners and westerners as possible.' Also noted by Carolyn Fluehr-Lobban, 'Islamization in Sudan: A Critical Assessment', *Middle East Journal* 44, no. 4 (1990): 610.

[96] Abusharaf, *Transforming Displaced Women in Sudan*, 66.

[97] Motasim, 'Deeply Divided Societies', 8, quoting Sharaf Bannaga, 'Al Shorouk'.

[98] This was articulated explicitly by several ex-residents of Khartoum: John Gau Riak, in Aweil, 28 June 2013; Riing Riing Lual, in Aweil, 3 September 2013; Anei Deng Akok, in Aweil, 13 August 2013.

[99] For examples of abuses and intimidation, see Gaspar Biro, 'Situation of Human Rights in the Sudan, Report of the Special Rapporteur', 1 February 1994, Transcript, IISH National Democratic Alliance Archive NDA.92, 21; Oxfam, 'Confidential Report', 3.

length.[100] Throughout research for this book, people described these government efforts as an exclusionary and silencing force: for these displaced residents, the government's cultural and social repression was part of a wider economic and physical violence, and which conspired with other pressures of urbanisation and exposure to global cultures to subjugate and desocialise.[101] These ex-residents explained Arabization and Islamisation as racism, economic exploitation, and cultural and physical violence, which specifically did not seek assimilation, imposed physical distance and difference, and led to marginalisation and personal loss.

2.4 Policing Public Space

The Khartoum government's civilising project focused most explicitly on public spatial control. As long-term southern residents of the city emphasised, state agents had 'always aggress[ed] people' in Khartoum.[102] As in similarly intensely racialised urban spaces in the United States and South Africa, stop and search policing and identity checks were routine throughout the late 1980s and 1990s because of paranoia over gun proliferation, gang violence, and urban unrest; southern and western Sudanese people were the main targets.[103] The expansion of the Criminal Procedures Act and the Law of Public Order in 1991, and their extension in the Public Order Act in 1996, extended state powers not only over practices considered 'un-Islamic' but also over public spaces.[104] These laws outsourced their powers of local policing and security to neighbourhood committees, partly because there was no money for state services, and this opened doors for local abuse.[105] The public order courts established in this period, according to popular southern opinion, 'had no written law' – 'so southerners ... suffered a lot [in those courts], they used to be judged ... they are

---

[100] Abusharaf, *Transforming Displaced Women in Sudan*, 33.
[101] 'Desocialisation' is the term used by Duffield, 'Aid and Complicity'.
[102] Chiefs' meeting in Maper Akot, 29 June 2013.
[103] Woldemikael, 'Southern Migrants in a Northern Sudanese City', 27.
[104] Willow Berridge, 'The Ambiguous Role of the Popular, Society and Public Order Police in Sudan, 1983–2011', *Middle Eastern Studies* 49, no. 4 (2013): 528–46; 'Nests of Criminals'; 'Under the Shadow of the Regime'; also see Motasim, 'Deeply Divided Societies'; Abusharaf, *Transforming Displaced Women in Sudan*, 65; Rone, *Behind the Red Line*, 132–37.
[105] Ahmad, 'The Neighbourhoods of Khartoum'.

2.4 Policing Public Space

basically trying to correct people according to the Islamic sharia, ... especially the ladies'.[106]

The Khartoum public thus had the power to enforce socially acceptable behaviour and performance from southern refugees who were, in Wendy James's term, 'ethnically visible'.[107] Women knew in which public spaces they would have to conform to alternative clothing standards, and men knew which neighbourhoods they could not safely walk in.[108] Local neighbourhood committees evicted southern residents with the justification that they should settle in 'separate' areas where they could drink or wear trousers.[109] In the early to mid-1990s, many non-Arab government officials were dismissed from service for failing to 'prove' their Muslim beliefs; applicants had to provide testimonials or confirm their religion in interviews.[110] But for most people this form of subsumption into politically Islamicised economic systems was heavy-handed, explicit, and superficial; one Islamic relief group would only accept Islamic-named food aid applicants 'on the understanding that this indicated conversion to Islam', and most people viewed their Arabic-language name as part of living in Khartoum.[111] This was a necessary pretence as part of finding employment; as a group of retired men explained, going to the mosque and wearing the jellabiya was 'just taking care of our lives ... in order to defend [ourselves] and our brothers'.[112]

Some men saw their rights to dress as they wanted, particularly in the very Sudanese jellabiya, as an assertions of their identification as Sudanese and a political statement of equality and citizenship; this southern claiming of Sudanese identity is arguably as neglected an issue as southern Sudanese nationalism. But many faithful converts

---

[106] Dhieu Kuel, in Mayen Ulem, 4 July 2013.
[107] Bjarnesen and Utas, 'Introduction: Urban Kinship', 4; Kameir, 'Nuer Migrants in the Building Industry', 456; James, 'War and "Ethnic Visibility"'.
[108] Angelina Majok, in Mayen Ulem, 16 July 2013; Michael Thiop Lang, in Aweil, 11 July 2013.
[109] Dhieu Kuel, in Mayen Ulem, 4 July 2013. Popular Committees were also created in 1990 but were not established in squatter or camp settlements, unless they were in *dar es salaams*. African Rights, 'Food and Power in Sudan', 164.
[110] Lesch, *The Sudan*, 139.
[111] 'Report by Rev. Dr. R. Rodgers for Light and Hope for Sudan Concerning a Visit to Khartoum', 22 June 1994, SAD.93/2/65-86; members of the Dinka Cultural Society, in Apada, 11 August 2013.
[112] Lual Agang Macham, in Apada, 8 June 2013; also Atak Akol Diing, in Aweil, 14 August 2013.

to Islam and non-Muslim displaced residents emphasised to me that conversion and public dress did not make a real difference. Outward adaptation to these Arab-Islamic standards – for example, dressing in a jellabiya or tob, the use of henna, co-opted marriage practices, attendance at the mosque, and taking up Arabic names – did not make a displaced person an assimilated and acceptable member of Khartoum society, even if 'some people [aspire] to be equal'.[113] Both locals and recent residents knew the limits of assimilation; this was not an 'open door' where one could convert, declare a new name and alter behaviour, and be seen by northern society as being 'Arab'.[114] 'Even if you pray in [the] Muslim religion, they are still thinking of [you as] being unbelievers.'[115] As a Darfuri man, quoted by Jok Madut, stated: '[Our Arab brothers in the north think] that they are better Muslims because their race brings them closer to the Prophet, and that Blacks can never make good Muslims.'[116]

This public order seemed – for these residents – to aim to alienate rather than assimilate, and to set out geographical, social, and behavioural exclusions. As James Garang, a young musician living in Haj Yousif in the early 1990s, emphasised: 'They don't need Dinka to enter into their customs like dancing, and dressing, and other things. [They say that] there are such things that are different from Black people ... when you want to be involved, ... they will tell you that this is not your custom.'[117]

For those on the receiving end in Khartoum, this was explicit psychological and physical abuse, intended to subordinate and demoralise through an unattainable promise of inclusion. This enforced public performance of this 'Sudanese-ness' was also commonly mocked in the endemic racist discourse in the city, which set out Black people and their war-torn and undeveloped peripheries as economically, socially, and intellectually subhuman: '[Local residents] try to say that – why arrange that petrol is to be taken to the south? Is it that they're going to

---

[113] Chiefs' meeting in Maper Akot, 29 June 2013; also David Dhieu, in Maper Akot, 4 June 2013, and Michael Thiop Lang, in Aweil, 10 July 2013, discussed 'pretending'.
[114] Sharkey, 'Arab Identity and Ideology in Sudan', 26, quoting a person called Nyombe.
[115] Lual Agang Macham, in Apada, 8 June 2013.   [116] Jok, *Sudan*, 4.
[117] James Garang, in Maper, 30 June 2013.

2.4 Policing Public Space

give it to the cows?'[118] Attempting to disprove these racist narratives was risky, as the school teacher Dhieu Lual noted: 'sometimes if you talk to them in Arabic they can accuse you of being a soldier in the south ... because they say why do you talk wisely in that language that does not belong to you, it means that you are a soldier'.[119]

The most obvious and insidious form of this intellectual racism was through state control of education, which also affected local self-run primary schools and evening classes through the systematic cancellation of scholarships, the posting of non-Muslim or non-Khartoum Arabic-speaking students to Omdurman Islamic University, the refusal to endorse school certificates or certify self- or church-run schools under the Sudan curriculum, and the unilateral closure of these peripheral schools by security and police forces.[120] Dhieu Lual emphasised: 'they said that – it is not good for us ... we the northerners, to witness you, you are learning, while your brothers are [killing] some people'.[121] This rhetoric was taken up in popular encounters in Khartoum, and was not the preserve of state officials. James Garang explained:

[When you] go to the restaurant to eat, you are asked – are you also a student? You say yes! What do you want to do when you finish and when you graduate?... some say I will be a politician; some say I need to be an engineer, I need to be a doctor, I need to be an officer in the police ... how they laughed at us! They said that – but what about your brothers in the bush now? They are killing people, and you are here eating our things.... Why do you refuse to join your brothers in the bush, and you are now affecting us in the market, even in the schools? Please, you join the bush, and you come with your brother and take this country from the Arabs, if you are able to do that.[122]

Peter Deng, the bricklayer, described this as a mental 'cold war'.[123] Many people remember being forcibly bussed to political rallies, where

---

[118] William Deng Aken, in Apada, 18 July 2013.
[119] Peter Deng Akok, in Maper, 29 June 2013; Dhieu Kuel, in Mayen Ulem, 4 July 2013; Lual Agang Macham, in Apada, 8 June 2013.
[120] The Information Committee of the South Sudan Students Alliance for Separation – Middle East, 'Report on the Compulsory Transportation of Students to Khartoum', 8 September 1992, SAD.93/1/74-5.
[121] Dhieu Kuel, in Mayen Ulem, 4 July 2013; Maper chiefs' court, 13 April 2013.
[122] John Gau Riak, in Aweil, 28 June 2013.
[123] Peter Deng Akok, in Maper, 29 June 2013.

they were 'discouraged' – 'especially on politics, they can say you will not succeed [in] what you are doing, even the Darfurians [will not succeed] ... you will be sorry if you refuse to become Muslims, because we are now going to Islamize this area; they even despair you [sic] by saying that the SPLM is not going to succeed'.[124] Many ex-residents' explanations of 'assimilation' into northern society were often based on acquiescence because of insurmountable inequality:

> when you request your rights in the court, ... you will not be given your right even if you are right. They considered Arabs to be the right person, who can say the right [sic]. It will not be possible for you to do a good thing: whatever good thing you do will not be considered by an Arab.[125]

2.5 The Utility of the Underclass

The racist social and exploitative economic pressures created apparently within *mashru al-hadari* hardly produced assimilation. But this was not necessarily the point of this Arab/Islamization work, or the point of the explicit racism itself; as Jok Madut observed,

> I no longer see the impact of race as being limited to what people think of one another or to the racial slurs mentioned above, but as a mechanism for allocation of rights, resources and social standing. It has to be seen as a reality built into the structures of government, the social and political institutions of the state.[126]

Creating silenced, politically and physically marginalised, and racially subordinate populations was extremely useful for Sudan's economic and political interests. The displaced in Khartoum – as across Sudan – were convenient, subordinate, and cheap labour.[127] A major impact – and aim – of war-induced displacement was to create a mobile labour reserve for Sudan's major agricultural investments. Resettling displaced people to rural labour sites was formal government policy since 1989. An aid report records that, in August 1990, the Council of Ministers' Resolution 56 announced that the problem of displacement

---

[124] Dhieu Kuel, in Mayen Ulem, 4 July 2013.
[125] James Garang, in Maper, 19 July 2013; also mentioned by Dhieu Kuel, in Mayen Ulem, 4 July 2013, and by Lual Agang Macham, in Apada, 8 June 2013.
[126] Jok, *Sudan*, 12.   [127] African Rights, 'Food and Power in Sudan', 172.

2.5 The Utility of the Underclass

would be eliminated in one year through repatriation, or through relocation of 'areas of production', particularly in the Kordofan and Central states.[128] As Peter Deng, a manual worker on construction sites in Khartoum and a seasonal agricultural worker in Gedaref, explained:

> All that hard work belonged to every Black tribe in Sudan. So this work belonged to the Black people in the first place – although if the Arabs found that it is going to create job opportunities for Black people and it will also provide them with experience, then they replaced them with Arab youth, yeah, in that work.[129]

Military and state planners were just developing older logics of peripheral labour exploitation, including the creation of 'peace villages', securitised camps near mechanised farming schemes where displaced populations were resettled throughout the wars; these 'peace villages' were also organised in the previous civil war from around 1965–72. By the late 1980s, government of Sudan planners justified these camps as a means for self-sufficiency and *salaam min al-dakhal* (peace from within).[130] Throughout the mid-1980s, the Khartoum state and national government termed new arrivals 'seasonal migrant labour'.[131] Under Sadig al-Mahdi's government, a 1987 committee on the displaced set out a policy to keep the displaced as an agricultural labour force, and to resettle people to agricultural schemes with labour shortages.[132] In 1991, a US House of Representatives committee recorded that the government of Sudan had forcibly removed tens of thousands of displaced residents in Khartoum to central Sudanese farms for the harvest season, and did not transport them back.[133] These projects worked well for many members and supporters of the al-Mahdi and then National Islamic Front (NIF)/National Congress Party (NCP) governments, who often had investments not only in these farms and

---

[128] Norwegian Refugee Council, 'Profile of Internal Displacement: Sudan', 119.
[129] Peter Deng Akok, in Maper, 29 June 2013.
[130] Norwegian Refugee Council, 'Profile of Internal Displacement: Sudan', 119.
[131] Haumann, *Travelling with Soldiers and Bishops*, 109.
[132] African Rights, 'Food and Power in Sudan', 163, 165; this discussion is also noted in Amnesty International, 'Sudan's Secret Slaughter', 23.
[133] House of Representatives by the Department of State, 'Report Submitted to the Committee on Foreign Relations US Senate and the Committee on Foreign Affairs', February 1992, IISH National Democratic Alliance Archive NDA.92, 390.

the banks and organisations that profited from them, but also in Khartoum space.[134] Jok Madut noted that squatter demolitions in Khartoum were often initiated after government-allied individuals had started to build in an area.[135]

2.6 Economic Pacification

The physical, spatial, and economic coercions and exclusions built generally unsystematically over the 1980s to early 1990s created overwhelming practical and immediate pressures on displaced people in Sudan. Secure living situations, food supply, and cash were all hard to come by. These stresses, and limited options, were extremely useful to local authorities and the state apparatus for ensuring people were forced to conform for their survival.[136] As noted at the time by Anthony Shahid: 'The shortsighted demolition policy ensures permanent crisis for the displaced. Farmers are made refugees, children are kept illiterate, and survival itself is made possible – barely – by aid delivered through relief agencies unprepared for the scenario.'[137]

In this context, work – despite the potential for abuse or the regular refusal of pay – on agricultural schemes elsewhere in Sudan, or in the Sudan Armed Forces (SAF) and later the Popular Defence Forces, was a financially sensible (or necessary) route for some men, as was working (for children and women) as domestic labourers.[138] Many accounts of life in Khartoum include periods of forced work or deception into trafficked labour outside the city.[139] Such economic coercion, by force or circumstance, was generally unsubtle, explained by many people as bribes, at the very least aiming to encourage a particular type of performance, for example, in exchange for publicly acting as a

---

[134] Thomas, 'Patterns of Growth and Inequality'.
[135] Jok, *Sudan*, 312, note 222.
[136] Sara Pantuliano, 'Responding to Protracted Crises: The Principled Model of NMPACT in Sudan', in Luca Alinovi et al., eds., *Beyond Relief: Food Security in Protracted Crisis* (Practical Action Publishing, 2008), 25–26.
[137] Anthony Shadid, 'Lurking Insecurity: Squatters in Khartoum', *Middle East Report* 216, no. 6 (2000).
[138] Anei Deng Akok, in Aweil, 13 August 2013; Michael Thiop Lang, in Aweil, 10 July 2013.
[139] Lual Agang Macham, in Apada, 8 June 2013; Arou Piol Adam, in Apada village, 22 July 2013; Maper chiefs' court, 13 April 2013; Lual Agang Macham, in Apada, 8 June 2013; Kuot Dut Kuot, in Apada, 3 June 2013.

2.6 Economic Pacification

Muslim, or to dress or act in ways socially acceptable to Arab riverain residents. Access to formal education in the peripheral official camps was through *khalwa* kindergartens, and most forms of paperwork could only be accessed through local government-affiliated committees.[140] As Mohamed A. G. Bakhit's study of a Khartoum suburb in 2011–12 notes,

> mobilizing political support for the government by means of the local committees, along with civil society organisations such as youth organisations, and some religious institutions, like the Zakat institute, ... [aimed] clearly to make political affiliation with the government the only way for shantytown people to participate in and influence the provision of government services.[141]

By the early 1990s, sorghum (a core Sudanese staple food) was rationed and distributed through these neighbourhood committees, which evolved under the NCP after 1991 into Popular Committees, managed primarily by NCP members and with a supervisory remit.[142]

At the same time, international aid theory and practice regarding displaced people was in many respects similar to that of the Sudan government. Mark Duffield and John Ryle, as contemporary observers, noted that aid agencies were essentially complicit with this exploitation and oppression.[143] In May 1987, when aid work in Khartoum specifically with the 'displaced' was legalised, these aid and development theories inadvertently conspired with the Relief and Rehabilitation Commission (RRC)'s own policy. Operational and funding decisions stuck – as they often do today – on 'how displacees are defined and how long a person is considered to remain a displacee'; the Khartoum government's efforts to redefine war-displaced people as squatters and urban migrants was useful for this apparent time-limited definition of displacement.[144] This was not helped by many international agencies' fundamental lack of understanding of 'southern

---

[140] Bruna Siricio Iro, 'The Situation of Sudanese Women', the First Sudanese Christian Women's Conference, Khartoum, 10–18 June 1994, SAD 306/7/94-111; Dhieu Kuel, in Mayen Ulem, 4 July 2013.
[141] Bakhit, 'Negotiations of Power and Responsibilities in Khartoum Shantytowns', 139.
[142] African Rights, 'Food and Power in Sudan', 142.
[143] Duffield, 'Aid and Complicity', 84, 93.
[144] Rogge, 'Relocation and Repatriation', 20; Malik, 'Displacement as Discourse', 3.

IDPs' in Khartoum.[145] Their lack of information was compounded by a particularly flattening terminology, as John Ryle and Yai Kuol noted at the time:

> Migrants of very diverse origins and backgrounds, speaking different languages, practising different religions and having different modes of livelihood become, collectively, 'the Displaced'. They are thus characterised only by their present condition, homeless, without identity, in limbo. This terminology tends to homogenise and dehumanise the inhabitants of the south. It conspires inadvertently with a strain in northern discourse about non-Muslim and non-Arab inhabitants of the Sudan which lumps all southerners together and defines them thus with negatives, as non-believers, without real religion, not fully deserving of moral respect.[146]

The NGO and multilateral community, like the regime, based their approach on a specific (homogenising and flattening) understanding of the IDPs in Khartoum. This was specifically a 'traditional and rural' homogeneity, and this kind of representation presented these new populations of urban Khartoum as vulnerable, not only to societal disintegration but to aid dependency.[147] Dr Rahman of the RRC emphasised in 1987 that 'we cannot just treat it as an emergency situation ... otherwise more and more people will come to the capital for handouts. Rehabilitation includes self-sufficiency.'[148]

The dominant international humanitarian idea of dependency theory thus aligned neatly with Khartoum government discourse and planning. Many aid agencies considered their energies better spent in the southern, or 'transition', region on the borderlands, where people were 'worse off' and also where populations could be controlled and aid distributed in an apparently more systematic manner. CONCERN re-focused on South Kordofan and Blue Nile partly because those places offered less stringent government restrictions and had settled camps to manage.[149] NGOs struggled to partition Khartoum into operational zones as they had done in the south, unfamiliar and

---

[145] Duffield, 'Aid and Complicity', 95.
[146] Ryle and Yai Kuol, 'Displaced Southern Sudanese', 34; for an example of this attitude, see Bannaga, *Peace and the Displaced in Sudan*, 37.
[147] Malik, 'Displacement as Discourse'.
[148] 'Meeting about Medical Assistance to Displaced People in Khartoum Region, Director General's Office, Commission of Health Affairs, Khartoum Region', 11 May 1987, MEDU 17/4/AID.
[149] Aid worker, in London, 6 February 2012.

2.6 Economic Pacification

unhappy with programming within 'urban sprawl communities' that 'look like' other areas, and the refugee camp-like but not-camp nature of urban living.[150] Many Khartoum programmes were closed in the early 1990s because (specifically 'emergency') feeding programmes were not considered necessary in the urban context.[151] This preference for formal 'IDP' sites unfortunately reinforced the government's strategic creation of formalised and securitised *dar es salaam* (peace village) camps on the outskirts of Khartoum, partly to maintain a dependent and impoverished labour pool for the city while removing unsightly and politically difficult populations from the city's suburbs: for UNICEF and Operation Lifeline Sudan, 'the reinstallation of some of the displaced persons in environments where they can recover self-sufficiency in basic food production and can have access to essential social services, the improvement of logistical facilities, should be among the top priorities of any rehabilitation and recovery programme'.[152]

This worked well for Sudanese governments' long-standing strategies of creating and maintaining a cheap labour class sourced from its peripheries. In South Kordofan and South Darfur, local government discussions focused on displaced people as agricultural labour.[153] In Khartoum, for example, food for work programmes lasted into the late 1990s, providing monthly food assistance to impoverished camp residents 'as they do work useful to their communities'.[154] The aid community was also worried that their efforts would undercut local enterprises like the donkey-drawn water carts.[155] For the UN

---

[150] Peter Feiden, Lynellyn Long, and Kathryn Stewart, 'Khartoum Displaced Assessment and Recommendations', USAID Sudan, 15 February 1990, MEDU 17/3/REF/17, 1.

[151] Ina Laemmerzahl, 'Report on Interviews with PVOs Engaged in Activities to Assist Displaced People in the Khartoum Area', USAID Sudan, 10 August 1987, MEDU 17/3/REF/6.

[152] James P. Grant, 'Operation Lifeline Sudan Situation Report No. 6', MEDU 17/4/AID, 20.

[153] UN Emergency Unit, 'Update of Displaced Persons in South Darfur and in South Kordofan', SAD.947/6/44-46.

[154] Amnesty International, 'Sudan's Secret Slaughter', 45; Joseph Beraki, 'PHRP for Displaced Population Khartoum Region, ECC/ED Supplementary Feeding and Food for Work Programme', Sudan Council of Churches, 10 September 1987, MEDU 17/4/AID.

[155] C. Farnsworth, 'Sudan – Displaced Persons in Khartoum: Telex Message, American Embassy in Khartoum to the Secretary of State, Washington', 17 May 1987, MEDU 17/4/AID/130.

Development Programme (UNDP) in 1990, 'relocation to the Transition Zone or to other areas where income-generation opportunities exist is to be encouraged and facilitated providing that it is completely voluntary'.[156]

Aid to Khartoum's displaced communities was always limited, and by the early 1990s programmes were increasingly restricted and frustrated. By 1990, aid assistance to Khartoum was overseen by a combination of the Commission for the Displaced, the RRC, the Ministry of Social Welfare, Zakat and the Displaced (MSWZD), regional governments, local popular committees, and the Khartoum Commission.[157] The Humanitarian Aid Commission (HAC), established in 1995, was the tenth institution created by the government for 'the displaced' since 1984.[158] Multilateral aid programmes were stopped or wound up in Khartoum by 1992, with the Ministries for Health and for Peace and Development blocking project proposals, and the Commission for the Displaced actively disrupted food deliveries and tried to blackmail aid agencies for vehicles in exchange for access to forcibly relocated camps.[159] Operation Lifeline Sudan operations effectively ended in 1992, leaving UNICEF and the World Food Programme.[160] Most remaining aid funds and programming were left to the Sudan Council of Churches or funnelled through local Islamic agencies.[161] Many remaining agencies were either expelled in the early 1990s or had little operational contact beyond their offices and 'the chiefs'.[162] Oxfam noted in 1993, 'There seems to be a well-coordinated policy by political and security authorities to isolate the displaced people from the international agencies. This "containerizing" of the

---

[156] Rogge, 'Relocation and Repatriation', iii.   [157] Ibid., 1.
[158] Sommers, *Islands of Education*, 216.   [159] Burr, 'Sudan 1990–1992', 26.
[160] Ibid., 26.
[161] Aid worker, in London, 6 February 2012. By 1990, NGOs were fighting a monthly battle to stay in Khartoum. The constantly changing government agencies responsible for registration of aid work were in control of permits and visas, and were apparently increasingly difficult to contact from 1989 to 1991. By the early 1990s, NGOs had to re-register every year, with visas and permits expiring annually around January, forcing international staff to leave for around three months each year, while also being expelled seemingly at random. Rogge, 'Relocation and Repatriation', iv; Grant, 'OLS Situation Report No 6', 2.
[162] Paul Eedle, 'Sudanese Refugees Dumped in Desert Camp', SAD.947/6/7-8, 8; aid worker, in London, 6 February 2012; Tearfund worker, in London, 15 February 2012.

southern population has contributed to the ability of the Islamic agencies to work.'[163]

For displaced residents of Khartoum at this time, this discourse and practice of fighting 'dependency', and promoting apparent self-sufficiency, were part of a wider history of state efforts to make southern people, in particular, impoverished, dependent, and enslaved to the demands of survival economics.[164] Being displaced (*naziheen*) was (and still somewhat is) a pejorative term, akin to being *abiid*, a slave, a term still associated with Black, southern-origin people.[165] Martin Kiir Wol, who fled to Khartoum in 1988 and later became a businessman and member of the Dinka Cultural Society, explained: 'You know, we were like people who ran to the enemy's house. You were fighting with me, and then I run to you. [We had to] stay with them, to become like – like somebody who is a slave.'[166]

2.7 The Limits of Acculturation: Direct Violence

This captive population were subject to direct violence. The crackdown on internal opposition by the post-coup Security Committee in 1989 targeted the Umma, Democratic Unionist, and Communist parties in particular, and 'suspected SPLA sympathisers (pejoratively known as 'Fifth Columnists')'. This crackdown followed infrequent but terrifying uses of Islamic legal (*hudud*) punishments against southern residents for theft and robbery, including John Chol from Wau, a man called David from Equatoria, and James Ran Nyek from Upper Nile, each of whom had a hand amputated for theft in 1984.[167]

From 1989, unemployed people and students were increasingly used or drafted as sources and informants, and detention sites popped up across Khartoum.[168] Police raids increased, including on alcohol

---

[163] Oxfam, 'Confidential Report', 3.
[164] Jok Madut Jok, 'The Targeting of Civilians as a Military Tactic', in Ann Mosely Lesch and Osman A. Fadl, eds., *Coping with Torture: Images from Sudan* (Red Sea Press, 2004) 23; Duffield, 'Aid and Complicity', 83.
[165] Malik, 'Displacement as Discourse', 13, 20; de Geoffroy, 'Fleeing War', 513; Jok, 'Post-Independence Racial Realities', 193.
[166] In Apada, 11 August 2013.
[167] Amnesty International Index, 26 February 1985, IISH AFR 54/15/85, 15; Amnesty International Index, 25 March 1985, IISH AFR 54/17/85, 85.
[168] Arop Madut-Arop, *Sudan's Painful Road to Peace: A Full Story of the Founding and Development of SPLM/SPLA* (BookSurge, 2006), 230.

brewers, who were overwhelmingly southern and western Sudanese women, and who often suffered beatings, repeated imprisonment, fines, and often sexual or physical violence from police.[169] Dhieu Lual and Michael Thiop both remember hearing of women having miscarriages from illness and rape in prisons, or from overwork.[170] Many women explained painful personal experiences of abuses, illnesses, and deaths in childbirth. By 1995, popular morality police worked at 120 police stations in Khartoum and in the *dar es-salaams* around the city.[171]

This violence included coercive or forced military and security work. From December 1990 onwards, all civil servants, teachers, professors, and students had to do military training for six-week periods, which was obligatory for enrolment in university and to obtain secondary school certificates.[172] This training became the Popular Defence Forces (PDF), established formally in the early 1990s as the 'school for national and spiritual education', according to Omar al-Bashir: 'through the PDF "the Sudanese citizen's mind can be remoulded and his religious consciousness enhanced"'.[173] Training was mostly targeted at northern populations, though the PDF did draw on financially or physically coerced recruits from elsewhere in Sudan, and many southerners experienced forced conscription or obligatory PDF training, essentially as cannon fodder in the intense fighting of the early 1990s. In 1992 this became a holy war: soldiers were *mujahidin* (holy warriors) and prospective martyrs, while rebels were *ahl al-harb*, the people of war, fighting against the world of Islam.[174] PDF training was extended to all men under thirty by 1995, with youths seized on the streets at 'checkpoints'.[175] In the words of Dhieu, who was trained in the PDF in the late 1990s,

---

[169] As detailed by Lual Agang Macham, in Apada, 8 June 2013; Dhieu Kuel, in Mayen Ulem, 21 August 2013. This violence is comparatively well-documented. See Michael Parker, *Children of the Sun: Stories of the Christian Journey in Sudan* (Paulines Publications Africa, 2000); African Rights, 'Food and Power in Sudan'; Lesch and Fadl, eds., *Coping with Torture*; Human Rights Watch Africa, *Children in Sudan*; Jok, *War and Slavery in Sudan*.

[170] Dhieu Kuel, in Mayen Ulem, 4 July 2013; Michael Thiop Lang, in Aweil, 11 July 2013.

[171] Lesch, *The Sudan*, 137.

[172] African Rights, 'Food and Power in Sudan', 233; Lesch, *The Sudan*, 136.

[173] Lesch, *The Sudan*, 135.   [174] Ibid., 130.

[175] Ibid., 135; Human Rights Watch Africa, *Children in Sudan*, 4.

2.7 The Limits of Acculturation: Direct Violence

Most of it is conduct training. They can train you by brainwashing you, by telling you that this is an Islamic country, and that Islam is under threat, and you're supposed to train yourselves to take up arms, and we are going to – even liberate Africa, ... Islamize Africa.[176]

Coerced recruitment also served as a tidying-up operation on the streets of Khartoum. From September 1992, city authorities started to round up 'street children', specifically to clean up the streets.[177] Many of these (mostly southern and Nuba displaced) children and young people lived with their families in the city, and were running errands, going to the cinema, or worked or begged on the streets to find food or basic income.[178] Human Rights Watch noted that officials probably 'genuinely feel they are acting in the best interests of the child'.[179] In 1994, during a second round of detentions, the Sudan government stated that it had established 'rehabilitation' camps for these children across Sudan, including in Khartoum, Kosti, Geneina, Abu Dom, and Durdib, with rumours of more brutal centres closer to the war front.[180] There is very little information on these camps, which were apparently run as forms of Islamic schools, with military drills and PDF instructors.[181] In 1995 Human Rights Watch reported one fifteen-year-old boy explaining that they were 'given an option of joining the army or remaining in a camp indefinitely'.[182] Prisoners, including women, were also targeted for these camps.[183] On Sudan's independence day in 1995, in Port Sudan, al-Bashir called for one million new PDF recruits to defend the country. In the following few months, widespread military conscription included checkpoints throughout the Khartoum area, where young men and teenagers risked arrest.[184]

---

[176] Dhieu Kuel, in Mayen Ulem, 4 July 2013.
[177] Human Rights Watch Africa, *Children in Sudan*, 18; African Rights, 'Food and Power in Sudan', 234; Madut-Arop, *Sudan's Painful Road to Peace*, 238; Norwegian Refugee Council, 'Profile of Internal Displacement: Sudan', 113.
[178] Norwegian Refugee Council, 'Profile of Internal Displacement: Sudan', 113, citing Amnesty International.
[179] Human Rights Watch Africa, *Children in Sudan*, 14.
[180] Norwegian Refugee Council, 'Profile of Internal Displacement: Sudan', 113.
[181] African Rights, 'Food and Power in Sudan', 233; Norwegian Refugee Council, 'Profile of Internal Displacement: Sudan', 113; Jok, 'Post-Independence Racial Realities', 200, 203.
[182] Human Rights Watch Africa, *Children in Sudan*, 2.
[183] African Rights, 'Food and Power in Sudan', 235–37.
[184] Human Rights Watch Africa, *Children in Sudan*, 4, 55.

2.8 On the Peripheries

These brutalities and unfreedoms structured how people could reconstruct their lives in Khartoum.[185] Fear and risk fundamentally delimited action, as an anonymous 'squatter' emphasised to Amnesty International in 1994:

> I am afraid to be caught and taken to prison or to be taken to somewhere else maybe to be hung or be ... I can tell you many things like that happen. People are taken but nobody knows their place. I am afraid to be taken to a place where nobody will know. This is the thing that led me to hide myself.[186]

Marc Sommers has described people's 'precautions designed to minimise potential interactions with government authorities', including not looking at landmarks on a commute through Khartoum, for fear of being perceived as suspicious or alien.[187] Mayen, Philip Akot, and a small group of other men who together had worked as bricklayers in Khartoum commented that it was better to (at least visibly) 'stay poor' in order to avoid notice; 'we don't talk strongly ... we don't want to show what we have'.[188] Hanaa Motasim Taha terms this 'camouflage', 'hoping at best to be overlooked and ignored'.[189] Long-term southern and other regional residents had contended with racialised prejudices and risks of violence in Khartoum for decades, feeling 'surrounded by hostility' and seeking to limit contact beyond fellow southern or ethno-local friends and colleagues.[190] Fear of government targeting and of

---

[185] Here the term 'unfreedom' is used following the literature on work, as imposed limitations on physical mobility, choice, conditions, access to resources and rights, and the imposition of surveillance and punishments for seeking to escape these boundaries. See Siobhán McGrath, Ben Rogaly, and Louise Waite, 'Unfreedom in Labour Relations: From a politics of Rescue to a Politics of Solidarity?', *Globalizations* 19, no. 6 (2022): 911–21; Benedetta Rossi, 'Dependence, Unfreedom and Slavery in Africa: Towards an Integrated Analysis', *Africa* 86, no. 3 (2016): 571–90.

[186] Amnesty International Index, video transcript, 22 November 1994, IISH AFR 54/55/94.

[187] Sommers, *Islands of Education*, 211.

[188] Maper chiefs' court meeting, 13 April 2013; Lual Agang Macham, in Apada, 8 June 2013.

[189] Motasim, 'Deeply Divided Societies', 12.

[190] Rehfisch, 'A Study of Some Southern Migrants in Omdurman', 92; Ibrahim, 'The Southern Sudanese Migration to Khartoum', 16. The fear of strangers and 'aliens' in Khartoum heavily informed Hale's studies of Nubian migrants in the city: Hale, *Nubians*, 5.

2.8 On the Peripheries

demolition campaigns pushed people to hunt more remote but less risky locations.[191] Going to the city centre was literally risky business – as people only went there for work, mostly menial or domestic labour. Motasim quotes bell hooks on this Black marginality: 'we could enter but we could not live there'.[192]

State and non-state pressures in Khartoum since the 1960s increasingly encouraged southerners not to assimilate, but to conceal their difference in central public spaces, remain in peripheral areas of the city, and hide their intellectual, political, and cultural interests, to avoid the worst of public abuses.[193] This self-minimisation created exhaustion.[194] Kuol Dut, who arrived in Khartoum in 1989 and was quickly directed at the train station to a Dinka-area neighbourhood in Haj Yousif 5, emphasised that

if they found people like the way we are seated here, they will just ... arrest all of us, because they don't want people to gather and share their opinion.... These people lose the appetite of staying [in Khartoum, and in the community] ... when they're tired.[195]

The Equatorian politician and veterinarian Jimmy Wongo invoked this exhaustion in describing how there was 'not much in the way of the lives of the people' throughout the war years in Khartoum:

They continued to live in the peripheries, ... pushed out. Every time they get pushed out, every time they get pushed out. As the war escalated and reached a point where now, they get pushed out, they go and squat somewhere, when services arrive then they are pushed further, to go and sit somewhere else, and then services reach there, they are pushed out – and they kept pushing us until, I think, peace came.[196]

But this pushing-out was also a fight for security. Kuol Dut also noted how repeated physical marginalisation in response to these risks meant that

---

[191] Rogge, 'Relocation and Repatriation', 30.
[192] Motasim, 'Deeply Divided Societies', 13.
[193] Lual Agang Macham, in Apada, 8 June 2013.
[194] This exhaustion is visible in the limited mental health records in Khartoum. In 1989, hospitals raised concerns about increasing cases of depression, schizophrenia, suicide, and alcoholism, particularly among southern Sudanese living on the outskirts of the city. Ibrahim, 'War Displacement: The Socio-Cultural Dimension', 64, citing 'The National Dialogue Report' (1989), 43.
[195] Meaning that they were tired of dealing with these pressures. Kuot Dut Kuot, in Apada, 3 June 2013.
[196] Jimmy Wongo, in Juba, 18 October 2013.

we collect ourselves and then we occupy one of the places for ourselves ... And this is how we protect ourselves, because sometimes if Arabs feel like taking one of our brothers in the presence of us, they feared us, but if they find you alone they will just kill you.[197]

Areas like Haj Yousif, Jebel Aulia, Wad el Bashir, Jabarona, Soba, Mayo, and Izba were 'all places for Black people', according to the newly made sultan Abaker Thelatheen: 'the poor Arabs, and some drunkard Arabs, they do stay with us there, because they don't have much concern with what is going on! [laughs]'.[198] Concerted pressures on peripheral and war-displaced new residents forged new peripheries where these disenfranchised residents could somewhat, and sometimes, assert themselves – for instance, when residents of New Extension resisted demolition campaigns in 1988, threatening, stoning, and wounding police and District Council staff when they tried to burn a shanty neighbourhood down.[199] As a young man told Woldemikael: 'During those times (in the past), we were few. They call you *abd* [slave], there was nothing you can do. But now when they say it, you beat them.'[200]

Khartoum's political geography and evolving forms of violence and control are the basic context for the rest of the book, delimiting and shaping what was possible to organise and discuss. These first two chapters have set out how the massive growth of Khartoum's population, particularly from 1988, and state and neighbourhood efforts to control and dominate these risky new residents, reshaped these Black, peripheral, exploited residents' understandings of themselves and their lives. This was a project not of assimilation but of exclusion, flattening, and labour exploitation that relied heavily on direct violence and impoverishment. The next chapter explores how these new residents worked to organise self-defence and community solidarities against this violence.

---

[197] Kuot Dut Kuot, in Apada, 3 June 2013.
[198] Abaker Thelatheen, in Apada, 8 August 2013.
[199] Amnesty International, 'Sudan's Secret Slaughter', 23.
[200] Woldemikael, 'Southern Migrants in a Northern Sudanese City', 27.

3 Community Space and Self-Defence

By 1990, the war in the south was escalating. As the SPLA became a significant force and gained territorial control, the war compounded the pressures of Khartoum's political geography and placed the city's new residents under intense political, societal, financial, and personal stress. Like embattled urban migrant populations around the world, they needed to create living space, to keep families, friends, and communities mentally, spiritually, physically, socially, and culturally safe. Many people invested significant energy from the early 1990s in making living room, and in doing so rebuilding their futures, within the hostile terrain of the city. This chapter is about this self-preservation.

Just living in Khartoum held immediate risks, not only from the violent state apparatus. In retrospect – as well as in surviving notes from the time – most people emphasised the core risk of societal disaster.[1] To many it looked like families and societies were imploding under the pressures of displacement, deaths, hunger, and fear.[2] A contemporary observer noted that 'everyone is fighting for his own survival and for maybe a few close relatives'.[3] The Khartoum Archdiocese education programme at this time was titled 'To Save the Saveable', and stated: 'there is simply no base from which to start. [The] Southern children ... today can be called a threatened species, physically, morally and intellectually.'[4] Hospitals and clinics reported a surge in psychiatric referrals from southern residents.[5] Church and

---

[1] See Ibrahim, 'War Displacement: The Socio-cultural Dimension', 65; de Geoffroy, 'Fleeing War', 517.
[2] Parents 'watch[ed] the family unit disintegrate': Jubara and Tawolde, 'Displaced Southerners in the Three Towns: A Survey Summary'. Also see Stockwell et al., 'Displaced Persons in the Khartoum Archdiocese', 23.
[3] Amnesty International, 'Sudan's Secret Slaughter', 12; Hutchinson, *Nuer Dilemmas*, 133.
[4] Archdiocese of Khartoum, 'To Save the Saveable', 2.
[5] Ibrahim, 'War Displacement: The Socio-cultural Dimension', 64.

human rights campaigners emphasised a pervasive state of shock and an 'atmosphere of helplessness and despair about the war'; a church observer wrote with urgency that 'if the war continues there will be nothing Southern to speak about'.[6]

There was a lot to organise. The risks of the city and the impacts of the war all demanded negotiation: of urban livelihoods and lifestyles, generational change and forms of loss, and new forms of information, socialisation, and cultural knowledge that were both challenging and necessary to understanding and navigating urban life. Associational cultures, arbitration systems, neighbourhood vigilantisms, gang cultures, new social spaces, and creative projects were all ways to re-establish lives and to support (and manage) the lives of others in reconstructing communities.

This chapter explores the work of the people who took up the possibilities offered by the city's new forms of self-expression and self-assertion, and who engaged in this work of educating, protecting, revolutionising, and organising these wartime urban community standards and orders. It was vital to discuss and plot out what must be maintained to keep hold of yourself, your community, and its futures, and how mutual reliance and moral order could be reset for these heterogeneous new suburbs. As within other populations under intense pressures of dislocation and violent authority, these new Khartoum residents were arguing about core issues of responsibility, social values, and trust, and investing in social and cultural projects to support their arguments.[7] These battles over community futures, moral standards, and acceptable societal change were often fought – as ever – on women's bodies and lives.

This work involved fundamental questions about the supposedly collective 'southern' displaced community. What were the limits of

---

[6] Amnesty International, 'Sudan's Secret Slaughter', 15; Stockwell et al., 'Displaced Persons in the Khartoum Archdiocese', 23; 'Encounter of Archbishop Gabriel Zubeir Wako with Christian Intellectuals: How Can Christian Intellectuals Contribute to the Peace Effort in the Country?', 18 September 1986, CAR 674/27/4.

[7] There is a huge literature here stretching in various directions, including Stephanie Newell and Onookome Okome, *Popular Culture in Africa: The Episteme of the Everyday* (Routledge, 2014); Lisa Malkki, *Purity and Exile: Violence, Memory, and National Cosmology among Hutu Refugees in Tanzania* (University of Chicago Press, 2012); Derek R. Peterson, 'The Intellectual Lives of Mau Mau Detainees', *Journal of African History* 49, no. 1 (2008): 73–91.

kinship, mutual support, and collaboration in these highly stressful and expensive neighbourhoods, within a confusing and fragmenting civil war? Who was a 'brother' in this struggle, and what were the ethnic, racial, and political limits to this solidarity? What and who should be defended, and for whom? Even while the loose geographical-political category of *junubiin*, southerners, was increasingly applied to Khartoum's war-displaced population, people were increasingly having to articulate what being *junubi* meant in practice, and the current and future political communities that could (and should) be created by southern, ethno-linguistic, or more generally Black and marginalised neighbours.

Displaced residents' responses to these challenges were not straightforward community 'resistance', but fraught, ambiguous, uncomfortable, and personal. These tensions are the focus of the rest of this book, complicating any idea of the 'southern community' acting in direct and antithetical reaction to Khartoum's violent hegemony. This is in contrast to a common retrospective idealisation of life in Khartoum – that people were together 'like one community against the north'.[8] Writing in retrospect, Amir Idris stated that southern community was forged simply by 'being collectively identified as Southerners'.[9] This is a common idea, that 'southern' identification emerged from this simple resistance, '[replacing] former ethnic and local identities' as a collective versus the 'one enemy, that is the "hakuma" [government]'.[10] These are James Scott's two false polarities, the apparent choice between resistance or acquiescence to assimilation.[11] This explanation is both reductive and implicitly passive. Instead, this chapter tries to detail the stressful (and to many, exciting) conversations and competing projects that tried to set parameters for possible political communities, including a southern community, and to determine the terms of a collective resistance to the violence of Khartoum.

---

[8] Anei Deng Akok, in Aweil, 13 August 2013.
[9] Idris, *Conflict and Politics of Identity in Sudan*, 64.
[10] Ibrahim, 'The Southern Sudanese Migration to Khartoum', 13; Woldemikael, 'Southern Migrants in a Northern Sudanese City', 30; Ibrahim, 'Southern Sudanese Women Migrants', 253–54.
[11] James C. Scott, *Weapons of the Weak: Everyday Forms of Peasant Resistance* (Yale University Press, 2008). For an example of this argument of basic 'resistance to assimilation', see Hale, 'Nationalism, "Race", and Class', 180.

3.1 Risks and Mutual Self-Help

Daily life in wartime Khartoum was fundamentally risky. The regular physical, financial, and mental abuses detailed in Chapter 2 – most particularly, the arrests, imprisonments, home searches, extortion, beatings, and harassment of street hawkers, market workers, women beer-brewers, and many others – were compounded by risks within displaced communities, particularly after the split of the SPLM/A in 1991 sparked massacres in Bor and violence between ethnically divided military factions.[12] After this split, people remember fighting in Arkawit between Dinka and Nuer residents, and fighting in the agricultural schemes in Kassala and Gedarif; Farouk, a Nuer engineer working in the city at this point, also remembers fighting between Nuer neighbours first, angry over families' involvements in government-sponsored militias.[13]

The other main risk, emphasised in people's retrospective accounts of this period, was a risk of societal loss, particularly as people became isolated in the city, families became fragmented, and loved ones remained missing. This risk was specifically articulated as a de-culturation, a de-saturation and loss, rather than a cultural change.[14] This was due to the impacts of state-sponsored alienation – as detailed in Chapter 2 – but also significantly because of people's own forgetting, new socialisation, and individualised coping mechanisms, such as drinking heavily. The adaptations necessary in Khartoum meant that 'since we left this area [Aweil] we were different people'.[15] There were wider pressures post-flight: trauma, urbanisation, poverty, the collapse of social ties and networks of mutual dependence, as well as sociocultural mixing, particularly with the advent of international media in the 1990s. Forgetting words in your mother tongue, picking up other languages, and learning 'the languages of the people who don't respect you' would mean someone was 'getting lost'.[16] Children born or raised

---

[12] Michael Thiop Lang, in Aweil, 10 July 2013.
[13] Lazarus Lual, in Juba, 19 October 2013; Diing Chen Diing, in Aweil, 12 August 2013; Farouk Gatkuoth, in Juba, 30 October 2013.
[14] Duffield, 'Aid and Complicity', 92. With reference to concept of 'cultural bereavement' of Maurice Eisenbruch, see Abusharaf, *Transforming Displaced Women in Sudan*, 16.
[15] Ngor Akol Jonkor, in Apada, 5 June 2013; also Abuk Deng, in Apada, 5 June 2013.
[16] Abuk Deng, in Apada, 5 June 2013.

3.1 Risks and Mutual Self-Help

in Khartoum generally became practically monolingual in a mix of southern and Khartoum Arabic.[17] Adults remember worrying about losing the ability to express complex ideas and emotions in their mother tongue.[18] Residents were well aware that 'something that stays in a place will resemble the environment'.[19] The social isolation of individuals as cleaners or guards, for example, would 'absorb' people like this: 'those who isolate themselves, are those to be lost to Arabs'.[20]

By 1991 and 1992, as the massive number of people who had arrived from 1986 to 1988 settled and established themselves in the city, managing and disciplining this community loss via 'controlling our language and our culture' became a priority for many within Khartoum displaced communities.[21] The most obvious of these concerns (for the community and observers alike) was the rise in numbers of street children (*shamasha*, or children of the sun) or gangs. These were catch-all terms for schoolchildren selling cigarettes to fund their education, pickpockets, homeless or destitute children, groups of youths in public spaces, and organised adult criminal activity.[22] Some children became vagrant or self-sufficient on the streets due to the death, abandonment, destitution, or mental health and addiction problems of their parents or guardians.[23] These were also physical, social, and moral risks to urban youth, particularly for angry, desperate, and depressed young people. Many emphasised the negative impact of emotional breakdowns, financial stress, and the monetisation of relationships on their communities, as people became 'tired' and 'lost appetite'.[24] As bricklayer-turned-pastor Michael worried,

---

[17] Miller, *Language Change and National Integration*, 59.
[18] Angelina Majok, in Mayen Ulem, 16 July 2013; members of the Dinka Cultural Society, in Apada, 11 August 2013; Diing Chen Diing, in Aweil, 15 July 2013.
[19] James Garang, in Maper, 19 July 2013.
[20] Michael Thiop Lang, in Aweil, 10 July 2013; Arou Piol Adam, in Apada village, 22 July 2013.
[21] Arou Piol Adam, in Apada village, 22 July 2013.
[22] Dhieu Kuel, in Mayen Ulem, 21 August 2013. In court, Dhieu said, these criminal groups were delineated as *shamasha*, small-scale pickpockets; *blathajiiya* or *balathaga*, big gangs of burglars, or *assaba*; and *rabathiin*, night gangs and drug smugglers.
[23] Marko Mathiang Deng, in Apada, 17 August 2013; Dhieu Kuel, in Mayen Ulem, 21 August 2013. See also Jubara and Tawolde, 'Displaced Southerners in the Three Towns: A Survey Summary', 10.
[24] See Harragin and Chol, *The Southern Sudan Vulnerability Study*; see also Luca Russo, 'Crisis and Food Security Profile: Sudan', in Alinovi et al., eds., *Beyond Relief*, 20. Mental health problems were recorded in 1989 in Ibrahim, 'War

Some people overload themselves in the drinking hall, some people take local brews and other spirits.... [There was] a group of girls, and young men, boys, sometimes they just move to ... places like the houses of the sex workers; many people gather there, and whoever doesn't have money may think of forcing other people.[25]

The practical and social risks of poverty, anger, and stress were interwoven with the issues raised by the new freedoms and social lives made possible in Khartoum, including from increasing access to global cultures through cinema, TV, and later through phones and the internet, over the 1980s to 2000s.[26] Poor, unmarried, and sporadically employed or unemployed young men increasingly looked to American Black cultures to assert an internationalised sense of difference and feeling of power, particularly through the frequently referenced 'n***a gangs' of the late 1990s and early 2000s.[27] And generally it was difficult (in the words of Dhieu, who was in his twenties in the early 1990s) to manage those youth 'who love drama'.[28] Many people remember (and still worry about) the effects of global acculturation, white supremacist beauty cultures, the impacts of racism and ideas of Black African inferiority, and the commodifying and destructive individualist forces of capitalism on the urban poor.[29]

Displacement: The Socio-cultural Dimension', 64; and also explained by Lual Lual Aguer, in Apada, 3 June 2013.

[25] Michael Thiop Lang, in Aweil, 10 July 2013.

[26] As noted by Wendy James, *The Listening Ebony: Moral Knowledge, Religion, and Power among the Uduk of Sudan* (Oxford University Press, 1999), 2.

[27] Members of the Dinka Cultural Society, in Apada, 11 August 2013. Many people emphasised that the name "n*gga" (or N***er, or N*ggaz) gangs developed in the early 2000s, including – in Khartoum – groups called 'West Coast', 'The Blacks', 'Backstreet Boys', 'Cash/Catch Money', and many others. This term, with various spellings, continues to be used to describe violent delinquency and immorality, particularly among young men in South Sudan, but is often described as a post-Comprehensive Peace Agreement (2005) phenomenon. See Cherry Leonardi et al., 'The Politics of Customary Law Ascertainment in South Sudan', *Journal of Legal Pluralism and Unofficial Law* 43, no. 63 (2011): 58–60; Mareike Schomerus and Tim Allen, 'Southern Sudan at Odds with Iitself: Dynamics of Cconflict and Predicaments of Peace', Development Studies Institute, London School of Economics (2010), 64–65; Katarzyna Grabska, 'In-flux: (Re) Negotiations of Gender, Identity and 'Home' in Post-war Southern Sudan', PhD dissertation, University of Sussex (2010), 11.

[28] Dhieu Kuel, in Mayen Ulem, 21 August 2013.

[29] For a global discussion of these themes, see Dimitrios Theodossopoulos and Elisabeth Kirtsoglou, *United in Discontent: Local Responses to*

3.2 Asserting Authority: Chiefs, Neighbourhood Committees, and Intermediaries

All of this demanded the reassertion of explicit, protective, and powerful values and personal identifications. People needed to make order, to keep things going. Most obviously, this involved societal management, particularly of familial disputes, marriages, debts, and fights. Clan, sub- and para-ethnic, and regional networks were reconstructed and repurposed in Khartoum, for social security, the organisation of justice and mediation, marital match-making, and spiritual self-management. These associational cultures were built on older organisations, often by the various 'chiefs' and spokespeople involved in the emergency relief and neighbourhood organisation work outlined in Chapter 1.

Neighbourhood committees began to reorganise themselves from the early 1990s, particularly 'since the blasting out of southerners' from slums and squatting in the centre of the city from the late 1980s.[30] Men were nominated (or nominated themselves) as committee members or sultans (the northern Sudanese term for chiefs), taking on aid coordination and state service provision in these new suburbs. These men became the 'focal points' for state authorities and international aid agencies.[31] This was encouraged by the Khartoum state: by 1991, Bashir's government wanted the cheap manipulability of a 'community-based government', distributing food through neighbourhood committees, and in return using committees and sultans to organise bussing people to rallies.[32]

These men drew their authority from various sources: some were tied to chiefly lineages and clan systems, others had military or state government experience or connections, and some were nominated by neighbourhood committees or by local security services as NCP-paid workers who could draw on connections to the Khartoum government.[33] These men were hardly liked; Saadia Izzeldin Malik's 2005 study cites a women's song that goes

---

Cosmopolitanism and Globalization (Berghahn Books, 2010); this argument is made by Duffield, 'Aid and Complicity'.

[30] Dhieu Kuel, in Mayen Ulem, 21 August 2013.
[31] Wijnroks, 'The Displaced People of Khartoum', 10.
[32] Kuel Aguer Kuel, in Juba, 20 January 2017.
[33] Duffield, 'Aid and Complicity', 96.

Nas al-Lajnna ijoloh lel miskeen ma bidoroh
Al-Mutgushshed le shotoroh, bagi al-Mukhzan holoh.
The people of the committee do not like the poor
The belly-god and greedy man, owned all that remained in the store.[34]

Many of these 'new' chiefs were 'not really chiefs of community'. Lazarus Lual, a teenager in the city in the early 1990s, emphasised that they were 'Islamic chiefs'.[35] He explained:

The chiefs were the most – they were the people who best understood the political, the political situation in Khartoum and they're like – they try to find a safe room for themselves. You find – you cannot find a chief who did not claim to be a Muslim. It doesn't matter whether he goes to the mosque or not. But he must dress like Muslim, wake up in the morning, behave like Muslim – uh, visit his Muslim brothers, sit down, plan to meet the big men in the government – and what he's going to say there is that: I have the people. I am the only one influential person whom they can listen to. If you have information to pass, why don't you share it with me? You see? They try to find a link between them and the government. They cheat, you know, they cheat the government, they cheat the community, they're cheating both.[36]

While of course plenty of men benefitted from this often self-interested intermediary work, many residents noted how useful this mediation was, particularly for negotiating or making payments to release some women arrested for brewing alcohol.[37] In establishing government-recognised alternative court systems, leaders could organise the resolution of local small-scale legal cases outside government courts (though, as in South Sudan today, robbery and murder 'belong[ed] to the government').[38] These intermediaries could negotiate down sentences and fines – for example, negotiating bail for a woman arrested for beer-brewing down from 1200 dinars to 800, or a prison sentence for brewing from three months to one month.[39] Chiefs who

---

[34] Malik, 'Displacement as Discourse', 17.
[35] Lazarus Lual, in Juba, 19 October 2013.
[36] Lazarus Lual, in Juba, 19 October 2013.
[37] Acien Acien Yor, in Aweil town, 11 July 2013; Michael Dau Mangar, in Apada, 5 June 2013; Lual Agang Macham, in Apada, 8 June 2013; see Cherry Leonardi, 'Violence, Sacrifice and Chiefship in Central Equatoria, Southern Sudan', *Africa* 77, no. 4 (2007): 535-58; Leonardi et al., 'The Politics of Customary Law Ascertainment'.
[38] Michael Dau Mangar, in Apada, 5 June 2013; Ngor Akol Jonkor, in Apada, 8 June 2013; Lual Agang Macham, in Apada, 8 June 2013.
[39] Michael Dau Mangar, in Apada, 5 June 2013.

3.2 Chiefs, Neighbourhood Committees, Intermediaries

knew Arabic could 'rescue people' more effectively, working with the local police partly in collaboration but also to stymie them.[40] Marko Majok, then a student and AYU volunteer, noted how chiefs' apparently parochial 'traditionality' was sometimes a useful performance when dealing with security or police officers in eviction negotiations or police stations: you 'could just tell them that South Sudan does not belong to me, I am just a representative of their voice. If you don't have [this] language to dodge them you will end up being killed in front of your family.'[41]

Those residents who were involved in, or approved of, this work echoed Cherry Leonardi's summary of the role of chiefs: that these men were intermediaries, working to hold the government at arm's length while drawing down the limited benefits it could offer.[42] By the early 1990s, too, the Khartoum city authorities barely invested in governing or even policing these Black suburbs. As Willow Berridge notes, Umbadda had only a very small and practically defunct police station by the mid-1980s, and the entirety of Haj Yousif officially had only two police officers in one police post. The central and city governments encouraged self-policing via vigilantism.[43] This active neglect (and encouragement of rather chaotic, locally organised security as 'community policing') chimed with some local interests anyway.[44] Dhieu Lual remembered how some chiefs '[selected] some youth to protect – to monitor the situation at night', and local gangs were expanded or incorporated into neighbourhood militias when camp relocations were imminent.[45]

These vigilantes' primary interest was 'to defend ourselves', as James, a 'community police' (and gang) member in Haj Yousif, explained:

[In] the time of war that when you talk in court, when you request your rights in the court as the Dinka boy or Dinka woman or Dinka girl, you will

---

[40] Lual Agang Macham, in Apada, 5 June 2013; for examples of this in Bor, see Tuttle, 'Life Is Prickly', 43, 49.
[41] Marco Majok Deng, in Khartoum Gedid, Kuajok, 28 August 2013.
[42] Leonardi, *Dealing with Government*.
[43] Berridge, 'Nests of Criminals', 244.
[44] Bakhit, 'Negotiations of Power and Responsibilities in Khartoum Shantytowns', 131.
[45] Dhieu Kuel, in Mayen Ulem, 21 August 2013; aid worker, in London, 6 February 2012.

not be given your right even if you are right. The youth were aiming to guard themselves against problems.... Our group was powerful because it included those who served national service, the educated class of people, and other physically strong people ... [and you know that] police cannot afford to come and arrest a person [who has served national service or is in the army], because they are soldiers, and that is police – so police cannot arrest them.... after something is heard over the whole of Khartoum, it brings a lot of people from that group, different groups of gangs, to come and investigate why their colleague was arrested.... the Dinka chiefs in Khartoum – you know, they were not happy with our group, but they like only that protection we made.[46]

For Dhieu, this self-policing was generally tolerated in remote areas by local state authorities because

they are taking care of their brothers. You see, if they do something wrong, they will not do it to an Arab. The government is not worried about them, because as long as they are working, they are working on their southerners. Even if they do it wrong, they do it to their people, because they have been isolated.[47]

The forms of neighbourhood protection, court, and committee systems varied even across residential blocks and suburbs, and between socioeconomic and ethno-regional communities. Both courts and gangs reflected the complex racial and ethnic dynamics of their neighbourhoods, with individual ethnic courts collaborating formally and informally, for instance, the Ashan Kom court, established in 1989 for Dinka Malwal, Nuer, and Shilluk in one area, with local sub-committees formed including Nuba, Baggara, and Darfuri members.[48] Residents originally from the Equatorias, particularly from Juba, were significantly fewer in these peripheral neighbourhoods, and more likely to be in Khartoum as students or formally educated workers in government, NGO, or other official positions, primarily because of the distance and difficulty of travelling to Khartoum from the southernmost parts of Sudan. Several Equatorian ex-Khartoum residents pointed out that they were more likely to involve the police and

---

[46] James Garang, in Maper, 30 June 2013; the impunity of security forces is noted in Rone, *Behind the Red Line*, 4–5.
[47] Dhieu Kuel, in Mayen Ulem, 21 August 2013.
[48] Ngor Akol Jonkor, in Apada, 8 June 2013; Marko Mathiang Deng, in Apada, 14 April 2013.

3.2 Chiefs, Neighbourhood Committees, Intermediaries 105

Sudan state courts in disputes, because of their proximity to (and familiarity with) formal structures and the language of government.[49] But many of these Equatorian residents were involved in, or knew of, Equatorian community courts and chiefs working in Khartoum as well.[50]

However, the majority of displaced people were from the northern areas of the south – from Dinka, Shilluk, Nuer, Dinka Ngok, Nuba, Jur Col, and other smaller ethnic communities, most of whom fled overland northwards in the mid- to late 1980s – and they lived and worked within this multi-ethnic suburban sprawl.[51] These complex new neighbourhoods required careful management, with conflicts over marriages, debts, domestic violence, divorce, and child custody sparked by the fallout of the traumatic flight to the city, as well as the stresses of divided or lost families; husbands who had died, fled, disappeared, or moved to seek work; and tensions between impoverished neighbours (although inter-ethnic fights and violence usually involved the police).[52] Khartoum-made chiefs like Lal Malou, a chief for Karton Kassala in Haj Yousif, were (according to him) nominated after the city authority ordered each residential block to select sultans to solve issues before they reached court, to represent their particular ethnic group.[53] Michael Dau, a member of a neighbourhood-elected Dinka Malual chiefly court from the early 1990s, emphasised that they had 'limited authority', but it was still important, focused on local disputes and relationship issues, all of which could escalate.[54] Men (and some women) from different clans and ethnic groups would convene to negotiate cases involving different standards and norms of restitution, for instance, forms and amounts of compensatory

---

[49] Alfred Taban, in Juba, 16 October 2013; this is reflected in Leonardi, *Dealing with Government*.
[50] For example, the uncle of Dor Tartizio Buni, interviewed in Juba, 14 October 2013.
[51] For example, some Shilluk communities coalesced in Soba around a Presbyterian church for 'nominally' Christian community meetings, and went to representatives of the Shilluk Kingdom based in Fitihaab for managing cases of witchcraft; Parker, *Children of the Sun*, 98, 108.
[52] Aleu Deng Dit, in Maper chiefs' court, 13 April 2013; Alfred Taban, in Juba, 16 October 2013.
[53] Lal Malou, in Khartoum Gedid, Kuajok, 27 August 2013.
[54] Michael Dau Mangar, in Apada, 5 June 2013.

payments and custody arrangements.[55] Courts like this were already working in Khartoum by 1980, for workers and other resident southerners to mediate, in particular, marriage disputes, intra-family loans, borrowing, and debts, in especially impoverished and therefore high-stress circumstances. Government courts across Khartoum already frequently referred cases back to neighbourhood chiefly committees when they involved issues of cattle debt and other locally specific compensation problems.[56]

Some men specialised in negotiating bride wealth and marriages among their own sub-clans and village members in Khartoum, and were experts in translating old standards of cattle debts into acceptable cash equivalents.[57] The ideal arrangement was part payment:

it was acceptable to pay money, as a dowry in Khartoum, but not all of the money ... you promise to pay cows when you come back to South ... It was told that a person must have to pay an amount that is equivalent to thirteen cows, and the rest of the cows will be completed in the South as a promise.... people always came from the South, and they were the ones to explain the rate of change of cows in the auction here. Then people must see which price is good for them.[58]

The cow-equivalent deposit varied, with most families unable to pay anything more than sacks of sorghum at the time; these agreements were recorded on paper, 'to be sorted after the war'.[59] This was a source of frustration to many people, but also entrenched the expectation of return southwards, and other forms of positive wealth- and family-filled futures beyond the war.[60]

With family members, old village neighbours, and ethno-linguistic communities now spread across refugee camps, 'peace villages', towns, and rural and migrant work routes, and in rebel movements and camps in Sudan and across its borders, these volunteer brokers and organisers

---

[55] For example, cases between the Luo Jur and Dinka; Joseph Ukel Abango, in Juba, 29 October 2013.
[56] Garang Atak Rieu, in Mayen Ulem, 20 August 2013; Ngor Akol Jonkor, in Apada, 8 June 2013.
[57] Angelo Arou Jel Deng, in Mayen Ulem, 22 August 2013; Kuel Aguer Kuel, in Juba, 20 January 2017.
[58] Santino Atak Kuon, in Mayen Ulem, 3 July 2013.
[59] Kuel Aguer Kuel, in Juba, 20 January 2017.
[60] Many conversations with women in Apada, June and August 2013; also Michael Thiop Lang, in Aweil, 10 July 2013.

3.2 Chiefs, Neighbourhood Committees, Intermediaries

built networks of middlemen across the region. Communication and movement linked these intermediaries, who often themselves worked on these migrant routes, or were in regional police or military jobs. These networks allowed for some useful solidarities and connections, for instance, in helping to track down missing family members, and to find and negotiate the release of relatives and children from abusive or servile conditions in houses and farms, particularly in Kordofan and southern Darfur.

The best example of this is Ashara Wilayat. Many Dinka and some Nuer people referenced Ashara Wilayat as a key example when discussing this type of community organisation and self-protection. Ashara Wilayat functioned as a networked arbitration system, literally meaning 'Ten States', referring to its supposed inclusion of community representatives from across the southern region. Many people remember this as the primary mixed-ethnicity southern judicial system organised in Khartoum, beginning roughly around 1988, with meeting places in Lafa'a Gufaa in Kalakla, Jabarona, and Haj Yousif; people had settled inter-ethnic dowry disputes, elopements, and other debt issues in these courts, where committees invoked southern legal standards (including the Nuer Fangak agreements and the Dinka legal standards agreed at Wad Alel) and settled cases in Arabic.[61]

This network was itself fundamentally male-dominated and made patriarchal and often-oppressive determinations. Equally concerning, the Ashara Wilayat court system's power to make case decisions stick was drawn from its government and military affiliations. These connections were not directly with the Khartoum regime, but with southern Sudanese government-allied militiamen in the city. Ashara Wilayat was partly structured around the personal compounds and offices of Paulino Matip, whose militia was based at Lafa'a Gufaa, and Abdel Bagi Ayii Akol, whose militiamen's family homes and offices were in Jabarona and Wad el Bashir. As such the court could enforce decisions, operating as a para-statal judicial and penal system, using the possibilities of intimidation and abuse that affiliation allowed.[62]

And Dinka cannot say no, I cannot go there ... because he is collaborating with Arabs. He was given the guns, the cars, he was given a stamp – and

---

[61] Abaker Thelatheen and court members, in Apada, 15 August 2013; Ngor Akol Jonkor, in Apada, 8 June 2013.
[62] Duffield, 'Aid and Complicity', 96.

there, if you refuse, then you will be killed. Yeah, that was it.... Yeah, some people tried to avoid [these courts]; but there's no alternative, cowardly people joined him. Those who fear, yeah.[63]

We will return to Ashara Wilayat in Chapter 7, to re-examine the 'protection' this system (and its ethno-military patrons) claimed to organise, and what this meant for societal order especially in the 2000s. But what many people involved across these early courts and committees said they were trying to do – in the words of Lual Lual, a chiefs' court worker and menial labourer in Jabarona – was to 'keep people safe', creating self-governed communities defended from direct state force.[64]

3.3 New Neighbourhoods and Making Community

Keeping people safe meant reorganising a sense of regularity and space for an insecure, criminalised, and unstable population – what the historian of labour and slavery Ahmed Sikainga terms 'taming the city'.[65] By the early 1990s, people had carved out spaces across Khartoum, setting up new football teams, leagues, and associations; childcare arrangements, youth groups, and community schools; savings collectives; dance events; workers' associations; and games clubs. These renewed associational and social lives fed people's own reconsiderations of themselves and their futures.

A lot of this involved reworking older institutions and using old rural-urban migrant knowledge and socialities.[66] People took up established rural-urban migrant methods of mutual help, for instance, the Sudani *sandouk* (box) group savings scheme, and *nadi* (club) cultures developed by Humr, Nubi, and other urban migrants over the 1950s and '60s.[67] Older clubs, mutual aid societies, and regional or ethnic associations had established 'particular political stances' and engaged in political organisation and local community projects. By the 1970s,

---

[63] Garang Atak Rieu, in Mayen Ulem, 20 August 2013.
[64] Lual Lual Aguer, in Apada, 15 August 2013.
[65] Sikainga, 'Organized Labor and Social Change', 9.
[66] See Pratten, *Return to the Roots?*; Bjarnesen and Utas, 'Introduction: Urban Kinship'.
[67] Farnham Rehfisch, 'Rotating Credit Associations in the Three Towns', in Pons, ed., *Urbanization and Urban Life*.

3.3 New Neighbourhoods and Making Community

older clubs were already centres for adult education classes, and some were increasingly multi-ethnic in membership.[68]

These social and urban associations were put under intense pressure by the arrival of so many new residents, as outlined in Chapter 1, and by the 1989 coup's banning of more formal professional associations and trade unions.[69] Options for civil organisation were few and risky. Some prominent migrant associations – such as the Fashoda Benevolent Cultural and Social Association – protected their institutional status by mainly limiting their work to Shilluk cultural activities.[70] But many other smaller, more peripheral, or new organisations founded in the late 1980s for emergency mutual aid and support survived and evolved. Many were initiated by students, civil servants, traders, and teachers within a given community, but were organised by and involved people from across class and educative backgrounds.[71] As Alfred, a Bari resident, observed,

these small, small organisations became quite big, involving many, many people – and for the first time, you would not only get like tribal ones, but the whole region or the whole south, in some cases. We were talking about the same language – that we are all suffering in the south, you know, and hunger, and they just want to drive us out of our land.[72]

Some people held membership in several organisations. For Diing, an organiser in the Aweil Youth Union, 'we have unions; we have associations; we have societies ... like myself, in Marial Bai, we have Ayat Youth Association', then the 'Tueny Youth Charitable Society', then the 'Ayat Sons Areas Association' as a subsection, with 'most of Tueny area living in Arkawit, in Gereif West'.[73] Continuing links to these ethnic associations' home regions created Khartoum-based echoes of 'village' events, such as counterpart funeral ceremonies for those who had died in the south, and vice versa.[74] These organisations allowed

---

[68] Asia Mahgoub Ahmed, 'Urbanisation and the Folk Verse of the Humr', in Pons, ed., *Urbanization and Urban Life*, 712 citing Fahima Zahir; Sikainga, *Organized Labor and Social Change*, 8.
[69] African Rights, 'Food and Power in Sudan', 146. [70] Ibid., 146.
[71] Miller, *Language Change and National Integration*, 121.
[72] Alfred Taban, in Juba, 16 October 2013.
[73] Marial Bai is a village area in Bahr el Ghazal. Diing Chen Diing, in Aweil, 12 August and 15 July 2013; Jimmy Wongo, in Juba, 18 October 2013.
[74] Miller, *Language Change and National Integration*, 38–39.

'people to know themselves'; as Lazarus Lual – who found his brother by walking between bakeries (see Chapter 1) – noted,

the most challenging thing is – how will people know themselves? That we are here, and they're from the same place, and they're brothers and they could help each other if they find each other, yeah. Because if you don't know anybody, then you are in trouble.[75]

This associational life allowed people to organise collective action, particularly around education, as children struggled to access Arabic-language classes or were forced to drop out of schools by economic pressures or discriminatory exclusions.[76] Over the early 1990s, the Aweil Youth Union (see Chapter 1) evolved into an education-focused organisation, organising night study and boxing clubs, aiming to divert young people from gambling and alcohol abuse. A significant amount of the funding for these associations, and a lot of the organisation, came from women and youth members, often those involved in street selling or beer-brewing.[77] Like dozens of other regional and ethno-regional associations, the Union organised graduation ceremonies and awards for young people passing exams, to encourage investment and pride in educational attainment. Martin Kiir – no longer doing emergency relief work at the train station, but an office clerk in Haj Yousif – explained:

We gave [the graduate] a diary, with a pen, and told him: these things are for you to remember Aweil. And those who have graduated their colleges, and universities, we give them honorary certificates, thanking him for making a great effort to graduate his university, and then – he is asked to come and help the people of Aweil.[78]

3.4 The Space Available

These projects were shaped by the space available: the clubs, market spaces, church spaces, multi-purpose centres, football pitches, and evening meetings in NGO-sponsored *rakubas* (thatched, open-walled shelters). These spaces were also rooted in older organisations since the 1940s, when the southern population in the three towns was

---

[75] Lazarus Lual, in Juba, 19 October 2013, speaking in English. [76] Ibid.
[77] Madut-Arop, *Sudan's Painful Road to Peace*, 248.
[78] Martin Kiir, in Apada, 14 August 2013, speaking in English.

3.4 The Space Available

comprised of a small number of young, mostly male labourers who socialised in church spaces and beer places.[79]

The centrality of Christian space to the Khartoum southern community since the 1940s was not necessarily due only to growing Christian beliefs or high rates of conversion among southerners, at least until the late 1990s.[80] A large majority of southern Sudanese residents had few to no church connections at all by the 1960s; for example, Jesse Hillman, an Anglican missionary, estimated that among the roughly 300,000 southern residents in northern Sudan, the Anglican Church was associated with maybe 300.[81] The various churches in Khartoum focused on catering to these new populations, particularly with the expulsion of foreign missionaries from southern Sudan in 1964.[82] By the 1950s, Christian institutions in Khartoum provided key accommodation, local information in the vernacular, education, job opportunities, and funding. The associations and clubs that the Catholic and Anglican churches housed and encouraged from the 1950s onwards provided a site for educational opportunity outside formal schooling, through religious training, libraries, night schools, games clubs, and reading and debate clubs, which were often only nominally religious.[83] They also provided space and security in a variety of ways for southern and Nuba Mountains migrants who spoke often poor or regional variants of Sudanese Arabic; Rehfisch's 1962 survey found a fifth of

---

[79] Mohammed Ahmed, 'Christian Missionary Activity', 3; see also Mark Nikkel, *Dinka Christianity: The Origins and Development of Christianity among the Dinka of Sudan with Special Reference to the Songs of Dinka Christians* (Paulines Publications, 2001); Bishop Allison to Africa Secretary, London, June 1949, Church Missionary Society Archives (CMS) CMS/G/Y/S; Rachel Hassan, diary entry, July 1956, CMS/ACC641.

[80] For discussion of this politically motivated growth of the Christian faith, see Jok, *Sudan*, 308, note 145.

[81] Jesse Hillman, CMS Nairobi, to Rev. Canon Bewes, CMS London, 29 October 1958, CMS AF35/59 G3 SN 1 Subfile 1.

[82] For a particularly vitriolic explanation of this work, see Mohammed Ahmed, 'Christian Missionary Activity', 1–3.

[83] Rev. Canon Bewes, diary entry for 1954, p. 29, CMS AF59 AFE AD3; 'Bible Society', Kenya National Archive (KNA) MSS 61/712 (A); Bertram to Hooper, 20 April 1938, CMS AF59 AFE AD1 729; Dr Roland Stevenson to Nuba Mountains Fellowship, January 1959, CMS AF35/59 G3 SN 1 Subfile 5; also see Rehfisch, 'A Study of Some Southern Migrants in Omdurman', 91; 'Gordon Memorial Sudan Mission Minutes of Mission Conference Held at Yei', KNA MSS61/712 (A), 4.

southerners in Omdurman kept their savings in church offices or with missionaries.[84]

By the 1980s, many of the old Christian club organisers and church workers from the 1950s and '70s were in charge of new emergency programmes and their own churches (e.g., the prominent Nuba politician and priest Philip Abbas Ghabboush, who ran a social club and Bible study group in Omdurman's Church Missionary Society [CMS] mission in the late 1960s).[85] The wave of Christian conversions among southern residents in Khartoum – like across southern Sudanese communities in the south and in exile elsewhere – is well-documented, giving people spiritual, intellectual, and practical resources to help manage the fundamental chaos and trauma of the war and displacement.[86] These church leaders and their teams established new centres and social outreach across Khartoum's expanding suburbs, prisons, and pubs, building on old literacy projects, counselling, Bible study, night schools, and mothers' unions, and making up new mixed-ethnicity local sports groups and tournaments, including the 'Olympic Team' for basketball.[87] These priests, lay members, and catechists from across southern communities were crucial in organising and caring for wartime arrivals in the late 1980s.[88]

By 1992, this organisation and funding rapidly expanded church congregations, including at the Roman Catholic St Matthew's Cathedral in the centre of the city, which was closed in 1988 but

---

[84] Hillman to Rev. Canon Bewes, 29 October 1958, CMS AF35/59 G3 SN 1 Subfile 1; Northern Sudan CMS Conference, Omdurman, 2–4 April 1957, KNA MSS 61.582; Rehfisch, 'A Study of Some Southern Migrants in Omdurman', 88.

[85] CMS Northern Sudan Mission, 'Minutes of Northern Sudan CMS Conference', 16–17 April 1958, KNA MSS 61.582.

[86] Jesse Zink, *Christianity and Catastrophe in South Sudan: Civil War, Migration, and the Rise of Dinka Anglicanism* (Baylor University Press, 2018), 1–7; 'Lost Boys, Found Church: Dinka Refugees and Religious Change in Sudan's Second Civil War', *Journal of Ecclesiastical History* 68, no. 2 (2017): 342; Tounsel, *Chosen Peoples*.

[87] Mohammed Ahmed, 'Christian Missionary Activity', 5, 13; Motasim, 'Deeply Divided Societies', 15–17; Rehfisch, 'A Study of Some Southern Migrants in Omdurman', 91.

[88] Members of the Dinka Cultural Society, in Apada, 11 August 2013; Mohammed Ahmed, 'Christian Missionary Activity', 14. Nikkel notes new translations of Dinka orthography and the Bible starting in the 1980s: Nikkel, *Dinka Christianity*, 20.

3.4 The Space Available

reopened in 1992.[89] In 1994, Abdelaziz Shiddo, then Minister of Justice and Attorney-General, reported 'alarming numbers of conversions to Christianity, or the proliferation of churches to the extent that Khartoum State has got 572 churches by February 1993'.[90] This period's boom in church organisation and attendance matched the corresponding intensification of Islamist justifications for state violence against the peripheries in the south and in Khartoum, as detailed in Chapter 2, and more broadly the rise to dominance of the overarching polarised narrative of Islam versus Christianity in Sudan's civil war.

These church-opened spaces were extensively used for secular ends.[91] But it is easy to be reductively materialist about the role of Christianity here: the proliferation of Bible studies, conversion, and regular worship provided resources for emotional, spiritual, and bodily needs, and new explanatory tools and personal fortifications.[92] These religious effects are beyond the space and ability of this book to explore here and are richly detailed in new work by Jesse Zink and Christopher Tounsel, among others, but many people explained to me that they turned to the church for healing from illnesses sparked by the violence, dirt, stress, and jealousies of the city.[93] Michael Thiop, the bricklayer who passed through Cic Adid in 1985 in Chapter 1, found the church after falling sick from witchcraft since arriving back in the city; he explained, 'I earned a lot of money and as we know traditionally in health here, if you have wealth, and you are not a good believer in God, you will be bewitched.... I was very happy after I get cured in the church, and I realised that it is God who is the most powerful, then I begin to serve God.'[94] Michael then became a healing pastor in a new evangelical church in Haj Yousif in the mid-1990s.

---

[89] To the possible surprise of Archbishop Gabriel Wako: noted in Madut-Arop, *Sudan's Painful Road to Peace*, 165. In 2000 the cathedral was turned into a museum.
[90] 'Statement by HE Mr Abdelaziz Shiddo', 25 December 1994, SAD 306/7/36-46.
[91] Santino Ayak, in Maper chiefs' court, 13 April 2013.
[92] Zink, 'Lost Boys, Found Church', 342.
[93] For this wide field of literature, see Zink, *Christianity and Catastrophe*; Tounsel, *Chosen Peoples*; Nikkel, *Dinka Christianity*; 'Aspects of Contemporary Religious Change among the Dinka', *Journal of Religion in Africa* 22, no. 1 (1992): 78–94; Christiane Falge, 'The Effects of Nuer Transnational Churches on the Homeland Communities', *Urban Anthropology and Studies of Cultural Systems and World Economic Development* 42, nos. 1–2 (2013): 171–205.
[94] Michael Thiop Lang, in Aweil, 10 July 2013.

A key resource of the church in Khartoum was space. The pressures of Khartoum's political geography made safe spaces more valuable. 'International security', as one man put it, was available in the Catholic Church–run Comboni Ground in the centre of Khartoum; various other denominations also provided space for cultural and teaching activities in the urban peripheries, and local communities established their own self-run church spaces in the suburbs.[95] These spaces multiplied and diversified as new 'multi-purpose' public structures, schools, clubs, and shelters were built by NGOs and through community funding.[96] A *rakuba* could serve, variously, as a dominoes hall and tea stand in the day, an evening school in the late afternoon, and an 'evening church' at night.[97]

This did not mean that political and cultural activism within these spaces was either monitored or encouraged by these churches. Aside from encouraging attendance and education, most people said that the international clergy 'didn't know' about political activism in church spaces.[98] Disputes with Catholic policies were frequent: the archbishop Gabriel Zubeir Wako walked a fine line, criticising the SPLA and attempting – controversially – to replace separate vernacular services with cross-community Arabic language programmes.[99] Catholic Church authorities were criticised by one literacy association for underrating and undermining community leadership skills.[100]

Christianity did not provide the only space for southern organisation in the city. *Nadis* (clubs) and old pubs and drinking streets tied newer southern migrants into older communities and geographies, documented in research into migrant communities in Khartoum since the 1960s. Rehfisch recorded that the beer houses were generally owned or operated by ex-slaves or their descendants. His 1960s study – recording spare time spent at mission clubs, night schools, libraries, the cinema, window shopping, visiting sex workers, and football – is

---

[95] Abaker Thelatheen, in Apada, 8 August 2013; Marco Akon Akon, in Apada, 11 August 2013; Diing Chen Diing, in Aweil, 15 July 2013; Maper chiefs' court, 13 April 2013.
[96] Mohammed Ahmed, 'Christian Missionary Activity', 14.
[97] For a disapproving note on unpermitted 'evening churches', see ibid., 116.
[98] 'Encounter of Archbishop Gabriel Zubeir Wako with Christian Intellectuals: How Can Christian Intellectuals Contribute to the Peace Effort in the Country?', 2–3; members of the Dinka Cultural Society, in Apada, 11 August 2013.
[99] Santino Akak Kuon, in Aweil, 3 July 2013.
[100] Members of the Dinka Cultural Society, in Apada, 11 August 2013.

echoed by descriptions of social life from older residents in the 1970s and new arrivals in the 1990s.[101]

Access to these spaces, and the spaces themselves, were shaped by economic class and by linguistic, educational, neighbourhood, and ethnic community ties and socialisations. As described by recent postcolonial studies elsewhere, these were spaces defined by intimacy, learning, and translation. Continued movement of people and information into, across, and out of the city provided what Waters and Jimenez call new 'raw materials'; neighbourhood histories, personalities, and public spaces shaped how new residents, new generations, and new organisations related to each other.[102] These spaces were the ground within which the huge refugee populations of the 1980s and 1990s organised, and which shaped their activities, theorising, and work.

3.5 Black Khartoum

The diversity of Khartoum's southern and otherwise peripheral Sudani communities and neighbourhoods created many different social lives across the city. It is common in (South) Sudanese literature to focus on divisions between ethnic communities, but class was at least as important as ethnicity in structuring relationships and dividing people in the stark socioeconomic geography of the city's first-, second-, and third-class areas and its slums and policed displaced camps. Many people emphasise the social and experiential gulf between generations of Khartoum residents, particularly between those settled in the city in the 1960s and '70s, and the war-displaced newcomers.[103] Deep differences of class, wealth, experience, and opportunity – as Dhieu Lual explains – divided people

into three sections. The first section is the life of those who are living [outside] the state of Khartoum, in rural areas, in Jabarona, Mayo, Haj

---

[101] Rehfisch, 'A Study of Some Southern Migrants in Omdurman', 90–91.

[102] Mary Waters and Tomás Jiménez, 'Assessing Immigrant Assimilation: New Empirical and Theoretical Challenges', *Annual Review of Sociology* 31, no. 1 (2005): 105–25; also see Louise Lamphere, 'Migration, Assimilation and the Cultural Construction of Identity: Navajo Perspectives', *Ethnic and Racial Studies* 30, no. 6 (2007): 1134.

[103] Atak Akol Diing, in Aweil, 14 August 2013; Sikainga, 'Military Slavery', 34. For a discussion of the Nuba Mountains urban experience in this period, see Ewald, *Soldiers, Traders, and Slaves*.

Yousif, and Jebel Aulia ...; and we have the life of those who are government officials and some other traders: they are living inside the city with Arabs, they are living in very good buildings or even they used to rent some houses with Arabs. And we have the life of those who are called Jongo, or the agriculturalists, the farmer workers: they used to migrate.[104]

These different lives structured neighbourhoods. Linguistic, familial, ethnic, and regional origins, as well as a person's time of arrival in Khartoum and ties among transiting communities created in Darfur, helped to develop patterns of clustered settlements. This was partly self-selecting, as impoverished newcomers were directed to neighbourhoods where extended family, people of similar linguistic groups, and otherwise helpful community members could support them. As Kuot Dut, a bricklayer and community representative noted, for Dinka people from the northern and eastern Aweil area this was generally Haj Yousif block 5, Kalakla, and in Jabarona in Omdurman: 'some people will just take you and – and show you the place where your Dinka people are residing'.[105] Another church worker remembered that 'you found people of Aweil[;] they are living in one place, people of Wau they're living in one place, people of Rumbek are living in one place'.[106]

This was partly also reflective of tensions around events in the conflict in the south, including clashes between Nuer Anyanya Two forces and Dinka fighters and migrants in the late 1980s, and particularly in response to the Bor massacre and other brutalities across the region in 1991.[107] By 1990, there was already localised conflict in Khartoum between angry residents, for example, clashes in Hillat Shook in 1989, a fight of 'Nuer against Dinka' in Arkawit in 1997, and between Dinka Parou, Lou Nuer, and Murle in one woman's neighbourhood, for example.[108]

---

[104] Dhieu Kuel, in Mayen Ulem, 4 July 2013. See Chapter 5 for the Jongo.
[105] Kuot Dut Kuot, in Apada, 3 June 2013.
[106] Riing Riing Lual, in Aweil, 3 September 2013; also see Miller, *Language Change and National Integration*, 48–50; Ibrahim, 'Southern Sudanese Women Migrants', 249.
[107] Aid worker, in London, 6 February 2012.
[108] Diing Chen Diing, in Aweil, 12 August 2013; Anei Deng Akok, in Aweil, 13 August 2013. For recorded inter-tribal violence, see Feiden et al., 'Khartoum Displaced Assessment and Recommendations', 10, 39–40; Amna Badri and Intisar Sadig, 'Sudan between Peace and War: Internally Displaced Women in Khartoum and South and West Kordofan', UNIFEM (1998), 21; Bannaga,

But these small ethnic enclaves were only one aspect of a massively dispersed new population that was often faced with little to no immediate choice in accommodation, and which was for the most part mixed together. For people with prior connections or experience of Khartoum – which was common – it was possible to live in compounds, for example, with Equatorian, Dinka, and northern Sudanese residents.[109] Religion (many people emphasised to me) was not necessarily important; in 1992 Catherine Miller observed families with members practicing a variety of faiths.[110] Personal conversion to Islam was not automatically politically or socially contentious, and could come in many forms. Most people divided Muslim converts in the community into those who 'joined' because of jobs or because of belief.[111] Initial or attempted ethnic and regional enclaves were generally confounded by the realities of Khartoum life: 'people were categorised in different places, but every tribe had to live together, especially the southern tribes, including the Darfurians'.[112]

The social effects of these mutual experiences and urban pressures are often remembered as very positive. In interviews, people across South Sudan recalled meeting other linguistic and ethnic communities for the first time, in schools, societies, and neighbourhoods, and learning bits of other Equatorian, Dinka, Luo, Nuer, and Shilluk people's languages.[113] Weddings, funerals, and dances provided opportunities to learn and observe other regional and ethnic dances and to try them out; one Dinka Malual woman remembered trying Shilluk, Zande, Nuer, Dinka Bor, Nuba, Fur, and Maasalit dances, as well as 'Bob Marley and disco', primarily with her Black neighbours.[114] This is not an entirely retrospectively imagined commonality; many people

Peace and the Displaced in Sudan, 131; Millard Burr, 'Khartoum's Displaced Persons: A Decade of Despair', Issue Brief, US Committee for Refugees, Washington, DC, 1990, p. 39.

[109] Melanie Itto, in Juba, 23 October 2013; lots of people, including women, noted the same throughout research.
[110] Miller, *Language Change and National Integration*, 51.
[111] Atak Akol Diing, in Aweil, 14 August 2013.
[112] Mathok Diing Wol, in Ariath, 21 August 2013.
[113] Michael Thiop Lang, in Aweil, 11 July 2013; Ayii Bol, in Aweil, 16 August 2013; Atak Akol Diing, in Aweil, 14 August 2013.
[114] Arou Piol Adam, in Apada village, 22 July 2013.

emphasised their frustration that they had lost phone numbers of friends from other Sudanese regions while returning to the south or with the change in national dialling codes in 2011, and women's photo albums from Khartoum were emotional records of their friendship groups of Zande, Dinka Bor, Dinka Malwal, and Darfur neighbours and colleagues, particularly with shared childcare arrangements.[115] Some women now living in Aweil fondly remember their neighbourhood meet-ups with Tishaat, Fur, and other southern women, to talk politics, watch TV, share childcare, or drink coffee.[116] Schools – particularly smaller, community-run ones – were often mixed-ethnicity.[117] While many people still married within their ethnic group, in part due to language and marriage standards, there was increasing intermarriage among Equatorians and between Sudanese communities in general.[118] Kinship expanded through friendships, business partnerships, and evening socialising.

As common as intra-ethnic or regional explanations of affiliation and friendship in accounts of Khartoum life is the assertion of a sense of racial collectivity. Pan-ethnic commonalities expressed through race – or Blackness, a term more reflective of the language used by people in Aweil and Juba – were constants in explanations of Khartoum community thought and everyday life, and an essential means of self-interpretation. The multi-linguality of communication even within a single neighbourhood in Khartoum provided plenty of space for ambiguity and overlaps in translation and terminology. 'Black people', 'southerners', and pan-ethnic or regional terms including Equatorian and Dinka run through accounts, but were used and translated between languages and dialects self-consciously, if flexibly; the most common term used across accounts in a variety of languages,

---

[115] At the independence of South Sudan in 2011, a national country dialling code was created (+211); this apparently resulted in many people's phone SIM cards failing, forcing people to change their numbers and lose contacts. Josephine and other women who requested anonymity, Maper Akot, 26 March 2013; and many others.

[116] Josephine and other women who requested anonymity, Maper Akot, 26 March 2013.

[117] Angelina Majok, in Mayen Ulem, 16 July 2013; Abuk Deng, in Apada, 5 June 2013.

[118] Jimmy Wongo, in Juba, 18 October 2013.

3.5 Black Khartoum

though, was 'Black people'.[119] This is exemplified by the famous song of Andrew Bol, a Dinka Malual labourer and singer:

> All the sons of the Black people do not sleep
> Even the women, they do not sleep
> Sons of the Black people everywhere
> Even in the land of Beja, they don't sleep, even their wives
> The land of Darfur is also crying, their women do not sleep
> The children of the Black people get up early and go out to find work
> And the children of others get up early to go to school.
> Aaah! All sons of Black people cry and even women cannot sleep
> Ooh! Every type of Black people cry and their wives cannot sleep
> That side of Beja is crying
> That side of Nuba is crying
> And that side of Darfur is crying as well
> Every child of the Black people looks for a job
> And every child of other people goes to school.[120]

Equatorian residents emphasised the importance of a Black social community in Khartoum; Tartizio, employed as a driver in Khartoum, remembered that 'we were there mixed with Arab, Burgu, Fellata, Massalit, and Nuba, yeah ... maybe at that time I will be able to say that – you are my brother, and you are my father. Yes, we sit together.'[121] Many Dinka people emphasised the historical nature of this Black solidarity, often with Saint Bakhita as a common example of mutual slaving histories, whose history, faith, and image as a Black Catholic slave saint was widely invoked throughout the 1990s.[122]

---

[119] A note on terminology: in Aweil, most informants spoke in a mix of Dinka and Arabic, using the terms *ran col* (black person), *monjiang/jieng* (Dinka person/ the Dinka, or sometimes translated by the person as 'people' in general), and *januubiin* (Sudanese Arabic for southerners); many Dinka people also used Dor as a collective term for Equatorians. In Juba and Aweil, those speaking Bari, Arabic, and English used the terms (in English or equivalent) 'Black people' and 'southerners' more frequently than ethnic categories. Awen Mayuon Macwac, in Maper Akot, 21 June 2013; Richard Tongu and Dor Tartizio Buni, in Juba, 14 October 2013.

[120] Presented on 23 August 2017 at a group meeting in Maper Akot Arou, translation by Joseph Diing Majok with permission.

[121] Dor Tartizio Buni, in Juba, 14 October 2013.

[122] See Christopher Tounsel, 'Two Sudans, Human Rights, and the Afterlives of St. Josephine Bakhita', *Christianity and Human Rights Reconsidered* (2022): 261. See also Figure 3.1, a photo of Josephine dancing in the Comboni school dormitory.

In coping with life in Khartoum, 'all the hard work belonged to every Black tribe in Sudan', which for many people included the Ingessana, Nuba Mountains, and Darfur residents – 'they were our people'.[123] A displaced Nuba woman, named in Malik's account as Shaikha, emphasised that 'we are Arab in ethnicity but not in deed'. 'If the government considered us to be Sudanese, we would not have been treated as strangers.'[124] One chief emphasised that the Khartoum government saw southern Darfuri people as non-Arab 'southerners'.[125] Some men dismissed 'southern' as an accurate marker – 'when I say I'm a southerner, it is a geographical direction' – but others emphasised a collective understanding: 'when we say southern Sudan, we became one tribe, the whole southern people ... But the Nuba and Fur ... we see as our brothers, they were colonised by Arabs, that is why they got lost.'[126] This marks the limits of some people's personal trust and solidarity, particularly for those new residents who had been brutalised by Darfuri and other Sudanese soldiers. Agany, a former cattle-camp leader and a young businessman in Khartoum at this time, drew the line with Darfuri residents. 'We were the same by the skin, but different in heart. They think that they are Arabs.... They don't want to be our brothers. For some time, they sat to be Arabs, and we sat as Dinka.'[127]

As such different residents drew different lines and shades of community across their neighbourhoods, not just on racial-political grounds but because of the limits of trust, respectability, and mutual aid in hard times. The dangers of such intimacy with strange neighbours are reflected in accounts of bewitchment and curses set upon naive, generous, or overly successful residents, echoing studies of modern witchcraft across Africa. Many people attended church as well

---

[123] James Garang, in Maper, 19 July 2013; Peter Deng Akok, in Maper, 29 June 2013; Michael Thiop Lang, in Aweil, 11 July 2013; Mathok Diing Wol, in Ariath, 21 August 2013; Juma Michael Atuko, in Maper Akot, 12 July 2013; members of the Dinka Cultural Society, in Apada, 11 August 2013.
[124] Malik, 'Displacement as Discourse', 9.
[125] Acien Acien Yor, in Aweil town, 11 July 2013.
[126] Members of the Dinka Cultural Society, in Apada, 11 August 2013; Acien Acien Yor, in Aweil town, 11 July 2013.
[127] Agany Macham, in Apada chiefs' court, 8 June 2013.

3.6 New Ideas and Free Women 121

as continuing to visit witch doctors and pay spear masters and other spiritual authorities for their work: 'we know that the spear masters and the church leaders perform the same thing'.[128] People often relied on traditional medicines and witch doctors, including across ethnic lines, for medical care, particularly after attempting courses of antibiotics.[129] Both men and women explained how they or others had been cursed or bewitched by people from their own or other communities. Ador, now an elderly woman in Maper Akot near Aweil, emphasised that there was a lot of southern witchcraft in Khartoum, mainly a 'matter of jealousy'. Most of the examples she gave involved spiritual violence against women's reproductive systems, including miscarriages and mysterious internal pain.[130] As ever, though, these bewitchments and possessions were not a society-wide phenomenon: '[Laughs] In Khartoum we were internally displaced people by the war, and everybody was busy looking for where to get food, and you cannot stand and shiver yourself like you have a spirit! Then you will not get food! [Laughs].'[131]

3.6 New Ideas and Free Women

These neighbourhoods were grounds for new ideas, self-expressions, habits, and opportunities. The second half of this chapter details how residents tried, in diverse and conflicting ways, to manage these new freedoms. These efforts were the foundations for more complicated projects of community-building and political expression that took root in these spaces in the early 1990s, and which will be the focus of the rest of the book.

These changes were not all seen as bad; viewed retrospectively from Aweil and Juba they were generally prosaically described as the

---

[128] Acien Acien Yor, in Aweil town, 11 July 2013; Michael Thiop Lang, in Aweil, 10 July 2013; chief's court in Mayen Ulem, 20 August 2013; see also Parker, *Children of the Sun*, 108.
[129] Ador Geng, in Maper Akot, 13 July 2013.
[130] Ibid. See also Christian Laheij, 'Dangerous Neighbours: Sorcery, Conspicuous Exchange and Proximity among Urban Migrants in Northern Mozambique', *Africa* 88, no. S1 (2018): 31–50.
[131] Mathok Diing Wol, in Ariath, 21 August 2013.

'advantages and disadvantages' of Khartoum.[132] Many people were positive about inter-tribal relationships, access to international news, and their relationships with non-southern work colleagues.[133] Most people's discussions of Khartoum – across gender, age, regional background, and economic status – demonstrated a core tension over these positive and negative impacts of modernity, for instance, between significant new economic opportunities for many, versus economic disempowerment (particularly of men), and over the changing social significance and moral weights of particular behaviours and skills, such as the capital gains offered through low-status, menial, and subordinate work like brick-laying.

There were deep disagreements about freedoms and standards among the heterogeneous classes and neighbourhoods of displaced and otherwise southern residents, as younger people in particular tested out new regional and global cultures and languages. As in new urban spaces across the world in the twentieth century, ex-residents of Khartoum remembered internal conflicts across southern, Nuba, and western Sudanese neighbourhoods over dances, fashions, sex, language, religion, gender norms, beautification, and intermarriage. This was a fraught conversation about how society should look, act, behave, and manage itself, during what was – for many residents – a period of societal disaster, and in circumstances that felt fundamentally at odds with their former understandings of the world and the futures of their families and communities.

Women's memories of these conversations are noticeably different to men's. Women were a marginal majority in Khartoum's peripheries since the 1990s, essentially because men were often migrant labourers or in rebel or Sudanese militaries.[134] As in most cities, there were more casual economic opportunities for women in small trade, housework, care, cooking, and market work than for comparatively unskilled

---

[132] Maper chiefs' court meeting, 13 April 2013; Apada chiefs' court meeting, 14 June 2015. Like Emily Callaci's urban residents of Dar es Salaam in the 1960s to early 1980s, movement, space, and money were all sites of opportunity and moral danger.

[133] Riing Riing Lual, in Aweil, 3 September 2013; anonymous woman, in Maper Akot, 3 September 2013; Angelo Arou Jel Deng, in Mayen Ulem, 22 August 2013; Diing Chen Diing, in Aweil, 12 August 2013.

[134] Norwegian Refugee Council, 'Profile of Internal Displacement: Sudan', 72, 74.

men.[135] Women therefore – as ever – did most of the work, both in the home and for family income.[136] Fouad Ibrahim relates the account of Nyagen, a twenty-five-year-old Aliab Dinka woman from near Juba, in his 1994 study:

> I am responsible for myself, my four children, my mother, my five sisters and four children of my sisters. Every day I go out to look for work. I go to the houses of the Arabs and ask for work. Last Tuesday I washed clothes the whole day and got £S100.[137]

For poorer women, living far out in the city's camps and peripheries, there were fewer employment options. The 1992 Khartoum State Public Order Act controlled the mobility of women in public spaces, banned them from selling food and drinks between 5 pm and 5 am, and gave authorities the authority to harass, assault, and detain women on spurious grounds.[138] Selling food required a council permit and a health office licence, and without it women ran the same risks of being raided by police and having their equipment stolen as if they were brewing alcohol. Many women relied on income from brewing beer and distilling aragi, often sold on wholesale through middlemen. This required borrowed capital (in 1993–94, about £S400, for double in profit). David Lukudu's short story 'Seiko Five', about a beer-brewing woman called Fatna in Dar es Salaam, explains how Fatna got into brewing after seeing

> how her neighbours, fellow Southerners, Sadiya and Nakuma, who came to the North almost two years earlier, fleeing from civil war, were doing far better than many. Rumour also did its spinning around Dar-es-Salaam that one of the two women had invested in the food business and was running a popular restaurant in Suk Juba, specializing in soups.[139]

In her study of displaced women in 1994, Bruna Siricio Iro listened to displaced women's accounts of the physical and mental stress of being the primary carer and breadwinner for extended families.[140] This

---

[135] Atak Akol Diing, in Aweil, 14 August 2013.
[136] Norwegian Refugee Council, 'Profile of Internal Displacement: Sudan', 160.
[137] Fouad Ibrahim, 'Hunger-Vulnerable Groups within the Metropolitan Food System of Khartoum', *GeoJournal* 34, no. 3 (1994): 259.
[138] Malik, 'Displacement as Discourse', 3.
[139] David Lukudu, 'Seiko Five', *Warscapes*, 6 August 2013.
[140] Siricio Iro, 'The Situation of Sudanese Women', 108.

included the risks of being 'caught by the kasha' for making alcohol: as Nyagen explained to Fouad Ibrahim, 'The first time I was given 30 slashes and had to pay £S500. I was imprisoned for a whole month. They ruin you completely.'[141] Siricio Iro wrote:

> Women show more concern for the children and the household in general. Thus, they are more willing than men to invest in building a house and providing their children with their basic needs of food and clothes. Men's priorities are more directed towards establishing a trade, pursuing an interrupted study or paying the bride-price for a concluded or a planned marriage.[142]

But many women also emphasised their new freedoms in the city. According to Raja, a young girl when she arrived in Khartoum from Wau in the late 1980s, 'women they go anywhere, they go to the theatre, they go to picnic, they go to anywhere in Khartoum'.[143] The stress of financial responsibility and the continued emotional and mental strain of the war, displacement, and other losses were – for some women – offset in the everyday by new self-determinations and forms of independence. Abuk, in her late twenties in 1991 with two children and a SPLA soldier husband missing in the civil war in the south, explained her joy at her ability to refuse her family's demands for her to re-marry, and her new independent life as a single parent: 'Khalas! [Laughs] Khalas intaa! I was really finished with marriage.'[144]

The economic power shift towards women in migrant communities has been well-documented: in Khartoum, men had absconded, had gone to fight or work on agricultural schemes, or were unable to find regular employment, and so most families depended on women's incomes, and often on women as heads of the household. This presented a serious challenge to male authority: as a group of chiefs emphasised, 'the women were free, because they were brewing local brew, they're working in Arab houses, and they get paid – they don't even ask where their man is!'[145] For these men, blaming women for

---

[141] Ibrahim, 'Hunger-Vulnerable Groups', 259–60.
[142] Siricio Iro, 'The Situation of Sudanese Women', 261.
[143] Raja, in Apada, 3 September 2013.
[144] Lit. 'Enough! (Completely) enough!' Abuk Ngor Deng, in Maper, 29 June 2013.
[145] Chief's court in Mayen Ulem, 20 August 2013; also Atak Akol Diing, in Aweil, 14 August 2013. See Ryle and Yai Kuol, 'Displaced Southern Sudanese in

this self-indulgent independence was (and is) likely a defensive response to how their masculine protective powers and responsibilities had been sharply undercut, leaving them, in the words of Sharon Hutchinson, 'incapable of defending themselves' – let alone their loved ones – from arrest, conscription, back-breaking and risky labour, or neighbourhood-razing bulldozers.[146] A contemporary news report quoted Barnaba, a resident in Mandela, explaining why his wife left him: '"She wants to eat and I'm jobless," he says. "How is she going to stay with me?"'[147]

Angelina, a young woman in Khartoum over the late 1980s into the 1990s, explained these fundamental shifts in economic and social balance during the civil war and displacement, and the strain on gender norms and relations. Lacking education and other options, many men displaced from the south were limited to socially stigmatised, low-wage manual labour or 'women's work' of laundry, cooking, and restaurant service. Being supported by a woman was (and is) difficult within most men's conceptions of their own social role.[148] Angelina emphasised how this led to some men stopping their wives from obtaining ID cards for work, or accusing their wives and daughters of sex work if they were cleaning houses or working in markets.[149] Younger men looked to other international Black masculinities, particularly African American Black urban and gang cultures, to help them articulate critiques of their circumstances and to work out their relationships with their subordinate and risky racial, economic, and political position; with the city space; with women; and with being modern Black men.[150] For one ex-gang member, 'the youth were

---

Northern Sudan with Special Reference to Southern Darfur and Kordofan', 40; for a more recent discussion of changing gender roles, see Grabska, *Gender, Home & Identity*.

[146] Sharon Hutchinson, '"Food itself is fighting with us": A Comparative Analysis of the Impact of Sudan's Civil War on South Sudanese Civilian Populations Located in the North and the South', in Vigdis Broch-Due, ed., *Violence and Belonging: The Quest for Identity in Post-colonial Africa* (Routledge, 2005) 150.

[147] Shadid, 'Lurking Insecurity', 6.

[148] Gabriel Deng Bulo, in Maper Akot, 22 June 2013.

[149] Angelina Majok, in Mayen Ulem, 16 July 2013; Atak Akol Diing, in Aweil, 14 August 2013; and many other casual conversations with women in Apada; Ibrahim, 'Southern Sudanese Women Migrants', 252.

[150] See also Jordanna Matlon, '"Elsewhere": An Essay on Borderland Ethnography in the Informal African City', *Ethnography* 16, no. 2 (2014): 145–65.

aiming to guide themselves against problems that will aggress them ... It was youth liberation.'[151] By the late 1990s, Angelina remembers gangs called West Coast, The Blacks, and Catch Money around her neighbourhood:

> they used to scatter the money in the air, whenever there is an occasion [laughter]. Some men were working in factories, some men were selling clothes in the market. Some men were laying bricks along the river. They just compete between themselves, to make themselves look as if they have a lot of money.[152]

Marital breakdowns, deaths, men in military work elsewhere, lost wealth, and missing parents all broke down family decision-making systems. Both older generations and younger men found bride-wealth systems difficult to maintain, especially for those who had lost parents and family and had no ability to negotiate formal agreements.[153] Casual arrangements, marriages through pregnancy, and marriages between Darfuri, Nubian, Beja, and other eastern and southern residents or between people of different religious backgrounds often caused tensions.[154] Angelina, from a Dinka Malual family, emphasised how the definition of intermarriage varied between families; her uncle emphasised to her that she was 'supposed to marry Dinka Ngok or Zande or Shilluk and other tribes of southern Sudan',[155] but nobody from further afield.

These stresses all played out on younger women's bodies and choices. Younger women were blamed more generally by older men and many women for making money through sex work, for drinking, and for smoking cigarettes, as well as being seen as morally questionable for attending picnics and parties.[156] Women's (and young men's) dress was socially policed. Some 'new' things, including henna designs described as 'Darfur style', were very popular, as were tobs

---

[151] James Garang, in Maper, 19 July 2013.
[152] Angelina Majok, in Mayen Ulem, 16 July 2013.
[153] Gabriel Deng Bulo, in Maper Akot, 22 June 2013.
[154] Miller, *Language Change and National Integration*, 53–54; Ador Geng, in Maper Akot, 13 July 2013; Dhieu Kuel, in Mayen Ulem, 21 August 2013.
[155] Angelina Majok, in Mayen Ulem, 16 July 2013.
[156] Atak Akol Diing, in Aweil, 14 August 2013; Angelina Majok, in Mayen Ulem, 16 July 2013; Abuk Ngor Deng, in Maper, 29 June 2013; Michael Thiop Lang, in Aweil, 11 July 2013.

3.6 New Ideas and Free Women

and other cheap and accessible fashion, such as kitenge fabrics from East Africa, and westernised suits and sportswear; hair and beauty salons were increasingly established and run by young southern men and women. Angelina explained that both men and women suspected that the tight wrap skirts adapted from a variety of southern Sudanese cultures (most often blamed on the stereotypically sexually risqué Zande people) were worn to trigger miscarriage as a form of abortion.[157]

This did not stop many young women, including Angelina, from testing out forms of power and possibility through global and internationalised Black cultures. By the late 1990s, girls would wear trousers and 'don't-sit' miniskirts, and a few dressed in American-style basketball shirts and urban streetwear, pushing hard against gender norms. As Angelina explains, 'we were pretending, dressing like a man'.[158] This was an explicitly hybridised, conscious game, not just a straightforward appropriation of Black American language and imagery. Angelina's photograph albums, carefully kept safe on the long journey to the south from Khartoum in 2010, show young people dancing, wearing various outfits of Western suits, Black-coded streetwear, and African kitenge cloth, in rooms covered in posters and newspaper cuttings of international figures including Nelson Mandela, Princess Diana, Bill Clinton, and Malcolm X, and Sudanese Christian figures like the formerly enslaved Black Catholic woman Saint Bakhita. Angelina and her friends might not have had access to the full canon of Malcolm X's speeches or a clear view of Reagan's politics, but they were working with fragments and creating interpretive political and creative cultures in Khartoum.

---

[157] Angelina Majok, in Mayen Ulem, 16 July 2013. Many people euphemistically used the term 'miscarriage' when discussing abortions in Khartoum. See Joyce Kinaro et al., 'Unsafe Abortion and Abortion Care in Khartoum, Sudan', *Reproductive Health Matters* 17, no. 34 (2009): 71–77; Jok Madut Jok, 'Militarism, Gender and Reproductive Suffering: The Case of Abortion in Western Dinka', *Africa* 69, no. 2 (1999): 194–212; Sharon Hutchinson and Jok Madut Jok, 'Gendered Violence and the Militarization of Ethnicity', in R. Werbner, ed., *Postcolonial Subjectivities in Africa* (Bloomsbury, 2002), 84–108.

[158] Angelina Majok, in Mayen Ulem, 16 July 2013. 'Don't sit' skirts, in common South Sudanese English, are skirts that are too short or tight to sit in without risking exposure.

Figure 3.1 Angelina (left) and friend, dancing in Comboni dormitory, late 1990s.
Reproduced with permission of Angelina Majok from her photograph album.

3.7 Women's Black Skin

Angelina and her friends in Khartoum were thus involved in constant debates and battles over personal agency, obligation, and moral judgement. These debates centred on how far changes to social cultures, languages, and life could or would affect moral integrity and personal values. While some people, both men and women, said that new urban socialisations were fundamental and irreversible – 'when something like rain falls down you cannot collect it again' – others argued that 'this is a world that can be worn and taken off'.[159] As both men and women emphasised, what mattered was proving continued moral integrity, mutual understanding, and, most particularly, a sense of self-awareness in political context.

Angelina herself argues – like Wendy James – that the process of appropriation and assimilation was not a passive process of taking up forms of cultural norms, behaviour, and style from northern and other Sudanese and global cultures. Some customs were adapted from local migrant communities, such as western and eastern Sudanese-style wedding convoys and large gifts of sugar, oil, and household goods, which fitted the urban context and were useful markers of formal marriage in circumstances where traditional practices from home were infeasible, unfashionable, or impossible.[160]

Racial-cultural hierarchies exerted powerful pressures on Khartoum residents – including setting new physical and sexual mores, such as female genital cutting and ideas of beauty. A key example of this intense racist pressure from global and local beauty standards was the controversial practice of skin whitening, which became common in the early 2000s.[161] Using bleaching creams on dark skin was both a localised part of the racial politics of Khartoum's society and a global

---

[159] Chiefs' meeting in Maper Akot, 29 June 2013; Mayo Mandela Circle, 'Dinka Displacement to the Northern Sudan and Other Stories' (SOLO Press, 2003), section 11.
[160] Members of the Dinka Cultural Society, in Apada, 11 August 2013.
[161] While there is increasing international anthropological scholarship on the practice of skin bleaching, there is little written on Sudan or South Sudan. See Caroline Faria, 'Styling the Nation: Fear and Desire in the South Sudanese Beauty Trade', *Transactions of the Institute of Geographers* 39, no. 2 (2013): 318–30.

racial-political issue. Angelina explained that people discussed the medical risks of bleaching, and how some people excluded women who had visibly bleached skin from certain jobs, implying, for example, that their chemically medicated skin would taint food preparation.[162] A group of older returnee men in Maper Akot emphasised that 'when our skin colour goes, what country will we belong to?'[163] For many people of all ages, 'those girls who have chemicalised themselves to be brown' were 'cases of despair' – although several men and women of various ages said they had tried it, often with ambivalence:

When they see the ladies, the girls of Arabs, are moving, they are so red, and that is why maybe they thought that if you change your colour, you will be loved by your boyfriend; so this is how they adapt, they want to change the colour. You know, even men are doing it.[164]

Another song from Andrew Bol is still sung in Dinka in South Sudan:

Why have you hated my homeland, lady?
Why do you hate Black skin, my homeland girl?
Why do you reject Black people, my homeland girl?
The face of a bleached girl looks like Fanta
And legs like Pepsi
The upper body looks Arab
The legs Black African
You girls that bleached with cream, what did you hate that made you bleach?
What have you hated that made you bleach, my homeland girl?
As God if he did not create you well, you bleached girl
The face is Arab, the legs as black as ajiec [a small black bird]
You girls of our Black people, have you forgotten your Black people?
You girls of our homeland, have your hearts forgotten your black skin?
The Dinka girls, the Nubian girls, the Maale girls, the Bongo girls have brown face and black legs.[165]

As Jemima Pierre notes, it is important to put skin bleaching into global as well as local histories of racialisation: this practice

---

[162] Angelina Majok, in Mayen Ulem, 16 July 2013.
[163] Chiefs' meeting in Maper Akot, 13 June 2015.
[164] Deng Atak Abuk, in Apada, 13 July 2013; Dhieu Kuel, in Mayen Ulem, 4 July 2013; members of the Dinka Cultural Society, in Apada, 11 August 2013.
[165] Sung on 23 August 2017 at a group meeting in Maper Akot Arou, in Dinka, translation by Joseph Diing Majok with the Rift Valley Institute.

is not just an aspiration to a lighter-skinned, potentially non-southern, ideal Sudanese (and potentially more 'Arab') skin tone, but a response to a complex combination of local, Sudanese, and international cultural hegemonies, and global white supremacy.[166] Angelina emphasised that this was a point of tension and arguments between young women, especially within friendship groups that included naturally lighter-skinned southern and Nuba women.[167]

Women themselves (as well as their families and neighbourhoods) argued over how best to appropriate, modify, and respond to these pressures.[168] Ex-residents struggled to articulate the differences between necessity, obligation, and personal choice in cultural adoptions of northern practices, as Rogaia Abusharaf observed in her anthropological study of displaced southern women in Khartoum in the 2000s.[169] But these struggles were not necessarily a case of negotiating specifically northern assimilation versus southern ethno-cultural resistance. Things like the use of henna and wearing tobs were both partly dominant Sudanese cultural adoptions and also part of a wider cultural expansion and exploration – of north-east African, eastern African, pan-African and global Black cultures, music, dress, and other self-expressions. Being able to code-switch, including using Sudanese and Juba Arabics and English, is a fashionable sign of modern, humorous, intelligent, youthful urbanity.[170] Some young women argued for fashion as an impermanent, rather than substantive, change and as an expression of their cultural knowledge, sense of self, and Black pride.[171] Angelina and her friends explained how they were proud of their learned ability to navigate multiple international cultures of modernity, asserting Sudanese-ness and southern-ness while also demonstrating global multiculturalism.

This demonstration of plural cultural powers could arguably be seen as a direct rebuttal of the mono-cultural elitism of upper-class

---

[166] Jemima Pierre, '"I Like Your Colour!" Skin Bleaching and Geographies of Race in Urban Ghana', *Feminist Review* 90, no. 1 (2008): 12.
[167] Angelina Majok, in Mayen Ulem, 16 July 2013.
[168] James, *The Listening Ebony*, 3.
[169] Abusharaf, *Transforming Displaced Women in Sudan*.
[170] Catherine Miller et al., *Arabic in the City: Issues in Dialect Contact and Language Variation* (Routledge, 2007), 21–22.
[171] Angelina Majok, in Mayen Ulem, 16 July 2013.

Khartoum, and potentially also of the patrimonial ethnic patriotism of some parents and community members.[172] Many young women now resident in Aweil were continuing discussions and practices, started in Khartoum, about Afro hair care and styling, Darfur styles of henna painting, and Chinese-made tight western T-shirts from the town market, a conscious balance of practical and aesthetic choices; cultural and political assertions of knowledge, individualism, and experience; and the negotiation of social judgement (see Figure 3.2).[173] It was also fun to learn all these things, including practicing, adapting, and mixing styles of dance, as Lazarus Lual remembers as a young teenager in the mid-1990s: 'it's a lot of fun and you find people asking so many questions ... like one of the best performances we made in the Aweil, Aweil Youth Association was when we were reflecting the Nuba dancing in our performance too'.[174]

This might be an idealist post-fact rewriting of social and racial pressures. But many people – from older men asserting elder status to younger single-parent and working women – emphasised that asserting Sudanese-ness was an explicit political statement, within an urban setting and a civil war that attempted to alienate and exclude, particularly southern residents.[175] Much like Siri Lamoureaux's surprise to find classical Arabic poetry exchanged by Nuba students in Khartoum, wearing supposedly elite 'Arab-Islamic' status markers and beauty trends was a casual way for displaced people to mark themselves as actually Sudanese.[176] Joseph Garang observed that 'whenever you put that jellabiya, ... then they will tell you no, this is not your dressing. Southerners dress in trousers.... But we want to wear jellabiya as a Sudanese, as Sudanese dressing, not to be Arabs.'[177]

[172] This is not specific to southern Sudanese communities in Khartoum, as Siri Lamoureaux's thesis 'Message in a Mobile' demonstrates.
[173] Grappling with this challenging cosmopolitan array of socio-political statements is likely the source of some ex-Khartoum residents' sense of exceptionalism, and sometimes also a sense of superior morality, skill, and experience, back in South Sudan.
[174] Lazarus Lual, in Juba, 19 October 2013; Miller, *Language Change and National Integration*, 124. Nuba wrestling and dancing were watched in Mayo, Umbadda, and Haj Yousif.
[175] Conversations with women in Apada; Angelina Majok, in Mayen Ulem, 16 July 2013; Abuk Ngor Deng, in Maper, 29 June 2013; James Garang, in Maper, 30 June 2013.
[176] Lamoureaux, 'Message in a Mobile', 104–5.
[177] James Garang, in Maper, 19 July 2013.

3.7 Women's Black Skin 133

Figure 3.2 Angelina (left) and friend, posing in African wax print tailoring, at home in Khartoum, mid-1990s. The photo has been stitched back together.
Reproduced with permission of Angelina Majok from her photograph album.

3.8 Managing Change and Controlling Behaviour

The early 1990s gave young people, in particular, room for new freedoms and self-expressions. But many people – including these young men and women – were also concerned about the risks of this self-realisation and social transformation, and what this might do to societies and families in the immediate years.

This was not just a ruralised reaction to the liberal individualist freedoms of the city; it was important to keep a sense of self, of history, moral order, and social standards for the sake of collective futures. Many people discussed the broad attempts to 'control' friends, family, and community in Khartoum from this period: Dhieu explained that 'we discussed so many things ... we keep on advising people to be careful when roaming around in the city', and many men emphasised the need for a 'very strict living'.[178] This organisation was framed by locals as civic and moral education and (self) control. In this context – against a background of systemic public abuses and risks, economic and intellectual subjugation, and opportunities for cultural innovation – many, particularly older residents, felt that 'we were going to forget dignity. We were about to forget it.'[179]

Of primary concern was a loss of mutual respect and moral standards, and a loss of social education, through the dissolving of family ties and new opportunities for creolisation, as one older man and part-time teacher explained:

When they come back to their grandmothers, who don't know these foreign languages, and call them *habooba*.[180] They will not understand, they will think it's an insult! They would say why don't you separate, if you are educated in English! When it is necessary, you want to speak in English – you speak English! Pure English, with those who want to understand. But when you come back to your family, don't make it as a class for your mother, for your father, and then you start pouring some foreign languages to them, they will not understand.... That is why we are advising our young men, our young people, that you have the right to assess all the other languages. But when it's time to come back to your house: you have to speak

---
[178] Deng Atak Abuk, in Apada, 13 July 2013; Michael Thiop Lang, in Aweil, 11 July 2013; Dhieu Kuel, in Mayen Ulem, 21 August 2013.
[179] Deng Atak Abuk, in Apada, 13 July 2013; also Angelina Majok, in Mayen Ulem, 16 July 2013.
[180] Sudanese Arabic for 'grandmother'.

3.8 Managing Change and Controlling Behaviour 135

with your people in your language. Let the young ones learn from you! Don't let them lose their ways, don't let them lose their culture, through you. Like ... these n***as, eh? That is why we were trying to control our – our tribe; our people; in order that to maintain our culture, that was the final thing.[181]

This concern over deculturation, acculturation, and re-culturation was articulated through these discussions and clashes over individualism, masculinity, women's sexual and social freedom, and the limits to broadening cultural repertoires, particularly from the early 1990s. The focus of this 'advice', as the teacher quoted above called it, was not ultimately on specific problematic actions, innovations, or ideas; these were flashpoints and tools in a discussion essentially about what James calls 'moral knowledge': the ability to make good and informed choices, and thus what constituted the right information and moral basis for these choices.[182]

This of course played out on women's bodies and choices, as the custodians of community morality and the next generation. There was significant social pressure on women not to get divorced despite the stresses of unsupportive or missing husbands.[183] This included another of Andrew Bol's more patriarchal Dinka songs, addressed to male elders:

> What are you doing about this destruction of culture
> Where a girl is married and a few days later, she's untied her womanly dress and gone back to the drum [dance]
> Now awat-yol moves in groups[184]
> The destruction of the South caused the girls to marry and later untie the tob, and go back to the drum
> And awat-yol move in groups

---

[181] Members of the Dinka Cultural Society, in Apada, 11 August 2013. The same concerns are noted in the colonial Zambian vernacular press in Harri Englund, 'Anti Anti-colonialism: Vernacular Press and Emergent Possibilities in Colonial Zambia', *Comparative Studies in Society* 57, no. 1 (2015): 240; and in Tanzania by Emma Hunter, 'Dutiful Subjects, Patriotic Citizens, and the Concept of "Good Citizenship" in Twentieth-Century Tanzania', *Historical Journal* 56, no. 1 (2013: 257–77.
[182] James, *The Listening Ebony*, 3.
[183] Ibrahim, 'War Displacement: The Socio-cultural Dimension', 63.
[184] Awat-yol: a young woman who divorced her husband and went back to the drum pretending to be single.

> The ladies of this war, even if you marry her, put her in the house, give her a child
> She will still hunt outside
> Your mother did not cut her marriage and go back to the drum
> Your stepmother did not cut her marriage and go back to the drum
> Your maternal aunt did not return to the drum and your paternal aunt did not return to the drum
> The destruction of our land, southern Sudan made it possible
> For a girl to get married and then take off her tob and return to the drum
> And now, awat-yol move in groups.[185]

This narrative was reflected in songs by Nuer, Shilluk, and Equatorian-community artists, such as General Paulino, who sings in Juba Arabic and Bari; he explained that his lyrics were against girls 'changing their colours' and 'changing their names from Keji to Kedija, Mejuan to Mejua'.[186]

Abuk Deng, a pre-teen in the early 1990s, explained how her parents sometimes told her to just pound sorghum for flour, rather than take it to the grinding mill, and occasionally to buy wood rather than charcoal, in order to learn the hard work and rural skills of cooking as opposed to the ease of urban life.[187] Women being 'softened' by urbanisation was a theme of other migrant Khartoum residents' songs, for instance a Humr song recorded by Asia Mahgoub Ahmed:

> Beware! You should not employ
> Bit [bint, the girl] Abbakar in grinding,
> You should not employ her in
> Pounding nor in bringing water
> You should not employ her in breaking wood,
> Nor should you employ her in husking.[188]

This is of course social shaming and a form of control over young women. But it also emphasises the importance of community knowledge and moral responsibility in the face of the individualist freedoms and casual living of the city. Khartoum offered access to global cultures and – possibly – opportunities for onward movement and personal

---

[185] Sung on 23 August 2017 at a group meeting in Maper Akot Arou, in Dinka, translation by Joseph Diing Majok with the Rift Valley Institute.
[186] General Paulino, in Juba, 23 October 2013.
[187] Abuk Deng, in Maper, 5 June 2013.
[188] Mahgoub Ahmed, 'Urbanisation and the Folk Verse of the Humr', 725–26.

advancement that encouraged the pursuit of individual success and freedom at the potential expense of collective obligations. For most people who contributed to this study – including, for instance, ambitious young men who headed on to Cairo, self-described gang members, as well as women like Angelina and Abuk – freedom, as Emma Hunter also observes, is not necessarily via individual autonomy, but a search for reciprocity, family responsibility, and security.[189]

3.9 Cultural Organising and Reasserted Patriarchy

This 'good' knowledge was negotiated through community projects of discipline and cultural entrepreneurship from the early 1990s onwards. As Catherine Miller observed in 1992, now that older migrants feel less isolated and have more opportunity to practice, traditions are being 'revalorise[d]'.[190] This was a conscious effort, as Jimmy Wongo emphasised:

To see to it that we don't, we don't get totally lost.... Yeah, we were very conscious of doing that, knowing that it is this identity that we wanted to maintain, and it is this identity that we were fighting for. And now – if we are going to fight for it, while it is fading in Khartoum, where there are four million people to keep it? Then we must bring these people back home, so that we don't totally lose it.[191]

One of Andrew Bol's most famous songs, written in about 1990, began:

> You elders of this land, the elders of this generation, it is to you that I ask this question
> You elders of the communities, what is your role?
> You elders who gave birth to us, what is your role?
> You chiefs of the communities, what is your role?
> What are you doing about this destruction of culture?[192]

The community, ethnic, and regional associations, church groups, university associations, and women's organisations established in the early 1990s, and their celebrations of collective heritage and pride in

---
[189] Hunter, *Political Thought and the Public Sphere in Tanzania*, 13.
[190] Miller, *Language Change and National Integration*, 123.
[191] Jimmy Wongo, in Juba, 18 October 2013.
[192] Sung on 23 August 2017 at a group meeting in Maper Akot Arou, in Dinka, translation by Joseph Diing Majok with the Rift Valley Institute.

the face of everyday as well as wartime violence and racism, were the foundation for political action detailed over the next three chapters. Even as neighbourhood tensions rose from 1991, with intra-southern violence in the south echoing in Khartoum and with the fall of the Derg regime in Ethiopia ending the SPLA Radio broadcasts from Addis Ababa every day at 3 pm, people from across class, linguistic, and ethnic backgrounds continued to meet and organise celebrations, meetings, and projects. This included the Aweil Youth Union; the Equatorian Union and Bari Community, formulated to discuss 'the problems they are facing, in their lives. They keep telling people exactly what they're supposed to do – so that they can remain in the right track'; and the Nuer Association, which encouraged collective investment in education and health projects ('and the moment it was politicised, then it became a very serious tool to the militias'; see Chapters 6 and 7).[193]

Being rooted in nominally 'traditional culture' and 'ethnic community' does not necessarily mean these organisations were entirely reactionary and parochial. As John Tomaney and bell hooks both note, grounding belonging in a sense of locality can give people 'a vital sense of covenant and commitment', and maybe a basis for broader collective action.[194] But it also gave many people tools for control and repression based on specifically reified ideas of cultural 'tradition' distilled as patriarchal rule. This was not just the preserve of elders working against the youth. The groups most explicitly attempting patriarchal control in the peripheral areas of Khartoum were (and are) what are commonly called 'traditional chiefs' courts' and local groups of young men often termed in South Sudan 'n***a gangs'. Maybe counter-intuitively, many among both groups were working to the same ends: they were engaged, and often allies, in explicit community policing of patriarchal power and women's lives.[195]

---

[193] Melanie Itto, in Juba, 23 October 2013; Farouk Gatkuoth, in Juba, 30 October 2013.

[194] John Tomaney, 'Parochialism: A Defence', *Progress in Human Geography* 37, no. 5 (2013): 663; bell hooks, *Teaching Community: A Pedagogy of Hope* (Routledge, 2003), 65.

[195] Warren Magnusson points out that urban control by gangs and militias is a kind of order in itself; this approach does not necessarily separate 'anomic' or 'immoral' policing activities from those more generally considered 'cultural' or 'traditional', such as chiefs' courts. *Politics of Urbanism: Seeing like a City* (Routledge, 2013), 12–13.

3.9 Cultural Organising and Reasserted Patriarchy 139

While many chiefs criticised 'the n****s' in Khartoum, they distinguished criminal associations from youth gangs: one sub-chief said that 'the youth ... are responsible people, that we give orders to, and they go and practice them. So they are right [*haq*].'[196]

Primarily, though, these groups' work centred on the control of women and marriage or, in one chief's words, 'wrong weddings and committing adultery'.[197] They worked with similar-minded family members to put pressure on women, particularly not to get divorced, or against marriages to men outside communities or the southern region; some women remembered others killing themselves when families blocked marriages, including marriage to Darfuri and Nuba Mountains men.[198] They also encouraged restrictions on other sexually risky behaviour, for instance, as Angelina explained, 'they were prevented even from using perfumed bathing soap; fake hair was prevented'.[199]

Many young men supported these efforts. The Tueny Youth Society's brief in 1992 focused on encouraging young women to go to school, stay at home or in Dinka spaces, and 'get married from our people'.[200] Girls who were 'not steady at home' were forced into marriages so that 'the man will take the responsibility of the girl'.[201] Some women worked as matchmakers, with some positive results,[202] but much of this 'relationship policing' was controlled by men.[203] Controlling some young women was made difficult by their access to alternative sources of finance, widespread poverty, and the limitations of the 'alternative' cash bride-wealth system in Khartoum.[204] This is why some men organised gangs, 'to monitor the situation of the girls ... that is why we created this gang, in order to liberate our girls from Arabs, because they [the girls] reject us'.[205] Unable to financially compete for bride wealth in Khartoum, James – a member of one of

---

[196] Lual Lual Aguer, in Apada, 15 August 2013.
[197] Agany Macham, in Apada chiefs' court, 5 June 2013; Anei Deng Akok, in Aweil, 13 August 2013; chief's court in Mayen Ulem, 20 August 2013.
[198] Ibrahim, 'War Displacement: The Socio-cultural Dimension', 63.
[199] Angelina Majok, in Mayen Ulem, 16 July 2013.
[200] Diing Chen Diing, in Aweil, 12 August 2013.
[201] Raja, in Apada, 3 September 2013.
[202] Josephine, in Maper Two, 26 June 2013.
[203] Angelina Majok, in Mayen Ulem, 16 July 2013.
[204] Chief's court in Mayen Ulem, 20 August 2013.
[205] James Garang, in Maper, 19 July 2013.

these groups – explained how they 'used to separate the girls ... whenever we see that the girl is walking with an Arab boyfriend':

They rejected their Black people, because they are poor, and they like the Arab northerners because they are rich.... when we see that a girl wanted a good dress and a phone, and we have money, we have to buy something and give it to her, in order to make her stay at home ... If you are Dinka, without knowledge of the Arabic language, you will not be considered as an important person.... We need to attract them towards us – such that we stay together, conversing together, because we are one.... After the Arabs saw that we have formed our group, the Arab youth also tried to form their group in order to control their girls.[206]

3.10 Conclusion

This neighbourhood, community, and cultural self-defence should not be romanticised as resistance. As Adolph Reed notes, this might 'presume that these conditions necessarily, or even typically, lead to political action. They don't.'[207] For the new residents of Khartoum's Black suburbs this was normal and necessary survival; people whom Richard Rodgers observed at the time were 'trying to do their best under difficult circumstances with a spectrum of willingness of collaboration'.[208]

This chapter has sought to complicate the idea that displaced southern Sudanese people in Khartoum, like their peripheral migrant neighbours, just constructed a counter-identity, a reactive antithesis to Sudanese cultures and political identity.[209] Instead, people who had lived a variety of lives across the city in the early 1990s emphasised their daily confrontations with the complex pressures of Khartoum's marketised, globalised urban cultures and economies; the questions and problems of organising mutual security and order in new heterogeneous neighbourhoods; and the stressful but necessary conversations over moral and practical responsibilities and freedoms. This was the basis for the long list of organisational, educational, and community-building projects that started around 1991–94. As both men and

---

[206] James Garang, in Maper, 30 June 2013.
[207] Adolph L. Reed, *Class Notes: Posing as Politics and Other Thoughts on the American Scene* (New Press, 2000), 9.
[208] 'Report by Rev. Dr. R. Rodgers for Light and Hope for Sudan', 85.
[209] Lesch, *The Sudan*, 213.

3.10 Conclusion

women became 'sad ... they discussed how to deal with it'.[210] Many of the people I spoke to agreed: they explained that this organisation was foundational. It provided the space and chance for what Lual Lual (a chiefs' court worker and daily paid labourer in Jabarona) called 'real work'.[211] This real work is the subject of the next chapter.

[210] Angelina Majok, in Mayen Ulem, 16 July 2013; Raja, in Apada, 3 September 2013.
[211] Lual Lual Aguer, in Apada, 15 August 2013.

4 | *Alternative Education*

Every child of the Black people looks for a job
And every child of other people goes to school.

Andrew Bol Deng [1]

The real work of Khartoum displaced life generally involved education. Education – for all ages, and of many kinds – was a major issue for residents in Khartoum, and a crucial form of political action. Most southern Sudanese people were (and are) excluded from state systems of education, including in Khartoum.[2] There is very little detail about education organisation within the displaced community in the city, even in humanitarian marginalia. But by 1990, USAID commented that 'education is surprisingly widespread and well-organised in the Khartoum displaced communities'.[3] By 2005, anthropologist and UN consultant Marc Sommers recorded a displaced literacy rate of 62.5 per cent, roughly the same as northern Sudanese rates, produced by complicated, disorganised, but self-run educative systems run by supposedly 'passive victims'.[4] But education as a key urban good, and as 'secondary resistance' in the war, was a well-understood concept within southern communities in Khartoum.[5]

Displaced people's accounts of education in 1980s and 1990s Khartoum often centre on what is colloquially called Comboni Majaneen, or Comboni ground.[6] In the centre of old administrative

---

[1] Song of lament sung at a group meeting in Maper Akot Arou, in Dinka, translation by Joseph Diing Majok with the Rift Valley Institute.
[2] Sommers, *Islands of Education*, 5.
[3] Feiden et al., 'Khartoum Displaced Assessment and Recommendations', 18.
[4] Sommers, *Islands of Education*, 218–19, 243.
[5] Anders Breidlid, 'Sudanese Images of the Other: Education and Conflict in Sudan', *Comparative Education Review* 54, no. 4 (2010): 568; Sommers, *Islands of Education*.
[6] For the long history of the Comboni Mission's involvement in Sudanese education, see Iris Seri-Hersch, 'Education in Colonial Sudan, 1900–1957', in

Khartoum, the wide courtyard of the old and historic Comboni mission church provided friendly free public space at the heart of a generally hostile and crowded city. 'Majaneen – It means just people who are staying without work. There different people collected, drunk people, people who are just talking.'[7] Like other Black-dominated public spaces on the edges of the city – including market spaces in Haj Yousif and Hai Baraka – Comboni ground was always extremely busy with a mix of people from 'every south', for dances, football, and conversation.[8] Through the late 1980s and early 1990s, though, in the early evenings, part of the ground was filled with tables and plastic chairs borrowed from the mission buildings. Here, Professor Yosa Wawa, a Kakwa historian at Juba University explained,

> We taught anything. I heard about it from a Nuer guy I was staying near in Souk al-Arabi, and visited with some Fur friends in about 1988. A Nubian friend, from Uganda, was a teacher there – Jamal – he survived from income from casual teaching there. He'd go with no money, pay for his bus, and return with a salary from donations. The learners did not know what they needed, they had different standards, and you got different learners every day, at about fifteen to twenty tables. Anyone could just come and join you – in groups of two, up to five. Most people were southern, mainly men, and a few women, mostly Nuer, Dinka, western and eastern Equatorians, and some Darfuris. English was the most popular subject, then literature and history. We taught from our heads; I taught English on and off over a few years. You didn't ask where people were staying, because this was the time of kasha, but they were ready to pay for knowledge. And at the end you get friendship, and you might have made a difference to someone's life.[9]

Southern residents had left the south in search of various forms of knowledge since at least the 1910s, and Khartoum was a major destination, not just for formal schooling but for learning a wider worldview, language skills, and knowledge of cash economies, paperwork, authorities, and state cultures. Many residents in the 1980s and '90s had long experience of being students in a variety of forms of schools, of teaching and organising educational groups and classes, and working without textbooks and space, including in refugee camps during the

---

Oxford Research Encyclopedia of African History (Oxford University Press, 2017).
[7] Deng Atak Abuk, in Apada, 13 July 2013.
[8] Anei Deng Akok, in Aweil, 13 August 2013.
[9] Yosa Wawa, in Juba, 26 June 2019.

1960s and '70s in Uganda and Congo, and in seasonal farming settlements in Gezira.[10] There were a lot of things to learn – not just to get access to certificates and qualifications, or to be able to communicate in the north, but to understand why and how Sudan worked as it did, and to teach children how to manage and think about their political, economic, and social-cultural conditions.[11] These educators were following Paulo Freire and Antonio Gramsci in working out education for critical consciousness, like their contemporaries in many other urban spaces and liberation movements elsewhere.[12] Many teachers were proud of their efforts in Khartoum to spread the ability to negotiate, triumph over, and critique state power and society, and to train a critically able new generation.[13]

There were far too many educational projects, including night schools, writing groups, and arts associations, encountered during research for this book to include here. The Rev. Marc Nikkel recognised this plethora of activities in Khartoum in 1994, noting that the enthusiasm of NGOs for providing 'psycho-social activities' for these poor IDPs was overshadowed by 'the most dynamic systems ... which refugees themselves create and sustain'.[14] Staying alive in Khartoum was exhausting, time-consuming, and complicated, but residents did not just want food aid. As Paul Kuel, a student and shopkeeper by the

---

[10] For example, Joseph Ukel Abango (interviewed in Juba, 29 October 2013) was a mid-level politician and primary school teacher; William Manyang Tong (interviewed in Apada, 17 August 2013) went to Khartoum in 1982 as a worker and student, then became a teacher.

[11] For example, in Somalia after 1991: Abdullahi S. Abdinoor, 'Constructing Education in a Stateless Society: The Case of Somalia', PhD dissertation, Ohio University (2007), 12.

[12] For example, Estêvão Cabral and Marilyn Martin-Jones, 'Writing the Resistance: Literacy in East Timor 1975–1999', *International Journal of Bilingual Education and Bilingualism* 11, no. 2 (2008): 149–69; Martha Caddell, 'Private Schools as Battlefields: Contested Visions of Learning and Livelihood in Nepal', *Compare* 36, no. 4 (2006) 463–79; John L. Hammond, *Fighting to Learn: Popular Education and Guerrilla War in El Salvador* (Rutgers University Press, 1998); Bruno Baronnet, 'Rebel Youth and Zapatista Autonomous Education', *Latin American Perspectives* 35, no. 4 (2008): 112–24; Mastin Prinsloo and Mignonne Breier, *The Social Uses of Literacy: Theory and Practice in Contemporary South Africa* (John Benjamins Publishing, 1996).

[13] Five teachers voiced their pride in having taught members of the SPLM elite, South Sudanese civil service, and SPLA officers.

[14] Mark Nikkel, 'Link Letter from Nairobi', 15 April 1994, SAD.105/91/3-4.

early 1990s and a member of both SANU and the Aweil Youth Union, remembered:

you know, I was reading *A Tale of Two Cities*, by Charles Dickens. And in it a small boy was asking his father, when the French were uprising, he said – daddy why are those people crying, what's wrong with them? He said they are very hungry, they want to eat. The boy said why don't you give them biscuits? The father said: why don't I give them something which will help them for life?[15]

This chapter explores how Khartoum's displaced residents organised their own schools, including adult night schooling, and taught their own syllabuses of critical political and social education. To do this, they used rewritten and self-written textbooks, language guides, and history pamphlets, in multiple everyday languages beyond Sudanese Arabic. The chapter first details the definition of education for these residents, which included practical and moral knowledge, political debate, language skills, and creativity. It then examines how people like Paul organised schools and educational spaces, how teachers worked, what they taught, and why they taught it.

4.1 A Critical Education

In South Sudan today, formal, school-based education is still a relatively new project, and efforts to promote it often emphasise the numbers of children and adults left supposedly uneducated. But there are deep histories of moral, social, political, ecological, and economic education across societies in the region, and competing (and still unreconciled) paths to adulthood, different standards for knowledge and enlightenment, and different definitions of ignorance.[16]

New wartime residents in Khartoum continued with educational work long-established within their communities but outside a formal school system. They had to teach their established knowledge of economic systems, responsibilities, collective histories, and social theories to their children. They also had to articulate new lessons, including various new languages, systems, and sociology of the city, and the skills and performance needed to navigate paperwork and offices.

---

[15] Paul Kuel Kuel, in Aweil, 9 August 2013.
[16] For a review of these histories, see Epstein, 'Maps of Desire'.

As Hanaa Motasim notes, this education was not primarily about finding jobs:

> education amongst the displaced is perceived as an essential component to becoming 'street wise' ... people who understand the written word become more oriented and confident in their dealings with officialdom. Night schools, to which the older youth go, are a centre for the discussion of politics, the discussions act as eye-openers.[17]

Formal written education and class-based schooling were an important part of this process for many residents. For most people across southern Sudan from the 1940s and 1950s, schools became an alternative path to wealth in new urban spaces or in the fraught political sphere. But school-educated adults were (and often are) viewed with some mistrust, as supposed 'elites' who have really been co-opted or otherwise alienated from their societies, who manipulate their rural families and 'trick' ordinary people, and who have frequently instigated political violence without suffering from it.[18] Cherry Leonardi observes that this is 'an expression of vulnerability in the politics of knowledge, as well as a moral criticism'.[19]

Real knowledge and learning was – for Khartoum's new residents – about emancipation from this position of intellectual and practical subordination. This position is best demonstrated by a fully improvised play staged in the late 1990s in Khartoum by the southern-led theatre group Kwoto (which will be discussed in more detail below). In the play titled *Haj Yousif*, two southern families arrive in Khartoum only knowing the name of the area Haj Yousif, where they have relatives. But – as the literary scholar Rebecca Lorins details in her record of a performance – when they call for their relatives on stage, the Dinka and Bari families are met with silence, as well as 'a few giggles and calls from the audience such as "ya fara" (oh, naive ones!)'. The families then have their things stolen from them by urbanised young southern teens, whom they cannot understand. The police then arrive – played by the same actors who played the teens, in an explicit association between criminals and government – and the families answer their questioning with only 'Haj Yousif', until they are arrested due to their lack of paperwork and lack of understanding.[20]

---

[17] Motasim, 'Deeply Divided Societies', 16–17.
[18] Epstein, 'Maps of Desire', 52–53.
[19] Leonardi, *Dealing with Government*, 135.   [20] Lorins, 'Inheritance', 205–10.

4.1 A Critical Education

Haj Yousif emphasises the most immediate education that people needed in Khartoum. Language learning was important not just for keeping community dialects in the family but for understanding and being able to use the Sudanese and South Sudanese Arabics of the city and the southern displaced community, respectively. Local vernaculars and ethnic languages were promoted at home and through associational cultures and church groups.[21] Angelina re-learnt how to articulate complex emotions in Dinka, and Raja remembers her mother singing Ngok Dinka songs from Abyei to her, and translating them into Arabic so she could understand them fully.[22] This was because, as the pamphlet *Dinka Customology of Marriage* noted, 'language is the human being, and it allows someone to be recognised'.[23] A Dinka-language teacher with the Dinka Cultural Society explained that vernacular language-learning was partly about maintaining a sense of pride and cultural confidence in the face of the prejudices and pressures of the city: 'we want our children not to lose their culture; not to lose themselves; we don't want a child to deny [their ethnic belonging] because of economics, or because of poverty or because of being ashamed ... or [because] their colour is black'.[24]

Language has always been a site of struggle in Sudan.[25] Supported by various Catholic foundations for education such as Sudan Open Learning Organisation (SOLO) and the Summer Institute for Linguistics, whose work was rooted in Bible translation since the 1970s, written vernacular literacy training was extended in Catholic programming from 1994, growing from seven to more than forty-nine centres by 1997, with the top-performing candidate (and their county in the south) feted after competitive exams.[26] Women's linguistic

---

[21] Garang Mayuen Mayuen, in Apada, 11 August 2013; Diing Chen Diing, in Aweil, 15 July 2013; Angelina Majok, in Mayen Ulem, 16 July 2013; Aguer Agor, chiefs' court at Maper Akot, 13 April 2013; also see 'Candle-Ends Sisterhood' constitution, Khartoum, ND, Justice Africa papers, SAD 89/5/18-20; Santino Ayak, in Maper chiefs' court, 13 April 2013.

[22] Angelina Majok, in Mayen Ulem, 16 July 2013; Raja, in Apada, 3 September 2013.

[23] Valentino Wol Akok, Joseph Garang Pin, and Santino Atak Kon (eds.), *Dinka Customology of Marriage* (SOLO Press, 2001).

[24] Members of the Dinka Cultural Society, in Apada, 11 August 2013.

[25] Sharkey, 'Arab Identity and Ideology in Sudan', 36; Miller, *Language Change and National Integration*, 104; Sommers, *Islands of Education*, 243.

[26] Members of the Dinka Cultural Society, in Apada, 11 August 2013.

education was encouraged in songs and texts.[27] 'People ... categorised themselves' according to sources of funding, spaces, and connections, with the Shilluk teaching in Moguren in Khartoum, Nuer-language schools being run by Catholic groups, and Zande often being taught by the Seventh-day Adventists.[28] Members of the Fur communities in Khartoum organised vernacular teaching, as well as smaller western and Nuba groups: 'every different Black tribe ... including Funj themselves were there'.[29]

This was a quite successful project over the 1990s. In 1992, Catherine Miller observed that the strong maintenance of ethnic mother tongues, especially among Nuer and Dinka communities and among the 36 per cent of young people born in urban environments, 'cannot be explained by their rural origin' alone.[30] Some 10–20 per cent of southern residents spoke English across different areas of the city, but many southern residents spoke other southern languages, including just over 16 per cent of southern residents who spoke more than three languages: 'this relatively high percentage of Southerners learning and speaking other vernaculars seems to challenge the assumption of the recession of vernaculars as lingua franca'.[31] Abdel Rahim Hamid Mugaddam recreated Miller's research in 2001, and found that over 80 per cent of adult southern residents and half of southern teenagers knew their vernacular language; this climbed to over 90 per cent for Dinka, Madi, and Shilluk adults especially.[32]

Most people learnt Sudanese Arabic and some English where possible, to access international and local news and discussion, particularly from newspapers and television.[33] There was very little access for most people to SPLM/A news outputs, particularly the SPLM/A *Update* magazine, which was the only official output after SPLA Radio stopped broadcasting from Addis Ababa in 1991, but John Garang's speeches in southern Sudanese Arabic were circulated by

---

[27] For example, 'The Magazine of Dinka Culture' (Khartoum, 2004), Story Two, 4; Story 23, 12; Story 35, 19.
[28] Arou Piol Adam, in Apada village, 21 July 2013.
[29] Miller, *Language Change and National Integration*, 110–11; Marko Mathiang Deng, in Apada, 17 August 2013.
[30] Miller, *Language Change and National Integration*, 61.   [31] Ibid., 69, 74.
[32] Mugaddam, 'Language Maintenance and Shift in Sudan: The Case of Migrant Ethnic Groups in Khartoum', *International Journal of the Sociology of Language* 181 (2006): 127–28.
[33] James Garang Ngor, in Aweil, 30 June 2013.

cassette (see Chapter 6) and BBC World radio reported on SPLA offensives.[34] Important here is the distinction between the Arabic of northern Sudan and this southern Sudanese Arabic, which is a distinct creole language structured by slaves, soldiers, traders, and interpreters over the nineteenth century, and which became the language of southern towns by the twentieth century. Many people emphasised how they learnt or improved their southern Sudanese Arabic in Khartoum, to talk with neighbours and colleagues across ethnicities. Southern Sudanese (or 'Juba') Arabic has never had the affective or anti-colonial prestige that ethnic languages or English have had in the propaganda of southern Sudanese liberation struggles, but it is an extremely useful common language distinct from the Arabic of Khartoum. By the 1970s and '80s, southern Sudanese Arabic was being used extensively in church and in southern broadcasting, including on the rebel station Radio SPLA from Addis Ababa, as a specifically southern means of communication.[35]

Teaching and learning southern Sudanese Arabic and southern vernaculars had some other benefits. Working in and on vernacular languages allowed people to claim their work was in the relatively apolitical space of 'ethnic cultural heritage', as well as to benefit from funding available for linguistic and cultural 'tradition', including from UNESCO and the Catholic Church. This de-politicisation was helped by common prejudices against this type of vernacular 'ethnic' work as backwards, unintellectual, and therefore unthreatening. Second, these vernaculars (and, to some extent, southern Sudanese Arabic) provided a relative amount of privacy and security. In 1992 Catherine Miller and Al-Amin Abu-Manga recorded a Nuba woman explaining that the vernacular offers 'a secret language', as under public organising laws it was only permitted to sing in Arabic.[36] Many writers and artists found space for critical and political self-expression through blending these languages, such as the Equatorian singer General Paulino's songs in a

---

[34] Stephen Ayaga, in Aweil, 8 August 2013.
[35] Catherine Miller, 'Language, Identities and Ideologies: A New Era for Sudan', *Proceedings of the 7th International Sudan Studies Conference* (2006), 7; 'Southern Sudanese Arabic and the Churches', *Romania* 3–4 (2010): 383–400; Cherry Leonardi, 'South Sudanese Arabic and the Negotiation of the Local State, c. 1840–2011', *Journal of African History* 54, no. 3 (2013): 351–72.
[36] Miller, *Language Change and National Integration*, 107; Dhieu Kuel, in Mayen Ulem, 21 August 2013.

mix of Bari and highly allegorical and abbreviated Juba Arabic.[37] Vernacular and southern language learning was a foundation for people to discuss, teach, and organise.

4.2 Educational Associational Life

This educational work was not primarily through formal school organisation. Many people did not have the time or money to attend classes, but they could spare hours around church, a Friday afternoon, or a few evenings. A lot of this work – such as language teaching, basic literacy, reading, song-writing, dance, and other creative art – was done through community associations, Bible study groups, vernacular language projects, choirs, and congregations.

As neighbourhoods shifted and reformed around the brutalities of *kasha*, by the mid-1990s church space, funding, and administrative support meant that (in the words of Alex de Waal in 1997) 'church membership and education became virtually inseparable'.[38] This funding and organisation was assisted by a significant number of southern organisers and employees in church structures across the city. Organisational infrastructure kept shifting depending on funding and practical politics. For instance, St Vincent de Paul, a Catholic social and benevolent organisation, was officially dissolved in Khartoum in 1994 but continued to operate informally, partly because there was nowhere else to rehouse the homeless children it was looking after.[39] Technically a prayer group and a cultural and mutual support church association, St Paul's Community partly grew out of the decline of St Vincent de Paul, and was a church-based attempt to create a more pan-ethnic organisation, with sub-communities of Nuer, Shilluk, and Dinka.[40] There were many other versions of St Paul's Community across Khartoum, some more specific to ethnic or linguistic group

---

[37] For discussions of code-switching, see Miller et al., *Arabic in the City*, 21; Leonardi, 'South Sudanese Arabic'; Miller, *Language Change and National Integration*, 101.

[38] African Rights, 'Food and Power in Sudan', 82.

[39] Santino Akak Kuon, in Aweil, 3 July 2013; Human Rights Watch Africa, *Children in Sudan*, 19; see the note on state abuses of St Vincent de Paul workers in Rone, *Behind the Red Line*, 180.

[40] Santino Akak Kuon, in Aweil, 3 July 2013; Arou Piol Adam, in Apada village, 21 July 2013.

4.2 Educational Associational Life

(such as the Dinka, Nuer, and Bari congregations).[41] Most encouraged youth groups, drama associations, an 'Olympics' for basketball and football between church clubs, and ceremonial parades at Christmas and Easter.[42] Neighbourhood committees helped by applying for permits for language schools.[43]

A significant amount of funding and organisational support for language teaching and writing came through the organisation of the re-translation of the Bible into many southern languages from the early 1990s.[44] This work built on a long history of vernacular orthography in southern Sudan, and Khartoum's residents were familiar with this history of dialect codification over the early twentieth century, especially the Rejaf conference on southern languages in 1928, and the work of the priest and scholar Arthur Nebel on the Dinka Rek grammar and dictionaries.[45] The various dialects of Dinka have had significant investment since the 1950s, and many newly displaced residents in Khartoum had previously had linguistic and teacher training during the southern regional administration period in the 1970s. Several of these men became key figures in reviving Dinka-language education in Khartoum, founding the Dinka Cultural Society in 1990, and using old primary-school Dinka textbooks to educate a new generation, as the teacher Martin Kiir explained: 'We didn't have public schools where you could teach Dinka, but we started in churches. So in churches we opened Primary 1 up to Primary 4. And then you will be graduated as a teacher, to teach another one.'[46]

This work was given new energy when the Summer Institute of Linguistics (SIL) began literacy programmes in the city in 1991.[47] The Dinka programme included Job Dhurai Malou, who had worked

---

[41] Lual Lual Aguer, in Apada, 15 August 2013; Jimmy Wongo, in Juba, 18 October 2013.
[42] Marko Mathiang Deng, in Apada, 17 August 2013; Mohammed Ahmed, 'Christian Missionary Activity', 13–14.
[43] Acien Acien Yor, in Aweil town, 11 July 2013.
[44] Dhieu Kuel, in Mayen Ulem, 4 July 2013; members of the Dinka Cultural Society, in Apada, 11 August 2013.
[45] Arou Piol Adam and friends in a group discussion, in Apada village, 22 July 2013; Hélène Fatima Idris, 'Modern Developments in the Dinka Language', *Göteborg Africana Informal Series* 3 (2004): 19.
[46] This history of Dinka linguistic development is written in full by Morwel Ater Morwel in the introduction to his textbook 'Dinka Course' (Khartoum, 1994). Martin Kiir, in Apada, 11 August 2013.
[47] Idris, 'Modern Developments in the Dinka Language', 22.

with SIL since the 1970s and who moved to Khartoum in 1991 when the University of Bahr el Ghazal was relocated to the capital.[48] Job Dhurai is well-known for restructuring the Dinka vowel system in 1988. A Dinka literacy team was established in Khartoum in 1993, and by 1994 those who had managed to completed Dinka Primary 4 were involved in literacy training, printing, and teaching in forty-eight literacy centres across Khartoum.[49] Many trainees went on to become church catechists and youth group leaders.[50] Some trainees went into Bible translation work, including Dut Anyak Dit, a teacher and poet in Dinka and southern Sudanese Arabic, who worked with SIL in a group translating the New Testament into Dinka.[51] Dut Anyak was introduced to SIL by Job Dhurai, who knew him from primary school teaching during the 1970s; Dut Anyak was then encouraged to start writing 'educative ideas' as poems and stories – 'I felt I shouldn't keep quiet, even if I don't have a forum for them.'[52] In 1995, Job Dhurai and Dut Anyak translated the Primary 5 core textbook into Dinka.[53]

This work produced a wide field of intellectual and educational projects beyond vernacular linguistic study and specifically Christian translations and publications. By the mid-1990s, for example, the SIL's Dinka Literacy Project began to compile Dinka stories, war songs, and proverbs in text; started publishing a quarterly literary review and a yearly calendar; and began organising writing workshops.[54] Small print shops as well as SIL's printer and church photocopiers were all useful in producing pamphlets and booklets of writing group output, personal poetry, and short histories and stories, which were sold and shared, and several of which have made it back to South Sudan today. The Dinka Cultural Society grew to include men, women, and those not in education, as well as secondary school and university students, and it held parties as well as formal discussions and writing groups in various suburbs.[55] The influence of this work reached well beyond

[48] Ibid., 20; Job Dhurai Malou, in Juba, 25 June 2019.
[49] Idris, 'Modern Developments in the Dinka Language', 22.
[50] Martin Kiir, in Apada, 11 August 2013.
[51] Dut Anyak Dit, in Kuajok, 28 September 2013.   [52] Ibid.
[53] Arou Piol Adam and friends in a group discussion, in Apada village, 22 July 2013.
[54] Idris, 'Modern Developments in the Dinka Language', 22.
[55] Atak Akol Diing, in Aweil, 14 August 2013; Arou Piol Adam, in Apada village, 21 July 2013; Santino Akak Kuon, in Aweil, 3 July 2013. For this project

4.2 Educational Associational Life

Khartoum. Other graduates of Dinka-language schools and writing projects (including Morwel Ater Morwel) made it to Cairo and founded the Dinka Language Institute there in 1995.[56] By the late 1990s, the SPLA (with Job Dhurai) was encouraging vernacular primary tuition and began to use Dinka Literacy Project materials in schools and literacy courses in liberated territories.[57]

For most people in Khartoum, the most important role of these self-made linguistic studies and vernacular education projects beyond Christian publications was to provide a rich basis for collective self-expression and discussion. Language skills were crucial in building a powerful artistic community in the city that could reflect, communicate, and debate the histories, stories, and current and future lives of the city's displaced residents. This required orality more than literacy (because, in one teacher and later politician's words, 'songs are the newspaper').[58] Early 1990s creative organisation was partly built on some people's experience of musical and cultural projects during the Nimeiri government and in the southern regional administration in the 1970s and early 1980s, when some artists and playwrights built experience in radio and theatre. And many people were self-taught songwriters, musicians, and poets; in 1992, Catherine Miller observed hand pianos and lyres as common possessions among Khartoum's southern residents, and noted the growth of amateur arts groups in Haj Yousif, Mayo, and Umbadda.[59]

James, a singer-songwriter now working in Aweil and Juba, started singing in his local church in Khartoum as a young teen, and by 1992 was involved in the professional music circuit in the city, when he took part in a group recording session in the Radio Sudan studio for the first time (recording the song 'I Ask You Mother, Is This the Land I Was Born In?'). James hung out in the Shabaab Club with the artists Fur Fur, Ajieng Mathiang, Deng Tahrir, Atak Deng Deng, General Paulino, the famous female singer Anyeth Dit, and Emmanuel Kembe. Sebit Bandas was a music teacher there, and Nyankol Mathiang had

---

I collected printed work from Mayo Mandela writing group members across Aweil and Juba.

[56] Idris, 'Modern Developments in the Dinka Language', 23.
[57] At university level, Dinka was taught in 2000 by Lino Kiir Kuony at the Institute of African and Asian Studies at the University of Khartoum. Ibid., 18.
[58] Manoa Aligo, in Koboko, 10 March 2017.
[59] Miller, *Language Change and National Integration*, 115, 117.

emigrated. This was a heterogeneous, multi-ethnic musical community: 'I was interested in other languages, and the Zande tribe's drumming style – I sang their songs.'[60] These musicians feature across my interviews for this project throughout South Sudan: '[Their] songs motivated us to take courage and also enable those that listen to change.'[61]

Some of these artists made a reasonable living from music teaching and performing, including the Bari singer General Paulino, who emphasised how grateful he was to Gino Barcelo, the director of Comboni College, who gave him space to practice and taught other students to play the guitar on the grounds of the college, commonly known as Comboni Ground. The Institute of Music and Drama, founded in 1969, started to take in a few southern students in the late 1980s, many of whom became involved in Sudanese street theatre and folk dance movements, and who later returned to the south to join the well-established arts scene around the Nyakuron Cultural Centre and Radio Juba.[62] General Paulino was a member of the Union of South Sudanese Musicians, who were paid by community associations to perform, although at student graduation ceremonies 'they didn't charge them a lot of money, only the cost of hiring the musical instruments and the PA system, because it was the right place for us to pass messages'.[63]

Probably the most famous of these Khartoum southern Sudanese artistic organisations is Kwoto.[64] Kwoto was a travelling theatre company and cultural centre since 1994, founded by Al Samani Lual Are, Derik Uya Alfred, and Stephen Affear Ochalla.[65] The centre had a library and courtyard with rehearsals and informal evening performances.[66] It auditioned its members, and grew to about forty male and female singers, dancers, and actors, mostly from southern Sudan and the Nuba Mountains. Kwoto refers to a Toposa sacred stone with spiritual unifying powers, a sign of the founders' intent to respond to

---

[60] James Garang, in Aweil, 15 June 2015.
[61] Deng Anyuon Ayuel, in Maper Akot Arou, 23 August 2017.
[62] Lorins, 'Inheritance', 189–93.
[63] General Paulino, in Juba, 23 October 2013.
[64] For this section, I'm hugely grateful to Rebecca Lorins and her thesis, and for discussions with Atem El-Fatih and Stephen Ochalla in Juba.
[65] Lorins, 'Inheritance', 142–43.
[66] Luke Dixon, 'Youth Theatre in the Displaced People's Camps of Khartoum', in Michael Etherton and Jane Plastow, eds., *African Theatre: Youth* (James Currey, 2006), 79.

4.2 Educational Associational Life

mutual distrust and wartime anger between displaced residents. Stephen summarised their feeling in 1994, that 'you as a people, you run from war, and you're going to another place but you still fight each other, for nothing. You have your own war behind you here, and how are you going to live as a people? How?'[67]

Ladu Terso described Kwoto's mission as 'a response to profound questions posed in the silence of the hearts of any right human being. It is the systematic loss of traditional cultural practices, intercultural bigotry, questions of identity, and lack of cohesion.'[68] But the purpose of the group was not simply to 'preserve culture' as artefacts of past glories in ethnic silos. Derik Uya argued at a lecture at Africa College in Khartoum in 2002

> that the preservation of cultures should not entail the purification of cultures, or the erasure of the process of hybridization. He warned against what he identified as the prevailing notion among southerners that 'culture is static' and the province of a particular group, and instead explained the importance of recognising the dynamism of any cultural tradition, adding 'there is no such thing as a pure culture'.[69]

As such Kwoto's dance and theatre work was comparatively radical. In performances in Square 42 in Omdurman, and in churches and football grounds across the city, Kwoto merged dance and music styles from across Sudan into single songs, and mixed stories, parables, and languages. Audience members often joined in, or the group stopped performances to incorporate a new move taught by an attendee. Only three of their performance songs were in Dinka, and the group used southern Sudanese Arabic extensively.[70] This sometimes 'left the audiences confused'.[71] But Kwoto is most often described by many audience members and casual observers of evening rehearsals, across secondary accounts, and in my interviews of daily lives in the mid-1990s as a 'learning' experience, and a kind of 'open popular university'.[72] Their performances had emotional power and political content, demanding self-reflection and analysis. Old songs were politically

---

[67] Stephen Ochalla, in Juba, 9 November 2013.
[68] Edward Ladu Terso, 'Kwoto in Holland (Part One)', *Khartoum Monitor*, 12 July 2003.
[69] Lorins, 'Inheritance', 164–65.   [70] Ibid., 255, 164.
[71] Ladu Terso, 'Kwoto in Holland'.
[72] Dixon, 'Youth Theatre', 79; Lorins, 'Inheritance', 248.

repurposed: for instance, Luke Dixon observed, 'one song had obvious resonance and was taken up by the audience. It was Baai, a song from the Dinka.... It means "Oh my land, you have been stolen."'[73]

Kwoto's plays were particularly useful for sparking and articulating political and social issues. Most plays were semi-improvised or fully improvised around a core plot, and commonly focused on self-critiques of the displaced community, particularly on class politics and inequalities, greed, and the use of violent power. The silent play *The Well*, performed with a drum soundtrack at Wad Ramli and recorded by Luke Dixon in 2005, saw

> a couple wearily draw the last water from a deep well and share it out. Then by a miracle the well springs with water. Everyone can drink. A soldier comes by on a bike and stops the celebrations. He pisses into the water and then shoots dead those who protest. The others take their revenge by strangling him with the rope that draws the water from the well.[74]

As Rebecca Lorins observed of Kwoto's complex reflections on southern life in Khartoum,

> Kwoto stages multiple and contradictory versions of the displaced southerner in the urban north – as a naïve rural self lost in an impersonal city, as an assimilated and corrupt criminal, street child, or agent of the law, as ethical witnesses to death and destruction, as a new, model citizen and as a figure potentially leading the way to a unified future and to the proper execution of the slogan 'unity in diversity' for so long promised to the Sudanese people by their leaders.[75]

Kwoto sparked a wave of cultural organisation across the city. Lazarus Lual, by then a teenage Dinka language student in the city, watched Kwoto's performances with friends and then registered a music group at the Cultural Centre (Markaz Sahafi) together. 'We were looking to have everyone but we could not, but we had some good few, we had people from Nuba, Dinka, Shilluk, Bari, Kakwa and Latuka. I played musical instruments including the kalimba and rababa; the kalimba is the traditional instrument from Western Equatoria.'[76]

---

[73] Dixon, 'Youth Theatre', 82. [74] Ibid., 83. [75] Lorins, 'Inheritance', 153.
[76] Lazarus Lual, in Juba, 19 October 2013. Lazarus attributed the kalimba to the south-west of southern Sudan, but it can be traced much further south to Zimbabwe.

4.3 Displaced Schools

Organised schooling was built on this educational foundation but was not separate from it.[77] As Marc Sommers observed in 2005, formal schools were 'one (of many) parallel education systems existing for the same population and in the same location'.[78] It was particularly difficult to establish formal schooling systems in circumstances of time-consuming poverty, political and administrative hostility and exclusion, and repeated neighbourhood destructions. In comparison to linguistic and cultural projects, formal schooling was much more closely policed. In 1990, al-Bashir announced a new education policy based on Islamic values, with a compulsory new curricula and university courses. The southern Sudanese–focused National Committee for Refugee Education, which had a half-southern executive administration and employed southern displaced teachers, was abolished in 1991 with displaced schools taken over by the Ministry of Education.[79] NGO education development programmes were few and underfunded.[80] Most schools in Khartoum were already beyond the physical and financial reach of Dar es Salaam camp residents.[81] A third of camp families reported no access to education, and camps were particularly subject to *kasha* demolition of schools and churches.[82]

But – as in southern Sudanese communities across the country over the 1980s to 2000s –residents invested intensively in establishing and promoting school-based education.[83] By 1992, schools had opened again or were newly established in the *dar es salaam* camps and in

---

[77] This chapter will not refer to these schools as 'informal' or 'private', as per education studies definitions, as many people paid in various ways for public or free church education via uniforms, books, and other expenses. I will differentiate with specifics rather than categories.

[78] Sommers, *Islands of Education*, 222.

[79] Breidlid, 'Sudanese Migrants in the Khartoum Area', 251; Sommers, *Islands of Education*, 220; Bakhit, 'Negotiations of Power and Responsibilities in Khartoum Shantytowns', 138.

[80] Bakhit, 'Negotiations of Power and Responsibilities in Khartoum Shantytowns', 139.

[81] 'Mission to Sudan: Thousands from the South Escape War, but Not Hardship, in Camps Near Capital; Fighting Forces Refugees to Live', *Pulitzer Center*, 6 February 2002.

[82] Norwegian Refugee Council, 'Profile of Internal Displacement: Sudan', 155–56.

[83] Epstein, 'Maps of Desire', 95.

peripheral neighbourhoods (particularly those that had organised systems of sultans and committees to negotiate with city authorities).[84] Volunteer teachers were recruited from among local residents, although only about one in ten had any formal training, and even by 2005 only one in ten schools had their own permanent structures.[85]

As usual, though, communities drew on long histories of school organisation in difficult circumstances in Khartoum. The expansion of Christian mission congregations in Khartoum over the 1960s and later was built on their educational provisions, as learning to read and write was a vital tool of self-protection and agency in the modern city.[86] The Omdurman Christian Club was built by 1968 specifically to provide classes.[87] The Church Missionary Society (CMS) Bible Society, formed in the early 1950s, was a catalyst for self-education, and was quickly taken over by Nuba Mountains priests (and later political leaders) Butrus Tia and Philip Abbas Ghaboush in their early careers.[88] Many residents who had previously worked in the city or as seasonal labourers in Darfur and central Sudan in the 1960s had attended night schools and evening classes at church centres, including for English, Arabic, comparative religion, and history courses.[89] In 1962, Rehfisch observed that 'many school teachers and other Sudanese are contributing much time and effort without pay to educate their fellow citizens'.[90] These intellectual labourers were Howell's 'in-betweeners', the partly educated southern interviewers Rehfisch employed to conduct his research.[91] William, a Dinka man who had

---

[84] African Rights, 'Food and Power in Sudan', 170; Amnesty International, 'Sudan's Secret Slaughter', 22.
[85] Wijnroks, *The Displaced People of Khartoum*, 14; Norwegian Refugee Council, 'Profile of Internal Displacement: Sudan', 156.
[86] Zink, *Christianity and Catastrophe*, 72, 91.
[87] Rachel Hassan, diary entry, 17 March 1968, CMS/ACC641 volume 1967–69; Khartoum University Annual Report 1958–9, SAD.562/12/5, 12/16.
[88] Church Missionary Society North Sudan Standing Committee minutes, April 1958, CMS ACC505 Z3, 3.
[89] Rehfisch, 'A Study of Some Southern Migrants in Omdurman', 65, 72. These religious debates had been notable at least since the 1950s; Rev. Eric Parry, Annual Letter 1951, CMS ACC/693 F2/1, 1; Lazarus Lual, in Juba, 19 October 2013. See also Daughtry, 'Conflict and Community', 41–43.
[90] Rehfisch, 'A Study of Some Southern Migrants in Omdurman', 72.
[91] Ibid., 50; Howell, 'Political Leadership and Organisation in the Southern Sudan'.

4.3 Displaced Schools

previously lived in Khartoum from the late 1970s to the early 1980s explained, in English:

It happened a long time ago that when your family have cows, then they cannot allow you to go for study. By there, we escaped to Babanusa in order to find the opportunity to go to school.... Before going north in 1982, we were just cattle keepers. We don't even know what's so called literature.... After I went to Babanusa, my friend came from Khartoum – this man was bilingual, he wrote in English and in his mother tongue. After that, I said I can also go and study. I went to Khartoum, and bought my exercise book that very day, and went straight to the school.... We saved our own lives. I was working in a sweet factory, then went to scheduled evening classes. That's how we get our power.[92]

By the 1980s, the biggest network of schools that southern residents could access were run primarily by the churches. In 1983, Mohammed Ahmed (writing very much in opposition to these schools) estimated that there were over 17,000 pupils in church schools, only a fifth of whom were formally Christian.[93] The Catholic Church ran prominent primary and secondary schools at Comboni College, the Sisters' School, Qiddis Saint Francis, and Comboni Girls and Boys in Omdurman, with the largest school having over 1,200 students. Church night schools spread across the city, including Eshash in central Khartoum and Karton Kassala evening school, both with about 200 students. Comboni Intermediate Secondary school was also an evening school with around 3,000 regular pupils in 1983.[94] Other churches had smaller projects; the Episcopalian Church specialised in girls' education, with around 700 pupils, and ran small night schools in displaced settlements around the city.[95] Educational work was organised partly by priests, such as Father Edward Brady, who founded the influential Christian Leadership course, but initiatives like the late night one-to-one teaching at Comboni Playground were sanctioned rather than led or controlled by the churches.[96]

By 1985, rapidly increasing numbers of prospective students forced local authorities to open special schools at Rufaa, Shiek Lutfi

---

[92] William Manyang Tong, in Apada, 17 August 2013; the same empowerment via urban migration is noted by Leonardi, *Dealing with Government*, 73.
[93] Mohammed Ahmed, 'Christian Missionary Activity', 11.   [94] Ibid., 8–9.
[95] Ibid., 10.
[96] Members of the Dinka Cultural Society, in Apada, 11 August 2013; interview with anonymous Tearfund worker, London, February 2012.

Secondary school, and then Maridi in Khartoum and Imatong in Omdurman.[97] In 1987 nine of these became 'IDP' schools, which ran strictly in the afternoons on government and private school premises.[98] By 1991, only ten 'IDP' secondary schools catered to just over 7,000 southern students, eighteen 'IDP' intermediate schools had over 8,000 pupils, and thirty-five 'IDP' primary schools catered to just over 19,000 southern students.[99] The Catholic Church and other religious groups took on the everyday management of most of these institutions.[100] In the late 1980s too, the three southern regional administrations (Bahr el Ghazal, Upper Nile, and Equatoria) founded ten basic-level schools, with community-built *rakuba* shelters; by 1993 these 'basic' schools grew to 143, with around 47,000 students across the city, and with generally good numbers of teachers and small classes.[101] The University of Juba moved to Khartoum in 1989.

Over the same period, many more community-financed and fee-paying evening and afternoon schools were established, including by community associations, former teachers, ex-politicians, and ex-civil servants.[102] Small schools often directly recruited their pupils from the local neighbourhood for low fees.[103] Abuk Deng, whose parents at the time were also teaching her how to cook over a wood fire and how to grind her own sorghum, attended a Dinka-language primary school for a year in Haj Yousif, organised by one of her neighbours who worked as a part-time teacher; she graduated Primary 1 after exams.[104] Josephine joined a Kalakla school called Saria ('Quickly'), learning in south Sudanese Arabic, organised by a Zande man, with Dinka-language teachers and a mix of pupils.[105]

---

[97] Stephen Akot Wol, 'Education of Displaced Southern Students and Pupils in Northern Sudan', in Eltigani, ed., *The Displacement Problem in the Sudan*, 70.
[98] As well as the Egypt scholarship scheme for 300 students.
[99] Wol, 'Education of Displaced Southern Students', 73–74; Sommers, *Islands of Education*, 220.
[100] Wol, 'Education of Displaced Southern Students', 71.
[101] Sommers, *Islands of Education*, 221–23.
[102] Diing Chen Diing, in Aweil, 15 July 2013; see Wijnroks, *The Displaced People of Khartoum*, 8.
[103] Feiden et al., 'Khartoum Displaced Assessment and Recommendations', 22–23; Sommers, *Islands of Education*, 222.
[104] Abuk Deng, in Apada, 5 June 2013.
[105] Josephine, in Maper Two, 26 June 2013.

4.3 Displaced Schools

At one point in 1986 school registration was doubling by the week.[106] These independently established schools came into their own in 1991 when regional schools and IDP schools were abolished. Government secondary 'southern schools' were closed down by 1994, with only three self-help secondary schools surviving by 2000.[107] Many students could not find places in other government schools or were excluded on the grounds that they had no documents or birth certificates to prove their eligibility. Joseph Ukel, an English teacher by training in the 1970s before becoming a politician and MP by 1989, worked in Khartoum in this period as an English teacher and underground politician; during this period, he helped to organise and fundraise for a 'remedial school' because 'most of our children did not go systematically: they jumped certain years and so even though they make attempts to go to university, they often didn't pass in sciences subjects and mathematics'. Joseph taught English and remedial science, so that teenagers could sit for the Sudan secondary school certificate and apply to university.[108]

Enrolment continued to increase over the 1990s into the early 2000s. The Catholic Diocese of Khartoum registered 60,000 students in 2001, with a very high pass rate at secondary level, higher than local government schools.[109] By 2005, even in Khartoum's IDP camps, over 40 per cent of children were enrolled in schools, and 67 per cent of displaced people in Khartoum between six and eighteen years old (compared with 38 per cent of nineteen- to twenty-five-year-olds) had been to primary school.[110] These are not great statistics, but the study only inquired about formal school-based education. Evening clubs also included language clubs and lectures, such as at Mari Girgis, Burri Lamab, the Catholic and Comboni Clubs, and the Coptic Library Club in Khartoum North.[111] Sommers saw these schools and educational projects as 'atomised', segregating the population along lines of ethnic

---

[106] Joseph Ukel Abango, in Juba, 29 October 2013; Deng Atak Abuk, in Apada, 13 July 2013; members of the Dinka Cultural Society, in Apada, 11 August 2013; 'Meeting of the Archbishop and the Director of the Coordination Office of Bahr el Ghazal Administrative Area, July 24 1986, in the Archbishop's Office', CAR 6734.21.1.
[107] Sommers, *Islands of Education*, 224–25, 228.
[108] Joseph Ukel Abango, in Juba, 29 October 2013.
[109] Sommers, *Islands of Education*, 229–31.
[110] Norwegian Refugee Council, 'Profile of Internal Displacement: Sudan', 155.
[111] Mohammed Ahmed, 'Christian Missionary Activity', 14.

origin, language, religion, and politics; however, many people remembered highly mixed classes of southern and Nuba populations, with many Darfuri classmates and teachers.[112] Fluctuating finances was really the primary determinant of parental or personal choices and opportunity.[113]

People's accounts of how they got their (heterogeneous, cultural, and political as well as curriculum-based) education in Khartoum reflect this history. Most young men split their time between factory shifts or other manual labour and a variety of forms of schooling; as James Akec (a founder of Akut Kuei, see Chapter 5) recalled, 'and then at three o'clock, we take our books and all these things and go to Comboni. Because we don't have anywhere to study, just we go to Comboni, and there in Comboni you study English and Dinka.'[114] Lual Lual explained how he struggled to get up to Primary 4, and then stopped to work full-time to support his mother and family; he wanted to get enough literacy to read the newspapers and listen to English-language radio.[115] Groups of young men rented housing together so they could better access intermediate and secondary schools in the centre of the city. John Riak, a young teenager at the time, graduated from primary evening school in 1989 and won a place at Jur River Intermediate School. With other teenaged boys, they organised renting a small room near the school, working in local shops part-time to cover transport and school fees.[116] For Lazarus Lual, Comboni schools were quite expensive and strict on past performance – he explained that the school he approached would not take him, because he had not finished Primary 1 and had skipped classes. Lazarus tried a community school called Juba Centre in Bahri, but felt it was disorganised:

you know there are some guys who established the private schools, like they rent some schools for short period of time, like in the evenings, and then they just teach and they like teachers organise themselves, and then they do the thing ... And then it was really like a free school, you come any time you want, you go any time you want, you do whatever – I said no no no, this one is not good. I went to Abraham School, somebody called Abraham from

---

[112] Sommers, *Islands of Education*, 222.
[113] Stephen Ayaga, in Aweil, 8 August 2013; Josephine, in Maper Two, 26 June 2013.
[114] James Akec Nhial, in Juba, 8 September 2013.
[115] Lual Lual Aguer, in Apada chiefs' court, 3 June 2013.
[116] John Gau Riak, in Aweil, 28 June 2013.

4.3 Displaced Schools

Lakes State, he organised a very nice school.... There were two Ghanaians who taught English, and otherwise there were southern Sudanese teachers. After school I went to the cultural dance places, then on Sundays church, then on Saturdays I'm in the Bible class, where they debate.

Lazarus got involved with the Khartoum Christian Centre, an evangelical new church, because of the opportunities to meet East Africans and white foreigners and practice his English.[117]

Many men (and a few women) who went on to become casual teachers in the same schools got their education through evening classes, such as Manyang Tong, who worked in a sweet factory in the day: 'that's how we get our power to teach the students'. Manyang worked as a Dinka-language teacher until 2011:

The main reason that we opened schools was to support the south. It supported them, mostly to facilitate their communication between different military companies in the south – the most important issue was to support the SPLA outside here, like those whom we trained, they came out and joined the SPLA. We encourage the children to study and be educated, telling them that your country will be liberated.[118]

This school education was explicitly political, but not (or not just) in the sense that many schools and teachers were explicitly pro-SPLA. The key was political education in the widest sense, to understand the politics and history of Sudan in the world, and how to critique and analyse. This was a key motivation for many new students: in the words of Lual Lual, to 'help me to understand the history, of why our people are fighting with people'.[119] Political figures organised lectures or worked as teachers, including Toby Maduot, Ghazi Suleiman, Ali Mahmoud Hassani, and Benjamin Marial, all of whom had different opinions on the war and the future of Sudan, and who prompted fierce debate amongst students who already discussed newspaper interviews and cuttings, including on the possible separation of the south or the prospective unity of the Sudan.[120] The war was brought home by repeated school closures and the politics of education itself in Khartoum. Dhieu Lual recounted how his small primary school (like many others) would be repeatedly closed by police during

---

[117] Lazarus Lual, in Juba, 19 October 2013.
[118] William Manyang Tong, in Apada, 17 August 2013.
[119] Lual Lual Aguer, in Apada chiefs' court, 3 June 2013.
[120] Dhieu Kuel, in Mayen Ulem, 4 July 2013.

the 1990s; security personnel, he said, would say that 'it is not good for us to witness you learning here, while your brother is killing us elsewhere'.[121]

Marc Sommers noted that schools were 'the central place where the issues of war, resistance and a sense of subjugation remain at or near the emotional surface of Southern Sudanese communities'.[122] Arou Piol, the student and part-time Dinka- language teacher, emphasised the importance of this emotional pain in schooling. He taught, he explained,

> things that make people sad. Because there were some students to be directed, not to get lost, within the school. About the south, we need to teach people about it. And to teach them about the Black people, also. And we need to remind them why we leave our land that time, we need to know it also. So these were the things we taught in the school, and these were also the things that made us sad.[123]

4.4 The Teachers

These educational organisations were generally not run by the (mostly) men who are frequently described as South Sudan's educated political elites. Since the 1950s in particular, southern Sudan had developed its own political class, usually comprised of men with post-secondary formal and often western postgraduate education, around East Africa and Khartoum. These men – often elected into national and regional government over the 1960s and '70s, or working in Sudan's civil service – were a tiny minority in comparison to their supposedly uneducated, illiterate, rural, parochial, and tribalised constituencies.[124] By the early 1980s, these highly educated men and their families were both politically marginalised and overwhelmed by the migration of

---

[121] Ibid. [122] Sommers, *Islands of Education*, 245.
[123] Arou Piol Adam and friends in a group discussion, in Apada village, 22 July 2013.
[124] Bona Malwal, 'The Military Regime (November 1958–October 1964) and Southern Sudan', October 1965, SAD.985/5/19-23. As Gordon Muortat asserted in 1966, 'it is the educated people who understand the wrongs committed against the South and it is they who can point out and speak against the sufferings of the Southern people. It is they who are the eyes of the illiterate masses in seeing that their political rights are secured and preserved.' 'Mourtat [sic] Addresses', *The Vigilant*, 24 February 1966, TNA FO 371.190417 VS1015.24.

their rural counterparts to urban areas, where their homes became doss-houses, schools, and social clubs for their extended family and community in the south.[125] But this did not narrow the 'large gulf' between themselves and the new migrant worker populations 'largely ignored by the politicians ... beyond limited contact along clan lines'.[126] As one highly educated southern politician living and working in Khartoum in the 1990s explained, 'we didn't need them – they couldn't give us anything'.[127] And Nyagen, the twenty-five-year-old Aliab Dinka woman from near Juba, emphasised to Fouad Ibrahim in 1994 that the southerners in government in Khartoum 'don't help us'.[128]

These cross-class solidarities were hard to organise even for those who wanted to. Educated, English-speaking, middle-class southern workers in NGOs and church organisations in the centre of the city had – in the words of one worker – 'no real interaction with the very poor southern Sudanese' even while they managed relief programmes to benefit them; local teachers and volunteers in the camps and suburbs were their key contacts and organisers.[129] Bridging the physical and class distance between middle-class residents and impoverished residents on the urban fringe was also potentially dangerous. Throughout the 1990s, prominent ex-politicians and other formerly politically active middle-class southern residents were under close surveillance.[130] In March 2004, for example, a group of Darfuri students at Khartoum University tried to visit newly displaced arrivals to the Mayo Mandela camp, and the police and security forces staged a violent intervention,

---

[125] This followed the 'government decision in late 1987 to close the co-ordination offices in Khartoum for Equatoria, Upper Nile, and Bahr El Ghazal and to freeze all their budgets pending investigation of alleged irregularities. Southern officials in Khartoum have been told to return to their regions, but lack the money to pay for tickets, even if any flights are taking place, and the lack of cash for southern students' fees and subsistence have left many stuck in Khartoum with no support.' Amnesty International, 'Sudan's Secret Slaughter', 45, 96; John Howell, *Political Leaders in the Southern Sudan*, manuscript, Durham University Library PamSC+00319, 14, 226.

[126] Howell, 'Political Leadership and Organisation in the Southern Sudan', 89, 146.

[127] Manoa Aligo, in Koboko, 1 April 2017.

[128] Ibrahim, 'Hunger-Vulnerable Groups', 259–60.

[129] Edward Jubara, in Juba, 14 March 2013.

[130] Biro, 'Situation of Human Rights in the Sudan', 36.

with tear gas and beatings. The following day the new residents were forcibly relocated, and some students were reportedly killed.[131]

Most everyday education work was organised, then, from within neighbourhoods and by residents themselves, including by some of these supposed 'elites' but much more commonly by poorer and informally educated locals. Many residents in Khartoum in the 1990s had previous experience of organising their own schools in difficult circumstances before, across east and central Africa and Egypt in the 1960s and '70s, as in the case of an ex-Khartoum University student who established and ran a refugee school at Niangara in Congo-Kinshasa in the mid- to late 1960s.[132] This was the work of teachers, students, ex-administrators, lay clergy, and waged workers: the people written off by John Howell in his 1978 doctoral thesis on southern politics in Khartoum as unrepresentative, apathetic, and apolitical, specifically because they worked outside the two understood 'spheres' of traditional chiefly authority and formal state politics.[133]

These organisers made up an alternative field of local intellectuals, those 'who knew how to survive' while also volunteering or helping to organise community work on less hierarchical and formal political grounds than the ostensible 'elites'.[134] These men and women are hard to label because their interests and incomes were often heterogeneous. Low-grade clerks and civil servants, traders, daily labourers, tea ladies, and brick makers on the banks of the Nile were variously involved with political parties like the Union of Southern African Parties (USAP), church organisations, village courts, and schools.[135] The most

---

[131] Norwegian Refugee Council, 'Profile of Internal Displacement: Sudan', 109.
[132] Agolong Col Agolong to Rev. Father Sina from Kisangani, 9 October 1970, CAR A/104/7/6.
[133] Howell, 'Political Leadership and Organisation in the Southern Sudan', 55; Elena Vezzadini notes this organisational work in 1920s Sudan: 'Spies, Secrets, and a Story Waiting to Be (Re)Told: Memories of the 1924 Revolution and the Racialization of Sudanese History', *Northeast African Studies* 13, no. 2 (2013): 166.
[134] Jimmy Wongo, in Juba, 18 October 2013; as argued by James Brennan of similar work in Dar es Salaam, Tanzania: 'Blood Enemies', 392.
[135] Examples include Anei Deng Akok, in Aweil, 13 August 2013; Lual Lual Aguer (in a discussion in Apada, 15 August 2013) debated who 'counted' as a 'local leader'. For discussion of this migrant plurality, see Hamidou Dia, 'From Field to Concept: The Example of Senegalese Multisited Villages', *Journal of Intercultural Studies* 34, no. 5 (2013): 580; Miller, *Language Change and National Integration*, 121.

4.4 The Teachers

active residents were variously and concurrently students, teachers, political activists, court workers, gang members, and poets.[136] Some men held multiple roles as teachers, chief court attendants, and church leaders; some teachers like Dut Anyak Dit were ex-government officials, who privately wrote songs, books, and poetry, often for church or ethnic association events.[137] Dut Anyak, whose real name is Protasio Dut Wol, took up his pen name while working as a teacher in the 1980s in Tonj. In 1986 he was sponsored by the Ministry of Education for teacher training at the University of Khartoum, where he completed undergraduate and master's courses while teaching in Immatong Secondary School for mostly southern students, and in Haher Secondary School with mostly northern students. Dut Anyak then became a lecturer at the displaced University of Bahr el Ghazal in Bahri until 2005. Throughout this, he wrote poetry 'to write something to encourage our youth', and worked also with SIL's language projects.[138]

Many military workers were also teachers, including Dor Tartizio, who started his life in Khartoum as a displaced student and part time donkey-truck worker in the 1970s, then a Dinka language teacher; after three years he joined the Sudan Armed Forces, worked in the military for six years, then left the army for school and manual labour again in 1989: 'because they are going to send all the Black people to come and fight with SPLA. But for me, I said no.'[139] In Catherine Miller's 1992 survey of Takamul suburb, 29 per cent of the male residents she interviewed were military or police workers, 28 per cent were manual labourers, 10 percent were drivers, 8.5 per cent were unemployed, 5 percent were junior civil servants, and 3 per cent were full-time students. All the military, police, civil servants, and manual

---

[136] For example, James Garang, Dhieu Lual, Santino Atak Kuon, and Lazarus Lual.
[137] Acien Acien Yor, in Aweil town, 11 July 2013; demonstrated by Santino Atak Kuon's authorial autobiography, printed in 'The Magazine of Dinka Culture', 22; Deng Atak Abuk, in Apada, 13 July 2013. Anei Deng Akok's uncle was in a political party, then became a teacher at a Comboni secondary school. One of the members of the highly political Dinka-language Akut Kuei song group worked as a language education coordinator – with Nuba and Nuer students – at a Comboni girl's school from 1994: James Akec Nhial, in Juba, 8 September 2013.
[138] Dut Anyak Dit, in Kuajok, 27 August and 28 September 2013.
[139] Dor Tartizio Buni, in Juba, 14 October 2013.

labourers she interviewed were southern or Nuba.[140] There was, in effect, no real category of 'students' in Khartoum, aside from those studying full-time at the university level; many people were perpetual students, exploring self-taught study in parallel with daily labour and other roles.[141]

This is not a fully masculine history, although women were generally under extreme pressure as key breadwinners, housekeepers, carers, and custodians of family values. But across accounts of educational organisation in Khartoum, women feature as teachers, organisers, and financial supporters. Women across the city are recorded – generally unnamed – as organising and fundraising for chapels and schools, community support groups, women's mutual aid societies, and family planning outreach, across the city.[142] Many men emphasised key female intellectuals in their neighbourhood – 'she is illiterate but she is intellectual' – taking on roles in community associations and fundraising.[143] Many women are extremely proud of their often dangerous work in Khartoum, which put their children and relatives through school.[144]

By the late 1990s, community organisation not only was funded significantly from women's earnings in Khartoum – particularly for child and adult education – but also included women as teachers. Marc Sommers records that by 2005, 52 per cent of informal or self-run community school teachers were young women, mostly with secondary school education, and this figure was roughly borne out through interviews with slightly more affluent women in Aweil and Juba who became teachers (as well as, in one case, a political candidate) in the late 1990s and early 2000s.[145] Melanie, a Bari woman from a Juba

---

[140] Miller, *Language Change and National Integration*, 31–32.
[141] For example, Stephen Ayaga, in Aweil, 8 August 2013; Maper chiefs' court meeting, 13 April 2013.
[142] Roland Werner, William Anderson, and Andrew Wheeler, *Day of Devastation, Day of Contentment: The History of the Sudanese Church across 2000 Years* (Paulines Publications Africa, 2000), 460.
[143] Stephen Ayaga, in Aweil, 8 August 2013.
[144] Abuk Ngor Deng, in Maper, 29 June 2013; also see Siricio Iro, 'The Situation of Sudanese Women', 105.
[145] Sommers notes that 7 per cent of formal schoolteachers employed by the state were women in 2005, but gives a far higher figure for women teachers in what he terms 'informal' education. Sommers, *Islands of Education*, 71, 252. Many women teachers contributed to this study, including Melanie Itto and Atak Akol Diing.

4.4 The Teachers

family who moved to Khartoum when she was only a few years old, started to teach in Jabarona in Jebel Aulia after she graduated from Ahliya University in 1999,

> to help and support our people. The songs but also the stories people used to narrate, about how the work was going on ... it played a very big role in our lives, so that we kept our culture. [The Khartoum Catholic Archdiocese] opened a lot of schools, primary schools, and they were in need of big numbers of teachers. That is why we respond to their call.... The freedom they had there was more than others in the residential areas [in the centre]. There were also big numbers of southerners in these remote areas. That is why they had the freedom to practice what they want, to sing, dance and do everything. You would travel out! [Laughs].[146]

Many secondary school and university students from Nuba, southern, and Darfuri communities were involved in educational activism, not just in student groups within schools but as teachers and fundraisers.[147] This organisation was given a boost in 1991 when the Sudan government cancelled its Egypt scholarship programme for southern students and recalled students on bursaries elsewhere, trapping students in Khartoum's university system, including in the displaced universities of Juba and Bahr el Ghazal.[148]

Many groups and social organisations, of various political persuasions and lifespans, formed or were reinvigorated in this period, including social organisations of the Nuba Mountains and Darfur, the Pan-African Socialist Society, Democratic Front, the African Thought and Cultural Society, and the more long-standing African National Front.[149] Despite many of these organisations being deeply affected by the split in the SPLM/A in 1991, with some fragmenting into Sudan unionist and South Sudanese separatist wings, the period after 1992 is

---

[146] Melanie Itto, in Juba, 23 October 2013.

[147] Jimmy Wongo, in Juba, 18 October 2013; Sommers, *Islands of Education*, 220, notes how displaced secondary school students started lobbying for further education and opened schools themselves in the mid-1980s.

[148] Information Committee of the South Sudan Students Alliance for Separation – Middle East, 'Report on the Compulsory Transportation of Students to Khartoum', 8 September 2002, SAD.93/1/74-76, 74–75.

[149] Philip Abbas Ghabboush, 'Growth of Black Political Consciousness in Northern Sudan', *Africa Today* 20, no. 3 (1973): 36. Also see Foreign and Commonwealth Office note, 30 October 1979, TNA FCO 93.2126, and memo from Youth Advisor to Director of Ministry for Southern Affairs, Khartoum, n. d., c. 1969, SSNA MSA 10.A.3/39.

(in hindsight) remembered as a period of 'renewal and revival' in Black Sudanese student organisation, and of more intense political education and articulation.[150]

University teaching was so frequently disrupted by funding and political suspensions that many students took well over three years to finish their courses. Kuel Aguer, who later worked for Save the Children in Darfur, was accepted into the economic and social studies program at the University of Juba in 1983, but finished his course only in 1990, as he had been suspended because of his political activities in 1985 and 1987.[151] 'In the meantime we went and opened displaced schools in the evenings in the classrooms. We named the schools controversially' – including Naam River, where the SPLA had defeated the SAF; Aggrey Jaden school, after the first civil war rebel group Anya Nya politician cum fighter; and Owinykibul, after the Anya Nya and then SPLA training camp and base.[152]

All of this teaching work carried risks. In reports through the 1990s, church catechists and volunteer education centre workers were detained and some disappeared, apparently because of their teaching. In 1993, Clement Deng, a Catholic catechist and teacher at a school in Arkawit, was arrested, beaten, and taken to a detention centre and tortured by local security. He reported being asked, 'Are you going to stop teaching at the centre?' and 'Have you been sent to Khartoum as an agent of the SPLA?' Other church workers, including Emmanuel Henry, Peter Malual, and John Bol, were also detained and disappeared over 1993. Clement later fled in February 1994, hitching lifts through Abyei into SPLA-held territory.[153]

---

[150] For a detailed discussion of subversive student politics, see Chapter 6. 'Renewal and Revival' is the title of the chapter covering 1992–2004 in Ajack Makor, *African National Front (A.N.F.): 50 Years of Political Struggle by Sudanese University Students* (Leesberg Enterprises, 2010), 19, quoting Bob Marley on mental slavery.

[151] Aguer was then in the southern Sudan administration and South Sudan government after 2005, and is now a university lecturer in Juba.

[152] Kuel Aguer Kuel, in Juba, 20 January 2017.

[153] 'Draft Preliminary Report: Christian Solidarity International (CSI) Visit to Sudan, January 19–25, 1995', SAD 94/7/1-10, 5. Amnesty International reported that Kamal Tadros, a deacon, was arrested on 19 April 1994; 'other reports claim that [his] arrest represents an attempt by the authorities to harass Christian church staff involved in relief and development work with people living in squatter camps around Khartoum'. IISH AFR 54/21/94.

Teaching and writing history were particularly dangerous. After 1992, history teaching was apparently reserved in state schools for Muslims only, and so was considered a risky profession in community-run schools.[154] Dhieu Kuel remembered his Fajulu and Latuka history teachers at his Comboni school, who were arrested repeatedly. They taught from the Sudan curriculum, 'but added some things' – including about the radical Islam of the Mahdist revolution and its legacies in the NIF and NCP governments, about the Abboud regime closing off the south, the expulsion of missionaries in 1964, and the 'assassination' of the southern Sudanese Communist politician Joseph Garang in 1971. 'He told us that this is not written in the book here, because the history is written by Arabs.'[155]

4.5 Rewriting the Curriculum and Making History

These educational organisations prompted a new wave of writing, poetry, publishing, and pamphlet sales. Many teachers, students, and residents had sporadic access to southern-run newspapers like the *Khartoum Monitor*, but these were heavily regulated and frequently shut down. Self-publishing features more prominently than these newspapers in poor displaced residents' accounts of educational work. By the 1990s Khartoum's suburbs had developed a vibrant publishing market, based on small pamphlets and the impact of the cheap photocopier. These DIY markets are often overlooked in newspaper- and book-focused research on literary cultures, but in Sudan they have roots dating back to at least the 1960s and in small southern-oriented bookshops and libraries in Khartoum.[156]

This self-publishing industry was partly a response to the al-Bashir government's Sudan curriculum, which provoked (and still provokes) real frustration from students and teachers. In the 1990s and 2000s, the history, geography, and civics primary textbook barely detailed

[154] Diing Chen Diing, written note on the government's introduction of a new education policy in 1990, referencing a new teachers' guide for history published by the National Committee for Curriculum Development and Educational Research for the academic year 1992–93; written by Diing and given to the author, 12 August 2013.
[155] Dhieu Kuel, in Mayen Ulem, 4 July and 21 August 2013.
[156] Lorins, 'Inheritance', 160. A Dinka Language Committee was formed in 1959 under the Rt. Rev. D. Atong: Gordon Memorial Sudan Mission Minutes of Standing Committee, 3–6 October 1959, KNA MSS 61/712 A, 3.

ethnic cultures, dated the arrival of 'man' to Sudan to the migration of Arab traders, made no reference to the slave trade, and used northern references for names, clothing, and food.[157] As Dhieu Lual emphasised, 'we doubted the textbook, because some explanations were forgeries – the history is not telling the real thing. Like the coming of Arabs, they write to be the coming of all people.'[158]

Southern residents needed a better curriculum. Sommers and Abdinoor both recorded that displaced schoolteachers frequently rewrote passages in textbooks, added Bible references, and translated whole courses into English.[159] Students used notebooks to rewrite their textbooks: Dhieu explained that, as an intermediary and then secondary school student, 'we sat together, and some realities which were faked in the Sudan history, we used to correct them'.[160] The Primary 4 reader in Dinka has sections on global geography, migration, government and taxation, indigenous flora, basic human anatomy and biology, the solar system, electromagnetism, Sudanese geography, and history. Fully amended alternative textbooks generally were only prepared for primary grades one to five, though, because by grade five teachers expected their students to be able to critique the Sudan curriculum themselves.[161]

Teachers, students, language groups, adult evening classes, and community association meetings discussed the history of the civil wars in the Sudan, the socialism of SPLM/A manifesto and John Garang, and the history of the Communist Party in Sudan, including the execution of Mahmud Mohamed Taha, and the history of displacement; cultural associations collected notes 'to make some texts', including on their own histories of violence, displacement, and marginalisation in Khartoum.[162] The singer-songwriter Deng Atak remembered books in production since the 1980s, including notes on 'the history of different events that took place in different towns, like the destruction of

---

[157] Breidlid, 'Sudanese Migrants in the Khartoum Area', 255.
[158] Dhieu Kuel, in Mayen Ulem, 21 August 2013.
[159] Sommers, *Islands of Education*, 247–49; Abdinoor, 'Constructing Education in a Stateless Society', 150–51, notes teachers explaining how they took chapters from various textbooks and re-compiled them.
[160] Dhieu Kuel, in Mayen Ulem, 21 August 2013.
[161] Sommers, *Islands of Education*, 248.
[162] Dhieu Kuel, in Mayen Ulem, 21 August 2013; Marco Akon Akon, in Apada, 11 August 2013; Diing Chen Diing, in Aweil, 12 August 2013.

Babanusa where people were burnt, and Daein also where people had been burnt in 1987', all in the Dinka language.[163]

This involved active research, including collecting news cuttings and human rights reports in the *Khartoum Monitor* office, and personal histories. Santino Atak, a member of the Dinka Cultural Society, founded a research group to collect oral histories for printing in pamphlets as histories – 'it was the same way you are doing now, was the way we were doing these things'. By 2000 he found funding for printing from SOLO.[164] Poets and singer-songwriters found audiences for political and historical works at association meetings and school graduation ceremonies, and sold cassette tapes of their work.[165] These tapes and pamphlet book collections were often part of people's most important luggage when returning from Khartoum over 2006–11. These books, songs, and poems are the focus of Chapter 5.

4.6 Linguistic Competition and Collaboration

With this cultural work mainly produced in vernaculars, it would be easy to characterise these networks as closed and Khartoum-based ethnic circuits, a self-contained mutual audience of the wealthier and time-rich.[166] For example, within the Dinka literature encountered in this study, there is extensive cross-referencing: the writer and church worker Lino Alëu Angic Dut's book *History* references a story on page thirty-seven of the civil servant and teacher Dut Anyak Dit's *Book of Stories*, as well as directing the reader to a proverb taught in the community-produced Dinka-language Primary 4 textbook, and citing a song by Akut Kuei (The Eagle Group), a popular Dinka-language song-writing duo.[167] The 'Reading Magazine of Dinka Culture', a

---

[163] Deng Atak Abuk, in Apada, 13 July 2013; likely in part referring to Lino Alëu Angïc Dut's book *Athör Käny* [History] (Khartoum, 2005), translated and discussed in Chapter 5.
[164] Santino Akak Kuon, in Aweil, 3 July 2013.
[165] For example, the writers Job Dhurai Malou, Morwel Ater Morwel, Dut Anyak Dit, (Lieutenant Colonel) Albino Akol Akol, and Atak Deng Deng; Deng Atak Abuk, in Apada, 13 July 2013.
[166] Sommers reports that 'most Southern Sudanese IDPs and IDP education officials had little or no knowledge of education taking place in southern Sudan or beyond'. They had never heard of the New Sudan Curriculum or the SPLM Secretariat of Education. Sommers, *Islands of Education*, 241.
[167] Lino Alëu Angïc Dut, *Athör Käny*, 2, 3, 24.

church-produced photocopied pamphlet written by a group of self-taught residents of Mayo Mandela, contains Dinka proverbs also printed in the Dinka Primary 4 textbook.[168] However, this is partly because of shared spaces for this work: Dinka Cultural Society members remember one compound holding five working translation groups, including the Luo, Dinka Rek, and Latuko teams.[169] A member of the Dinka Cultural Society also noted that, from the mid-1990s into the 2000s, a prominent Dinka Rek poet and ex-civil servant chaired Rek-dialect Bible translation work in the same office as the (Malwal dialect–speaking) Cultural Society's Dinka literacy textbook drafting programme, and Joseph Modesto – a prominent Luo politician – ran a translation team in the same office space.[170]

Major figures, such as the textbook and story writer and poet Dut Anyak Dit, the song group Akut Kuei, the pan-ethnic theatre group Kwoto, and the Bari singer General Paulino, were referenced by many people in Aweil and Juba, including people with no formal education. Pan-ethnic dance groups boomed in the late 1990s, following Kwoto's example, where performers would translate and explain songs 'from Nuer or from Anuak or from Zande', generally through southern regional Arabic.[171] Stephen Ochalla explained that Kwoto organised the 'collection' of songs from older community members and family, and the boom in similar church-based dance and song groups in the mid-1990s meant he toured schools and churches as an advisor. Like local self-supporting schools, arts and literacy groups had a broad support base: one of the Akut Kuei artists cited the Abyei Youth Union and a group of university graduates and civil servants who provided financial backing, and referenced the singers Atak Deng Deng and Teresa Nyankol as supporters and artistic influences.[172] The renowned Bari-origin singer General Paulino performed with other southern musicians at graduation ceremonies, and cited as influences Nuba, Nuer, and Shilluk male and female performers; Akut

---

[168] 'Reading Magazine of Dinka Culture' (SOLO, 2004), 25, 22; Dinka Reader 4 (Khartoum, c. 2004), 12.
[169] Members of the Dinka Cultural Society, in Apada, 11 August 2013.
[170] Ibid.
[171] Stephen Ochalla, in Juba, 9 November 2013; Catherine Miller, 'Juba Arabic as a Way of Expressing a Southern Sudanese Identity in Khartoum', *Proceedings of the 4th Aida Meeting* (2000), 118.
[172] James Akec Nhial, in Juba, 10 September 2013.

4.6 Linguistic Competition and Collaboration

Kuei; and the Wau-origin artist Emmanuel Kembe, who was forced to leave Khartoum in 1994 after performing his song 'Shen-Shen' – about the day-to-day violence of life in Khartoum shanty towns – at a major Khartoum music festival.[173]

This collaboration did not necessarily prioritise or strive for some kind of pan-southern integration. Many Dinka artists and writers use 'Dinka' as a shorthand for 'southern' as well as for the pan-southern Dinka collective, often emphasising pan-Dinka moral, linguistic, and cultural strength while also referencing other southern groups and 'Black people' in general, sometimes all within the same paragraph or verse. The song group Akut Kuei are a good example of the complexity of this affiliation and focus: singing entirely in Dinka, their songs often focus on pan-Dinka unity and draw on community stories and sayings, but their content emphasises collaboration and common cause between 'col Junub' (the Dinka term for southerners) and includes references to the Shilluk, Nuer, Nuba, and the Dor (Equatorians) as 'Southerners with the same skin colour'.[174] An Akut Kuei artist emphasised that 'it was really very good' when Nuer song groups began to translate and write in parallel with Akut Kuei songs around 1998.[175] There was a spectrum of collaboration that, to most participants, was not supposed to be ethnic and insular, but worked in (and emphasised the need for) confederated efforts. As one Bari man commented:

I attended several of the Dinka events, whether they were Dinka Twic or Dinka Aweil, I attended! And I attended the people of Western Bahr el Ghazal having their cultural days, and they attended ours.... We worked as a team ... we had the same agenda which we were carrying out.... The Dinka had better methods of passing information, through songs ... the messages in the songs – the Dinkas are very crafty when it comes to them.... We needed to create more activists within the ethnic groups, but they knew that they were all southerners, and that we were actually doing the same thing, except in different languages. But it was the same.[176]

---

[173] General Paulino, in Juba, 23 October 2013; 'Emmanuel Kembe Profile', *The Sixty One* (2009).
[174] Lino Alëu Angïc Dut, ed., *Diet Akut Kuëi* [Akut Kuei Songbook], 'trial edition' (Dinka Cultural Society Committee Khartoum Workshop Programme, 2003); see Chapter 6 for a full discussion of this work.
[175] James Akec Nhial, in Juba, 10 September 2013.
[176] Jimmy Wongo, in Juba, 18 October 2013.

These people, and their wider networks of supporters and financiers, were attempting to formulate an audience both within and beyond their own personal sphere.[177] All this work wove ethno-linguistic and regional specificities with broader ideas of overarching commonalities of politics and moral community. These are Peterson and Macola's 'local historians', who are speaking both to a specificity of knowledge, such as folk tales, local histories, and dialect-specific shorthands, and trying to contextualise their ideas to a wider community. This cultural and educational work itself was a fundamental discussion over whether messages could be broader than ethnic language group, clan, and locality; whom they should include; and how.

4.7 Conclusion: Education and New Knowledge

Education was fundamental to displaced southern communities' work in wartime Khartoum. This was an education in the broadest sense, and was fundamentally reflective and political.[178] As then youth organiser Madut Tong put it, 'we were encouraging youth to go to school in Khartoum, and others to go to Jongo and into the Movement [the SPLM/A]. We would tell the youth painful points, to focus them to join the movement. We said – even if you finish your education, there are no jobs, so it's best to fight; we encouraged some to finish education and then go to fight.'[179] This intellectual war was part of displaced southern organisation across the region in this period. In his research in Kakuma refugee camp in northern Kenya, Andrew Epstein records a group of young men singing a school song for him:

> Have you seen the nation?
> It does not make itself
> Even if we get finished (from the struggle)
> One person will remain
> We will need the pen to promote it.[180]

But this self-consciousness did not clearly, directly, or passively create a straightforwardly 'southern' consciousness, a 'supra-southern-Sudanese identity replacing the former ethnic and local loyalties' of

---

[177] Peterson and Macola, *Recasting the Past*, 8.
[178] Joseph Ukel Abango, in Juba, 29 October 2013.
[179] Madut Tong, in Khartoum Gedid, Kuajok, 28 August 2013.
[180] Epstein, 'Maps of Desire', 241.

4.7 Conclusion: Education and New Knowledge

the kind Ibrahim argued existed in 1991.[181] The economic pressures, racial geography, violence, and pluralism of Khartoum created a range of complex responses within family and community life. This did not necessarily exclude their other regional neighbours. Non-southern local residents were not all considered to be the politically dominant and hostile 'Arabs'; often they were 'their own co-citizens who suffer with them from the complete negligence and hostile attitude of the "hakuma"'.[182] As the Nasir-born Nuer political activist Yïen Matthew explained,

> I finished my secondary school and joined university over there. And there are no words actually to describe this. I just had anger in me, and it was like a kind of psychological agony that was – I was undergoing, seeing my people under persecution. Allow me to call it persecution. I used to listen to the SPLM/SPLA radio, when I was very young, especially the songs, you see. All the songs, I can sing them to you if you want! In Khartoum we were also given a lot of freedom to research for ourselves. We were not confined to certain things. And that's why you see, so many of us are very mature today politically, because we were given these freedoms of research, not like normal political limits. We were not given certain political lines and just stop there.[183]

These educational projects contained a confusion of ideas and arguments about the form and future of a potential Sudanese and/or southern Sudanese community. They were a way of working out these ideas, a practical politics of community-building during war. Their content is the subject of Chapter 5.

---

[181] Ibrahim, 'The Southern Sudanese Migration to Khartoum', 13.

[182] Ibrahim, 'Southern Sudanese Women Migrants', 253–54. *Hakuma*, a southern Sudanese Arabic term, generally refers to the broad sphere of military, urban government. The term is best explained by Cherry Leonardi: '"Liberation" or Capture: Youth in between "Hakuma", and "Home" during Civil War and Its Aftermath in Southern Sudan', *African Affairs* 106, no. 424 (2007): 394.

[183] Yïen Matthew, in Juba, 10 September 2013.

5 | Intellectual Work and Political Thought on the Peripheries

So you are saying
That we are going to survive;[1]
No one will survive
If we don't leave *rueeny* behind.[2]
No one will survive if we don't forget our jealousy.
So that we unite ourselves to be one
We unite ourselves to see
This calamity that is killing us, the Southerners
It is a disaster that will spare no one,
Even if you give up your chair and say,
That you are my friend – it will not spare anyone.
Even if you change your name to Mohammed
So you pray, and take his totems as yours,
If you change your black colour –
It is a disaster that will spare no one.
This killing of Dinka, is divide and rule.[3]
Akut Kuei, 'Ka ye Bëny thëëth' (The spearmaster will regret his prophesy)

Educating and arguing over political futures and political communities needed extensive authorial and editorial work, and this chapter explores the contents of this diverse array of work. Residents of Khartoum's displaced peripheries produced an array of handwritten, photographed, printed, recorded, and re-typed work over the 1990s and 2000s. Street sellers and bookshops across the city sold and resold textbooks, reference books, pamphlets, and cassette tapes

---

[1] By being in Khartoum, away from the war; a justification for being in exile was to stay safe to help with reconstruction.
[2] 'Rueeny': deception, trickery, two-faced behaviour.
[3] Nak aburdit kou: literally, the targeting of the biggest first.

(see Figure 5.1), and people built up carefully curated photograph albums. Many southern residents brought their personal libraries back south from Khartoum in their limited luggage space after peace in 2005.[4]

This chapter focuses on the content of the self-produced works, cassettes, photocopied pamphlets, song sheets, and lyric books that I collected across the former Northern Bahr el Ghazal and Warrap states and in Juba over 2012–17. These songs, short books, and poems recorded and translated for this chapter were part of a miscellanea of photograph collections, documents, membership cards, and work and training certificates that made up the material references of interviews in South Sudan. Because of my research locations – working across the predominantly Dinka area of Northern Bahr el Ghazal because of its comparative stability over 2012 to mid-2013, and then in Juba until December 2013 – the majority of the texts and songs discussed in this chapter are written by Dinka residents. I saw (and bought) many Nuer, Dinka, Bari, and Arabic hand-printed versions and cassette tapes on sale in markets in Aweil, Wau, and Juba, but I focused on finding work explicitly referenced or written by my interviewees.[5] Because of my research time in Northern Bahr el Ghazal, these texts and songs use primarily written Dinka, as well as blended Sudanese and Southern Sudanese Arabic, a mix still used by returned Khartoum residents in the south today. I regret not having more time and ability to reach other communities' intellectual heritage from Khartoum, and am continuing to search, collect, and translate as much as I can.

Many people were similarly frustrated by how little they now had of this invaluable archive. Women had lost photograph albums, diaries, and tapes in transit; several men's libraries had been eaten by rats or destroyed by rain; video tapes were unplayable without electricity or destroyed by heat. Dhieu Kuol's book collection was partially burnt.[6]

---

[4] Stephen Ochalla, in Juba, 9 November 2013; Dia also observed this in Senegal: Dia, 'From Field to Concept', 574.
[5] See the Bibliography for a full list of texts, authors, publishing details, and translators.
[6] Dhieu Kuel, in Mayen Ulem, 4 July 2013.

My discussions often involved references to photograph collections, history textbooks, remembered documents, songs, speeches, and cassette tapes, sometimes to the point of comedy: one man, in response to a question about his employment in Khartoum, laughed and went to look up his personal history in the 'authors' section of a book he had edited in the early 2000s.[7]

I focused on trying to trace the texts, songs, and books most referenced during research. This includes the works of Dut Anyak Dit, Morwel Ater Morwel, Akut Kuei, Kwoto, General Paulino Mesaka, and Lino Alëu Angïc Dut. This included various versions of Dut's book *History*, which was popularly referred to as the 'debt book', as its focus is on 'compensation' for 'our debts from Arabs'.[8] I was given the 2005 edition, which was published as a pamphlet and whose credits note Dinka teachers as proofreaders and financial supporters. Lino Alëu, Dut Anyak, and Morwel Ater were named throughout research as influential Dinka writers, historians, and teachers in Khartoum, and I thus tried to trace them. In Kuajok, Dut Anyak provided me with the handwritten versions of nineteen of his poems composed since the early 1990s in Khartoum, which he was transcribing and translating into English himself, from his own notes and from some photocopied pamphlets. James Akec, one of the two singer-songwriters who made up the well-known song group Akut Kuei (The Eagle Group), provided me with a printed song book with twenty-four typed song lyrics spanning songs written from 1992 to 1997, with illustrations.

Several teachers, members of the Dinka Cultural Society, catechists, and part-time students provided me with various copies of books or with short bibliographies of texts they recommended that I trace. An ex-resident of Mandela neighbourhood provided copies of three texts. The first was 'The Dinka Customology of Marriage', printed by the Sudan Open Learning Organisation

---

[7] Santino Akak Kuon, in Aweil, 3 July 2013; also see Diana Coben's discussion of Gramsci's ideas of 'cultural journalism', *Radical Heroes: Gramsci, Freire and the Politics of Adult Education* (Routledge, 2013) 23.

[8] Lino Alëu Angïc Dut, *Athör Käny*, 3–4; Arou Piol Adam, in Apada village, 21 July 2013; Dhieu Kuel, in Mayen Ulem, 21 August 2013; Diing Chen Diing, in Aweil, 12 August 2013.

(SOLO), a Sudanese national NGO focusing on literacy – which printed many of these texts as basic photocopied pamphlets with a soft card cover – and which was written as a 'trial edition' by the Mayo Mandela Dinka Rek Group, made up of teachers from a Mayo Mandela school, established in 2000. It was published in 2000, and reprinted again in 2001, both times for a local Khartoum audience. The same group then wrote the pamphlet 'Dinka Displacement to Northern Sudan and Other Stories' in October 2003, assisted by the International Extension College and SOLO. By 2004, the Dinka Mayo Mandela group had expanded and published the 'Reading Magazine of Dinka Culture' – in Dinka, titled 'Kuën' (Reading) – with short passages from a variety of authors drawn from a wider consortium of reading and writing groups, based in markets and churches across Khartoum.[9]

A Dinka schoolteacher gave me the Dinka-language 'Primary 4 Reader', a vernacular school text produced on a photocopier and adapted from various sources. I was also given, variously, Dinka and Equatorian-origin song lyrics written and sung in Khartoum, including song lyrics written by southern university students in support of the SPLA and other northern and Nuba rebellions, and notes of plays, photograph collections, comedy group programmes, and tape recordings of other songs. These pamphlets and song and poetry collections are a tiny and unsystematic sample of the field of Khartoum's cultural and educational literature, including individual leaflets and reference materials, songs, and poems. In these works, the problems of constructing a pan-southern community, and the moral crises and failings of Khartoum's wartime residents, were expressed via robust self-criticism and dark humour, including improvised comedy, satirical plays, and songs.

---

[9] These contributors were Santino Atak Kuon from the group of St Paul, Khartoum; Angelo Anau Mohammed from the group of Diaar Suk (Ladies' Market), Mayo; Garang Dut Kuol from the group of Riengthii Abiem, Mandela; Joseph Agany Majak from the group of Guir Latueng Cieeng Monyjang (Dinka Cultural Development), Khartoum; Jemith Kuc Anei from the group of Choir, St Kizito; Volantino Wol Akok from the group of Writers and Readers of Mandela; and Ajok Akol Run from the Group of Writers in Mayo Mandela. The editor and convenor was Garang Apiin Akok.

Figure 5.1 Friends of Angelina selling their books of writing and poetry on a stall in Haj Yousif, c. 2000.
Reproduced with permission of Angelina Majok from her photograph album.

5.1 Texts and Translation

A methodological note on the collection, translation, and editing is needed here before turning to some key themes that cut across these texts. This chapter is built on limited and somewhat indeterminate material, because it is difficult to establish 'original' lyrics and texts, their provenance, authors, and dates for much of the material I heard of and came across.

This is because the texts produced by the mid- to late 1990s were cheaply stapled into cardboard covers with photocopied pages showing glue and scissor marks and handwritten edits. Several introductions in the texts collected during research emphasise the importance of the illustrations drawn by contributors, which are often comedic or dramatic and are photocopied into the text alongside photographs cut from human rights reports or news articles on the civil war. Some pamphlets are compilations of previous printouts or mix standard state-issued textbook pages with typed-out Amnesty International citations (see below). Many more pedagogical texts (of language and primary education, for example) contain long lists of previous printings and versions in their frontispieces. This self-publishing apparently became very popular by the early 2000s, with the growing availability of computers and printers, creating a diversity of these reprints and edited versions. Song lyrics, recordings, and poems were even harder to pin down, with the publishing and re-publishing of personal and edited collections of popular songs, as well as the songs' oral circulation in southern bars.[10] This compounds the challenge of interpreting this work here, particularly because authors worked in expressive and emotive rather than specific terminology, and used parables and metaphor (in the words of Dut Anyak Dit, 'putting a blanket on it' for minimising political risk).[11] Authors also assumed the ability to cross-reference: as Lino Alëu wrote in the preface of his Dinka-language book *History*,

---

[10] Nikkel, *Dinka Christianity*, 297, 300. One popular 1970s song by a mechanic, Jacob Jot, is quoted by Nikkel: 'We were nearly lost in the wilderness / we had disappeared far away. / ... / We had vanished in a bad place. / No temptation will have victory over us.' Ibid., 302.

[11] Dut Anyak Dit, in Kuajok, 28 September 2013.

If you want to know how to encourage people, read the story about encouragement in Book of Stories written by Dut Anyak Dit page 37. If you get it, read the 'Thokriel's mother' story. What did Thokriel's mother do to her children?[12]

These printed texts were essentially composite works and in their own words demanded further work. The introduction to 'The Dinka Customology of Marriage' states: '[This] book is selected out of books which are written by the Rek Dinka who are living in Mayo Mandela; it is written so that other books will be written too.'[13] These texts continue to evolve today. During research, people emphasised they would re-edit, re-record, and re-publish if they could find the funds in South Sudan. Their authors also emphasised that their work must be discussed, and must be maintained as a living debate, as the Dinka-language 'Reading Magazine' introduction notes:

Women and children who have gone to school should be told to read in the evening (to attend evening classes). And ... those who have attended education but did not complete it, and they are not able to attend morning lessons, must also join the evening classes in order to finish [their] education. Because if you are just reading some books and articles outside without attending classes, you think yourself someone who is educated, but those things cannot take you anywhere. This is not because it is bad to read novels and some other articles, but one has to attend classes.[14]

Songs were the most common reference point in working people's accounts of their political awakenings, as catchy and emotive shorthands, but their provenance is often hard to mark out. Fluid editing is the most obvious in song recordings and lyric pamphlets.[15] Recordings of some of the songs mentioned here can be found on YouTube and on community websites, although it is hard to know their provenance. Some songs' lyrics match exactly with the 1990s and 2000s transcribed versions used here, but others have been altered or follow different patterns of chorus and verse. For example, although I met one of the

---

[12] Lino Alëu Angïc Dut, *Athör Käny*, preface.
[13] 'The Dinka Customology of Marriage' (Khartoum, 2001).
[14] George Garang Ngong, 'Evening Teaching', in 'Reading Magazine of Dinka Culture' (SOLO, 2004).
[15] For further discussion of academic worries over mutational sources, see Angela Impey, 'The Poetics of Transitional Justice in Dinka Songs in South Sudan', *UNISCI Discussion Papers* 33 (2014): 65.

two singer-songwriters who together created Akut Kuei, a Dinka-language political song group, and who provided me with a photocopied booklet of collected song lyrics he helped to edit in Khartoum in 2002, I heard many, slightly differing versions of the same songs – and of other Akut Kuei songs not recorded in the booklet – including versions sung by the Akut Kuei singers themselves. And although Akut Kuei was made up of two men working primarily between 1992 and 1997, it was more commonly and variously described by other informants as being a large group of artists, a general phenomenon of political singer-songwriters, or a 'political party': some young men described their attempts to become the 'next generation' of Akut Kuei in Khartoum, by performing versions of Akut Kuei songs as well as their own new compositions.

These tensions over versions, authorship, and meaning continued into the translation work for this chapter, which I worked on with Joseph Tong Ngor in Aweil town, with a group of young Dinka- and Arabic-speaking young people in Kampala in 2015, and with the authors of the texts themselves, where I could find them. This produced multiple translations and multiple arguments for phrasings and interpretations. Even when the author had given me their literally authoritative version, colleagues would argue for their interpretation or an alternative pattern of chorus and verse. This reflects the actual nature of this intellectual and cultural sphere. The songs and poems recorded here were written down as pamphlets, or copied out by their authors, as part of a process of clarification, editing, and improvement that still continues today. The translations of Dut Anyak Dit's writings and Akut Kuei's songs that we produced during this research project are currently being debated by the Dinka Cultural Society, now re-formed in Aweil, with continuing disputes over translation of specific words. This chapter finds no methodological resolution to this, but instead understands the translation and transcription process for this book as part of this ongoing work.

5.2 Discursive Worlds

The southern Sudanese creative and literary world boomed across eastern and north-eastern Africa from the 1980s onwards.[16] New

---

[16] Miller, *Language Change and National Integration*, 74, 79; Nikkel, *Dinka Christianity*, 271, 276–77.

cassette recording technology, literacy and school projects, the rise of cheap photocopiers, and the posed photography studio (with its props and backdrops) allowed more people than ever to document and illustrate their wartime worlds. But this was not a new creative field. These artists, writers ,and their audiences were building on (and referencing) vast oral historical resources and creative histories, including generations of parables, folk-tales, dance beats and song lyrics, and oral histories.

Only a tiny amount of this intellectual sphere was incorporated into emerging print cultures by the 1940s (and print and online text culture in South Sudan is still only a small part of this wider discourse today). But urban spaces like Khartoum were key sites for new print opportunities. By the 1940s, handmade pamphlets, flyers, and 'wall newspapers' (one-page posters) were circulating in towns and schools, alongside a limited circulation of newspapers, religious texts, and imported publications. 'Candour', a hand-written weekly wall newspaper at the prestigious Rumbek Senior Secondary School, appeared in 1951. By the mid-1950s, Rumbek also had the 'Spark', and the University of Khartoum had the English-language wall newspapers 'Negro' and 'The Observer', with Othwonh Sabino and Ezboni Mondiri as contributors.[17] These drew on socialist ideas and texts circulating at Rumbek Senior Secondary, and ideas from African nationalist movements and pan-Africanism by the 1960s. In 1965 Joseph Garang revived the Sudanese Communist party's English-language daily newspaper 'Advance'.[18] In his speech to an open audience of southern residents of Khartoum North on 10 April 1965, convened by the Southern Front Executive Committee and recorded in 'The Vigilant' newspaper, Hilary Logali recalled how with his fellow students

we began to read about such names as Dr [Nnamdi] Azikwe, about Dr Aggrey of Achimota and the Pan African movement... Soon such people like Dr Nkrumah came into the scene and his speeches were food for thought for the Southerners.... I hope that I have sufficiently shown where we belong. I think and believe that our national movement in the South has its intellectual origins in the great Pan-African movement and in the great

---

[17] Howell, 'Political Leadership and Organisation in the Southern Sudan', 142.
[18] Kuyok Abol Kuyok, *South Sudan: The Notable Firsts* (AuthorHouse, 2015).

continental movement for liberation from domination from anyone who wanted and who wants to be our master.[19]

This literary field continued to expand in the 1970s, particularly after the peace agreement in 1972. Key textbooks had (according to John Howell in 1978) 'unusual influence', including T. R. Batten's series *Tropical Africa in World History*.[20] People who were refugees and Anya Nya fighters in the Congo and northern Uganda in the 1960s and '70s emphasise the importance of copies of *A Short History of the Sudan* by Mandour el Mahdi (published by Oxford University Press in 1965) in political and historical debates. In 1974, Peter Adwok Nyaba became co-author of 'The Alternative', 'the voice of Southern progressives, a leftist outfit with a sizeable following among the students' at the University of Khartoum. Atem Yaak Atem wrote for 'The Mirror', the voice of the African National Front student group in Khartoum. George Maker Benjamin, Arop Madut Arop, and many other later SPLM/A propagandists were involved in the 'Nile Mirror' newspaper, the 'Heritage' magazine, and Radio Juba until the late 1980s. Marxist and anti-government leaflets by Lokurnyang Lado's Southern Sudan Patriotic Front circulated in secondary schools and among university students in Khartoum and Upper Nile.[21] Socialist literature (some of which was brought by students travelling to Western and Eastern Europe on scholarships) continued to circulate through the 1980s through towns and schools across Sudan.[22] Mohammed Ahmed recorded (with concern) how churches had 'recruited large numbers of sons of depressed regions as sellers of books in the corners of the United Nations Square and on the markets of Khartoum North and Omdurman', selling pamphlets at 'economical prices' to 'families and children in the peripheral areas', some of which dealt with inflammatory topics such as women's rights and the history of slavery in Sudan.[23] Egyptian and British newspapers were circulated; copies of Reuters bulletins were shared by employees in post rooms; and pamphlet culture expanded.[24]

---

[19] 'Logali Addresses Southerners', *The Vigilant*, 10 April 1965, CAR A/86/21/1/ 119-20.
[20] Howell, 'Political Leadership and Organisation in the Southern Sudan', 112.
[21] Kuyok, *South Sudan*.   [22] Ibid.
[23] Mohammed Ahmed, 'Christian Missionary Activity', 16.
[24] Elena Vezzadini, 'The 1924 Revolution: Hegemony, Resistance, and Nationalism in the Colonial Sudan', PhD dissertation, University of Bergen (2008), 118–20.

This abbreviated history of southern Sudanese print cultures should not be overstated. Most people beginning literary and creative careers in Khartoum in the early 1990s were not wealthy, were not from formally educated families, were new to publishing, and were mostly disconnected from this generally middle-class print history. As the editor Achirin Nuoi Mou introduces the 'Reading Magazine of Dinka Culture': 'The authors of this book do not know whether they are great writers, because many of them have just started writing and reading. They have written these books without hope that they would continue.'[25]

In discussing their work, most people explained that they had access to fragments of this field – to some Sudanese and BBC radio, some books (such as el Mahdi's *A Short History*), copies of the Sudanese state curriculum, and some newspapers and religious texts. Sudanese media was also increasingly surveilled and embattled by the mid-1990s, with repeated newspaper closures and arrests of journalists including Bona Malwal, Alfred Taban, and Nhial Bol. After the closure of SPLA Radio in Addis Ababa after the fall of the Derg regime in 1991, Khartoum residents had much more limited access to SPLA speeches, organisational information, and propaganda (although there was a strong oral information circuit about the progress of the war). Marc Sommers notes that in 2005, the southern Sudanese teachers and educational workers he interviewed had 'little or no knowledge of education taking place in southern Sudan or beyond', and had never heard of the New Sudan Curriculum or the SPLM Secretariat of Education.[26] Many southern publications such as 'Heritage' magazine, 'Southern Sudan Bulletin', and the 'SPLM/A Update' operated from Nairobi and the United Kingdom, and copies that reached Khartoum did not seem to circulate far. And there was a real risk of having even innocuous documents, as Sommers found when trying to give out past reports on education planning in 2005 in Khartoum.[27] Circulation of information was limited because of the dangers of security services targeting anyone as suspected SPLA insurgents. Dhieu Lual, by then a

---

[25] Achirin Nuoi Mou, 'Reading Magazine of Dinka Culture' (SOLO, 2004).
[26] Sommers, *Islands of Education*, 241.
[27] Ibid., 32; personal accounts were also given by John Gau Riak, in Aweil, 28 June 2013; and Nhial Bol, in Juba, 18 October 2013.

court clerk and part-time teacher, remembered newspapers holding printouts of international news about Sudan as 'carton news' at the *Khartoum Monitor* office, called that because it was stored in a box to be read on the premises and shared by word of mouth.[28]

For Elena Vezzadini, 'uneducated political activists' acting in or commenting on Sudanese national politics and history have had 'very few channels to express their own views of the past'; at least on English- and Arabic-language national platforms.[29] But the artists and authors of new histories, textbooks, pamphlets, and lyric books – including some of the writers discussed in this chapter – were also not necessarily aiming to speak to this wider news circuit. Many authors were explicitly anti-elitist and focused on their own, local audience.[30] Their (avowed) egalitarian intentions are most obvious in the acknowledgements and introductions to textbooks and histories. Two books' editors emphasised the accessibility of authorship: the conclusion to 'The Dinka Customology of Marriage' states of its writers, 'their highest level of study is this: twenty four people have read other languages plus Dinka, and ten people read only Dinka language ... One person has reached high school level.'[31] The same book calls for new members to 'join the group of your brothers, and we move forward, preaching the culture of reading and writing together'.[32]

5.3 Brave Writing

This writing, publishing, and archiving was very risky. Dinka Cultural Society members noted that before the mid-1990s, 'no one started to develop the history ... about how people [came] to Khartoum. Because people were afraid [laughs].'[33] This publishing and archiving was an attempt at laying out and giving substance and definition to histories,

---

[28] Dhieu Kuel, in Mayen Ulem, 4 July 2013.   [29] Vezzadini, 'Spies, Secrets', 65.
[30] This is articulated most explicitly by a (potentially self-deluding, but still notable) comment by a student on a scholarship to Wisconsin: 'It is not my ambition to go as far the academic title of the doctor of Philosophy. This kind of degree tries to isolate you from the people where you can be effective.... I must go back [to Sudan]. Everything is not in our own hands.' Zacharia Deng to Bishop Eduardo Mason, Stout State University, Wisconsin, 11 June 1971, CAR A/104/37/4/7.
[31] 'The Dinka Customology of Marriage' (Khartoum, 2001), 13.   [32] Ibid., 3.
[33] Members of the Dinka Cultural Society, in Apada, 11 August 2013.

debates, and community changes, as 'acts of persistence' in the face of silencing, lost stories, and unrecorded histories.[34]

But this work has often not been studied as such. Vernacular community work – particularly Dinka songs – has broadly been studied either as ethnographic evidence of a particular society, such as the work of Francis Deng, or as general local comment on war and state crisis: as a way of 'resistance' to maintain an ethnic identity and a specific sense of community until 'hometime', a standard line in Sudanese scholarship on urban migration.[35] Education research has focused on formal education systems and curriculums, where this form of self-publishing and textbook editing has been interpreted as essentially anti-state and against 'Islamic influence'.[36] These interpretations are valid, but understanding this creative work as a reaction to displacement from a rural and ethnic 'home' and against Arab-Islamic state impositions is too narrow.[37] The dominant language of these texts is ethnic because of the use of vernaculars to describe common historical experience: their authors often use idioms as generalisable, often-ambiguous demonstrations of common knowledge, and as a means of euphemising, variously, political critique, direct threats to the regime, or information about the war, for example: 'the eagles have landed on the road', or 'the doctor is coming with his medicine'.[38]

While 'future return and present-day resistance to the Islamic state' is a convenient shorthand explanation, it glosses a far broader understanding of these complex projects. These many projects were

---

[34] 'Reading Magazine of Dinka Culture' (SOLO, 2004) 3; Shevaun E. Watson, '"Good Will Come of This Evil": Enslaved Teachers and the Transatlantic Politics of Early Black Literacy', *College Composition and Communication* 61, no. 1 (2009): 70.

[35] Francis Mading Deng, *The Dinka and Their Songs* (Clarendon Press, 1973); *Dinka Folktales: African Stories from the Sudan* (Africana, 1974); Nikkel, *Dinka Christianity*; 'Jieng "Songs of Suffering" and the Nature of God', *Anglican and Episcopal History* 71, no. 2 (2002): 223–40; Bert Remijsen et al., *A Collection of Dinka Songs* (University of Edinburgh Press, 2012); Impey, 'The Poetics of Transitional Justice'. For this interpretation of 'education as resistance,' see Sommers, *Islands of Education*, 243; see also Breidlid, 'Sudanese Migrants in the Khartoum Area'; Anders Breidlid, 'Education in the Sudan: The Privileging of an Islamic Discourse', *Compare* 35, no. 3 (2005): 247–63; Breidlid, 'Sudanese Images of the Other'. For a summary of this literature, see Leonardi, *Dealing with Government*, 5–7.

[36] Breidlid, 'Education in the Sudan'; Sommers, *Islands of Education*, 247.

[37] For example, see Miller et al., *Arabic in the City*, 21.

[38] That is, Dr John Garang de Mabior, leader of the SPLM/A.

5.3 Brave Writing

fundamentally internal, focused not on the grand Other of the Sudanese regime but on the various politically dubious or ignorant edges of what was considered as the community. If these are studied only as forms of resistance to the Sudanese Islamic state, then these texts and songs often appear to just present a relatively straightforward patriarchal ethnic nationalism, policing and judging women, and eulogising broad-brush ideas of lost community lands. They do this, but they also do other things; the majority of songs written and performed in Khartoum, for instance, were about love.[39]

This chapter seeks to take a broad view of the content of this work. In the interests of space, it looks beyond the immediate familial and interpersonal: all these texts contain questions about personal honesty, love, sexual relationships, forms of respect between members of the community, and the challenges of homosexuality, female circumcision, and the risks of blood poisoning through scarification, heavy drinking while pregnant, and skin bleaching (concerns detailed in Chapter 3).

But these pamphlets, songs, and poems were also seeking to highlight competing political philosophies; critiques of their current economic, political, and social circumstances and conflicts; and ideas of the future, agreeing with Stuart Hall that the key question in a world of movement is 'How can people live together in difference?'[40] This was a work that built beyond ethnic nationalism. By the 1970s, for example, John Howell noted with surprise that even among the Dinka (whom he considered 'the most conservative of all southern people'), '"jur mathiang" ("other people") was sometimes replaced by "Wuok koc col": "we Black people"'.[41] One Dinka-language writer explained this conversation as centring on 'the four things to be put in mind ... if people want to be in peace: 1. Truth (yic), 2. Equality (thongnhom), 3. Love (nhier), 4. Freedom (Nhom laau)'.[42] The truths, equalities, love, and freedom these texts detail is not coherent, but evidences a discussion over the possible shape and extent of a political community of

---

[39] James Akec Nhial, in Juba, 8 and 10 September 2013; Atak Deng Deng, in Aweil, 17 August 2013; Stephen Ochalla, in Juba, 9 November 2013; General Paulino, in Juba, 23 October 2013.
[40] Stuart Hall, 'Rethinking the Multicultural Question', a conversation with Nira Yuval-Davis, presented at 'Racisms, Sexisms and Contemporary Politics of Belonging' conference, London, August 2004.
[41] Howell, 'Political Leadership and Organisation in the Southern Sudan', 256.
[42] Santino Atak Kon, 'Peace in the World', 'Reading Magazine of Dinka Culture' (SOLO, 2004), section 14.

'Black people', of 'southerners', and of 'brothers' in a common political, historical, and cultural experience of being exploited, marginalised, and peripheral 'Sudanese'. This work, for some people, was the explication of John Garang's nebulous idea of New Sudan.[43]

5.4 Painful Histories

Common across this work is the expression of pain. Despite its attempts to speak to and about the past and future of a political community, this literacy and educational work was not meant to be comfortable or positive. One chapter of Lino Alëu's *History* is titled 'My heart Burns with Sadness throughout the Day and Night', and Dut Anyak writes

> We hear the old words
> We know they repeat themselves
> And they hurt in our hearts when we think on them.[44]

Community-run literary and artistic education was difficult and emotionally draining work: the texts, poems, and songs drawn on for this chapter all directly address the history of pain and loss of their audiences, and explicitly demand emotional and intellectual self-reflection and response. Isolation, loss of family and friends, and the individualising brutality of city life are recorded across songs and poetry in the 1990s and 2000s. Dut Anyak's July 2000 poem 'Manh cïn nhom tëde' (A wandering child) details life in Khartoum:

> My mother goes to work,
> When she came back,
> She saw the smoke from a distance.
> Our shelter is being burnt,
> It was lit with fire.
> The s[h]ack, our house is burnt down.
> They don't like us to be near people –
> They isolate us.

---

[43] For a full discussion of the history of the idea of New Sudan within the SPLM/A, see Øystein H. Rolandsen, *Guerrilla Government: Political Changes in the Southern Sudan during the 1990s* (Nordic Africa Institute, 2005), 118–22.

[44] Dut Anyak Dit, 'Diet e muooc' (Bravery song"), written c. August 2004, Khartoum; the song's translator noted that this pain is meant to act as encouragement. Dut Anyak Dit, in Kuajok, 27 August and 28 September 2013.

5.4 Painful Histories

> We people who are not needed,
> They isolate us.
> They isolate us in Ras Satan –
> and Jabarona,
> They say a hen is better than us.[45]

As Lino Alëu explained in his preface, 'What is happening now all the Black people are in despair in this war time. They even forgot their good future of the lands of the South.'[46] General Paulino's song 'Nan Be Kolo Jongo' (I am crazy) contains a similar lament:

> I became crazy from being lonely
> I am tired of staying alone,
> No one to comfort me or even to heal my wounds,
> The wounds inside me, do you remember me?[47]

The Akut Kuei song 'Ka Col Ater Cie Ke Yeku Puöl Yok Muonyjän' (The Dinka don't give up the fight) includes the lines

> It is paining me, it is paining me if I think of all this destruction
> I don't sleep
> I wish I could divide my heart
> To divide it amongst all the people
> It pains my heart,
> I wish I could divide it among all the southerners.[48]

These records of pain and experience are part of a wider global history of literacy work among marginalised and abused people. Shevaun Watson, writing of African American slavery and post-redemption literacy work, emphasised the 'ambivalence' of literacy, as a means both of self-determination as well as 'indoctrination [and] disillusionment'; she notes that literacy brought alienation, dissatisfaction, and frustration.[49] But this pain was important, both for recording an accurate emotional history of wartime experience and society and for building a full and critical understanding of the political system that created and maintained this suffering and exploitation. The

---

[45] They kept chickens in the place where they were displaced from.
[46] Lino Alëu Angïc Dut, *Athör Käny*.
[47] Khartoum, 15 July 2000. Translated by Melanie Itto.
[48] Written c. 1994–95, Khartoum.
[49] Watson, 'Good Will Come of This Evil', 68.

songwriters of Akut Kuei agreed. Their song 'Rïnydan Junub' (This southern generation) is a cry of masculine anger:

> This southern generation,
> Is the angry generation – all of us.
> The generation of Wau is annoyed – all of us.
> The generation of Juba is angry – all of us.
> The generation of Malakal is furious – all of us.
> And being always angry makes you a man
> And being always angry makes you a man
> If you're a man who is not enraged
> Then you are not a man
> Then you are not a man
> Whoever doesn't help[50]
> Is not a man
> Is not a man
> Where will you have a say?
> You don't have a say in this southern land of ours.
> You don't have a say in this southern land of ours.[51]

Malcolm X – whose ideas were invoked by several men during interviews – also agreed that this rage should push a person into action: 'embracing our suffering is key to our resisting it. We should not wallow in our pain, or be consumed by it. We must use it as the driving force to push us into building a radical alternative. Once we get too comfortable, we stop struggling, but struggle is the only route to freedom.'[52]

Dhieu Kuol, at the time pursuing secondary school studies and working as an office clerk, explained to me how these songs 'saved the southerners, very much, because they touched all types of life'. With Joseph Tong, who helped me translate some of the texts here, the two now middle-aged men explained how these various literary and musical projects were about both morale and morals: 'especially we the students, when you are hungry, you have no money – you remember! The song to create the morality for you, so that you can [go on].' They sang and quoted me lyrics from songs I then managed to track down

---

[50] That is, in the fight. [51] Rïnydan Junub ('This southern generation').
[52] Quoted in Kehinde Andrews, *Back to Black: Retelling Black Radicalism for the 21st Century* (Zed Books, 2018) 223, note 12.

5.4 Painful Histories

and cite here, including the Akut Kuei song 'Alany Deng Nhial Arom' (The majesty of [William] Deng Nhial will be taken) (see below), which demanded that the listener maintain dignity in the face of abuses and poverty, turning Khartoum's racism against supposedly backwards and undignified displaced people on its head. During a chat with me and Joseph Ngor, Dhieu explained that Deng Nhial

> said that he will not be captured by the north! Whenever, whatever they used to do, he said that they will not succeed! [Laughs] [Sings] – he said that, the Black man [*ran col*] is really suffering. That is a question – *guop pial? Ce ran col?* Who is unlucky like a Black man? In the chorus, all tribes, you sing their names, and then you end up in Alany Deng Nhial Arom. The majesty of Deng Nhial – is going to be taken. Yes, he's wanting to tell people to go, come outside to rebel to take the authority from the north. You want to remind the southerners about the situation which is taking place. And even he talks of food – he said you eat the food of the big people, and your – [Joseph: like official food] Yes, you go with officials who support – [Joseph: and the majesty of Deng Nhial is taken away. That means that people are just eating with Arabs, they don't think of what is going on in the south.]
>
> ... some of these songs, we used to put them in cassette, so that you can put them on, wear them in headphones, yes, you can take them with you. [Joseph: to keep on reminding you.] Yes, yes, they can remind you.[53]

By invoking common Blackness, wartime suffering, ethnic identity, and southern-ness, this work did not consistently or solely set out a 'southern Sudanese' communal identity, or even argue that southern-ness should take a kind of precedence over ethnic, regional, or racial affiliations. The historical and political content of this work was not (or not only) pushing a clear 'South Sudan nation-state' political community. Instead, these texts and their authors encouraged a consciousness of broad affiliations of Black political and historical consciousness, and emphasised the critical discussion of the nature of Black, southern and Sudanese identification, and the importance of self-reflection in this context; as Dut Anyak's poem 'Kongku röt deet' (We must study our souls) says,

> We must study our souls, and come together
> We first study ourselves, then we will become one

---

[53] Dhieu Kuel, in Mayen Ulem, 4 July 2013.

196   *Intellectual Work and Political Thought on the Peripheries*

> Let's not be misled by blackness
> But let's be united by facts.[54]

Lino Alëu wrote that knowledge is to 'understand our hearts', to 'cooperate', and to 'select out those with poor vision among us'.[55] The most obvious manifestation of this focus on practical education are the frequent tests, questions, and mottos strung through the books. These are not straightforward questions but demands for critical thought:

Questions:

1. What is the lesson we learn from the above?
2. Is there anybody who has ever done this?[56]

The pamphlet 'The Dinka Customology of Marriage' has a revision section with twenty-two questions on the content of the book, including 'which things are not in order in Khartoum?'[57] The story pamphlet 'Dinka Displacement' demanded that 'a person ... read [and] analyse,' and 'think about [the stories] carefully'.[58] This should be a collaborative education, according to the 'Reading Magazine': 'if you are just reading some books and articles outside without attending classes, you think yourself someone who is educated, but those things cannot take you anywhere'.[59]

These exams could be seen as tests of character, not knowledge. Their central demand for personal and collective responsibility and self-regulation is common across histories of southern Sudanese political thought.[60] This demand is commonly conceptualised in the Dinka texts and songs here as *yic*, commonly translated or co-opted into

---

[54] Dit, 'Kongku röt deet' (We must study our souls), written in Khartoum on 6 December 2003.
[55] Lino Alëu Angïc Dut, *Athör Käny*, 12.
[56] 'Reading Magazine of Dinka Culture', 13; also see Lino Alëu Angïc Dut, *Athör Käny*, 10; 'Reading Magazine of Dinka Culture', 13.
[57] 'The Dinka Customology of Marriage', 12.
[58] Mayo Mandela Circle, 'Dinka Displacement to the Northern Sudan and Other Stories', sections 4 and 10.
[59] 'Reading Magazine of Dinka Culture', 12.
[60] Cherry Leonardi, 'The Poison in the Ink Bottle: Poison Cases and the Moral Economy of Knowledge in 1930s Equatoria, Sudan', *Journal of Eastern African Studies* 1, no. 1 (2007): 34–56; Tuttle, 'Life Is Prickly'.

English as 'right' or 'the right'. Godfrey Leinhardt translates *yic* as 'truth which is arrived at and stated by a communal intention'.[61] Cherry Leonardi's discussion of 'rights' focuses on its application for advocacy and 'claiming one's right', an educated person's 'creolised and multivalent term, an interpretation both of Western notions of legal rights and of vernacular concepts like yic in Dinka'; she defines *yic* as an objective truth 'which transcends the subjective truths of disputants'.[62] Here, in Dinka and English (used by both Dinka and Equatorian people), these terms go beyond claim-making into explanations of political consciousness and self-management, a 'right' and 'rights' that are understood through this educational work: 'when you are exposed to education then ... you realise your right'.[63]

Realising this right and responsibility required the painful knowledge presented in this work, which spurred people to not lose hope or become immersed in day-to-day economic and leisure activities. Dhieu explained:

[These songs were] enlightening the southerners to remember the situation they are [in]. Because ... some of them have even given up.... And because of this despair – this song was the one [to] restore the hope.... The singer wanted to remind people that if you behave like this now, then what Deng Nhial died for is going to become zero. You're supposed to be aware ... you eat the food of important people here in Khartoum – and majesty of Deng Nhial is going to be taken. You walk in the street like free people – but the majesty of Deng Nhial ... which means: he wants to tell them that even though you walk freely inside the streets of Khartoum, you are still enslaved, you are a stranger here.[64]

5.5 A Political Education

These texts and songs emphasise the importance of cultural knowledge and moral standards, but they do not necessarily promote (or do not only promote) a return to 'ethnic traditional' values, or demand that

---

[61] Godfrey Lienhardt, *Divinity and Experience: The Religion of the Dinka* (Oxford University Press, 1961), 139, 247–48; for the Nuer equivalent, see Douglas H. Johnson, 'Judicial Regulation and Administrative Control: Customary Law and the Nuer, 1898–1954', *Journal of African History* 27, no. 1 (1986): 59.
[62] Leonardi, *Dealing with Government*, 101.
[63] Riing Riing Lual, in Aweil, 3 September 2013.
[64] Dhieu Kuel, in Mayen Ulem, 21 August 2013.

everyone aim for westernised education and enlightenment through modern employment and urban success. These artists, writers, and teachers intended to inspire a very specific type of political education, in Paulo Freire's term, focused on critical consciousness. All the texts and songs I encountered in research explicitly criticised those whom Cherry Leonardi calls 'modern, urban intellectuals': the Black and/or southern Sudanese individuals who presented themselves as superior to 'tribal' things, who called Garang a 'savage', or who criticised the continuing war. These men were criticised in turn as being ultimately uneducated – despite their university degrees – and focused on 'eating'.[65] This vocabulary is directly referent to broader discourses of eating and the politics of the belly in African political discourse, with this language of eating resources, power, and social futures meshed here with the Dinka taboo against selling cows for food.[66] 'Eating' is a common metaphor both for individualistic greed and for politically ignorant action across this Khartoum literature, for example, in Akut Kuei's songs 'Anyoot yic' (It has not started yet) and 'Abuk jal tïng, ku abuk jal tïng' (We shall see – we'll see), the latter of which includes the lines

> Now that we are like the ticks on the cows
> The tick that sucks at the cow
> Now that we are like the fly on the meat
> ...
> It is food that is killing us,
> It is eating that we are fighting.
> We were made to fight
> And you agree to go and fight with your brother
> Just because of food
> ...
> Do not sell your right because of food –
> Don't sell your land for food,
> Don't waste your lives for food.

Their texts argue for a critical self-awareness based on rewritten community histories, aiming to promote an understanding of the individual

---

[65] Leonardi, *Dealing with Government*, 148.
[66] Most notably, Jean-Francois Bayart, *The State in Africa: The Politics of the Belly* (Longman, 1993).

5.5 A Political Education

and communal place of southern people in Sudanese political and historical context. The content of this education, and the type of knowledge taught, would need to stop someone from being fooled – in the common language of these texts and songs, being blind.[67] Many of these songs and texts involve cynical, wry, or sarcastic comment on Khartoum circumstances, asserting a high level of knowledge about how the world worked. This literary community were arguing for a 'real education' based on intra-community dialogue and a critical factual basis for self-knowledge in context: 'when you see yourself, you can find that you are already marginalised'.[68] These cultural activists were thus indirectly disproving James Scott's claim 'that subalterns always perceive clearly the reality of elite domination'.[69] They argued instead that this understanding required work.

Thus a theme of all of this work was the preservation of internal integrity, a personal inner 'front', and a core of social and moral responsibility and understanding, expressed through variously translated ideas of 'the right', 'knowledge', 'respect', and 'heart'. This was not necessarily self-definition against a set (Arab, northern Sudanese) other; this literature was frequently concerned with critiquing a growing individualism and the need for personal control in the pressures of the Khartoum economy and geography. This was based on the common fear of 'getting lost', including in the day-to-day demands and opportunities of city life. These texts and stories are punctuated by demands for self-awareness and factual knowledge, and their direct questions to their audience – as actual quiz tests or as rhetoric – tried to set the terms and content of this self-awareness. This is probably best exemplified by Dut Anyak Dit's poem 'Adhuöm Akan!' (There is a hole!), written in February 1992 as he saw displaced people settle into the life of the city among northern Sudanese residents:[70]

---

[67] For example, Dut Anyak's poem Panda ('Our Country'):

> The blind man can now see
> Days are not the same, the blind man is throwing away his walking stick

[68] Deng Atak Abuk, in Apada, 13 July 2013; Arou Piol Adam, in Apada village, 22 July 2013.

[69] James C. Scott, *The Art of Not Being Governed: An Anarchist History of Upland Southeast Asia* (Yale University Press, 2009); *Weapons of the Weak*; see Fletcher's problematisation of 'resistance studies', *Beyond Resistance*, viii.

[70] Dut Anyak Dit, writing in Khartoum, 25 February 1992.

> Have you just forgotten –
> look at the struggle that is going on.
> Can't you see the blood that has not stopped being shed –
> Have you forgotten –
> how many people that are not with us.
> ...
> We are not one, know your people, the peace is yet to come.
> Don't just forget,
> know your type[71] –
> The peace is far.
> The children and the women that were abducted are not there,
> No peace.
> Even if you meet and laugh,
> it is divide and rule.[72]
> Thousands are watching,
> Don't just forget, peace is like a star.
> ...
> Even if he laughs with you, the truth is the bone[73]
> and the heart is a stranger.
> Even if you are friends and share things,
> what you say – he doesn't do.
> Even if you are friends, it is friendship between hyenas and dogs
> He knows you as a leaf that moves with the air,
> you are light –
> You are just that water hyacinth that floats on water,
> you are light.[74]

These moral messages were lodged in histories and emotive songs and poetry. These were not explicitly ethnic projects but were aimed at reframing and challenging the standard hegemonic order of Sudanese 'national history', re-casting and redefining whose history was national. Their often contradictory or ambiguous language about the linguistic, local, regional, racial, and political lines and layers of community inclusion were arguments about the parameters of alternative political collectives. The rest of this chapter will focus on the content and aims of this work Freire calls 'conscientization,' as an attempt to

---

[71] Race, people, also spelled *kuatdu*.
[72] Literally, 'they are killing the strongest first'.
[73] Just seeing smiling teeth is no proof of inner feelings.
[74] That is, worthless to him.

5.5 A Political Education

create mutual and critical self-awareness.[75] Compared with formal child education and literacy programmes, these writers held a very different understanding of basic skills.

These texts primarily emphasise the importance not of a broad westernised liberal schooling but of a comprehensive and critical worldview.[76] This was explicitly anti-hegemonic historical work, challenging the narratives put forward by the state, as detailed in Chapter 4. Arou Piol specifically collected a small library of books that 'talk about history, and the politics'.[77] Dut Anyak's poems frequently deal with this erasure of history and truth-telling, including 'Yic acie kuöt nyin bï lëu' (You can't bury the truth):

> You've put truth aside
> And you begin blaming the native people
> That they mismanaged the land.
> That's why we have these grudges like this.
> ...
> The truth you are denying today,
> You will get to know it when the Black people have broken the bondage.[78]

Rebecca Lorins details the theatre group Kwoto's play *Warnish* (Varnish, about street children – *shamasha*, children of the sun), including the children's quest to tell their history against the dominant History – personified by one of the *shamasha* – who leads them from an idealised precolonial world into 'a time when there is no History'. History cannot remember what happens after the arrival of the Arab people, and begins to drink heavily to cope, as the children become stressed over this loss of the past.

As a group, they declare: 'The face of our dangerous history', and 'the truth of the homeless, who know no mother nor father nor country', and 'Varnish the History'. The play ends with a warning … 'You will never find a substitute to the Varnish. Nothing there except a lot of dust. Nothing. Varnish.'[79]

---

[75] Paulo Freire, *Literacy: Reading the Word & the World* (Routledge, 1987).
[76] 'Primary 4 Reader' (Khartoum, c. 2004); also Santino Atak Kon, 'Equality', in 'Reading Magazine of Dinka Culture', 10: 'If one wants to be the only educated one, and others with whom they are sharing the country are not educated, then there will be no peace.'
[77] Arou Piol Adam, in Apada village, 21 July 2013.
[78] Written in Khartoum, 25 May 2004.   [79] Lorins, 'Inheritance', 231–32.

The majority of these texts and songs focus on old regional histories, writing southerners into a longer history of Sudan, or recording their own subaltern of the civil wars. This history writing was so important that a research methodologies section is included in the Dinka 'Primary 4 Reader'.[80] The Reader details a history of the Nubian kingdom, Merowe, Greek migration, and the gradual arrival of Christianity, but emphasises that

> The history of the people who have lived in your land where there are black people – we do not know it. There are no records in the books, but we have them on rocks and caves.... The stories of our grandparents are of a few years past. Which means we have only discovered the history of the people who stayed at the riverside where Khartoum is now.... There are no records, we do not have remains, the words they spoke orally are not from long ago and they are unclear.[81]

The Reader suggests future archaeological projects will reconstruct this hidden peripheral Sudanese history:

> We shall also get to know things from other tribes through remains which are left and things which are covered by the soil long ago. You find remains of those people when we try to dig the land, and they remind us about those older generations. Others show us where we have built up our houses.[82]

The pamphlet 'Dinka Displacement to the Northern Sudan' begins with a history of the Northern Bahr el Ghazal famine, with the opening sentence, 'What took them away from their country?' It then details the start of the famine in 1985, what people were forced to eat, including plant names, and the route through Meiram, when events were so terrible that 'a person who died on the road can be overlooked'. This was so that children could know 'how you came to northern Sudan,' and so that others would '[not] forget all the past and present events'.[83]

These history books had, therefore, very different foci and timelines – both to national history textbooks and also in comparison to southern elite histories of the 1983–2005 war. Teachers emphasised this alternative history as a fundamental part of their curriculum: 'these were the things we taught in the school, and these were also the things that

---

[80] 'Primary 4 Reader', 7.   [81] Ibid., 8–10.   [82] Ibid., 10.
[83] Mayo Mandela Circle, 'Dinka Displacement to the Northern Sudan and Other Stories', section 1.

5.5 A Political Education

made us sad'.[84] Lino Alëu's book *History* listed the presidents and prime ministers of Sudan and then stated: 'all these presidents had oppressed Black people and sold them'. His history of (specifically) South Sudan starts by writing 'every Black' into the struggle for independence in 1956, and includes the Closed Districts order controlling southerners' movements in the 1920s, a short mention of the 1947 Juba Conference, details of the southern regional administration in the 1970s, and a section on the Babanusa and Daein massacres.[85] He details the reasons for Kerubino Kuanyin Bol's mutiny at Bor that sparked the SPLM/A rebellion, including the lack of equality in Sudan's administration and education, the lack of regional development, and violence against Black people in general.[86] Texts and songs also referenced international texts, such as Lino Alëu's reprinted first-person accounts of atrocities compiled by an international human rights organisation (probably Human Rights Watch), as well as popular sustained metaphors from SPLA propaganda – such as Dr John Garang's medical 'needles' for AK47s in one Akut Kuei song – and traditional songs and stories, such as Dut Anyak's shorthand reference to an Aweil-area Dinka war song.[87]

Songs included references to a continuous history of slavery, and many of the books found in Aweil included photocopied images of atrocities, such as the back-page image of the 'Primary 4 Reader' of shackled men, and Lino Alëu's *History* including a picture titled 'abducted children', and one of men with amputated hands.[88] There was significant power in articulating experiences of forced labour, mass violence and abductions in villages in the south, and labour

---

[84] Arou Piol Adam, in Apada village, 22 July 2013.
[85] Lino Alëu Angïc Dut, *Athör Käny*, 16–17, 23.   [86] Ibid., 17.
[87] Ibid., 19; Akut Kuei, 'Piny cï Deng nök' (The land that killed Deng); Dut Anyak Dit, 'Diet e muooc' (Bravery songs). Similar referencing is observed by Cabral and Martin-Jones, 'Writing the Resistance', 159.
[88] Lino Alëu Angïc Dut, *Athör Käny*, 32, 27; Dut Anyak Dit, 'Wek cää bï ben tïng' (I will not see you again):

> This slave peg that we've been tethered to,
> The black race wants to uproot it
> ...
> The people among us still hammer the peg further
> They will not manage it.
> The hammer they are using is being taken from their hands.

exploitation in Khartoum specifically as slavery. Lino Alëu's *History* emphasises the continuities of slavery as a common experience for, variously, Dinka people, southern people, and Black people in the Sudan since the 1800s to the present day, and notes international authority on this:

> The Human Rights Watch has conveyed the message to Dinka youth, women and children that many people have been abducted by Baggara and categorised them into two:
> 1. Groups of men and women to work on their farms as slaves
> 2. Groups of other young men and children to take care of their cattle as slave shepherds.[89]

The Dinka 'Primary 4 Reader' includes a cut-out photograph photocopied into the text, of uncertain provenance, depicting two handcuffed men and captioned 'slavery in Wau where people are chained'.[90]

These texts also included extensive detail about the recent history of displacement and settlement in Khartoum itself. The pamphlet 'The Dinka Customology of Marriage' details the background of disputed local place names:

> When people were chased out of Khartoum, where they settled was once called Mayo Sahara, after some time in that place it was renamed Kawaja Dagath (the mistake of the white man), and the people who named this were the Arabs (Juur) that were given money by the Kawaja such that the black people stayed there, such that the white man could get annoyed and stop helping the black people.
>
> The people came to realise that that name was not good; so they decided to name their own country (*panda*) as Mandela, as the name of the President of South Africa. The government came and talked to the leaders of that area, and told them to rename it was Mayo Salam, and it was first re-named as Mayo Mazarii. Have you seen, the name which has been accepted by the entire country (*baai*) is the name which is being used now [Mandela] – that unites the people.[91]

Even if this was recent or lived history for its students, as some of the members of Dinka Cultural Society said, 'you want somebody to remind you'[92] and to put individual or relatively distant experience

---

[89] Lino Alëu Angïc Dut, *Athör Käny*, 19.   [90] 'Primary 4 Reader'.
[91] Wol Akok, Garang Apin, and Atak Kon, 'The Dinka Customology of Marriage'.
[92] Members of the Dinka Cultural Society, in Apada, 11 August 2013.

5.5 A Political Education

into a broader historical narrative, as one young woman who was born in Khartoum said: 'we realised it was colonial – because we were slaves to the Jur, to Arabs'.[93]

This work emphasised comparisons of life before the 1983–86 famine and wars, versus life in Khartoum, in the wider context of Sudanese history – 'we want to show ... the change'.[94] Comparative histories and sustained metaphors are common in the predominantly Dinka texts and songs examined here, but also in Equatorian versions seen and collected during research. 'The Dinka Customology of Marriage' is a sustained comparison between Khartoum and pre-war southern 'traditional' gender relations and marriage norms. Songs particularly – probably because they were more commonly written than books, and recited in conversations and gatherings, including among women – put personal histories of displacement in wider historical context and with a narrative arc.[95]

This work aimed to produce an overarching historiography and core narrative, with major historical figures, periods, and events on which local histories and references could be hung, as an implicitly nationalist teleology. These songs and texts emphasised a broad heroic southern history, often beyond ethnic or clan boundaries. The pamphlet 'Dinka Displacement' includes a long story of how the late and famous Dinka Rek paramount chief Giir Thiik of Luonyaker, Warrap State, became a chief.[96] The 'Primary 4 Reader' references the historic northern Sudanese state of Alwa as a root of its national Sudanese history; Alwa was also used by Nuba Mountains politician Philip Abbas Ghabboush and his party, the United Sudan African Liberation Front (USALF), as their name for the imagined future state of a united Black Sudan.[97] And Dut Anyak Dit references the King of Zande – likely a reference to King Gbudwe, who died in 1905 of wounds received in a clash with Condominium forces in Western Equatoria – as one of

---

[93] Atak Akol Diing, in Aweil, 14 August 2013.
[94] Santino Atak Kuon, in Mayen Ulem, 3 July 2013.
[95] See Malik, 'Displacement as Discourse'; for example, General Paulino's song 'Problems Have Come', a version of which was rewritten and sung by the Gbaya singer Emmanuel Kembe.
[96] Mayo Mandela Circle, 'Dinka Displacement to the Northern Sudan and Other Stories', section 6.
[97] 'Constitution of USALF,' May 1970, CAR uncatalogued Bresciani papers, A/90.

many martyred 'forefathers' in his epic poem 'I will not see you again':[98]

> I will not see you again
> I will not find you again.
> You will not leave my heart
> I will never forget you
> Our forefathers have ever fallen
> They have ever fallen like you
> Freedom killed Kon[99]
> And also killed Gbudwe.[100]
> And Deng followed them[101]
> ...
> Your remains are left at the frontline,
> To bring freedom.
> You offered your soul,
> So that freedom comes.
> You offered your blood,
> To gain freedom.
> The freedom we wanted, we have not yet received!
> ...
> This slave peg that we've been tethered to,
> The Black race wants to uproot it.
> They are still hammering the peg in further.
> The people among us still hammer the peg further
> They will not manage it.
> The hammer is being taken from their hands.
> Even if you have died!

The most heavily referenced and invoked hero in the Dinka Bahr el Ghazal texts and songs is William Deng Nhial, a politician from Tonj, then part of Bahr el Ghazal state. As he caused a split in the SANU party in 1965 during the first civil war and advocated federalism under a united Sudanese government before being murdered by government forces in Cueibet in 1968, William Deng seems an unlikely martyr figure. However, his name has been invoked in Dinka songs – particularly from Greater Bahr el Ghazal – since his death, and a song

---

[98] Edward E. Evans-Pritchard, 'A History of the Kingdom of Gbudwe', *Zaire* 10, no. 5 (1956): 451–91.
[99] Dinka man who resisted the coming of missionaries.
[100] Late king of the Zande.   [101] William Deng Nhial.

addressing William Deng is recorded by Francis Deng in his 1973 text *The Dinka and Their Songs*.[102] Akut Kuei's songs reference William Deng frequently, particularly his death as sacrifice and his judgement on the current apathy or lack of valour of southern people.[103] Dhieu Lual remembered and sang a version of this song with the lyrics (cited above) 'who is unlucky like a Black man?':

> Dinka! The majesty of Deng Nhial will be lost
> Shilluk! The majesty of Deng Nhial will be taken
> Nuer! The majesty of Deng Nhial will be gone
> Zande! The majesty of Deng Nhial will be lost[104]

William Deng Nhial is most heavily invoked as one of several southern owners of the land, for instance, in Akut Kuei's famous song 'Duk ben la wël-wël':

> Why did you come and step on the land of Deng Nhial?
> And the land of Ajang Duot?
> And the land of Ayel Baak?
> And the land of Tookmac?[105]
> And the land of our maternal uncles?
> ...
> People live on the land but they have to know the owner.[106]

And in Akut Kuei's song 'Piny cï Deng nök' (The land that killed Deng):

> If it is not this land, the land that has killed Deng,
> If it is not this land that will be compensation for Deng -

---

[102] 'We Are the Dinka,' including the lines: 'it is the land of Morwel Malou and William Deng Nhial. We shall avenge the evils of the past.' Deng, *The Dinka and Their Songs*, 216–17.

[103] 'Duk ben la wël-wël' (Don't panic), 1994; 'Pienyda, pienyda, pienyda' (Our land), 1992; 'Ku na kocka' (What of these people?), 1997; 'Aya yii ye ping, ye ping' (I'm hearing – I'm hearing), c. mid-1990s; 'Ke col ater ci ke yeku puol yok muonyjang' (The Dinka don't give up the fight), c. mid-1990s; 'Abi thok terrek' (It will finish, one by one), c. mid-1990s; 'Piny cï Deng nök' (The land that has killed Deng), c. mid-1990s; and 'Cien kedie ka alei' [sic] (I have no problem with foreigners), c. 1996.

[104] This chorus can be repeated through a list of tribes; as sung by Dhieu Kuel, in Mayen Ulem, 21 August 2013, as well as by Akut Kuei in Juba: James Akec Nhial, in Juba, 8 September 2013.

[105] Likely, my translators noted, a code name for an Anya Nya or SPLA leader local to the area.

[106] 'Duk ben la wël-wël' (Don't panic), 1994.

> Then we shall avenge with one hundred people,
> One hundred, tens of thousands, we shall not count.
> Even if I'm given food, I will not accept -
> The life of Deng Nhial is not food ...
> The life of Deng Nhial is not worth money ...
> The life of Deng Nhial is not thirty-one cows.[107]

The word used for land is *baai*, or *baai panda* – a territorial expression of a permanent homeland that runs through these books and songs. As Zoe Cormack details, the term *baai* 'has been infused with strong associations of liberation war, nationalism and independence' and 'provides a way of expressing the nation and political identification with the state,' but – more importantly – this use of *baai* subsumes the central state of southern Sudan to a local, rural, and 'moral centre'.[108] This is true of the sustained moral analogies that run through the books of children's stories, poems, and songs, with wolves and hyenas attacking the *baai* and outsiders stealing from it.[109] Intrinsic to the idea of *baai*, and as common in the Dinka songs and books, is the idea of ownership of land. Many people emphasised the true meaning of the name 'Sudan' as the land of the Blacks – 'because of this colour of ours' – marking their authentic ownership of *baai panda*; Nikkel records a female songwriter singing in 1991: 'we are the real owners of the country ... is there a soil which does not know its owner? The country resembles us.'[110] This is reinforced by the common representation of Arab-origin Sudanese as immigrants, as 'the land they entered is an African land ... I studied this history in the school.'[111]

> Sudan is the land of the Black people
> We shall struggle for it
> ...

---

[107] 'Piny cï Deng nök' (The land that has killed Deng); thirty-one cows is the sum paid by Dinka people as *dia*, compensation for murder, under the legal codes set out at Wanh Alel in 1984. See Leonardi et al., 'Local Justice in Southern Sudan', 27.
[108] Cormack, 'The Making and Re-making of Gogrial', 187, 189–90.
[109] Akut Kuei, 'Junub pandan' (The South our country), c. early 1990s.
[110] Members of the Dinka Cultural Society, in Apada, 11 August 2013; Nikkel, *Dinka Christianity*, 332; also see Akut Kuei's use of the term 'visitor', in 'Duk ben la wël-wël' (Don't panic), 'Pienyda, pienyda, pienyda' (Our land), and 'Thudän ee Panda' (Sudan is our country), c. mid-1990s.
[111] James Garang, in Maper, 19 July 2013.

> It is God who created us and placed us in Sudan and said this is your land. You are a visitor – you go.[112]

There are comparative ideas of land, homeland, and ownership in the Equatorian and Arabic-language work from Khartoum, including the work of General Paulino Mesaka and Emmanuel Kembe, although this really needs further exploration beyond the scope of this book.

These songs and books, however, do not focus on a clear future nation-state of South Sudan, but on political identification with a broader territorial moral collective. In establishing a historical homeland – even if the parameters were vague – this literary work was challenging readers to imagine an alternative political community. Many poems and songs emphasise the war between north and south, but do not necessarily consistently refer to a southern (*junubi*) war of independence. Dut Anyak's poem 'Yomdït Mëi' (The dry season thunderstorm is rising, written in 1992) locates the rising winds of war between the two rivers, the Blue and White Niles, in the centre of Sudan:

> The wind is strong
> It has driven away the cowards, and those who could not face its trials.
> Those with weak hearts are driven away by the wind that blows
> where the two rivers meet.[113]

Dut Anyak's continuation of this poem, written later the same year and titled 'Kër lioi aacï yom buok' (The weak branches of the tree are broken), repeats the wind metaphor:

> A person who already knows about this wind doesn't get scared. An elder of the land, who knows the truth about the past, doesn't get concerned.... Do not fear, though it rises high, it will stop in time: work together, and sometime it will stop.[114]

5.6 Building Political Community

The texts, songs, poems, and pamphlets collected in this project all emphasise the importance of building community solidarity. These

---

[112] Akut Kuei, 'Thudän ee Panda' (Sudan is our country).
[113] Written in Khartoum, 5 February 1992.
[114] Written in Khartoum, 10 February 1992.

authors also put forward inconsistent political claims in different songs – for instance, Akut Kuei's two songs 'The South Our Country' and 'Sudan Our Country'. In the latter, they sing:

> Sudan is our country, our country
> Sudan is the land of the Black people
> We shall struggle for it.[115]

This included struggling to define a series of core questions about the political community and future of these Black people. Who could be included in this political community, how could solidarity be built, on what grounds, and in what space? How could people fight together for multiple homelands? And how could people learn to work together in the immediate war?

Basic practicalities constrained efforts at broad community-building. Work in vernacular languages was generally easier to organise, was safer than working in Sudanese Arabic, could draw on musical and rhetorical traditions and motifs, and as such was often more emotionally powerful for its audience. But while Akut Kuei mostly sang in Dinka for the Dinka, they worked to translate and perform their songs for wider audiences, and several non-Dinka speakers I met were familiar with (and sometimes could sing) Dinka songs. And despite being written in Dinka and often about Monyjiang, the Dinka collectively, the songs and texts studied here (Dinka and Equatorian) use generic 'people', Black people (*ran col* in Dinka), and *junubi* (southerner, in Sudanese Arabic) as well.

This was not necessarily just a case of interchangeable terminologies. These projects, and their authors, aimed specifically at complexity and interpretation, creating ambiguous works of broad emotional strength that were often the opposite of more common dogmatic, unequivocal political propaganda. For instance, Lazarus Lual took the lead in our meeting with one of the Akut Kuei songwriters, James Akec Nhial, to discuss his own interpretations of their work:

LUAL: The information you have in your songs is more than what you saw in your eyes, I believe. You might have seen ten things but what you have put down here is ninety. [We laugh]
JA: So now, like what you said, the meaning of songs here, is really powerful, more than –

---

[115] Akut Kuei, 'Thudän ee Panda' (Sudan is our country).

5.6 Building Political Community

LUAL: What you saw.
JA: What I saw. These – deep things coming from my heart.[116]

All the authors I met were well aware of the contradictions and problems of mutual affiliation as 'southerners' or as 'Black people' in their work. Most songs, poems, and texts here complain about the lack of broader pan-ethnic unity and political community, and the lack of common ground beyond skin colour and suffering. The most obvious example of this is in the Akut Kuei songs 'Yen Adhiau' (I'm crying) and the provocatively titled 'Jiëëng ameen wuöt' (Everyone hates the Dinka):

> Something's gone wrong in this South Sudan of ours
> Look at Africa –
> They are different, but southerners have the same skin
> The Nuer of nyantoic speak and act differently
> But we, the people of the South, have the same skin
> The Dor[117] and the Nuba are different
> But they are also Southerners, with the same skin
> The Shilluk are also Southerners with the same skin
> But the heart – the heart is not the same
> If it was one,
> We would not have problems between us,
> Scrapping over the remains of the carcass
> We have chaos over the carcass
> And we leave a person eating the meat,[118]
> Dipping their hands into the Dinka for their blood.
> It is better to go hungry.[119]

And in 'Yen Adhiau', the songwriters lament:

> The entire Dinka –
> All eyes are on them –
> The Black people, all eyes are on the Black people
> But despite this, these Black people don't realise our own problem
> They don't know – they still go ahead
> They take knives and murder their own brothers

---

[116] Lazarus Lual and James Akec Nhial, in Juba, 8 September 2013.
[117] A Dinka term for Equatorians.
[118] The carcass: the remains of power and wealth in the south, while eating the 'meat' of Sudan's wealth.
[119] 'Jiëëng ameen wuöt' (Everyone hates the Dinka), 1992.

And they leave the foreigners
The person who has murdered his brother,
If he faces a problem later, he will be killed by it alone.
You Black people,[120] leave this internal fight
Fighting at home, fighting in the community
Let's abandon it, and face one enemy in this big war.[121]

Tensions in the suburbs of course reflected the anger and inter-ethnic violence of the 1990s civil war, as well as of local conflicts and inter-family feuds. Plenty of war and praise songs aggrandised clans and ethnic groups, laid claim to both personal and military supremacy, and supported violence against other communities. These songs, poems, and writings likely contributed to sporadic intercommunal violence between gangs of young men in the city. More broadly, they were also part of a wider kind of mutual competition between linguistic groups and self-identified ethnic communities, over creative and social power and success.

However, many of these songs – even those engaged in this kind of competitive ethnic art – emphasised a need for mutual respect and solidarity in these projects: as Santino Atak wrote in the 'Reading Magazine of Dinka Culture', 'if [someone] only loves to promote this own culture, and does not want other people's culture to develop, then there's no truth'.[122] Dr Jimmy Wongo, the Equatorian veterinarian and politician, explained how

> we attended the Dinka's organisation and the Dinka activists, who were intellectuals, attended ours. Like, anybody. I attended several of the Dinkas' events, whether they are Dinka Twic or Dinka Aweil, I attended! And I attended the people of Western Bahr el Ghazal having their cultural days, and they attended ours.... Yeah, we worked as a team. But – but coming from different ethnic groups in Southern Sudan, but we worked as a team. We had the same agenda which we were carrying out.[123]

---

[120] Most people thought this was translated as Black people, but *jieng* can also be translated as more specifically Dinka people, as it is a Dinka term for people.
[121] Akut Kuei, 'Yen Adhiau' (I'm crying).
[122] Santino Atak Kon, 'Equality', in 'Reading Magazine of Dinka Culture', 10; also 'The Culture in Northern Sudan', in 'Reading Magazine of Dinka Culture', 5; 'The System of Marriage among the Dinka,' and 'What Is Marriage?', in 'The Dinka Customology of Marriage', 7–8.
[123] Jimmy Wongo, in Juba, 18 October 2013.

5.6 Building Political Community

People now living in South Sudan are proud of their friendships with other black Sudani colleagues and neighbours, and lamented the loss of old SIM cards and phones with friends' numbers. Mark Mathiang, a labourer and neighbourhood committee representative in Lafa'a, emphasised that 'people are still keeping that spirit' of friendship, 'even' with Nuer people, and Dor explained: 'at that time I was able to say that you are my brother, and you are my father. We are sitting together. We were there, mixed with Arabs, Burgu, Fellata, Masaalit, and Nuba.'[124]

These friendships reflected the changing political community in Khartoum. This was partly based on the political geography that emerged by the early 1990s (see Chapter 2), building mutual understandings and social solidarities in new neighbourhoods. It also reflected the politics of the civil war, as conflict spread across southern and eastern Sudan and popular discourse about the war developed. For many residents, despite localised fighting between southern factions, the war was still about colonisation and exploitation from a Sudanese elite who saw themselves as racially and politically dominant.

Sudan's history of racist exploitation and violent marginalisation of its politically Black populations – regardless of the complexities of actual Sudani skin colours – created a Black political community.[125] This shifted the language used in Khartoum. Lazarus Lual explained how the songs he sang as a young teenager drew on Black nationalism beyond Sudan, including a song that 'a Black man can never be ashamed – you should have learned from Nelson Mandela'.[126] The songwriter Deng Atak explained:

The most important thing I know, my father is a Dinka. And my mother is a Dinka. And they are Black. And they are in the southern Sudan.... So I thank God for that, because the skin, the black skin, it was not given to us by human beings but by God.... So the black colour is the most important thing and that is the one that I am most happy about. The most important, the most important thing. And that was the key issue that we form our [song] group. Because the Arabs always rejected the black-skinned people. Even they tried, indeed, to change the Dinka's colour by giving them some [skin-

---

[124] Marko Mathiang Deng, in Maper chiefs' court, 3 June 2013; Dor Tartizio Buni, in Juba, 14 October 2013.
[125] As explained by Awen Mayuon Macwac, in Maper Akot, 21 June 2013.
[126] Lazarus Lual, in Juba, 19 October 2013.

bleaching] chemicals to chemicalise themselves, to become brown-skinned people.[127]

A Dinka person interviewed by Tekle Woldemichael in 1985 explained:

> We are black. They claim to be white or they are brown.... There is hostility deep inside us. The hostility is because of domination. They want to dominate us. We want to control our country.... They have more education, more industries, more people in government because they are more advanced than us. They control the economy.[128]

Popular political discourse in the suburbs reflected the fundamental question resulting from this analysis: Who are 'we', and what are we fighting for?

5.7 Fighting for What?

The literature and intellectual cultures produced by Khartoum's Black residents in the 1990s and 2000s often centred on this question of who could and should be part of this Black political community. This 'deep horizontal comradeship', as Benedict Anderson called national community, in this work was more frequently explained as brotherhood. As ever, different people set different limits to their local, regional, linguistic, ethnic, and Black solidarities, and they could invest in ethnically specific projects at the same time as identifying as Black nationalists.

These investments were often compared (in discussion and in these texts) through the language of trust, in the broadest sense of the term as truth, responsibility, mutual safe-keeping, and common hope. Tekle Woldemikael's interviewees in Wad Medani town in 1985 referred to 'northerners' as *mundukuru*, now a common derogatory term in South Sudan for Arab northern Sudanese people but in Woldemikael's translation meaning 'untrustworthy'. Saadia Izzeldin Malik records a Kordofan woman resident of a slum area as being afraid that 'one day they [southerners] will come to kill and eat me' (although her friend corrected her that southerners could be trusted, unlike the

---

[127] Deng Atak Abuk, in Apada, 13 July 2013.
[128] Woldemikael, 'Southern Migrants in a Northern Sudanese City', 26.

5.7 Fighting for What? 215

Nuba).[129] Similarly extreme accounts of a lack of trust punctuate explanations of relationships with Darfur and Arab northerners in my interviews and texts,[130] most obviously in the multiple accounts I collected of northern Sudanese doctors murdering patients to remove their blood, organs, and bones: 'some good things for his medical activities'; 'even they steal babies sometimes'.[131] Throughout these discussions, 'Arab' is often used as a shorthand for those people falling outside racial, ethno-linguistic, and political lines of trust.

In the texts collected here, this hard line – the 'Arab' northern elites who exploited and monopolised, and who could not be trusted – demanded what James Brennan calls 'a politics of enmity'.[132] This collective animus needed to be reinforced. Lino Alëu's *History* lists atrocities and acts of discrimination against Dinka and southern people, including photographs of amputations and enslaved men.[133] Lino Alëu's *History* is explicitly violent and retributive, calling not necessarily for financial restitution but for direct violent repercussions against the Khartoum regime and its supporters by generations to come. It directly asks for this to be taught to future generations:

> Ask the child like this:
> – Do you know what Arabs did to us?
> Explain it properly to the child, if he understands, ask him or her:
> – What shall we do to Arabs?[134]

This work was connected to wider regional wartime discourse. Khartoum poor and displaced migrant communities were tied into the network of information and misinformation from the various conflicts, fronts, propagandists, and growing regional and international diaspora over the 1990s and 2000s. This was mainly through personal movement and discussion, as well as through growing

---

[129] Ibid., 30; Malik, 'Displacement as Discourse'.
[130] For example, Peter Deng Akok, in Maper, 21 June 2013; Dhieu Kuel, in Mayen Ulem, 4 July 2013; Abaker Thelatheen, in Apada, 8 June 2013; Maper chiefs' court meeting, 13 April 2013.
[131] Arou Piol Adam, in Apada village, 22 July 2013; Dhieu Kuel (in Mayen Ulem, 4 July 2013) also told stories of blood- and bone-selling. For regional histories of blood-sucking and body-snatching, see White, *Speaking with Vampires: Rumor and History in Colonial Africa* (University of California Press, 2000), 37.
[132] Brennan, 'Blood Enemies', 389.
[133] See Lino Alëu Angïc Dut, *Athör Käny*, 26. [134] Ibid., 11.

communication networks. Ideas and debates were passed through the same network, and the creative work discussed in this chapter was often understood as part of their authors' war efforts – as Dhieu explained, to 'inform those who were living in the north, so that they can leave Khartoum, and come back to liberate the country. Even they preached to us about the coming of the SPLM inside Khartoum city' (for more on this political organisation, see Chapter 6).[135] Songs from southern conflicts and battle-fronts were shared in Khartoum, for example, a famous Turalei song from Warrap that lamented the fighting of their leaders (Kerubino Kuanyin against Garang's SPLA) while the country is being invaded, sung by Dinka communities outside Turalei and that particular conflict. As Dhieu said, 'because we were there in the far north, and we don't know exactly what was going on ... that is why we sing this song for a memory of the south's situation'.[136] City-based writers and artists discussed recent events and dry season offensives in their work: for example, Dut Anyak's poem 'Adhuöm Akan' (There is a hole), about the series of political agreements in the late 1990s that he saw as compromising the principles of the war.[137]

Khartoum's field of political debate reflected regional discussion of the future political community that people were fighting and hoping for. As in all heterogeneous political communities, residents and writers articulated layers of political commonality, moral proximity, and mutual understanding, and this fed into their ideas of the aims of the war. Across southern accounts and texts, Nuba and Darfur neighbours and communities at large were peripheral 'brothers' – although for many people, while 'all the south Sudanese in Khartoum [were] brothers together', people from the Nuba Mountains and particularly from Darfur were 'brothers' of a different kind.[138] This made explanations of political work complicated, as Riiny Lual noted: 'when you talk about the rights, even if you are not from that [area], you get people supporting you ... [the SPLA was] addressing every problem which is facing any Sudanese people in general. And south Sudanese in particular.'[139]

These tensions – over constituting and defending a specifically 'southern' Sudan or seeking a wider Black Sudanese future, and who

---

[135] Dhieu Kuel, in Mayen Ulem, 21 August 2013.   [136] Ibid.
[137] Dut Anyak Dit, in Kuajok, 28 September 2013; also see his 'The Dry Season Storm' poem.
[138] Anei Deng Akok, in Aweil, 13 August 2013.
[139] Riing Riing Lual, in Aweil, 3 September 2013.

5.7 Fighting for What? 217

was Black or southern – were partly catalysed by SPLM/A political theory under John Garang. Alfred Taban explained that 'it was only during the SPLA movement when the SPLA begin to say well, we are talking for the marginalised people of Sudan, and the Nubas are marginalised, the people of Darfur are marginalised, that is when things began to change. And southerners began to consider these people as their brothers.'[140] As Santino Akot put it, 'Dr John realised that there is [a unity] of the Black people.'[141] Lazarus emphasised:

we discussed Black as a community, and then we discussed about the general situation in the country, we discuss about all the marginalised people ... I think most of the people came to understand marginalisation through John Garang.... When you talked about the whole Sudan, that's when you talk about marginalisation.[142]

Discussions of the constitution and defence of Black or southern Sudan often echoed or directly took up John Garang's ideas of New Sudan. A core term in the SPLA's ideological rhetoric from its first use in the SPLM/A manifesto of 1983, 'New Sudan' was initially used to describe an imagined Sudan that would emerge after the overthrow of the regime, becoming unfashionable after the 1991 SPLA split but then re-emerging in 1994 at the first SPLA National Convention.[143]

Khartoum communities – probably unsurprisingly – had a much stronger discourse around New Sudanese Black unity than in other southern towns and refugee camps through the war. Most of the texts collected here, and the discussions around them, emphasised the historical and political inclusion of eastern and western Sudanese people.[144] Although a history of Darfur, Nuba, and Beja activism in

---

[140] Alfred Taban, in Juba, 16 October 2013.
[141] Stephen Ayaga, in Aweil, 8 August 2013.
[142] Lazarus Lual, in Juba, 19 October 2013.
[143] Rolandsen, *Guerrilla Government*, 118–19.
[144] See Dut Anyak Dit, 'Yok cï yoköth tuööm' (We have gone opposite ways):

> What you are looking for is not what I'm looking for
> We are going different directions
> You have missed me ...
> Look your way – the road is there.
> I have turned my back on you.
> I am going to the border
> I will sit at the border and demarcate it.

Khartoum is not included here, these communities were frequently seen by southerners as partners in the peripheral power struggle for ownership of Sudan – in theory, if not always in practice. This was, most people explained, because of the heterogeneity of crowded neighbourhoods, the common experience of discrimination and violence from the Khartoum state because of their blackness, and the collective multi-ethnic educational provision in impoverished areas of the city.[145] Many Khartoum southern residents at least studied alongside these other 'black marginalised' populations in Khartoum, particularly the Nuba residents.[146] 'The students we taught [were] not from Dinka alone, but from various states, including the far north, and western Sudan, Darfur. It's a mixed school, but [we] used to tell in classes that – you are our people.'[147]

This was based on a subjective personal spectrum of inclusion, trust, and collaboration with collectively titled Nuba, 'easterners', and Darfuri neighbours (mostly in that order). Khartoum's residents drew on a very different, and possibly wider, field of Sudanese political education than many residents in the south and in eastern Africa had access to, including the Nuba movements led by the priest-turned-politician Philip Abbas Ghaboush. Several people I spoke to had attended the Nuba politician Philip Abbas Ghaboush's rallies because 'we want to learn politics'.[148] There was significant intermarriage between southern and Nuba residents. The place of the Nuba Mountains peoples within a political community was emphasised in many of the texts here; for instance, a chapter in Lino Alëu's *History*, was titled 'William Deng Nhial and Philip Abbas Ghaboush': '[They] were the first leaders who begin the struggle for the south against Arabs. They met and discussed to find a solution about Arab colonialism in Sudan.'[149] Lino Alëu also included now-marginal political thinkers in his history of political thought, like Joseph Garang – a Communist and anti-secessionist southern politician, executed in 1971 following the failed Communist party coup against Nimeiri:

---

[145] John Gau Riak, in Aweil, 28 June 2013.
[146] Dhieu Kuel, in Mayen Ulem, 21 August 2013; also Atak Akol Diing, in Aweil, 14 August 2013.
[147] Marco Akon Akon, in Apada, 11 August 2013.
[148] Dhieu Kuel, in Mayen Ulem, 21 August 2013.
[149] Lino Alëu Angïc Dut, *Athör Käny*, 27; this section is probably referring to General Union of Nuba meetings with the SANU leadership, c. 1965–69.

'Arabs also kill the wise and educated Black person: for instance, Joseph Garang was a wise South Sudanese whom Gaffar Mohammed Nimeri targeted and tried to kill him. No sooner than he killed Joseph Garang, said Garang, "kill me and you will find another Garang."'[150]

There was no consensus about where the south ended, as well as what political community people were fighting for. John Garang's problematic pronouncement on the reach of the civil war – in the words of one Bari man, 'those of you who want to fight for South Sudan, fight and then when you get to Kosti – you stop there, we will continue' – resonated with many people engaged in this mutual and personal definition of the limits of *baai panda junub*.[151] As James said, 'whether I came from the north to join them in Kosti or not, or whether I perished there it didn't matter – my people would stop at Kosti and come back to what is theirs'.[152] Topologies of violent confrontation characterise these mobile borders in these accounts, for instance, in Akut Kuei's song 'Abyei, Abyei, the wut of Deng Kuol':

We no longer want to be in the north ...
Twelve years Abyei has fought with these sons of dogs
And we have allowed them to suffer
If we had realised this
We would have told the youth from Dor[153] to run to the border ...
And the youth of Dor would run in,
And the message would be taken to Nuer ...
Then this war of ours would have finished at the border ...
Let's respect Aweil and Abyei,
They have managed to keep the nightmare at bay ...
If it were not for them, then the Arabs would have gone deep into the south for the border.[154]

---

[150] Lino Alëu Angïc Dut, *Athör Käny*, 27.
[151] Literally, our 'homeland, the country of the south'; Jimmy Wongo, in Juba, 18 October 2013.
[152] Jimmy Wongo, in Juba, 18 October 2013; another version of Garang's statement is recorded by Jok Madut Jok, 'Diversity, Unity, and Nation Building in South Sudan', US Institute of Peace (2011), 9: 'anyone not convinced about the liberation of the whole Sudan can stop when we reach Kosti and leave me to march to Khartoum alone if I so choose'.
[153] Dinka term for Equatorians.
[154] 'Abyei, Abyei wut e Deng Kuol' (Abyei, Abyei, the wut of Deng Kuol), c. mid-1990s; Lino Alëu makes similar statements in *Athör Käny*, 11. *Wut* means a section of the Dinka, more easily translated here as the 'people' of Deng Kuol.

The area of 'the south' – or of 'Black Sudan', which is sometimes correspondent – is a historically and politically shifting concept across these texts: the Dinka 'Primary 4 Reader', for instance, includes a map of the 'land of the areas of Dinka' but juxtaposed this with the explanation that, just south of Jebelein, 'the southern part of Sudan is for black people [*koc col*],' including the Nuer, Luo, Shilluk, Nuba, Zande, Bongo, and Ndogo.[155] And while many people debated where the borderline of southern Sudan fell, people also made wider claims to Sudan. Claims to ownership of northern Sudan in genealogies and origin mythologies not only were an expression of ethnic nationalism but were often – for the teller – a claim to ownership of an original Black Sudan.[156] One pan-Africanist student activist emphasised that he wanted 'to re-Africanise those people in the north parts'.[157] These conversations, including in the texts here, were often linked to discussions of the heritage of pre-colonial non-Muslim regional states such as Nubia and Alwa, and to pro-southern and pro-Black historical work in general.[158] The 'Primary 4 Reader' states that 'we assume our grandparents were also the ones near Khartoum', but the textbook goes on to briefly explain textual, oral, and archaeological historical sources, the limited source material on southern and pre-colonial Sudan, and the importance of research and record-keeping.[159]

5.8 The Limits to Solidarity

There were limits to this complicated solidarity. The Darfur populations of Khartoum are a good example of these limits; their young men often joined the Sudan Armed Forces and Popular Defence Forces under al-Bashir's 'jihad' in the 1990s and early 2000s.[160] The presence

[155] 'Primary 4 Reader', 6.
[156] These origin myths are not limited to Dinka people; see Leonardi, *Dealing with Government in South Sudan*, 22; Nikkel, *Dinka Christianity*, 41–43. For example, see the introduction to 'The Dinka Customology of Marriage', 5; Lino Alëu Angïc Dut, *Athör Käny*, 9.
[157] John Gau Riak, in Aweil, 28 June 2013.
[158] Beswick, *Sudan's Blood Memory*.
[159] 'Primary 4 Reader', 10. It is possible that the author of this section of the textbook was drawing on the colonial Sudan Government District Commissioner and Governor A. J. Arkel's 1940s writings that described excavations in northern Sudan apparently finding skeletons resembling Dinka and Nuer physiognomy; see Nikkel, *Dinka Christianity*, 41.
[160] Arou Piol Adam, in Apada village, 21 July 2013.

5.8 The Limits to Solidarity

of Darfuri locals in Khartoum's neighbourhoods blurred these lines of brotherhood and social inclusion as 'co-citizens who suffer with them'.[161] People from Darfur were often described as 'Black but', being racially but not consciously politically, socially, or intellectually part of a broader Sudanese Black collective, unlike those who were 'Black and': 'we are Black and we are south Sudanese,' in that order.[162]

We were the same by the skin, but different in heart. They think that they are Arabs.... So for Darfurians we don't mix with them sometimes, because for them they used to steal our things and they don't want to be our brothers. For some time they sat to be Arabs, and we as Dinka.[163]

For many residents of Khartoum, Darfur people's political and social loyalty was suspect, undermined by some Darfur groups' claims to Arab genealogies, forms of Islam, and political Islamic ideas. For many southern residents, their Darfur neighbours further challenged pan-Sudanese solidarity in the Khartoum suburbs because of personal memories of extreme violence at the hands of Darfuri armed groups. This is particularly true for Dinka Bahr el Ghazal communities, who suffered atrocious violence in massive Rizeigat and Misseriya armed raids, driven initially by famine in western Sudan in the mid-1980s and then fuelled by government assistance as proxy *murahaleen* (Misseriya militia) warfare against the SPLA in the late 1980s and early 1990s, which killed tens of thousands of people and depopulated large parts of northern Bahr el Ghazal.[164] Many of the poorer and newer residents from greater Bahr el Ghazal and Abyei had suffered significantly in Darfur and the Nuba Mountains on the way to Khartoum, losing relatives and children; some had been kidnapped or forced by violence or circumstance into enslavement or exploitative labour by local landowners or cattle and camel herders between 1986 and 2005. There are many examples of extreme vitriol against Darfur communities in the literature collected here, not necessarily restricted to Muslim groups or those claiming Arab ancestry. The most extreme example is Lino Alëu's introductory comments about the nature of the civil war in his *History*:

---

[161] Ibrahim, 'Southern Sudanese Women Migrants', 253.
[162] Bruce Berman, 'Ethnicity, Patronage and the African State: The Politics of Uncivil Nationalism', *African Affairs* 97, no. 388 (1998): 306.
[163] Lual Agang Macham, in Apada, 8 June 2013.
[164] Mawson, 'II Murahaleen Raids'.

We will punish Darfuris, and they will know that Garang was fighting for the freedom of a Black person ... it is good for God to show Darfurians how the disaster occurred in the south. It is good for God to show them the disaster, to see it with their own eyes in Darfur ... what let us be conquered by the Arabs was Darfur, they are those who let us be conquered ... I will thank God if He will show Darfurians disaster.[165]

Most texts and people emphasised why the Darfuri community were 'stooges' of the Khartoum regime: they were 'duped', not politically conscious, or not fully understanding of their deeper political and historical position in Sudan – 'they are black, but they are brainwashed by [the] Islamic system'.[166] Many people, as well as Lino Alëu's *History*, explained that Darfur people were misled into thinking that they were fighting for the cause of Islam. Gatkuoth, a Nuer business manager in the late 1990s, told me that 'the Darfurians didn't really understand their position ... It was just recently that they have realised.'[167] They were, as a member of the Dinka Cultural Society emphasised, 'black in colour but their heart is different'; 'Darfuris don't understand that they are also black.'[168] As Lino Alëu's *History* and many interviewees stressed, John Garang 'enlightened those of western Sudan ... to know themselves also as a black people, and that Sudan belongs to them'.[169]

All these debates over political consciousness and community returned to the question of trust. As the pamphlet 'The Dinka Customology of Marriage' explained,

you consider being related as when you share ideas, and you share wealth. If one finds you in a problem, and he doesn't help you, then you are not related. Now as we no longer share things with Arabs [*weet e nyankai*, literally, the sons of my sister], and we no longer give each other help, our relationship has turned to be a simple thing, and now the conflict is too great.

---

[165] Lino Alëu Angïc Dut, *Athör Käny*, 8.
[166] Diing Chen Diing, in Aweil, 15 July 2013. Also Chiefs' court meeting in Mayen Ulem, 20 August 2013; Ayii Bol, in Aweil, 16 August 2013.
[167] Farouk Gatkuoth, in Juba, 30 October 2013.
[168] Members of the Dinka Cultural Society, in Apada, 11 August 2013; Anei Deng Akok, in Aweil, 13 August 2013; Ayii Bol, in Aweil, 16 August 2013.
[169] Stephen Ayaga, in Aweil, 8 August 2013; also Ayii Bol, in Aweil, 16 August 2013; chiefs' meeting, 20 August 2013; Lino Alëu Angïc Dut, *Athör Käny*.

You have to realise that you have separated from your people. Calm down to share ideas peacefully with your people, so that they know that you are related to them. In a country where ideas are not shared properly, God is not with the people and there is no peace there.

This community-building needed equity, common wealth, and freedom, as Santino Atak explained in the 'Reading Magazine of Dinka Culture'.[170] 'In a country where people share ideas and resources, it brings progress, luck, and other good things to the people there. Love has two things: faith [*gam*] and hope [*ngoth*]. With love, they work together.'[171]

This literary and artistic work was part of a debate over the content and form of wartime moral and political community. This work rarely set out an answer. Instead, it demanded its audience engage in political thinking and practical action.

5.9 On Sell-Outs and New Societies

There were some Black people who were beyond the pale (so to speak), but they were not necessarily Darfuri. The people most explicitly criticised in all this work were the southern and otherwise non-Arab residents of Khartoum's Black suburbs who were intellectually lazy, were dismissive of these political and cultural projects, and had sold out to the elite, capitalist, individualist lifestyle of the city.[172] All the writing and songs studied here are explicitly anti-individualist, warning against the risks of the commercialisation of relationships and daily living in Khartoum, and becoming isolated and thus 'lost' in everyday pressures of survival. This work is not anti-change per se, but emphasises the importance of social systems and political awareness, as Dut Anyak's poem 'Ala käk yo tek yiic' (There are things that separate us) explains:

> He doesn't know the rights of other people.
> Otherwise we wouldn't be here fighting![173]

---

[170] Santino Atak Kon, 'Freedom,' in 'Reading Magazine of Dinka Culture'.
[171] Santino Atak Kon, 'Love among the People,' in 'Reading Magazine of Dinka Culture'.
[172] This is also a demonstration of what Leonardi describes as 'the widespread discourse of selfish 'townese': Leonardi, *Dealing with Government*, 157.
[173] Written in Khartoum, 25 March 2002.

224   *Intellectual Work and Political Thought on the Peripheries*

The Akut Kuei song 'Everyone hates the Dinka' includes the lines:

> Haven't you heard anything, you Dinka?[174]
> You are told but you don't listen
> You are shown, but you don't want to see
> This is something even the Dinka deaf have heard,
> And the Dinka blind have seen.
> So you Dinka, what are you waiting for?
> Are you waiting for your paycheck?
> Are you waiting for your paycheck?
> If it's your payment
> If you're waiting for your pension
> We'll be like donkeys, just waiting for our paycheck.

The Dinka work here often draws this distinction between 'hard'- and 'weak'-hearted people, where weak hearts give in to individualist profit and pro-government apologism in defence of their comfortable lives.[175] Comedy groups commonly satirised 'how the leaders are behaving in the community'.[176] All accounts used the term 'bribery'. This was turned particularly against southern elite politicians and businessmen who appeared to be profiting from the al-Bashir government and war economy (see Chapter 7). Akut Kuei wrote several songs about these men, including 'Ku Na Kockä?' (What of these people?), which makes reference to an old parable about greed and comeuppance, where a man in a hunting party – so desperate to get to the best meat on the inside of a slain elephant – climbs inside the carcass, but then has his testicles cut off by the efforts of the group cutting the meat from the outside:

> How about these people, what about this gentleman?
> They have put their heads together with the Arabs,
> And share their understanding,
> What will happen to them?
> Will their testicles not be cut off, when we start stabbing at the Arabs?
> Better – better a man who was skinning the elephant,

---

[174] *Jieng*; this was commonly interpreted to mean specifically southerners, within the song.
[175] For example, Akut Kuei, 'Köngdiën ë cuëc' (My right hand) and 'Ka ye Bëny thëëth' (The spearmaster will regret his prophesy); Dut Anyak Dit, 'Yomdït Mëi' (The dry season storm is rising), c. 1992.
[176] Angelina Majok, in Mayen Ulem, 16 July 2013. Miller records text from several plays on this theme: Miller, 'Juba Arabic', appendix 3.

5.9 On Sell-Outs and New Societies

Because he avenged his testicles using his spear
And you, what will you avenge yourself with?
I won't be a witness, even if your testicles are cut off.

The group's song 'Ka ye Bëny thëëth' (The spearmaster will regret his prophesy) argues against the comfortable apologism of the urban Black upper classes:

So you are saying
That we are going to survive;[177]
No one will survive
If we don't leave *rueeny*[178] behind.
No one will survive if we don't forget our jealousy.
So that we unite ourselves to be one
We unite ourselves to see
This calamity that is killing us, the Southerners
It is a disaster that will spare no one,
Even if you give up your chair and say,
That you are my friend – it will not spare anyone.
Even if you change your name to Mohammed
So you pray, and take his totems as yours,
If you change your black colour –
It is a disaster that will spare no one.
This killing of Dinka, is divide and rule.[179]

But for the majority, food was both a metaphor and a real concern in the extremely poor and desperate displaced suburbs. As Lino Alëu's *History* explained,

> many people were bribed by money ... and forgot their future. Black people talk in Arabs' voice because of money. The money Arabs give people has blinded them.... Didn't you see these people, our people? What Black people are doing in the North, these are people who were bribed to fight against their brothers. They are not fighting against John Garang, they are fighting against their hunger. Because whenever you felt hungry you can even fight your father or mother when there is no food today.[180]

---

[177] By being in Khartoum, away from the war; a justification for being in exile was to stay safe to help with reconstruction.
[178] Deception, trickery, two-faced behaviour.
[179] Nak aburdit kou, literally, targeting of the biggest first.
[180] Lino Alëu Angïc Dut, *Athör Käny*, preface.

This manipulation of poor and desperate people was well understood. In Lino Alëu's words, 'Dinka and Nuer were coopted by the Arabs in the oil field to fight these same southerners, because Arabs need to delay and blindfold these people to be able to steal their oil to northern Sudan, and the southerners didn't realise that Arabs are killing them secretly, as Akut Kuei said.'[181] Many plays and songs criticise and satirise the brutal commodification and everyday violence of Khartoum life and the civil war.[182] This included 'turning marriage into a business', forcing marriages on daughters for the promise of bride-wealth payments; 'The Dinka Customology of Marriage' notes that when marriage is 'flowing like money', 'it's this process that has broken families'. The Akut Kuei song 'Abuk jal tïng' (We'll see) says that this violent economy is at the root of the dragging war:

> The truth is here – I have discovered the truth[183]
> I have discovered the truth
> It is here – it's in my hand
> It is food that is killing us,
> It is eating that we are fighting.
> We were made to fight
> And you agree to go and fight with your brother
> Just because of food
> And food can be grown in the land of the South
> It is full of food,
> The stomach is God's plate[184]
> Let's not leave our corpses for the birds because of food.[185]
> Do not sell your right because of food –
> Don't sell your land for food,
> Don't waste your lives for food.

This economic analysis has implications for the future in these texts and songs. The article in the 'Reading Magazine of Dinka Culture' titled 'The Nationalist' (literally, the person who loves his land, *pan-dan*) notes how Sudanese peripheries have been consistently exploited by other countries, and residents had 'sold off the country's resources'. 'If one is careless, and wastes his wealth, leaving his relatives and brothers suffering and favouring others, then this retards

---

[181] Lino Alëu Angïc Dut, *Athör Käny*.   [182] Lorins, 'Inheritance', 245.
[183] Literally, 'word', *wet*.
[184] Leave food up to God, don't worry about tomorrow.
[185] Don't die without burial for food.

development.'[186] The section in the Dinka 'Primary 4 Reader' on economics emphasises that academic education alone is not a remedy for underdevelopment.[187] In the 'Reading Magazine', Santino Atak writes an article titled 'On Equality':

Education, leadership, culture, equal sharing of resources, and development are all involved. If all these things are put into practice, then there will be no problems. But if one person wants to be the only educated one, and others with whom they are sharing the country are not educated, then there will be no peace. And if he likes to rule other people, and he doesn't want to be ruled, then there is no equality.... If he loves to be the one to distribute resources but he doesn't want others to do the same, then there's no freedom. And if he loves to do everything and he forgets others, then there's no love. The peace that was made in 1972, what spoilt it then? What spoiled it is the absence of those four words.[188]

5.10 Conclusion

The creative and literary projects gathered and discussed here are only a fragment of a wider intellectual circuit and discursive sphere that grew and evolved in Khartoum's Black suburbs over the 1990s and 2000s. This chapter highlights some of the political, educational efforts of this work. The artists and writers studied were trying to work out what Wendy James calls a minimum common moral ground: the basis on which people see themselves and understand their circumstances.[189]

These artists and writers did not strive for consensus but were engaged in (and promoted) debate. They encouraged people to have internal critical lives, in the face of heavily policed public space and expression. One man remembered using headphones and a cassette player to listen to these subversive songs while on a long commute to work and school on public transport.[190] A 1998 song by an unknown author, recorded by Marc Nikkel in 2001, summarises the importance of having a sense of political self in this way:

---

[186] The nationalist (the person who loves his land, *pandan*); 'Reading Magazine of Dinka Culture'.
[187] 'Primary 4 Reader'.
[188] Santino Atak Kon, 'Reading Magazine of Dinka Culture'.
[189] James, *The Listening Ebony*, 149.
[190] Dhieu Kuel, in Mayen Ulem, 4 July 2013.

> I must struggle to adjust my life
> For best advantage,
> Both in the way of our ideals
> And in actuality.
> If it does not proceed like this,
> Then my life and my existence
> Have no meaning
> In the flow of the stories of my people,
> In the history of the world.[191]

This work complicates the idea that there was only a 'hazy notion' of southernness during the second civil war, fought essentially as a reactive opposition to 'the North'.[192] There was much deeper critical thought beyond this fundamental opposition. People of course knew that, as Jok Madut said, 'nations are made, not born ... creating such a nation ... requires a vision, a plan, and honest and participatory actions, not just the pronouncements of politicians': these local intellectuals were doing this work in Khartoum already.[193]

The texts and songs in this chapter also show how focusing on the 'southern' specifically constrains any analysis. The South is not a clear or pre-existing category. Similarly, this work does not just outline a competition between neatly ethnic and nationalist identifications.[194] These are not static or atavistic personal labels, of ethnic group, for instance – these identifications, people knew, needed also to be reconstructed and discussed in Khartoum. This work therefore deals with the complexity of the idea of an ethnic group in an urban, capitalist, and migrant context, as well as debating the concept of 'the South' and the idea of a Black nation. These debates over the nature and scope of political commonality and community are key to all types of

---

[191] 'Deng and Mohammed in the Land of Sudan', in Nikkel, *Dinka Christianity*, 281.

[192] Quoting Jok, 'Diversity, Unity, and Nation Building', 2; Jok, *Sudan*; Ole Frahm, 'Defining the Nation: National Identity in South Sudanese Media Discourse', *Africa Spectrum* 47, no. 1 (2012): 21–49; Peter Harengel and Ayantunji Gbadamosi, '"Launching" a New Nation: The Unfolding Brand of South Sudan', *Place Branding and Public Diplomacy* 10, no. 1 (2014): 35–54; Christopher Zambakari, 'South Sudan and the Nation-Building Project: Lessons and Challenges', *International Journal of African Renaissance Studies* 8, no. 1 (2013): 5–29.

[193] Jok, 'Diversity, Unity, and Nation Building', 4.

[194] Frahm, 'Defining the Nation'; Jok, 'Diversity, Unity, and Nation Building'; Copnall, *A Poisonous Thorn in Our Hearts*.

5.10 Conclusion

mobilisation and political action. Here, this community-building depended on trust and mutual understanding: writers were concerned that 'the heart is not the same' and were intent on encouraging people to take up a particular perspective on the war and the world, including as 'Black people united on the one vision – [who know that] the Sudan belong[s] to them.'[195]

Most importantly, these intellectual projects demanded critical engagement beyond self-ascription as a 'southern nationalist'. People needed to discuss the economics, politics, and morality of any future political community. This is an example of what John Lonsdale calls deep political work, drawing up civil societies and challenging the civic virtue of the wealthy, apathetic, culturally promiscuous, and politically ignorant.[196] Many of the authors of these pamphlets, school readers, plays, and songs did not demand that their readers subscribe to their particular world-view, but instead emphasised the importance of political self-consciousness and critical engagement. These texts and songs – and their authors and writing groups – were focused on a recruitment to consciousness. They challenged readers and listeners to define themselves. Those who failed to participate in this self-education project were told: 'know that you're colonised now'.[197]

---

[195] Akut Kuei, 'Jiëëng ameen wuöt' (Everyone hates the Dinka); Stephen Ayaga, in Aweil, 8 August 2013.

[196] John Lonsdale and Bruce Berman, *Unhappy Valley: Conflict in Kenya and Africa* (James Currey, 1992).

[197] 'The Dinka Customology of Marriage', section 6.

6 | *Akut Kuei and Wartime Mobilisation*

The societal reconstruction and defence work, education, and intellectual projects of displaced residents of Khartoum intended to build political consciousness during the war; it also demanded action. This chapter examines the actions and political organisation encouraged in particular by the educational and intellectual work detailed in the last chapter. This is what makes up the content of wartime resistance and rebel mobilisation through the 1980s and 1990s.

This 'underground politics' is not romantic or exceptional. Through the war, living in Khartoum was generally stressful and intimidating. In these circumstances a lot of everyday discussion – like getting updates on family in the south or elsewhere – could be a kind of subversive activity, and many people drew on 'cell systems' of small meetings and points of contact, old and well-known ways of having political conversations, sharing information, and organising on the quiet in urban Sudan since at least the 1900s.[1] This chapter demonstrates the divides of class and gender that cut across this 'underground politics'.

This chapter first traces explicitly rebellious forms of political organisation and subversion, within banned and opposition parties, student spaces, and opposition coalitions. This comes with caveats. It would be relatively easy to build an image of a vibrant and coordinated subversive anti-Bashir political movement in Khartoum, thanks to the availability of opposition documents, such as the National Democratic Alliance and Communist Party archives in Amsterdam, the occasional bombastic political party or student manifesto in national archives, and the emphatic descriptions of organised spy cells in many politicians' autobiographies, homogenised as covert SPLM activity under

---

[1] Vezzadini, 'The 1924 Revolution', 32–33; Abbas Ghabboush, 'Growth of Black Political Consciousness', 1; Howell, 'Political Leadership and Organisation in the Southern Sudan', 196–98; 'Police Conspiracy in Equatoria Province,' newspaper cutting, 20 August 1969, TNA FCO 39.480.

other names.[2] These narratives were echoed in my interviews (with men) in South Sudan, of spying and being betrayed by 'collaborators'.[3]

This creates a problem of representation. This chapter could present this history as some of its narrators would like, as a seemingly united field of action, with brave rebels making bold stands in the National Assembly and universities, speaking out for peace and honest negotiations, and organising subversive fund-raising and information-passing to 'the South' (in general). Alternatively, the chapter could follow others who argue that there was no evidence for rebel mobilisation among displaced people and that the manoeuvrings of self-described politicians and elite university students, breaking alliance after alliance with infighting and corruption allegations, generally had little relevance to the progress of the war.

Both of these summaries have some truth, but they focus primarily on comparatively well-off or at least well-educated and well-connected (mostly) men engaged in explicitly political activity. The second part of this chapter briefly explores the class divisions – the formal educational attainment and employment, access to middle-class and university spaces and homes, and gendered time – that were needed to participate in this 'leadership' work. It then explores other, more peripheral revolutionary actions, including the mobilisation songs of the Akut Kuei music group, and organisation of recruitment drives and information-sharing, among the majority of poorer working residents (which included some of these students, journalists, and political activists mentioned above; there was no real line between these forms and spaces of action). Many people organised funds and networks of information and support to help others travel to join the SPLA or to go back to home villages to join local defence militias, out of conviction or to escape the pressures or direct targeting of the brutal urban state.[4] Generally referred to as the *jongo* (a colloquial Sudanese Arabic term for casual or seasonally employed agricultural workers, particularly on

---

[2] Elijah Biar Kuol, in Juba, 12 September 2013; Joseph Ukel Abango, in Juba, 1 November 2013; Nhial Bol, in Juba, 18 October 2013. For one of the more ambitious accounts of this subversive history, see Abbas Ghabboush, 'Growth of Black Political Consciousness'. There is substantial material available in the Communist Party, National Democratic Alliance, and Amnesty International archives, all held in the International Institute of Social History, Amsterdam.

[3] These accounts are always by men: Raja, a young woman, pointed this out in Maper Akot, 2 September 2013.

[4] Jok, *Sudan*, 78.

large commercial farms), many of these recruits made up the rank and file of the SPLA's New Sudan Brigade battalions formed in 1995.

Within all this work, this chapter tries to explore what people wanted to do with this work, what they wanted to change, and how they thought they could do it. A lot of scholarship has focused on the intentions of the war: whether people were aiming for the secession of the south, a radically new Sudan, the specific liberation of their homeland or a community, or a combination or shifting array of these rough ideas. But people's actions were generally shaped by what spaces and forms of action were possible, whether these actions matched up with their aims or not. There were many different ways to fight, for some kind of liberation.

6.1 Underground Politics

Political groups opposed to the Sudan governments of Nimeiri and then Sadiq al-Mahdi proliferated since the late 1970s, centred around the homes, study spaces, and offices of southern white-collar workers, school and university students, and the growing class of businessmen, politicians, and journalists, in Juba, Khartoum, and Cairo.[5] The Southern Sudan Liberation Movement; the Juba, Wau and Malakal African People's Organisation; the National Action Movement; and the African National Front all printed leaflets and organised rallies and protests, taking up various reformist, secessionist, and communist approaches to collective anger at the division and fragmentation of the southern regional government, abuses of central government powers from Khartoum, and the idea of national unity and a new Sudan.[6]

---

[5] Following his coup in 1969, Nimeiri banned party politics by the early 1970s under his new socialist national project, rendering these foundering parties and their politicians relatively redundant. Other forms of open organisation – like university unions, trade unions, and the Communist party – were shut down or restricted in the early to mid-1970s. Sikainga, *Organized Labor and Social Change*, 16.

[6] Young, 'Intellectual Origins', 203; this particularly involved Matthew Obur, Lam Akol, Wani Igga, Abraham Wani, and many other prominent political figures. See (with a critical view) Lam Akol, *Southern Sudan: Colonialism, Resistance, and Autonomy* (Red Sea Press, 2007), 3–6; James Wani Igga, *Southern Sudan: Battles Fought and the Secrecy of Diplomacy* (Roberts & Brothers, 2008), 10–17.

6.1 Underground Politics

During the popular uprisings that brought down Nimeiri in 1985 and in the parliamentary democratic reconstruction that followed, some of these established politicians and long-term Khartoum residents – old hands from the Southern Front and SANU parties of the 1960s – formed the Southern Sudan Political Association; mostly younger or more recent arrivals and academics grouped themselves as the Southern Sudanese in Khartoum.[7] These fractured into a host of parties and groups, known by various acronyms, including the People's Progressive Party (PPP), founded by the MP Eliaba James Surur in 1986, and the Sudan African People's Congress (SAPCO), the Sudan African Congress(SAC), the Sudan People's Federal Party (SPFP), the new incarnation of SANU, and others.[8] The Nuba Mountains priest and politician Philip Abbas Ghaboush led the Sudan National Party, and El-Amin Hamouda led the General Union of the Nuba Mountains.[9] Altogether, these parties – with the Darfur Development Front, the General Union of the Ingessana Hills, the General Union of Southern Funj, and the General Union of the Northern and Southern Funj – represented the peripheries of Sudan, via support from migrant workers in Sudan's cities; they had a brief coalition as the Sudan Rural Solidarity movement, holding a rally in Khartoum in December 1985.[10]

Many of the leaders and organisers of these groups had met repeatedly through 1985 in political detention at Kober prison (where Lam Akol and Edward Lino, the late politician from Abyei, organised history teaching during detention).[11] Southern and Nuba political groups organised into the Union of Southern African Parties (USAP) in July 1987, including other technically non-southern opposition parties such as the Communists and Democratic Unionists. Led by Philip Abbas and Eliaba James Surur, USAP organised a dramatic

---

[7] Akol, *Southern Sudan*, 43. The Southern Sudanese in Khartoum became the Sudan African Congress, holding its first meeting at the University of Khartoum; Madut-Arop, *Sudan's Painful Road to Peace*, 192.

[8] Close family members of Eliaba Surur, in Juba, 24 March 2017.

[9] CMS Newsletter No. 352, September 1971, SCF A173 Sudan.

[10] Akol, *Southern Sudan*, 65, 70: the 1985 elections caused extensive splits, including Philip Abbas Ghabboush winning the majority-displaced constituency of Haj Yousif, standing as the Sudanese National Party (SNP) against Sudan Rural Solidarity (SRS) and according to Lam Akol splitting the vote across the city.

[11] Akol, *Southern Sudan*, 61.

procession to the June 1986 opening of parliament (apparently dressed in Kenneth Kaunda–style safari suits) to announce their boycott of the undemocratic and unrepresentative parliamentary session, in part due to the growing war in the south.[12] Their procession was reportedly supported by displaced and other poor residents, and members of the Rural Solidarity organisations. By the mid-1990s – particularly after Eliaba James Surur was repeatedly arrested then moved into exile in 1994 – the National Democratic Alliance (NDA) became the nominal collective for opposition organisation.[13] Established as an exile opposition coalition by twelve political parties – including many of the above – and fifty-one unions in October 1989 following the coup, the NDA is broadly characterised as a failure.[14] Its elite political coalition fragmented from 1999, but the organisation continued in theory and name.[15] From a local perspective within Khartoum, the NDA was a collective term for those organising discussions and debates around the war and Sudan's future.[16]

The archival record of these parties and groups – of splits, jockeying for political position, and accusations of bad faith and money-grubbing, generally – disguises how displaced workers and poor residents engaged with these organisations and their meetings and discussions. Many people I met across South Sudan produced minutes, records, and descriptions of seminar circuits and political meetings held in schools and church centres, as well as in the Comboni Playground and Khartoum's university campuses.[17] Men and women detailed the speeches and debates organised by southern and Darfur

---

[12] The Democratic Unionist Party had southern members; Dhieu Kuel, in Mayen Ulem, 21 August 2013; Madut-Arop, *Sudan's Painful Road to Peace*, 171, 144–45.

[13] Diing Chen Diing, in Aweil, 12 August 2013; NDA Comprehensive Political Settlement Committee (CPSC), 'Memorandum to IGAD Secretariat,' 10 August 2000, IISH NDA.41.

[14] Lesch and Fadl, *Coping with Torture*, 2; Johnson, *The Root Causes of Sudan's Civil Wars*, 122, 138.

[15] Canada, Immigration and Refugee Board of Canada, 'Sudan: National Democratic Alliance (NDA); Location of International Offices; Role and Mandate of Branch Office in Washington; the process NDA Follows When Verifying Claims to Party Membership; Description of Stamps and Letterhead; Presence of NDA in Sudan', 17 April 2003, SDN40323.E.

[16] The Sudanese Victims of Torture Group, 'Annual Report on the Human Rights Situation in Sudan', March 2001–March 2002, IISH NDA.90, 3–5.

[17] Diing Chen Diing, in Aweil, 12 August 2013; Dhieu Kuel, in Mayen Ulem, 21 August 2013.

6.1 Underground Politics

movements such as the United Popular Front, as well as other parties or associations that are untraceable in wider literature and archives.[18] Atak, who was brought up in Khartoum in a middle-class family, remembered how she attended various conferences and house meetings; by 2010 she was standing as a USAP candidate in Aweil.[19]

These meetings and discussions were accessible to at least some of Khartoum's poorer residents partly because many of their organisers were local residents and workers anyway.[20] Many ex-MPs and political activists were employed in Catholic school and church networks, in local businesses, and in low-level civil service positions.[21] Many prominent politicians, including James Surur, Joseph Okel, Philip Abbas Ghabboush, Hilary Paul Logali, and Toby Maduot, either made their living by teaching or working in churches or in religious organisations like the Sudan Council of Churches, or visited schools and churches to take part in discussions.[22] Attendees and participants were not just educated young men with enough income to have spare time, but included less-literate market workers and women.[23]

The most active group among the large school and university student community in Khartoum was the African National Front (ANF). The ANF was an old organisation, having been recreated and the name reused several times since the 1960 and '70s.[24] Two now-prominent ex-students of a Khartoum-based university said that they re-established the ANF with a group of students in the late 1990s, using university records to find notes on the founding of the 'original' Southern Students Welfare Front in 1958 as a means of establishing themselves as part of this student heritage.[25] Its membership was drawn from university students and graduates, who became teachers, legal clerks, and church workers, many of whom now live and work

---

[18] Anei Deng Akok, in Aweil, 13 August 2013; Stephen Ayaga, in Aweil, 8 August 2013; Dhieu Kuel, in Mayen Ulem, 21 August 2013.
[19] Atak Akol Diing, female USAP candidate, 14 August 2013.
[20] Including those with positions within the NIF and NCP administration; see Chapter 7.
[21] Diing Chen Diing, in Aweil, 12 August 2013.
[22] Diing Chen Diing, in Aweil, 15 July 2013.
[23] Dhieu Kuel, in Mayen Ulem, 21 August 2013; Atak Akol Diing, in Aweil, 14 August 2013; Jimmy Wongo, in Juba, 18 October 2013; among many other accounts.
[24] John Gau Riak, in Aweil, 28 June 2013.
[25] Ibid.; Yïen Matthew, in Juba, 10 September 2013.

in regional towns in South Sudan.[26] Members shared pamphlets and books, put up posters and bulletins, screened films made about the war in the south, and sang SPLA and Nuba Mountains rebel songs.[27] Students organised mutual welfare, and petitioned for better conditions at universities. Membership included northern, Nuba, and Darfur students, as well as students from the Communist party.[28]

Much like the NDA, the ANF was explicitly a conglomeration of political ideas and aims. 'It is a shelter that student southerners are hiding themselves [under] to fight the system ... the ANF is the umbrella.'[29] Student members' politics ranged from demands for liberal parliamentary democracy to Nyerere's ideas of African socialism.[30] Some members were straightforwardly pro-SPLM/A, seeing their membership in the ANF as a proxy for the SPLM, and supporting either secessionist aims or Garang's ideas of a New Sudan and a democratic revolution in the country; the language of marginalisation found Nuba and Darfur student support.[31] Alfred Taban, a prominent journalist in Khartoum through the 1990s, noted that ANF students – who generally lived in Haj Yousif and other neighbourhoods of the mostly displaced – were very active in encouraging residents to be 'conscious of their rights', partly by working in adult and evening education classes.[32] As increasing numbers of women joined secondary schools and universities by the mid-1990s onwards, the ANF's female membership expanded.[33]

As an umbrella for dissent, the ANF contained serious divisions. It broke into factions after the 1991 split in the SPLM/A, dividing

---

[26] Yïen Matthew, in Juba, 10 September 2013.
[27] Anei Deng Akok, in Aweil, 13 August 2013; Anei provided me with a battered copy of SPLA songs, written in Sudanese Arabic and containing a lot written by Nuba and Darfur authors, specifically in support of the SPLA's pan-Sudanese revolution. Makor, *African National Front*, 18.
[28] Yïen Matthew, in Juba, 10 September 2013; John Gau Riak, in Aweil, 28 June 2013.
[29] John Gau Riak, in Aweil, 28 June 2013.
[30] Makor, *African National Front*, 17.
[31] Lazarus Lual, in Juba, 19 October 2013; Yïen Matthew, in Juba, 10 September 2013.
[32] Alfred Taban, in Juba, 16 October 2013.
[33] See the list of women activists at Makor, *African National Front*, 15; including Victoria Yai Akol, Ida Musa, Mary Sokoji, Nyanjur Ibrahim, and others.

unionist and secessionist student members.[34] Groups got into fights with each other and with other student groups, and members were arrested (and some disappeared). By 2001, the main ANF had been pretty much torn apart by ethnic and political factionalism and accusations of corruption.[35] From this period on, ostensibly in response to John Garang's call for southern students to return to the south to support the SPLM and build the rebel government, many students and graduates left Khartoum for SPLM/A-held territories or organising spaces in east Africa, some travelling through the Nuba Mountains with help from the SPLA.[36] These men and (some) women produced a stream of discussions, texts, songs, and groups over these two decades.

6.2 Talking Shop

Across these two decades, the main political activity in Khartoum was talking.[37] This should not be interpreted as all talk and no action; sharing information was a crucial political action in the securitised circumstances of Khartoum. As Lual Aguer explained, 'when we talked to non-northerners, we talked about what is our right and what is not our right, and this was also struggling – it means you are fighting. Because the person is supposed to find the right way – when he finds the right way from us, then he has to join us.'[38] Teachers shared updates on military operations in the south, and people met at homes and parties, including during religious days at Comboni Majaneen, in schools in Mayo Mandela, and at the Comboni schools at Bahri and St Peter & Paul, to talk about events in the war and about the future.[39] As Angelina remembers of parties at Comboni Majaneen: 'so that's like the time when people were discussing about SPLA, how people will go back to the South, and how they will also stay normally with the

---

[34] Makor, *African National Front*, 7, 19; separatist wings formed different student groups with a variety of multiple splinters.
[35] Incorporated into the SPLM as part of the Youth League after 2005. Anei Deng Akok, in Aweil, 13 August 2013.
[36] John Gau Riak, in Aweil, 28 June 2013; Yien Matthew, in Juba, 10 September 2013.
[37] Paul Kuel Kuel, in Aweil, 9 August 2013. Academics and political observers have long criticised Sudanese domestic opposition politics as a 'talking shop'.
[38] Lual Lual Aguer, in Apada, 15 August 2013.
[39] Diing Chen Diing, in Aweil, 15 July and 12 August 2013.

Arabs in Khartoum, secretly'.[40] This talking was part of political and historical education. Atak described how at these parties she learnt from secondary school students about the two southern civil wars, and the idea of a 'cold war': 'we realised what was happening in the south'.[41] Discussions included histories of famous southern figures like the prophets Ngundeng, Awuo Kon, and Arianhdit; the Anya Nya fighters and chiefs Tafeng, Ali Gbatala, Lohide, and Akuei; and many others.[42]

As large groups and parties were forbidden without security permission, outside of schools and churches people passed news and ideas through chains of conversations. 'So you talk to one person, and that one will go to talk with another person, and on and on.'[43] Better-off residents met up in cars, driving round in small groups to buy time for political discussion, and passing information on to schoolteachers and church organisers to spread the word.[44] Not all of this information was necessarily correct: 'you know, there were times when we told lies ... even when, at times, the SPLM and SPLA was at lowest ebb, we kept their hopes up, by saying no, you know, they've acquired more weaponry there now, they're moving and you'll soon hear this will happen, and you know, just keep raising their morale'.[45] Discussion groups debated the SPLM/A's manifesto in the 1980s, and made notes on Garang's speeches and other announcements and factional statements through the war.[46] Plenty of critical history books, booklets and photocopied documents, speeches, and song lyrics made their way around, often 'a little worn out' or faint from re-photocopying,

---

[40] Angelina went to parties at Comboni Majaneen: 'Whenever there are some political activities, that are to be discussed, so they like to call the young men to listen, because these people are getting old and these young people will remain, so they need these people to listen for the future.... So that's like the time when people were discussing about SPLA, how people will go back to the South.' Angelina Majok, in Mayen Ulem, 16 July 2013.

[41] Atak Akol Diing, in Aweil, 14 August 2013. Atak was a USAP candidate as a young woman in Khartoum.

[42] Lazarus Leek Mawut, 'The SPLM's New Sudan Vision and Southern Sudanese Nationalism: Are They Compatible?', Current Conditions in the Southern Sudan conference, Oxford, 13 February 1999, 16, 20.

[43] Lual Lual Aguer, in Apada, 15 August 2013; Nhial Bol, in Juba, 18 October 2013.

[44] Jimmy Wongo, in Juba, 18 October 2013; Marko Mathiang Deng, in Apada, 17 August 2013; Diing Chen Diing, in Aweil, 12 August 2013.

[45] Jimmy Wongo, in Juba, 18 October 2013. [46] Akol, *Southern Sudan*, 27, 42.

6.2 Talking Shop

including the Darfur opposition's Black Book in 2003, translated into English locally and re-circulated.[47] As Dor Tartizio laughed, it was all about passing things, 'pass, pass, pass, pass'.[48]

Accessing and discussing this information was a subversive act in its own right by the mid-1990s in Khartoum. Security forces conducted raids on private homes and offices; confiscated books, photocopiers, and fax machines; and detained at least one person for the unauthorised possession of a fax machine.[49] Journalists, editors, and press workers, as well as teachers and university staff, were most exposed to these abuses, but also best positioned to make use of photocopiers and early computers to share information and print flyers and rebuttals of government statements.[50] Some residents of Haj Yousif and other predominantly displaced peripheries called people at the English-language *Khartoum Monitor* and other friendly journalists to record testimonies of thefts, beatings, and sexual assaults, to print and pass on to human rights monitors.[51] Dhieu remembers visiting the *Khartoum Monitor* offices to read the 'carton news': 'they are the glue, the facts! But not to be printed – you read them and you leave them there. You can find if the SPLA recaptured some town, or about the death of Arab [Sudanese] soldiers.' These printouts of international media were just stored – 'they put them in cartons, in a closed box, inside the office. That's why we named them that.'[52] Nhial Bol, Albino Okeny, Edward Lado, and Alfred Taban, the most well-known journalists and reporters for Reuters, the BBC, and the *Khartoum Monitor*, were repeatedly arrested, detained, and fined throughout the 1990s and early 2000s for various critical articles and infractions.[53]

---

[47] Stephen Enock Tombe got his copy of the Darfuri Black Book in February 2003, translated into English in Khartoum; there was also a book written by Professor Suleiman Mohamed Suleiman in 2000 circulating titled 'The Sudan: Wars of Identity and Resources'. Stephen Enock Tombe, *In Hope & Despair: Serving the People, Church and Nation of South Sudan* (2015), 81; Akol, *Southern Sudan*, 17; 'The Black Book,' anonymous translation, March 2000, MEDU 17/3/GEN/67.

[48] Dor Tartizio Buni, in Juba, 14 October 2013.

[49] Rone, *Behind the Red Line*, 161–62.

[50] Akol, *Southern Sudan*, 26–27, 42–43.

[51] Dhieu Kuel, in Mayen Ulem, 4 July 2013.   [52] Ibid.

[53] Nhial Bol, in Juba, 18 October 2013; Alfred Taban, in Juba, 16 October 2013; the Sudanese Victims of Torture Group, 'Annual Report on the Human Rights Situation in Sudan.' For a wider background on Sudanese press history, see Heather Sharkey, 'A Century in Print: Arabic Journalism and Nationalism in

This was not just security service paranoia; Garang's mainstream SPLM/A and SPLA factions had been circulating information and propaganda through Khartoum since the 1980s. From 1983 to 1991, this was primarily via Radio SPLA, broadcast from Naru in Ethiopia at 3 pm every Friday and listened to carefully by residents of all backgrounds.[54] Teachers arranged listening meetings in the Khartoum University Staff Club.[55] Melanie, originally from Juba and growing up as a young girl in Khartoum, remembers:

> my father used to open this Radio SPLA. It was in 85. 84, 85. He used to open the radio inside, even if it was very hot. They sat inside. That is when we [kids] started to realise that there is something bad [going on]. Yeah, we listened – we just kept quiet, we don't comment. After that, they discussed – they always sent us outside.

Later, at school, Melanie discussed what she heard with other girls, 'about the killing, the starvation, and the evacuation of people to neighbouring countries'.[56] Tapings of the broadcasts were carefully circulated and hidden.[57] When Radio SPLA went off-air in 1991 with the fall of the Derg regime in Ethiopia, Garang's speeches and other messages from SPLM/A and NDA leaderships continued to circulate as copied-out text and, later, mobile phone recordings,[58] helped by organisers across the city.[59]

This information flowed both ways, particularly from southern and Nuba workers within universities, government services, and the military – a large minority of displaced residents in Khartoum. Elijah, a radio operator in government service, explained that he was 'getting

---

Sudan, 1899–1999,' *International Journal of Middle East Studies* 31, no. 4 (1999): 531–49.

[54] Madut-Arop, *Sudan's Painful Road to Peace*, 92.
[55] Akol, *Southern Sudan*, 41.   [56] Melanie Itto, in Juba, 23 October 2013.
[57] Michael Thiop Lang, in Aweil, 10 July 2013.
[58] John Garang de Mabior, 'Khartoum Press Conference by Telephone', 17 November 1999, in IISH NDA.125: 'I greet all the marginalized Sudanese everywhere in the countryside from Nimule to Halfa, from Genneina to Kassala, in the streets and in camps for displaced people around the capital.' The SPLM/A Update was distributed within liberated areas of Sudan and in the diaspora. Christopher Tounsel, 'Khartoum Goliath: SPLM/SPLA Update and Martial Theology during the Second Sudanese Civil War', *Journal of Africana Religions* 4, no. 2 (2016): 133–34.
[59] Atak Akol Diing, in Aweil, 14 August 2013.

6.2 Talking Shop 241

fresh news' from army employees in particular.[60] This was nothing really new; John Garang was himself living in Haj Yousif in 1983, before the Bor mutiny and the start of the war, and held regular gatherings at his house with teachers and military staff.[61] As Garang said in a speech in March 1986, 'we are inside the Sudan, inside the General Headquarters of the Army. This is how we get our information. How do we know that two battalions have left Khartoum? We are not an external force and this is a misconception.'[62]

While the scale and expertise of this informant work is likely exaggerated, it was a common practice to try to share potentially useful information, either with known SPLM/A contacts or with intermediaries (like USAP and ANF members, or church leaders) who might be able to do something with it, and to help people who wanted to join the rebellion. Many people's relatives were already fighting either within the SPLA or in militias near home. Emmanuel's brother was fighting with the SPLA in Abyei in the 1990s, and fighters visited friends and family in Khartoum from the south, sometimes to try to recruit, including at Comboni Majaneen: 'people tried to tell us to go to the SPLA, what are you doing here, when your people are dying there?'[63] Dhieu was active with the National Democratic Alliance and its meetings in the mid-1990s, and during his work in a local court as a filing clerk would try to look for potentially useful information in paperwork and pass it on to NDA colleagues.[64] Middle-class residents generally had contacts outside Khartoum; for example, office staff in the Sudan Council of Churches collected information and funds through meals and work meetings with southern colleagues in the police and schools, and transferred them via friends in London, as well as occasionally booking flights and arranging exit permits for people leaving Khartoum to join the opposition.[65] Members of USAP included civil

---

[60] Elijah Biar Kuol, in Juba, 12 September 2013; Elijah was a radio operator in government service. Also discussed by Emmanuel Deng Anei, in Apada, 3 June 2013; and Dhieu Kuel, in Mayen Ulem, 4 July 2013.
[61] Madut-Arop, *Sudan's Painful Road to Peace*, 43–44; Akol, *Southern Sudan*, 19–21.
[62] John Garang de Mabior's speech at opening of Koka Dam Conference with National Alliance for National Salvation, 20 March 1986, in Wël, *The Genius of Dr John Garang*, 100.
[63] Emmanuel Deng Anei, in Apada, 3 June 2013.
[64] Dhieu Kuel, in Mayen Ulem, 21 August 2013.
[65] Clement Janda, in Arua, 6 March 2017; Akol, *Southern Sudan*, 21–23.

servants and church workers, who helped to arrange and fund the travel of medical staff and military personnel to join various SPLA groups, including the Nuba wing under Yousif Kuwa, via colleagues working in aid agencies or as local police or farm workers across Kordofan and Kassala.[66] A university lecturer from central Equatoria had several Darfuri friends who helped members of their displaced communities leave Khartoum to join the SPLA 'to fight Arabism in Sudan', and his regular bookseller 'used to disappear for a few weeks to take guns to fighters in Darfur'.[67]

This is where spy stories become very hard to substantiate. People shared hundreds of stories of dramatic acts of sabotage and subversion, often involving prominent SPLA and SAF commanders and civil servants. I heard several stories of women employed to pass maps and stolen information to contacts in Darfur and Kordofan, travelling on buses with notes hidden in their vaginas.[68] Some spy names and accounts did echo across conversations, repeated in different locations and by men who did not know each other. There are obvious caveats; they were all given by men, many of whom worked within the Sudan government civil and military services through the war. The group 'Black Fox' (named in English and translated as *awan col* in Dinka) was apparently a group of southern Sudanese government and police staff who worked on buying information and transferring it to London and Addis through the early 1990s.[69]

The most common 'spy stories' that I heard centred around a general Dinka-language code name for subversive work: Diin Ajer or Katip Ajer, meaning either the stone religion or the stone battalion, implying that it was impossible to break; its Dinka name was used by non-Dinka interviewees as well.[70] The phrase was used to refer to people engaged

---

[66] Jimmy Wongo, in Juba, 18 October 2013; Ayii Bol, in Aweil, 16 August 2013.
[67] Yosa Wawa, in Juba, 26 June 2019. This included Yahiya Bolat, the Darfur SPLA leader, before he left to join the rebellion. Dhieu Kuel, in Mayen Ulem, 21 August 2013.
[68] Jimmy Wongo, in Juba, 18 October 2013; Albino Madhan, in Aweil, 9 August 2013; Dhieu Kuel, in Mayen Ulem, 4 July 2013; Abaker Thelatheen, in Apada, 14 April 2013.
[69] Paul Kuel Kuel, in Aweil, 9 August 2013; also Marko Mathiang Deng, in Apada, 17 August 2013.
[70] Marko Mathiang Deng, in Apada, 17 August 2013; Paul Kuel Kuel, in Aweil, 9 August 2013. The SPLA apparently called it Katip Ajer, 'the Stone Battalion'. See Chapter 8 for more on Katip Ajer.

6.2 Talking Shop 243

in deeply subversive work across Khartoum and Sudan government-held territory. This includes stories of South Sudanese officials working within the Khartoum regime sending information to the SPLA – 'they will say this news, we [got] it from Diin Ajer! [Laugh]' – and stories of SPLA recruiters working in Khartoum, or about spying within the SAF.[71] Marko, who had fought in Kerubino Kuanyin Bol's Anyanya Two unit and then was integrated into the SAF as a driver, explained how he worked with Katip Ajer: 'there were difficulties of getting clothes for the SPLA, and I was responsible for the store and everything in it, so the people I've trained I used to give them money and the clothes, and they came [south] with it. And when they reach a place called Jebelein, so they gave [the clothes] to a certain lady called Asunta.' Marko also sent small parcels of stolen supplies and information on troop movements through *jongo* workers via the Damazin road (see the next section of this chapter). Some of Marko's SAF colleagues were also involved, including a Nuba man who was arrested and disappeared; 'most of the people that [we worked with] were women, especially the tea makers'.[72] Across accounts, the work under the name Diin or Katip Ajer ended in 1996 with sustained security pressure, although other subversive work continued.[73] The name Katip Ajer re-emerged in 2005, and is detailed in Chapter 8.

In retrospect, from the comparative safety of South Sudan after the war, these spy names and spy stories might feel like fictions that help non-combatants to feel like they were part of the fight. But while likely a bit embellished, people probably did do this work, and I have now met hundreds of SPLA and militia fighters who at various points had lived and worked in Khartoum, or were recruited in the city and travelled south to take up arms. Code names were reasonable in circumstances of real risk. Throughout the 1990s and early 2000s, people explained how loved ones and neighbours went missing, and how others (or they themselves) were detained, beaten, and tortured on suspicion of rebel activities. Amnesty International's archives are filled with reports of detentions, disappearances, torture, and murders, including southern SAF soldiers and officers, lecturers,

---

[71] James Akec Nhial, in Juba, 8 September 2013; Emmanuel Deng Anei, in Apada, 3 June 2013.
[72] Marko Mathiang Deng, in Apada, 17 August 2013.
[73] James Akec Nhial, in Juba, 10 September 2013; Paul Kuel Kuel, in Aweil, 9 August 2013.

teachers, ex-politicians, civil servants, church and aid workers, and everyday workers.[74] Makoi Wol Manuer, the head of the Sudan Council of Churches' relocation programme, was detained and held incommunicado on suspicion of recruiting people to join the SPLA.[75] Moses Machar and Richard Kalam Sakit, two lecturers at the University of Juba (transferred to Khartoum in 1990), were arrested in 1991 and detained at Kober Prison, suspected of contacting the SPLA, along with hundreds of other residents, particularly from Dinka and Nuer communities.[76] And earlier, in October 1989, a nurse named Buthina – originally from southern Sudan – was detained in Omdurman prison for two months, accused of passing information to foreign diplomats and the SPLA.[77] There are hundreds of other reports; as a veteran politician and Khartoum resident said, 'go to Kober – inside there, you can read the history of South Sudan on the walls'.[78]

Most people who said that they were involved in this – from sharing information, to recruiting and fundraising – explained to me that they were working for Garang's SPLM/A. Sometimes they were also organising to recruit and fund local militias defending communities back home, including from the SPLA; this was not necessarily mutually exclusive. People also worked to support other militias and factions, including those of Riek Machar, Kerubino Kuanyin, and Paulino Matip, who were (particularly from the mid-1990s) supported by

---

[74] For example, Amnesty International recorded a series of southern Sudanese detainees accused of SPLA involvement over 1989–90, including Emmanuel Doku Joseph, engineer with National Electricity Corporation, arrested 2 December 1989, and Deng Macham Angai, chairman of the banned Southern Sudan Farmers' Union and 'chief of chiefs' detailed in this book, arrested January 1990 after a dispute with a security official. Others detained in Kober included Lt Col Dr Charles Yor Odhok, arrested 5 May 1990; Abraham Ngor Luong, an accountant arrested on 28 June 1990; Peter Panwil Yata, manager of a church relief organization, arrested 11 November 1990; Gabriel Matur Malek, a former minister in the Bahr el Ghazal regional government, arrested 26 November 1990; and Mou Bol Akot, a UNHCR employee arrested on 24 November 1990 and reportedly left very ill after beatings in prison. Amnesty International report for April 1992, IISH AI 03/92, 4.
[75] Ibid., 9.
[76] Amnesty International report for 1991, IISH AI 09/91, 27, 29–30; this echoes Amnesty's 1989 reports.
[77] Amnesty International Index, 22 November 1989, IISH AI 54/21/89.
[78] Jimmy Wongo, in Juba, 18 October 2013.

6.2 Talking Shop

Bashir's government as proxy forces, and who also mobilised recruits from Khartoum; this work is the focus of Chapter 7.

Working to support Garang's SPLM/A did not necessarily mean everyone was working towards the same ends. Many residents, from impoverished and wealthy backgrounds alike, were seeking friends and alliances with Nuba, Darfur, and other Sudanese residents and rebel movements, working to imagine a revolutionary democratic New Sudan and to bring people together on this basis: 'we were just discussing: how can Black people unite?'[79] Other residents, particularly those originally from the Equatorias but generally from across displaced society, believed that they were working towards the secession of the south – often because there had been too many abuses and atrocities to imagine a united Sudan.[80] And many other people changed their minds or held complicated and equivocal positions, through the long and confusing war. USAP is representative of this. Over the 1980s and 1990s, its membership in general hoped to work towards a New Sudan, working with other Black Sudanese opposition 'in the struggle against state directed racism, religious bigotry, cultural imperialism and historic injustices'; by the early 2000s, with the failure of the National Democratic Alliance and a resurgent SPLM/A pushing forward the possibility of secession, USAP's position had mostly changed.[81]

But even if residents had ideas of how the war could and should end, it was very hard to know what actions might actually be helpful or make any difference at all. For some people, this meant that marginally 'subversive' actions were essentially pointless, outweighed by the risk of even being suspected of dissident work. For others, this meant acting in the faith that it might potentially help – 'because the information I get – even a single bit – could help at least 100 people ... [but if I don't,] if I'm happy, my stomach is full, and all those people are starving – what have I done?'[82]

---

[79] Stephen Ayaga, in Aweil, 8 August 2013; also Albino Madhan, in Aweil, 9 August 2013; Paul Kuel Kuel, in Aweil, 9 August 2013.
[80] Peter Adwok Nyaba, *South Sudan: The State We Aspire To* (Centre for Advanced Studies of Africa, 2011), 155.
[81] Kunijwok Gwado Ayoker to Daniel arap Moi, n.d., c. 2002, SAD 89/10/106-111.
[82] Paul Kuel Kuel, in Aweil, 9 August 2013.

For a few others, taking action on principle was the point. Some people engaged in open political defiance, with few revolutionary consequences other than their own punishment by the police and security services. A prominent example are the actions taken by the ANF group at Nilein University over April and May 2002, explained to me in 2013 by Dhieu, the Dinka office clerk and teacher in Aweil, and Yïen Matthew, a Nuer political organiser then working in Juba, both of whom had been involved (and who had not seen each other since). Dhieu explained:

> We raised the SPLM flag in Nilein University, me and some others. We made a celebration for the anniversary of the SPLA['s founding].... We raised it up on the university campus, and we were arrested, we were twenty-five in number. We spent twenty-two days in jail in security cells.... We denied all the accusations that we belonged to the SPLA.[83]

These celebrations were part of the ANF's celebrations across Khartoum, partly intended to eulogise the late SPLM/A Nuba Mountains commander Yousif Kuwa Makki, who had died in March 2001. Yïen Matthew, a leader of one of the ANF factions at the time, led a previous parade in April at Ahlia University. Those who were not released with Dhieu were sentenced to a few months' imprisonment in Dabak Prison and subject to heavy fines. The raising of the SPLM/A flag at Nilein University was, according to ANF member Ajack Makor, about 'a spirit of defiance against subjugation, intimidations and threats by the Ingaz regime and readiness to confront it within Khartoum city'.[84]

6.3 Class Privilege, Social Divides, and Separate Political Spaces

Most displaced people in Khartoum did not have the time, funds, literacy, or access to university spaces where a lot of this explicitly 'political' organisation took place. Many residents also could not

---

[83] Dhieu Kuel, in Mayen Ulem, 21 August 2013; Yïen Matthew, in Juba, 10 September 2013. These events are corroborated by Amnesty International reports AFR 540092002 SUDAN UA 15402 Fear for Safety: Incommunicado Detention: Possible Prisoners of Conscience (POCs): 25 Students – Members of the African National Front (ANF), May 2002, and SOUDAN: 25 étudiants membres du Front national africain (FNA): Further information on UA 154/02, July 2002, AI IISH UA 154/02.

[84] Makor, *African National Front*, 26.

6.3 Class, Social Divides, Political Spaces 247

afford to expose themselves to the risks of arrest and violence that even the suspicion of political involvement could bring. Women in particular were already navigating abusive police and local authorities with the tea selling, beer brewing, and domestic work that kept families afloat and children fed.

Differences of class relationships and privilege shaped political thought and action across the southern displaced communities in Khartoum.[85] The explicitly political and rebellious organisation detailed above was mostly the domain of formally educated, wealthier, male residents within an extremely small student, teacher, civil service, and industrial worker class that had emerged over the 1930s onwards.[86] There were still only a few thousand university-educated southern people – mostly men – even by the early 1980s. Otherwise, the other space where collective organisation was possible was the military, and this is where revolutionary action has repeatedly come from in Sudan's peripheries, in mutinies, uprisings, and rebel movements. These are the (mostly) men who made up the southern political class in Khartoum by the 1990s, and who were in the position to gain access to waged jobs, business opportunities, and time for social and political organisation. Most ex-MPs and other prominent members of this educated class of men were under surveillance through the 1990s and early 2000s.[87] Some of them took up paid but politically dubious roles within Sudan government administration, often on the claimed grounds that they would be more benevolent officials than others, or they might be able to do some spying as above.[88] The primary

---

[85] See Marta Iñiguez de Heredia, 'The Conspicuous Absence of Class and Privilege in the Study of Resistance in Peacebuilding Contexts', *International Peacekeeping* 25, no. 3 (2018): 325–48.

[86] See Lilian Passmore Sanderson and Neville Sanderson, *Education, Religion & Politics in Southern Sudan 1899–1964* (Ithaca, 1981).

[87] Biro, 'Situation of Human Rights in the Sudan'; Jimmy Wongo, in Juba, 18 October 2013.

[88] Many of these men have documented and justified their working lives. See Gérard Prunier, 'Sudanese African Political Parties', 1988, SAD 938.11.41-60; Howell, 'Political Leaders in the Southern Sudan'; Justin Willis, 'The Southern Problem: Representing Sudan's Southern Provinces to c. 1970', *Journal of African History* 56, no. 2 (2015): 281–300; Elijah Malok, *The Southern Sudan: Struggle for Liberty* (Kenway Publications, 2009); Akol, *Southern Sudan*; Nyaba, *Politics of Liberation*; Jacob Akol, *Burden of Nationality: Memoirs of an African Aidworker/Journalist, 1970s–1990s* (Paulines Publications Africa, 2006); Mawut Achiecque Mach Guarak, *Integration and Fragmentation of the Sudan: An African Renaissance* (AuthorHouse, 2011); Bona Malwal, *Sudan and*

constituency for their politics were university students, essentially the successors to this employment and political space, and they moved in a specific space too, in the better-off central suburbs and university campuses of the city.[89] Many of these men and their families supported immediate kin and clan members, paid some student fees and funded some ethnic and cultural associations, and acted as speakers at associational, school, and university events: 'whenever they have a rally, especially at Juba University, we are asked to speak as guests of honour'.[90]

Generally, though, the southern political community across Khartoum was divided and disconnected, by ethnicity, language, and literacy; by educational experience and knowledge; by gender and poverty; by the costs and risks of travelling across the sprawling city; and by experiences of and exposure to the brutalities of the war. This was true in the 1970s, before the second civil war, when these educated elites had little in common, and little connection, with growing numbers of migrant workers and the primary and part-time education they organised for themselves.[91] This disconnection grew with the displacement of hundreds of thousands of impoverished and traumatised people during the wars over the 1980s and 1990s. Focused on survival and constrained to new, remote suburbs by poverty and political risk, these new residents had very different experiences of both the city and the war to older residents.[92] This generally shaped very different attitudes to life in Sudan, local authorities, and political community, as one man born and raised in the city before the war observed slightly condescendingly: 'they were different; they told us the way we speak is like the Arabs, and that "you want to colonise us like

---

South Sudan: From One to Two (Palgrave Macmillan, 2014); Steven Wöndu, *From Bush to Bush: Journey to Liberty in South Sudan* (African Books Collective, 2011).

[89] Howell, 'Political Leadership and Organisation in the Southern Sudan', 143; Willis, 'The Southern Problem'; Howell, 'Political Leaders in the Southern Sudan', 4; Jimmy Wongo, in Juba, 18 October 2013.

[90] Farouk Gatkuoth, in Juba, 30 October 2013. Philip Abbas Ghaboush attended various southern community graduation ceremonies. Stephen Ayaga, in Aweil, 8 August 2013; Diing Chen Diing, in Aweil, 15 July 2013.

[91] Howell, 'Political Leadership and Organisation in the Southern Sudan', 89, 146; Howell, 'Politics in the Southern Sudan', 165.

[92] Kuot Dut Kuot, in Apada, 3 June 2013.

6.3 Class, Social Divides, Political Spaces

Arabs". At that time they wanted to fight Arabs when they met them. And they hated that [they couldn't].'[93]

This disconnection was not a worry for some of these self-described elite politicians, who had little need for these new working poor in their politics. One politician-businessman, a long-term resident and homeowner in Khartoum and after peace in 2005 an SPLM representative to the National Assembly, explained that 'we didn't need them': 'they couldn't give us anything. We only used them for rallies, sometimes.'[94] Connections with the government were more important, as was the more extroverted work of opposition messaging. Archives are full of statements, minutes, and messages to the UN, the United States, and other states and 'to the Sudanese Nation,' generally speaking for but not to their ostensible southern community.[95]

There were some long-term residents and educated middle-class workers who bridged this divide; many poor displaced workers remembered the political discussion and educational work of people including Yousif Kuwa, Eliaba Surur, Philip Abbas, Joseph Ukel, and Joseph Modesto, among other prominent political opposition figures, who often worked in church spaces, in displaced schools, and with the Sudan Council of Churches, Sudan Aid, the Catholic Agency for Overseas Development, and other aid agencies.[96] Some of these middle-class working families were helped with house rents and business capital from relatives in the US and Canadian diaspora by the late 1990s, and many of them worked as teachers in the formal school system.[97] But this working connection did not necessarily overcome the distances, political surveillance, and experiential divides of the city, as Edward Jubara, long-time Sudan Council of Churches worker,

---

[93] Anei Deng Akok, in Aweil, 13 August 2013.
[94] Manoa Aligo, in Koboko, 1 April 2017.
[95] Letter from 'Concerned Southern Sudanese', signed by Abel Alier, Ezekiel M. Kodi, Joseph Ukel Abango, Isaiah Kulang Mabor, and Henry Tong Chol, titled 'Peaceful Resolution of the Conflict in Sudan: Open Appeal to the National Salvation Government, Sudanese Political Forces, the Sudanese Army, Sudan People's Liberation Army (SPLA/SPLM)', October 1995, IISH NDA.121. Also letter from Southern Sudanese in Khartoum to the People's Revolution, 'From the Southern Masses', 7 April 1985, CAR 674/24/2.
[96] Diing Chen Diing, in Aweil, 15 July 2013; Stephen Ayaga, in Aweil, 8 August 2013; Jimmy Wongo, in Juba, 18 October 2013.
[97] Anei Deng Akok, in Aweil, 13 August 2013.

noted – there was 'no real interaction with very poor southern Sudanese'.[98]

6.4 The Working-Class Underground

People living in Khartoum's impoverished peripheries had their own rebellious work. Most ex-residents had had no connections to these politicians and their parties, although some had heard of them.[99] Regardless, from the perspective of people living in Khartoum's slums and *dar es salaams*, 'we saw they were of no importance'.[100]

Previous chapters have detailed the extensive political organisation that residents of these peripheries were engaged in. There was also plenty of information about the war. Most people knew someone, or had a relative in the Sudan Armed Forces, the SPLA, or another militia (or all three).[101] Political discussion was also shaped by what John Garang called being 'educated into the situation by the dynamics of the situation itself'.[102] Throughout the 1990s, people took decisive rebellious actions against the Sudan government – through small acts of resistance, speaking out, and leaving the city to take up arms. These came at people's own breaking points, including hearing of a particular mutiny or local government incident, the destruction of a whole family's herd or village, or the repeated provocations of life in Khartoum.[103] For many young men in particular, leaving the city to join the SPLA was a reasonable response to this provocation. James, gang member and part-time student in the 1990s (see Chapter 3), finally left Khartoum to join his uncle's SPLA battalion in 1999, and argued that this was essentially a response to continued police harassment, poverty and arrest:

This recruitment was supported by the Arabs themselves.... Why I say that – at that time, if [police or authorities] met like three young people from southern Sudan, sitting together, they could arrest them, beat them, and when you ask – why do you beat me and why you arrest me – he said yes,

---

[98] Edward Jubara, in Juba, 14 March 2013.
[99] Kuot Dut Kuot, in Apada, 3 June 2013.
[100] Dut Anyak Dit, in Kuajok, 27 August 2013.
[101] Garang Diing Akol, in Maper Akot, 22 June 2013.
[102] John Garang de Mabior, presentation to the Brookings Institution, Washington, DC, 9 June 1989, in Wël, *The Genius of Dr John Garang*, 161.
[103] Jok, *Sudan*, 36.

why are you sitting here? They say okay, go now, but you be careful – okay, I will be careful, but I didn't do anything! You find me at my house, without anything, I don't have anything, I stay with my kids! And why do you accuse me like this? I'm not a politician! I'm a young person, looking for where I can get food to eat, to feed my family, and now you involve me in politics, you arrest me all the time, you ask me silly questions and I don't know.... So that's why I said the Arabs themselves are supporting the movement. That's why, you see, everyone arrested will go to join SPLA. Even myself, once I found a way to get out from there, I joined the SPLA.[104]

When discussing the history of this recruitment to rebellion, most people I spoke to highlighted two linked events in the 1990s. First and within Khartoum, the song group Akut Kuei was explained as fighting the system from within, inspiring SPLA recruitment and other rebellions, and spreading criticism of these middle-class southern party politicians and civil servants. Akut Kuei 'used to hold occasions, celebrations, in places in Jabarona and even in Comboni ground … they used to sing these songs so that the youth can hear them, [so] they will rebel. These songs, they are the ones that led to the rebellion of battalion called *jongo* in the SPLA.'[105] The next sections detail these two forms of action.[106]

6.5 Akut Kuei

Akut Kuei, meaning literally Eagle Group in Dinka – a coded reference to SPLA battalion names – was discussed as 'the fifth column of the SPLM/A' by people across Aweil, Gogrial, and Juba's formerly displaced communities.[107] Akut Kuei's work formed a significant part of Chapter 5, and the core of Akut Kuei was made up of two singer-songwriters. Many people gave a variety of other histories of Akut Kuei, though, because the name 'Akut Kuei' and many of their songs have been appropriated and reinvented by various young Dinka men and some women, and translated into Nuer and Shilluk versions,

---

[104] James Akec Nhial, in Juba, 10 September 2013.
[105] Dhieu Kuel, in Mayen Ulem, 21 August 2013; also noted by members of the Dinka Cultural Society, in Apada, 11 August 2013.
[106] This history is particularly focused on Dinka narratives, because of my lack of time to explore other communities' histories of rebel recruitment before the civil war started in 2013.
[107] Athian Kuol Malith, 'Top 12 Famous South Sudanese Artists of All Time', PaanluelWël.com, 20 April 2018.

across East Africa and further afield.[108] A Nuer dance group worked with Akut Kuei in 1998 on performing and reworking songs together.[109] Various other prominent Dinka writers, as well as some Nuer activists and singers, were included by Akut Kuei fans in their lists of members of its core 'committee'.[110]

Akut Kuei were 'like a political party' in Khartoum's displaced camps and settlements because they also focused on political education and radicalisation.[111] Arou Piol, a big fan, explained how Akut Kuei was formed 'to teach people': 'they had seen all the Arab colonialism that was taking place between the Black people and the brown-skinned people. And they used to advise Black people, especially the southerners.'[112] Akut Kuei's songwriters and performers were part of the educational work explored in Chapters 4 and 5: they were Dinka-language teachers who owned a cassette recorder, and then – like hundreds of other artists – sold these homemade albums to people in displaced camp markets.[113] As Madwok, another teacher who owned several of their tapes, said:

> actually these were political musicians. They were there to preach messages, about how bad we are treated, and what they should do, for those who are strong – and how lion-hearted people must join the SPLA and fight for the people. They also – when they were there together, they talked about SPLA indirectly, how the SPLA activities are being run there, who has taken what and who is doing what, and how are they doing there.[114]

This political song writing was partly because the two founding members wanted to fight for the SPLA. James, one of the founders,

---

[108] A few people said that the member I spoke to had died in Australia. This translation work was noted by several people, and English translations of Akut Kuei's song lyrics are often used online and cited as key source material, for instance, by a commenter on the online article by Hamid Eltgani Ali, 'Darfur War Crimes, Changes in Demographic Composition, and Ethnic Displacement,' *Sudan Tribune*, 1 October 2012: 'if you know someone that can translate the songs in Akut-Kuei's Cassette for you from Thuongjang/Dinka to Arabic or English, please look for this cassette'. Arou Piol Adam, in Apada village, 21 July 2013. Akut Kuei songs were generally agreed to be some of the best; 'they had very good songs – even now they are present here in the cassettes, we have them'. Dhieu Kuel, in Mayen Ulem, 21 August 2013.

[109] James Akec Nhial, in Juba, 10 September 2013.

[110] Dhieu Kuel, in Mayen Ulem, 4 July 2013; Arou Piol Adam, in Apada village, 21 July 2013.

[111] Arou Piol Adam, in Apada village, 21 July 2013. [112] Ibid. [113] Ibid.

[114] Madwok Diing, in Juba, 3 August 2013.

6.5 Akut Kuei

explained that he started writing songs because he was already in Khartoum when the war started, as a student, and he had read some of the writing explored in the previous chapters: 'I started to read Morwel Ater Morwel's book, it was really powerful, and also Dut Anyak Dit.' James worked in schools for the displaced teaching the Dinka and English languages, and wanted to head south to join the SPLA, but

> the way was blocked – there was no way to come to South Sudan ... I tried with the *jongo*, but I became fed up, there is no way to get out. So I went back to Khartoum, I said okay, I can fight inside here. Because fighting is not only to take up a gun – you can fight in different sections, you know? You can fight with songs ... you can fight with business, you can do business and support people with money, and all these things.[115]

James partnered with his friend Peter Bol, after several other singers apparently refused – 'they were saying that this song is dangerous and I cannot involve myself in these things' – and started writing and recording in about 1992.[116]

Akut Kuei's songs explicitly aimed to get people angry. This anger was of course directed against northern Sudanese people, and particularly their leaders, like their famous song 'Duk ben la wël-wël' (Don't panic), with the lyrics:

> Now, you are the disease that kills me – you're my problem
> Hated by the children of this land
> Forcing me to believe in your totems
> You're touching the floor with your head – this is hated by the children of this *baai*
> When you came and you found my pot on the fire,
> You took the calabash and distributed the food
> You sat, taking ownership,
> And you put only a small portion in my hands
> It is not your food.

Similarly, the song 'Pandan Pan Theer Wadit ke Madit' (Our grandmothers' and grandfathers' home) is addressed to the Black people of Sudan about the unforgivable atrocities of the Sudan government, the breakdown of Black societies (reflected in the loss of children and

---

[115] James Akec Nhial, in Juba, 8 September 2013.
[116] James Akec Nhial, in Juba, 10 September 2013.

the sense of missing generations), and the resulting impossibility of compromise:

> There's no talking, there's no talking –
> We have closed the door
> You're left with what you've seen
> You're left with what you've seen
> You Black people
> We have seen –
> The lack of the newborn child,
> You see – there's no talking, there's no talking –
> We have closed the door
> You're left with what you've seen.
> You – the entire Black people – we've seen –
> The lack of the newborn child,
> The lack of the newborn,
> And we've seen – there's no talking,
> There's no talking –
> We have closed the door.

But most of Akut Kuei's songs directed their anger towards two economic brutalities of the war: the stripping of land and resources from southern Sudanese people, and the complicity and profiting of other southern supposed 'leaders' who turned their people against each other while they profited from the war and from government pay and pensions.[117] Their song 'Pienyda' (Our land) says:

> Our land of Deng William has been divided into people's pockets[118]
> And people laugh.
> You have broken it up into your mouths and laugh
> You have cut it up on your plates and laugh
> You have cut it up on your plates and laugh
> We have to put it back in the pot and divide it ourselves
> ...
> If you don't put it back into the pot,
> Then we shall pour it out.

Akut Kuei's lyrics and musical styles echoed old Dinka war songs and mimicked the lyrics of SPLA war songs that could not be sung in the city.[119] Much more aggressive than the poetry and songs explored in

---

[117] See Chapter 5. [118] William Deng Nhial; see Chapter 5.
[119] Madut-Arop, *Sudan's Painful Road to Peace*, 92.

6.5 Akut Kuei

previous chapters, Akut Kuei's work demanded action and accused Khartoum's Black communities of cowardice. The song 'Wa Ye Ke Nyiei Wen' (What took the cows) sets out (macho) moral imperatives to fight:

> What took the cows? ...
> And killed the women?
> Orphaned the children?
> – And we are still here, so that we can die a death, any way it comes –
> There is only one death,
> It is the same death and the same grave.
> What has killed the old man and old woman,
> And they cry, where have the children gone?
> We are still here – struggling, only to die the same death later –
> There is only one death,
> It is the same death and the same grave.
> The brave die in war;
> The coward remains.
> He will die the same death later;
> It is the same death and the same grave.
> They refuse – they are helping people to cry, every year, like a woman –
> Why are we sitting crying like a woman?
> A woman who screams when bad things befall her –
> You coward with a frown on your face,
> If you're afraid now, you should go back to your mother's womb:
> People are not supposed to hide from death.
> Even if we hide, it will still claim us.
> People are not supposed to run from death:
> Even if we run, it will still claim us.

Akut Kuei, like other political songwriters, wanted to spark personal rebellions through their work.[120] Teachers and songwriters organised music events and collected money for recording sessions.[121] Many people were arrested, beaten, and fined for this. The Bari singer General Paulino was jailed for his songs (particularly his song 'Wen Waja Wen') in 1997, and his cassettes were burnt; after he was released, he left the country.[122] Peter and James in Akut Kuei were

---

[120] There are many stories of how this worked, especially from Ayii Bol, in Aweil, 16 August 2013; and from Atak Deng Deng, in Aweil, 17 August 2013.
[121] Lino Alëu Angïc Dut, *Athör Käny*.
[122] General Paulino, in Juba, 23 October 2013; similar to Emmanuel Kembe's personal history.

famously 'betrayed' by people who translated 'Ku Na Kockä', 'Duk Ben la Wël-Wël', and other inflammatory songs, particularly the ones that insulted southern political collaborators.[123] James has a prominent scar on his shoulder from a period in detention in Khartoum, before he left for Egypt in 1998. As Arou explained, 'it finished, there remained only cassettes, and all the people who formed Akut Kuei have scattered'.[124]

But Akut Kuei – like other political songwriters in this period – is a success story: in common discussion, their work fuelled the rebellion of the *jongo* from 1993 to 1997.[125] They encouraged 'the youth, and sound-minded people – who know what is going on' – to join the SPLA through *jongo*. As the teacher and writer Santino Atak explained: 'every Southerner who understands what is going on in the South gets that feeling of joining the SPLA … They just move as workers. That's why they were called *jongo*.'[126]

6.6 *Jongo*

Jongo is a colloquial Sudanese Arabic term for casual or seasonally employed agricultural workers, particularly on large commercial farms. These workers live as squatters in seasonal *kambos* (camps), most often housing displaced people too, across the Sudanese agricultural belt of Gedarif, Kordofan, and southern Darfur.[127] This waged agricultural work was, and still is, the main source of income for displaced people across Sudan.[128] Going to work in the Gezira as *jongo* was part of most people's explanations of how they survived in wartime northern Sudan. Through the 1990s, working in the

---

[123] Named by Arou Piol Adam, in Apada village, 21 July 2013; Diing Chen Diing, in Aweil, 12 August 2013.
[124] Arou Piol Adam, in Apada village, 21 July 2013. [125] Ibid.
[126] Santino Atak Kuon, in Aweil, 3 July 2013.
[127] Magdi Al-Gouni, 'For Whom the Bells Toll: Kambo (18): Fifty Years of Solitude', *Sudan Vision*, 9 March 2014; Justin Ambago Ramba, 'The Kambo and Jongo Business in the Sudanese Relationships', *South Sudan News Agency*, 12 October 2012; Magdi El Gizouli, 'South Sudanese Labour: Refill the "kambo"', *Sudan Tribune*, 8 October 2012.
[128] African Rights, 'Food and Power in Sudan', 161; Nicki Kindersley and Joseph Diing Majok, 'Monetized Livelihoods and Militarized Labour in South Sudan's Borderlands', Rift Valley Institute (2019); Abraham Diing et al., 'South Sudan: Youth, Violence and Livelihoods', Rift Valley Institute (2021).

6.6 Jongo

commercial farms and market trades that serviced these workers was a way to build investment capital for life in Khartoum.[129]

But there were two meanings to the term *jongo*:

> Is it *jongo* for work or the *jongo* that goes to Ethiopia?... So the *jongo* were the workers who go into agricultural scheme for work, and that is also where they get that SPLA *jongo*. So when you go to the agricultural scheme, you leave the field and then you go to Ethiopia to join the army. And that is why they were called *jongo*.[130]

Jongo was the pathway for the movement of political information via migrant workers, and through the 1990s also the way to join the SPLA. Because roads back to many areas of the south were blocked or extremely dangerous, people – mostly men, but some women – would 'go underground' to Gedarif and into Ethiopia via the border markets at Basinda and Lubdi.[131] People who didn't want to join the SPLA used the roads directly south to their home villages, 'but for those who want to join the army, they just take the road of *jongo*'.[132] Many migrant agricultural workers took those roads but didn't sign up with the SPLA recruiters: 'we crossed to Ethiopia, working in the *simsim* scheme. For me, I went back to Khartoum and said that maybe I think the soldiers do not need me [laughs].'[133]

Most people timed the beginning of SPLA recruitment via *jongo* to about 1993; '*jongo* 2' – a second wave of recruitment – was generally said to be in 1996.[134] There were people who organised meeting points

---

[129] Gabriel Deng Bulo and Garang Diing Akol, in Maper Akot, 22 June 2013; Paul Kuel Kuel, in Aweil, 9 August 2013. This is borne out by statistics on cane-cutters in Gezira from a sample survey conducted by Hassaballa Omer Hassaballa in 1991: people from Darfur made up 52.4 per cent, Upper Nile 8.9 per cent, Equatoria 3.6 per cent, Bahr el Ghazal 10.1 per cent, and White Nile 10.3 per cent of labourers. 'Displacement and Migration', 45.

[130] William Deng Aken, in Apada, 18 July 2013; also explained by Diing Chen Diing, in Aweil, 15 July 2013. Peter Deng Akok was a *jongo* worker in Gezira for 24 years; interviewed in Maper, 21 June 2013.

[131] Lual Lual Aguer, in Apada, 3 June 2013; Diing Chen Diing, in Aweil, 15 July 2013; Garang Diing Akol, in Maper Akot, 22 June 2013. News was also transferred via southern workers in the civil service: Gabriel Deng Bulo and Garang Diing Akol, in Maper Akot, 22 June 2013.

[132] Abaker Thelatheen, in Apada, 8 June 2013.

[133] William Deng Aken, in Apada, 18 July 2013.

[134] Santino Atak Kuon, in Mayen Ulem, 3 July 2013; Arou Piol Adam and friends in a group discussion, in Apada village, 22 July 2013; William Deng Aken, in Apada, 18 July 2013; Peter Deng Akok, in Maper, 21 June 2013. Most were

and funding, but also 'whoever becomes set [in their mind] – goes to mobilise the rest of his colleagues, in order to find a way to Gedarif and then they cross over'.[135] Abuk, as a very poor young married woman brewing beer and cleaning clothes to keep her young family afloat in Jabarona, knew several women who took this path, including her sister-in-law, who 'escaped' Sudan and travelled to family working in SPLA-held territories in the south by taking the *jongo* road.[136]

Garang, a seasonal worker himself, gave money to friends to pay for the bribes and transport costs for their journey to SPLA training camps. He explained how this 'setness comes as a result of the war, when your brother has been killed in the south, and the rest of your relatives, then you become set and you intend to go. Sometimes your father will be killed; when you hear about that, you get yourself into this group.... We gave them money and send them to Gedarif.'[137] There were both organised recruitments and individual choices. When Lual, working as a bricklayer at Jebel Aulia, heard that two of his brothers had died in the SPLA in the south, he said something changed in his mind: 'I was not actually good, until I escaped myself from Khartoum' on the *jongo* road.[138]

Lual headed for his brothers' old division, but others had different destinations, and generally people referred to recruitment into an imagined umbrella SPLA, depending on where they got to after crossing into Ethiopia: a demonstration of the agglomeration of political mobilisation, communication, and associational efforts in fighting for 'the cause'.[139] 'People went to war themselves,' as Kuol Dut, a

    keen to define three periods of 'Jongo battalions' recruitment. Jongo 1, the oldest and least organised, was dated by several people to the time of Sadiq al Mahdi in roughly 1989, with Jongo 2 in 1992–93, and Jongo 3, the largest movement, in 1995–96: 'Bashir has two *jongos*, Sadiq al Mahdi has one *jongo*.' Quoting Abaker Thelatheen, in Apada, 8 August 2013; also William Deng Aken, in Apada, 18 July 2013; Gabriel Deng Bulo and Garang Diing Akol, in Maper Akot, 22 June 2013.

[135] Paul Kuel Kuel, in Aweil, 9 August 2013; Diing Chen Diing, in Aweil, 12 August 2013; Abaker Thelatheen, in Apada, 8 June 2013; Dhieu Kuel, in Mayen Ulem, 21 August 2013; Stephen Ayaga, in Aweil, 8 August 2013; Garang Diing Akol, in Maper Akot, 22 June 2013. James Garang Ngor has friends who went together: interviewed in Aweil, 30 June 2013.

[136] Abuk Deng and female friends, in Apada 20 June 2013.

[137] Garang Diing Akol, in Maper Akot, 22 June 2013.

[138] Lual Lual Aguer, in Apada chiefs' court, 3 June 2013.

[139] This was noted in Khartoum by similar-minded revolutionaries: el Gizouli, 'South Sudanese Labour'.

6.6 Jongo

community court member and manual labourer in Mayo Mandela, explained, precipitated by repeated abuses in the city; 'people grow a lot, they lose the appetite to stay. Once they have experienced this kind of situation, they will just collect themselves and find a way of leaving.... Some people leave their parents, some others leave their brothers, and they just go, when they're tired.'[140]

This 'setness' was a generic point across accounts of *jongo* recruitment. Haj Yousif neighbourhood representative and small shop owner Abaker said that – having seen looted cattle marked with his own clan's brandings for sale in Omdurman – many men, including himself, wanted to go to Ethiopia to join the fighting.[141] Most of the people I met who stated that they went to join the SPLA through travelling via Ethiopia, or whose family members went, travelled in 1995 or 1996.[142] Many people knew friends and neighbours from the Nuba Mountains, Darfur, Blue Nile, and Dongola who joined the SPLA through *jongo*.[143]

Retired senior SPLA commanders explained how these recruits were also generally referred to within the SPLA as *jongo*, but officially made up the New Sudan Brigade. John Garang declared the formation of the New Sudan Brigade on 21 February 1995, under his own direct command via the Ingessana Front veteran commander Malik Agar.[144] The Brigade was the fighting force of the National Democratic Alliance, a demonstration of the idea of a Sudan-wide revolutionary army, and a way to try to threaten Khartoum by moving the war northwards.[145] It had some brief success – attacking and

---

[140] Kuot Dut Kuot, in Apada, 3 June 2013.
[141] Abaker Thelatheen, in Apada, 8 June 2013; also Santino Atak Kuon, in Aweil, 3 July 2013.
[142] For example, Arou Piol's cousin went to join Jongo 2 in 1996 after spreading Akut Kuei songs and becoming frightened for his life; Arou Piol Adam, in Apada, 21 July 2013. Other similar accounts were given by Mathok Diing Wol, in Ariath, 21 August 2013, and Stephen Ayaga, in Aweil, 8 August 2013. Stephen went to join Jongo in 1998 after he graduated, but he returned directly to Aweil and said that he tried to support the SPLA regionally.
[143] Paul Kuel Kuel, in Aweil, 9 August 2013; Dhieu Kuel, in Mayen Ulem, 4 July 2013.
[144] 'Row over the "New Sudan Brigade"', *Sudan News & Views* 7, 6 April 1995.
[145] Elijah Biar Kuol, in Juba, 12 September 2013. For notes on the activity of the New Sudan Brigade, see Johnson, *The Root Causes of Sudan's Civil Wars*, 207–8, 211, 213–15. The organisers involved were apparently Alier Ayom, James Osmail, and Nathaniel Agoot: John Garang de Mabior, presentation to

capturing Khor Yabus in southern Blue Nile on 4 April 1996 – but by the early 2000s, with the collapse of the idea of the National Democratic Alliance and shifting military priorities in the SPLA, *jongo* fighters were dispersed across other SPLA battalions.[146]

6.7 Conclusion

There is not enough space here to detail the wide range of kinds of resistance described to me during research for this book. These also included legal challenges and efforts to work within and against local neighbourhood committees; protests and arrests at churches and cathedrals, at printing presses, and in schools; young women wearing T-shirts, skinny jeans, and knee-length skirts; and, more vaguely, performances of passivity: 'we went to the centre of Khartoum dressed like we went to the forest like rural villagers, not like those who are going to the town'.[147] 'If you pretended to be a beggar in Khartoum – you are even affecting their economic situation.'[148] Cheats, thieves, and cultural performers could all be contributing to the struggle; joining the security services or converting to Islam could be justified as finding ways and means to educate your children independently, 'for the south'.[149] Pretty much anything, including receiving Islamic food aid, could be justified this way – people explained how they took aid and support as pretend converts, and re-distributed it among needy friends.[150] These small insurrections might not register as political resistance, but this book follows other scholars in giving up on the artificial divide between 'the realm of politics and the everyday'.[151] Surviving as Black migrants in Khartoum was (and still is) fundamentally political, and people themselves determined what constituted their

---

the Brookings Institution, Washington, DC, 9 June 1989, in Wël, *The Genius of Dr John Garang*, 200–201.

[146] Guarak, *Integration and Fragmentation of the Sudan*, 389; Madut-Arop, *Sudan's Painful Road to Peace*, 318.

[147] Patrick Augustine, 'Horror in the Sudan', 22 April 2001, SAD.891/1/1-3; Lual Agang Macham, in Apada, 8 June 2013; similar stories were told by Lazarus Lual about returning to the south in the late 1990s through Abdel Baggi Ayii Akol's territories in Southern Kordofan; interviewed in Juba, 19 October 2013.

[148] Ayii Bol, in Aweil, 16 August 2013.

[149] Ayii had worked for Sudan's National Intelligence Service for a few years.

[150] Arou Piol Adam, in Apada village, 21 July 2013.

[151] Heredia, 'The Conspicuous Absence', 7.

resistance – from acts of dramatic symbolism at Nilein University to inflammatory songs, passing a friend some money to leave for Ethiopia, or wearing a shorter skirt in a suburb. All of these are attempts to change things, if you include changing your sense of subservience and passivity.

It would be relatively easy to try to classify political activity in this period as a spectrum of action to inaction, and of iconoclastic nationalists to anti-secessionist collaborators. Ascribing these labels is less important, though, than exploring what people actually wanted to change, what actions they took, and what these actions were meant to do. Fighting against the Sudan regime, or even for the SPLA, encompassed a range of motivations and ideologies behind often politically ambiguous actions. Holding political discussions in beer houses might not appear to be participating really in any material way in the civil war effort, but was an act of political resistance to the men and women involved. For most people – not leaders of political parties or active combatants in one of the SPLA factions – it was very difficult to know the consequences of political actions like, for example, passing on information about events in the south, or donating money 'for the SPLA'. Even for the men who crossed into Ethiopia to join the rebels, it was not clear to them where they would end up and whom they would be fighting.

Explicitly rebellious actions were a lot more uncertain in this context. Some people took significant personal risks in organising what they believed were actions for the 'total liberation of the country' – 'so that the Islamists will be smashed out of the country and the country will remain united – and people can practice democracy'; but it was hard to know if any actions, like collecting cash or protesting at the universities, really helped this cause.[152] Other people, particularly Equatorian residents, 'had a different interest, to see this country [the South] independent'.[153] But many Equatorian residents were happy to work alongside NDA and revolutionary Black activists, while also supporting people to fight for 'what is theirs, South Sudan'.[154] Like most people, residents had shifting and sometimes contradictory ideas about what should happen, over the span of the war: by the early

---

[152] Dhieu Kuel, in Mayen Ulem, 21 August 2013.
[153] Melanie Itto, in Juba, 23 October 2013.
[154] Jimmy Wongo, in Juba, 18 October 2013.

2000s, with the idea of southern self-determination gaining momentum within Garang's SPLM/A, people felt 'they failed to conceptualise the pan-African thing'.[155] What was generally understood was that the debate and fair resolution of Sudan's violent racisms, political cultures, economic exploitations, and histories of abuse needed to be part of any political outcome: 'there is no short cut in the future'.[156]

---

[155] Dhieu Kuel, in Mayen Ulem, 21 August 2013; Kuel Aguer Kuel, in Juba, 20 January 2017.
[156] Gwado Ayoker to arap Moi, SAD.89/10/110.

7 Military Independence and Khartoum's Warlord Communities

By the late 1990s, a generation of children had been born in Khartoum, and neighbourhoods were well-established against the backdrop of a long, shifting war. Multiple peace negotiations since the 1980s, endless splits and factions, and stories of clashes and victories made discussing the fight for, and definitions of, self-defence, self-rule, and independence very complicated, and often hopeless. Despite the radical, imaginative, liberationist ideas and work outlined in the previous chapters, for many displaced residents of Khartoum, working within government systems and in Sudan's military forces was a necessary part of survival and everyday working life in the increasingly austere and militarised economy by the mid-1990s. This chapter explores this work of these supposed 'sell-outs' of Chapter 5 within Khartoum's military and militia systems that grew through the 1990s and 2000s.

This work was important. Schools, churches, and safe family spaces in policed camps and squatter settlements were protected – many people emphasised – by southern workers in Khartoum's local authorities, police, and the army, and by southern militias in the city. These workers included some of the writers, political activists, evening school teachers, and artists of the previous chapters; like people everywhere, they balanced family welfare and good employment against their political beliefs and activities, and their compromises were not (to them) necessarily contradictory. Formal employment in the Sudan Armed Forces was relatively secure salaried and pensioned work. For many poor displaced men, recruitment into the SAF or into other government militias, police and security services, and militias run by southern warlords were part of their limited employment options (or hard to avoid).

Southern militia leaders like Paulino Matip built local political and military presence in Khartoum from the late 1990s, as the al-Bashir government sought to co-opt their usefully divisive military and political power. Many of these militias were called self-defence forces: ostensibly fighting against the SPLA and other armed factions for the 'protection' of an ethnic community and homeland. Their leadership and fighters were not necessarily pro-Sudan government, but partly relied on their weaponry and backing. This supported their localised militias in the south, who justified their violence against and economic exploitation of local residents, and their fight against the SPLA and other factions, by claiming their fight was to defend and liberate their specific ethnic homeland and community. This was these militias' version of fighting for southern political independence.

This chapter does not focus on the political deals of these militias' leaders and the Sudan government. It looks specifically at their systems and effects in Khartoum. Empowered by their bargains with the Sudan government particularly after the Khartoum Agreement in 1997, southern militia leaderships created localised para-governmental systems, setting up their own barracks, court systems, and militia economies in neighbourhood strongholds around the city's peripheries. These systems worked on the same aggressive self-defence principles as their militias in the south: for their ethno-regional community, these militiamen could broker with the regime and local government and could provide forms of work, security, law, and order on familiar terms for 'their' people in the city.

This was another version of self-rule and independence, rooted in ethnic solidarity, armed power, and self-defence. It was a practical alternative to the more radical forms of collective Black or pan-Sudanese liberation, and ideas about radically changing the structures of violent power in Sudan, that were explored by people in previous chapters. For many displaced people in Khartoum, these militia projects – while still brutal, exploitative, and antagonistically ethno-nationalist – were more practical and realistic pathways to some kind of independence out of the war. Many residents, exhausted, brutalised, and angry after years of violence, grief, and exploitation, lacked the time or desire to imagine beyond the terms and structures of armed governance that they had lived within for generations. At least these were their own armed regimes, operating with a language and principles that could be understood and engaged with. Working with these militia groups in Khartoum was therefore reasonable, even while they were *maraziin* (betrayers) committing atrocities against communities at home and morally corrupt in their bargains with al-Bashir.

This chapter traces the impacts of government and military employment and the growing power structures of southern militia leaderships across Khartoum from the late 1990s. It sets the sometimes-radical work of the previous three chapters back into the context of the changing city and war from the late 1990s into the early 2000s. This period saw rising prices, conscription and national service, and a war that ground on after a dozen years with waves of splits, misinformation, and bad blood, despite rounds of high-level bargaining and supposed peace agreements and ceasefires. It is understandable that many people saw the only possible route to a better future through their own armed struggle for the secession of the south; this was a way to self-rule, even if it would be self-rule by the gun.

7.1 Everyday Self-Defence and Government Employment

Education, writing projects, music, theatre performances, political meetings, and social lives were all dependent on maintaining a safe distance from state scrutiny and its policing. Managing this required people who worked within the state in some form: in local neighbourhood committees, as clerks in courts, in the police, military, and regional administration, for example. Like the chiefs in Chapter 3, some people justified their work in neighbourhood Popular Committees, in the police, and as government-paid sultans for displaced camps as a method of self-defence, even if it meant outwardly denouncing Garang and the SPLM/A.[1] Taking up these positions gave these men the ability to influence land allocations for displaced people (in theory, fairly), to find out where someone's relative was detained, or to negotiate with local courts on fines.[2] Government connections were useful in all aspects of everyday life. When the Episcopal then-priest and Sudan Council of Churches worker Enoch Tombe got married in Khartoum in 1993, he ran out of time to get a police permit and authorisation from the Local Area Popular Committee, so organised his wedding at his SAF soldier relative's house in a military barracks.[3]

---

[1] Ayii Bol, in Aweil, 16 August 2013.
[2] Mathok Diing Wol, in Ariath, 21 August 2013; Awen Mayuon Macwac, in Maper Akot, 21 June 2013; Joseph Ukel Abango, in Juba, 1 November 2013.
[3] Tombe, *In Hope & Despair*, 61.

Employment within the systems and military forces that were killing one's relatives and exploiting your communities was discussed during research for this book with a range of equivocation, amusement, anger, and sympathy. These employees were 'just in between'.[4] Of course, not everyone had the ability or inclination to take on radical work of the previous two chapters – and plenty of people worked for and within the Sudan government, using a variety of justifications, for their own careers and survival. Some of these workers – as politician and teacher Joseph Ukel summarised – 'succumbed to the requests of the system', which asked southerners in the government job market to at least superficially be anti-SPLA and Islamist.[5] Many men had already invested in their careers in the Sudanese military during peace in the 1970s and continued their work, supporting large families and homes; with national security vetting, employees could even buy houses in the city.[6] Many highly educated southern men worked in the southern regional administration, established by the Revolutionary Command Council in 1989, although staff were repeatedly marginalised or dismissed.[7] These middle-class government workers were described in Aweil in terms of a common child's tale of the *lueth* fish in the Lol River; the *lueth* looks terrifying but has no teeth, and (stupidly and gullibly) told this to the crocodile.[8] The song that apparently led to the detention and flight of the Akut Kuei songwriters in 1996 specifically targeted these collaborators:

---

[4] Chiefs' court in Mayen Ulem, 20 August 2013; Albino Madhan, in Aweil, 9 August 2013; Atak Akol Diing, in Aweil, 14 August 2013; Riing Riing Lual, in Aweil, 3 September 2013; and many other discussions over 2013. For example, Diing Chen explained that people were 'exhausted' in Khartoum; interview in Aweil, 15 July 2013.

[5] Joseph Ukel Abango, in Juba, 1 November 2013; Madut-Arop, *Sudan's Painful Road to Peace*, 248. Regardless, most southern government and military employees were not fully trusted in their offices or professions anyway: Awen Mayuon Macwac, in Maper Akot, 21 June 2013.

[6] Madut-Arop, *Sudan's Painful Road to Peace*, 86–87; Dhieu Kuel, in Mayen Ulem, 4 July 2013.

[7] See Madut-Arop, *Sudan's Painful Road to Peace*, 228–32, 243, for a list of the Revolutionary Command Council members and other assignments. Lesch, *The Sudan*, 116–17, 122, 126.

[8] 'Dinka Reader 4', 3; and the song 'Dut Anyak Dit, Adhuöm Akan!' (There is a hole!).

7.1 Everyday Self-Defence and Government Employment 267

What will happen to them?
Will their testicles not be cut off, when we start stabbing at the Arabs?[9]

But more prosaically, working-class residents knew why these men and their families were making this compromise. As Arou Piol explained: 'they know that there is not going to be a peace again. And they need a good life, in order to get a house, and a car, and his children need a good life and they're studying, that was what they need ... they just need to get their better life. And these were the people whose children are now studying in universities.'[10] For the impoverished majority, work was work. As Pastor Michael – the bewitched and healed brick-layer-turned-evangelist – emphasised: 'they want to live! They have children! People are suffering! No food to eat! Yes – if you are given a position, you can go and work, get your money, eat!'[11]

In the middle of all of this were the chiefs and sultans who had been nominated, or named themselves, in the reconstruction of southern neighbourhoods in the late 1980s and early 1990s. Some of these 'traditional' representatives benefitted from the al-Bashir government's investment in 'customary authorities' from the early 1990s, partly as a way to extend state control into neighbourhoods and to cut down the expense of state bureaucracy.[12] Residents of Khartoum's squatted neighbourhoods and remote *dar es salaams* knew the pragmatic utility of a government chief: for brokering aid, credit, and assistance, for instance, with land claims at the town-council level.[13] To do this effectively, representatives had to at least perform northern-ness in their lifestyle, image, dress, and name, even if they were not Muslim.[14] For example, Fouad Ibrahim noted in 1990 that

---

[9] See Chapter 5 for a full discussion of this song.
[10] Arou Piol Adam, in Apada village, 21 July 2013.
[11] Diing Chen Diing, in Aweil, 15 July 2013; also Michael Thiop Lang, in Aweil, 10 July 2013.
[12] These southern intermediaries have been discussed briefly in Chapter 3, but here I am focusing on their political positionality by the late 1990s onwards; for a discussion of the ambiguous position of chiefs specifically, see Leonardi, *Dealing with Government*, 140.
[13] Tuttle, 'Life Is Prickly', 49. Explained by Santino Atak Kuon, in Aweil, 3 July 2013, and Ayii Bol, in Aweil, 16 August 2013. Mathok Diing Wol, in Ariath, 21 August 2013, echoed ideas in Christian Lund, 'Twilight Institutions: Public Authority and Local Politics in Africa', *Development and Change* 37, no. 4 (2006): 689.
[14] Bakhit, 'Negotiations of Power and Responsibilities in Khartoum Shantytowns', 139–40.

the squatters of Abu Siid have elected Ali Faragalla, a Mondari Muslim to be their sheikh and speaker before the town council ... Ali is being supported by a committee of 16 sheikhs representing the main ethnic groups of the shanty town.[15]

These government chiefs, sultans, and sheikhs – depending on location and preference – have always been political middlemen, and in Khartoum they had to balance community demands for support via fair and useful representation with their need to stay on the right side of government.[16] Chiefs were expected to mobilise supporters to be bussed to al-Bashir's political rallies; they could also advocate for detainees at police stations, and influence government and NGO service provision, such as the siting of water points.[17] Echoing notes in the marginalia of Darfur and Kordofan emergency aid reports through the 1990s, some people explained that chiefs worked with southern aid workers and police officers to locate and reunite abducted relatives and children.[18] All of this meant that while these community representatives were not necessarily trusted – and often benefitted personally from their work – they were part of the slow work of mitigating the brutal economic and political realities of life in Khartoum, and were useful at moments of crisis: they 'can defend a person'.[19]

7.2 Ashara Wilayat

Tapping into state power provided opportunities for some men to build larger-scale justice systems for southern displaced communities that had the ability to settle and enforce cases in parallel (and as a recognised alternative) to the Sudanese state justice apparatus. These systems extended the local arbitration of chiefs and clan leaders set up

---

[15] Ibrahim, 'Southern Sudanese Women Migrants', 251.
[16] Leonardi, *Dealing with Government*, 141; Dhieu Kuel, in Mayen Ulem, 21 August 2013.
[17] Duffield, 'Aid and Complicity', 96; Ibrahim, 'Southern Sudanese Women Migrants', 251; Bakhit, 'Negotiations of Power and Responsibilities in Khartoum Shantytowns', 139.
[18] Awen Mayuon Macwac, in Maper Akot, 21 June 2013; Acien Acien Yor, in Aweil town, 11 July 2013; Albino Madhan, in Aweil, 9 August 2013. For independent examples of this assistance with emancipation, see 'Non Athway Escapes Slavery', SAD 307/6/5; and Human Rights Watch Africa, *Children in Sudan*.
[19] Riing Riing Lual, in Aweil, 3 September 2013.

7.2 Ashara Wilayat

in the immediate disasters of the 1980s and early 1990s, which tried to settle family disputes, marital crises, extra-marital pregnancies, theft, and assault between displaced neighbours outside state judicial and police intervention. These systems have longer roots in colonial native administration and chiefs' courts and policing under British and Ottoman rule, and often still make reference to this history through titles, terminology, and uniforms.[20]

Over the late 1990s, though, more powerful 'customary' court systems were set up, with official state sanction. The one most commonly referred to in my research was Ashara Wilayat, meaning 'Ten States', reflecting the ten states of southern Sudan's administrative area and the various regional and ethnic representatives who constituted it.[21] The court had offices at Lafa'a Guba and Jabarona in Haj Yousif, where cases would be heard and then referred to the leadership of Ashara Wilayat if they could not be resolved.[22] There were contradictory stories about how it was established, how it operated, and who led it, but the chiefs on its books drew their salaries from the Khartoum government.[23] For this reason, Ashara Wilayat was generally understood as – morally – 'not a good court' because of its proximity to the state.[24] But at the same time, its state sanction meant official recognition of court judgements, and therefore the authority to resolve cases definitively.[25] And it was also preferable to take a case to Ashara Wilayat, when more local mediation had failed, because the court's judgements took community standards and realities into

---

[20] For this wider history, see Leonardi, *Dealing with Government*.
[21] Gabriel Deng Bulo, in Maper Akot, 22 June 2013.
[22] Garang Atak Rieu, in Mayen Ulem, 20 August 2013; Peter Deng Akok, in Maper, 21 June 2013; chiefs' court in Mayen Ulem, 20 August 2013; Ngor Jonkor, in Apada, 8 June 2013; Dhieu Kuel, in Mayen Ulem, 4 July 2013; Acien Acien Yor, in Aweil town, 11 July 2013.
[23] Deng Macham claimed himself as chief of chiefs under this system, under the NCP ('so they became a pressure group'); he mobilised people for political rallies for al-Bashir's political moves, to demonstrate 'southern support' for government policies; and is known locally as a dodgy trader with some government loan debts. He even managed to be a signatory on the CPA. Chapter 6, Section 6.2, records his arrest and detention. These activities were also described by Joseph Ukel Abango, in Juba, 29 October 2013; Kuel Aguer Kuel, in Juba, 20 January 2017; Sadig Abdel Bagi, in Juba, 23 January 2017; and Ayii Bol, in Aweil, 16 August 2013.
[24] Dhieu Kuel, in Mayen Ulem, 4 July 2013.
[25] According to the 'formal codes' of Nuer Fangak punishment, or Dinka Wanh Alel punishment: Ngor Jonkor, in Apada, 8 June 2013.

consideration, unlike state justice systems. The court would not imprison people who could not immediately pay fines, and would hear out cases that involved poisoning, witchcraft, or complex issues of inter-ethnic or inter-clan marriage and child custody disputes that needed to be solved carefully on community terms.[26] And at least all proceedings would be done in a language that people of all ages could understand: 'it was a translation place'.[27]

However, Ashara Wilayat – like other courts with decisions that could stick, thanks to their bargains with the state – was partly a product of southern militia power in the city by the late 1990s. Its state approval and funding were, by many accounts, connected to southern militia leaders including Paulino Matip, Kerubino Kuanyin, and Abdel Bagi Ayii Akol.

7.3 Southern Militias: Independence on Other Terms

Running these parallel legal systems in the capital needed power, and not just from southern civil servants and police within the state bureaucracy. Ashara Wilayat, like many other community associations over the late 1990s and early 2000s, drew on power and protection from the southern militia leaderships that consolidated bases across the city over 1996–97.

Southern militias were funded and puppeteered by al-Bashir's government throughout the second Sudanese civil war. Successive Sudan governments since the 1960s worked to fund competing militias and divide southern armed leaderships over local and ethnic issues of land, power, and tit-for-tat atrocities as a counter-insurgency strategy. Over 1983 to 1991, a series of Sudan governments supported the Anyanya Two insurgency, in direct conflict with Garang's SPLA, led by Paulino Matip Nhial from around Mayom in Western Upper Nile with predominantly Nuer fighters and supporters; the Anyanya Two had an office and press briefings in Khartoum, and provided relief aid from humanitarian agencies to displaced Nuer communities in the city.[28] When the SPLM/A split in 1991, Riek Machar and Lam Akol failed to find enough support and funding for their faction and turned to the

---

[26] Dhieu Kuel, in Mayen Ulem, 4 July 2013.
[27] Gabriel Deng Bulo, in Maper Akot, 22 June 2013; also Dhieu Kuel, in Mayen Ulem, 4 July 2013.
[28] Amnesty International Index, 12 December 1989, IISH AFR 54/17/89, 23.

Sudan government for support in 1992, joining two other major militia leaders funded by the government, Paulino Matip and Kerubino Kuanyin Bol, another SPLM/A defector.[29]

Splits within the SPLM/A factions and other militias continued to 1996, when the government reinvested in attempts to divide armed southern factions through its Salam min al-Dhakal (Peace from Within) strategy, negotiating directly with individual commanders.[30] In April 1996, the government signed a political charter with six rebel groups, including Riek Machar's Southern Sudan Independence Movement, Samuel Aru Bol's faction of USAP, Theophilus Ochang's Equatoria Defence Forces, and Kerubino Kuanyin; Riek Machar and Paulino Matip became Major-Generals in the SAF under the agreement, and moved part of their command centres to Khartoum.[31] In April 1997, under the Khartoum Agreement, this group was collectively termed the Southern Sudan Defence Forces (SSDF) and announced an end to the war.[32] The Agreement set out an interim Coordination Council for running southern Sudan, with a referendum on independence after four years. The government (and many of these militia leaders) aimed to counter the apparent growing strength of the National Democratic Alliance and the Garangist SPLM/A's New Sudan by explicitly setting out a path to regional state independence. While the SSDF's militia leaders continued to fall out and fight each other, in April 2001, a conference convened by Gatluak Deng, chair of the Coordination Council of the Southern States, brought many more southern militias at least nominally into the SSDF and elected Paulino Matip as chief of staff, unopposed, with deputies including Theophilus Ochang and Clement Wani Igga. By 2004, the SSDF was a loose coalition of about twenty-five militias.[33]

Much has been written about the SSDF and its various militias' politics and brutalities across the south, especially for the period 1996–2004. As well as building stronghold areas on southern

---

[29] Madut-Arop, *Sudan's Painful Road to Peace*, 298.
[30] African Rights, 'Food and Power in Sudan', 161.   [31] Ibid., 304.
[32] In April 1997; this united the Southern Sudan Independence Movement headed by Riek Machar, the Sudan People's Liberation Army Bahr al-Ghazal group under Kerubino Kuanyin Bol, the independent rebel group led by Kawac Makwei, the Equatoria Defence Force commanded by Theophilus Ochang, the Alliance of Bor Citizens led by Arok Thon Arok, and the Union of Sudan African Parties headed by Samuel Aru Bol.
[33] Arnold, 'The South Sudan Defence Force', 491.

borderlands, they also built space within the city.[34] Paulino Matip's compound was in Lafa'a Gufaa, for example.[35] Disagreements between leaderships played out in the streets: in June 1998, two men were shot dead by their militia colleagues as part of the ongoing fight between Paulino Matip and Riek Machar.[36] Displaced communities' attitudes to these armed factions were apparently very mixed, and still are. Most people 'didn't like them – because they destroyed the south'.[37] But the systems they built, including the Ashara Wilayat court system that Paulino Matip was directly involved with, were useful for people who needed to find backing against a neighbourhood demolition or to try to get a relative out of prison, even if they approached these men with caution.[38] As Gabriel Deng, resident in Jabarona at that time, explained, you went 'in order to receive power from that government in order to help your people'.[39]

7.4 Abdel Bagi Ayii Akol

To explore the workings of militia power in Khartoum over the late 1990s to early 2000s, this chapter focuses on a much lesser-known leader, Abdel Bagi Ayii Akol, who alongside Paulino Matip and a variety of other militiamen from across Equatoria, Upper Nile, and Bahr el Ghazal built his own bases, legal system, and power structures in Khartoum over the late 1990s and early 2000s. Abdel Bagi was an obscure figure through the war, with his militia and activities barely recorded through the conflict and very little understood about his organisation by the peace agreement in 2005.[40] However, in the Aweil region on the southern Darfur border, where I began research for this project, Abdel Bagi is – in the words of Dhieu Kuol – both 'the

---

[34] John Young, 'The South Sudan Defence Forces in the Wake of the Juba Declaration', Small Arms Survey (2007), 17.
[35] Garang Atak Rieu, in Mayen Ulem, 20 August 2013; Diing Chen Diing, in Aweil, 12 August 2013.
[36] 'Situation Report: The South Sudan Defence Force – A Challenge to the Sudan Peace Process', Institute for Security Studies, 8 April 2004.
[37] Dhieu Kuel, in Mayen Ulem, 21 August 2013.
[38] Abusharaf noted that Paulino Matip's court system was approached with caution by Khartoum locals: Abusharaf, *Transforming Displaced Women in Sudan*, 48.
[39] Gabriel Deng Bulo, in Maper Akot, 22 June 2013.
[40] Young, 'The South Sudan Defence Forces'.

most popular one; and he's the leader that destroyed this area'.[41] This section reconstructs Abdel Bagi's career since his youth during the colonial period, as a foundation for the following discussions of his militia and court organisation in Khartoum.

Abdel Bagi is from a small sub-clan of Dinka Abiem of Aweil East, called the Paluil; he died as a very old man on 6 June 2020. His family members have recounted to me how he worked as a young man in Abyei at the court of the powerful and famous Dinka Ngok chief Deng Majak after the Second World War ended, which is where he converted to Islam. On his return to his homeland of Abiem, Abdel Bagi – by then a literate translator with good connections – was appointed a tax collector by the postcolonial Sudan government in the mid-1960s, just as the Anya Nya conflict grew into the first civil war in Bahr el Ghazal.

The next part of Abdel Bagi's warlord origin story is a popular tale across Aweil East. The common facts are these: that because of their government loyalty, Abdel Bagi's brother Akol Agany and Awan Anei were killed (along with another man) by Anya Nya rebel fighters in Malualkon. Some people say their ears were cut off, a punishment recorded elsewhere in the Anya Nya wars for accused informants.[42] In response, Abdel Bagi organised his own militia to fight the Anya Nya. Recruiting from young men working on farms in southern Darfur and locals wanting to defend their herds and villages, he drew on arms and funding from the Sudan government in Aweil as part of the Haras Watani (National Guard), although his fighters were also more disparagingly called Aram Col (Black Arabs). The civil war – collectively an expression of rage against government marginalisation, economic exploitation, lack of services, and racism – was a useful instrument for local power struggles among powerful men, in both the Anya Nya and government-allied forces. In Aweil East, Abdel Bagi's forces fought his chiefly rival Malong Yor's Anya Nya faction, and at the same time Abdel Bagi stood for national election in 1965 and 1967 against (much-disliked) Santino Deng Teng, winning the MP seat from

---

[41] Dhieu Kuel, in Mayen Ulem, 21 August 2013.
[42] Sadig Abdel Bagi, in Juba, 23 January 2017; for other examples of this same Anya Nya punishment, see Øystein H. Rolandsen and Nicki Kindersley, 'The Nasty War: Organised Violence during the Anya-Nya Insurgency in South Sudan, 1963–72', *Journal of African History* 60, no. 1 (2019): 87–107.

Santino in 1967.[43] Abdel Bagi used these tools of electoral systems, militia organisation, business investments, and Islamist politics throughout his career.

The Addis Ababa Agreement ended active conflict in 1972, and Abdel Bagi returned to work as a local chief and businessman in his home region of Abiem on the southern Kordofan border. But in 1980, ex-Anya Nya fighters including Kawac Makuei started organising against increasing armed raids from the famine-stricken Rizeigat and Misseriya communities across the border. In response, Abdel Bagi raised another local militia – personally justified, some say, by some of his relatives being killed by these 'Anyanya Two' – to fight both the Anyanya Two and the Misseriya militia raiders, and then to fight the locally predatory SPLA when they formed in the region from 1984.[44] His local recruits were told that these were criminals, come to destroy the country for their own profit, and that the militia was organised in defence of their homes, herds, farms, and land from growing destruction.[45]

In this early war, the militia apparently financed their weapons by their own local raids and donations by members of the Islamist movement in Khartoum and by the local Sudan Armed Forces. Abdel Bagi's son Sadiq organised gun-running from Chad along the border roads.[46] The family built an arrangement with the local Sudan government and its army, on similar terms to the first civil war: they would defend Abiem villages from the *murahaleen* as well as the SPLA, and in exchange for weapons and government sanction, would run an armed escort for SAF's trains moving to Aweil from Darfur.[47] The militia

---

[43] This story is the founding narrative of many local military men in the region, including Albino Akol Akol, Kawac Makuei, and Salva Kiir, who all fought as young men in the Anya Nya there. Awan Anei – killed alongside Abdel Bagi's brother – was the father of Paul Malong Awan, later SPLA commander and governor of the region, and a rebel warlord in his own right.

[44] Sadig Abdel Bagi, in Juba, 30 August 2017; Abdel Bagi moved his family to Meiram town across the border in southern Kordofan, and to Khartoum.

[45] The first wave of SPLA in the area were locally called 'locusts' because of their looting and exploitation, so this armed self-defence is potentially understandable. Lual Malong, in Madhol, 26 August 2017.

[46] Sadig Abdel Bagi, in Juba, 30 August 2017.

[47] 'Situation Report', 8 April 2004; soldiers walked on foot, looting as a coping strategy for families at home. Interview with executive chief, Ariath, 17 August 2017. Julie Flint, 'Beyond "Janjaweed": Understanding the Militias of Darfur', Small Arms Survey (2009), 13; Nicki Kindersley, 'Politics, Power and

officially called itself Liwa Salaam (Peace Brigade), although because of its looting style it was locally nicknamed *ee laac ku beric* (piss and go).[48]

Alongside other armed southern militias, the *murahaleen*, and the Sudan Armed Forces, Abdel Bagi and his fighters perpetrated atrocities on local populations in this period: directing SAF raids on other communities and looting cattle, women, and children for sale to farm owners in southern Darfur and Kordofan.[49] This horrific profiteering drew in local men as fighters, as a chief from the area explained;

> We had no power.... A man who has not enough courage, who has a weak heart, would run to a man who has the power to shelter and protect him in order to live and survive well. [Abdel Bagi] could delegate someone who knows the areas well to lead the *murahaleen* into the villages to raid. If you joined him, he would award you with a rank, and also give you food.[50]

By the 1990s Abdel Bagi had built his family's economic, military, and political power in the borderland at Abiem and in family homes in Khartoum. Over the 1980s, he worked in all directions: militia-running, building business and economic interests and networks, acting as judge and chiefly arbitrator, and engaging in electoral politics and aid distribution via Dawa Islamiya.[51] In the 1985 elections, Abdel Bagi contested Constituency 27 in Ombadda in Khartoum and won, joining Sadig al-Mahdi's parliament, and apparently working to allocate displaced settlements in the city in the late 1980s.[52] At the same time, he recruited young men from the Madhol area who had reached Khartoum, taking them for training with SAF forces at El Obeid and other sites, and building his militia in Aweil East from his base at Meiram (see below).[53] By 1996, when the Southern Sudan Defence Force was built in Khartoum, Abdel Bagi was working in collaboration

---

Chiefship in Famine and War: A Study of the Former Northern Bahr El Ghazal State, South Sudan', Rift Valley Institute (2018).

[48] Or Peace and Protection Battalion, or Peace Battalion for Protection. This was not associated with Tom al Nur: 'everyone had their own separate army.' Sadig Abdel Bagi, in Juba, 30 August 2017; Nicola Ariik, in Madhol, 26 August 2017.
[49] Jok, *War and Slavery in Sudan*, 49; Garang Diing Akol, in Maper Akot, 22 June 2013.
[50] Dut Maper, in Juba, 15 August 2017.
[51] Ayii Bol, in Aweil, 16 August 2013.
[52] Malou Tong Tong, in Juba, 16 August 2017.
[53] Lual Malong, in Madhol, 26 August 2017.

with the Nuer militia commander Paulino Matip,[54] and had been elected again in that year's national elections.[55]

All of this is why Abdel Bagi was (and still is) spoken about with deep ambivalence. Jok Madut writes that

> when I visited Warawar in the summers of 1998 and 1999, people spoke about Abdel Baggi with mixed sentiments. Some said that his presence in the North is good for the Dinka because he keeps track of Baggara movements and on the eve of a raid, he sends one of his men to inform the Dinka so that preparations can be made against the raiding force. Other people, although acknowledging his positive role, said that his residence with the Arabs has blurred the whole image of the southern struggle because the Arabs use him as an example of Arab-African coexistence, even though he is only a figurehead.[56]

Abdel Bagi's militia manned checkpoints from Abiem to Meiram from the 1990s to early 2000s, providing some form of safety for desperate displaced Dinka people on the road and keeping paths open for people to check on family and farms at home.[57] As Luka Longar, a community representative for a small neighbourhood of mostly Dinka people in Khartoum at this point, said: 'he was also useful, he helped us. His militias strongly stood with us and they give a safe passage to those moving in the border – like one man, called Anyaar Dut, went up to Gokmachar and Nyamlel to collect and bring us information on missing people. Abdel Bagi was a true Haras Watani [national guard, translated by Luka as a traitor]; but he is a Dinka.'[58]

Abdel Bagi's career reflects the economic and political realities of the conflict, in which most families had very little power of self-defence, and few ways to make enough money to feed families, put children in school, or get medical care for elderly relatives. Most options for work were exploitative, violent, and involved personal risk, whether in the unpaid rebel armies, in government-allied militias, or in casual physical labour under scrutiny in Khartoum. As Arou Piol Adam, at that point working as a part-time teacher and labourer in the city, explained: 'if people were in the north, you'd better attach yourself to Ayii, because

---

[54] Emmanuel Deng Anei, in Apada, 3 June 2013; Young, 'The South Sudan Defence Forces', 36.
[55] Ayii Bol, in Aweil, 16 August 2013.   [56] Jok, *War and Slavery in Sudan*, 50.
[57] Lazarus Lual, in Juba, 19 October 2013; Wol Akol Agany, in Amar-Jal, Madhol, 26 August 2017.
[58] Luka Longar Deng, in Jebel Dinka, Juba, 17 August 2017.

he has power from the Arabs – you'll not be a traitor, but just to protect yourself'.[59] At least Abdel Bagi Ayii was 'our militia'.[60]

7.5 Militias and Economic Organisation

This is how Abdel Bagi ended up with armed power in Khartoum. As a less-powerful affiliate of the now-deceased Nuer commander Paulino Matip in Khartoum's Lafa'a Gufa'a area, Ayii based himself in Jabarona, with militia bases apparently outside Fitihaab in Fatasha, in Wad el Bashir, as well as in Meiram near the southern border.[61] Even when these forces were officially sanctioned under the SSDF in 1997, this caused some tensions; for example, in 1998, 117 of Abdel Bagi's Peace Forces were arrested for organising military training on the outskirts of the city without apparent authorisation (although they were later released after their commanders testified in court).[62]

The forces recruited among young Dinka men, particularly from the Aweil East area as they could justify their recruitment on the grounds of local self-defence.[63] Recruits included ex-SPLA fighters who had fled the famines and wars in the 1990s or who had come looking for wives and families in the city, men who had cases brought against them in Khartoum or within SPLA-held territories, or those who needed the job for bride wealth or businesses.[64] Many militia leaders worked to find scholarships and employment in Khartoum and abroad for young men from their militia-administered regions.[65] And militia work was potentially an easier way to make money than being in the SPLA.[66] For young men who had been in the SPLA, or who could be suspected of SPLA support on the basis of their southern appearance alone, joining the militia mitigated some risks: there was no way, as an ex-SPLA soldier, 'for them to survive in the north here, unless they joined a militia'.[67] Recruitment expanded fast in the early 2000s, reflecting the

---

[59] Daniel, in Apada, 22 July 2013.
[60] Ngor Akol Jonkor, in Apada, 5 June 2013.
[61] Dhieu Kuel, in Mayen Ulem, 4 July 2013; Sadig Abdel Bagi, in Juba, 23 January 2017; Kuel Aguer Kuel, in Juba, 20 January 2017.
[62] Deutsche Presser Agentur, 26 May 1998.
[63] Agany Macham, in Apada chiefs' court, 5 June 2013.
[64] Dhieu Kuel, in Mayen Ulem, 21 August 2013; Ayii Bol, in Aweil, 16 August 2013.
[65] John Gau Riak, in Aweil, 28 June 2013.
[66] Dhieu Kuel, in Mayen Ulem, 21 August 2013.   [67] Ibid.

re-intensification of the Sudan government's war effort.[68] Abdel Bagi's forces were critical in the SAF recapture of Gogrial in 2002 and in defending the oil fields until 2005.[69]

By 2000, Abdel Bagi's armed power allowed him to carve out an alternative legal and governmental network in Khartoum and across the country, back to the southern Kordofan town of Meiram, and into his home village of Abiem across the putative southern border in Bahr el Ghazal.[70] A senior aid worker from the Aweil area summarised it as 'a miniature government' in Khartoum – 'he had his own custody unit. Abdel Bagi was a commander from afar, Agany (his son) was commanding the militia, and Nurudiin (another son) was coordinator between the militia and SAF.'[71]

Some residents emphasised the need for this armed rule of law in southern displaced communities. Fights, family disputes, feuds over accidental pregnancies, sexual assaults, and domestic violence all needed resolutions that would be fair and would stick. Northern courts could not solve these issues properly, and exposed litigants to the abuses of the state system. But the community courts set up in displaced communities since the 1980s had no coercive power. As Agany, one elderly court worker in Omdurman's Jabarona, explained of these state courts: 'you can just go and press your view, but you talk like a woman in front of a man. And for you, you have to talk to them in a cowardly way, like you're just asking for help.'[72] One of Abdel Bagi's sons agreed. 'No one could accept a decision if you were weak.'[73] In Agany's words, Abdel Bagi Ayii was 'given guns by the Khartoum government in order to make the Dinka people afraid – even if you just don't pay attention to him, he can even shoot you'.[74] This meant that Abdel Bagi had the power to make judgements that would be followed; for Riing Riing, a basketball-playing civil servant, 'this was the positive side' of Abdel Bagi's military power.[75] The Ashara Wilayat courts

[68] Chiefs' court in Mayen Ulem, 20 August 2013; Arou Piol Adam, in Apada village, 22 July 2013; Stephen Ayaga, in Aweil, 8 August 2013.
[69] 'Situation Report', 8 April 2004.
[70] Arou Piol Adam and friends described it as a government (Apada village, 22 July 2013) as did Kuel Aguer Kuel, in Juba, 20 January 2017.
[71] Kuel Aguer Kuel, in Juba, 20 January 2017.
[72] Agany Macham, in Apada chiefs' court, 8 June 2013.
[73] Sadig Abdel Bagi, in Juba, 23 January 2017.
[74] Agany Macham, in Apada chiefs' court, 8 June 2013.
[75] Riing Riing Lual, in Aweil, 3 September 2013.

leant heavily on Abdel Bagi and Paulino Matip's armed men as police.[76] Ngor Jonkor, who once took an inter-family dispute to the Ashara Wilayat courts and who himself worked as an arbitrator when cases were heard, explained that 'we sometimes reported to Abdel Bagi and Paulino Matip whenever the Arab police used to aggress the Dinka people – because they were just rebelling against the SPLA, but they were still defending Dinka people in the north. And they are the ones to refer the case to the high top government in Khartoum.'[77]

By the early 2000s, Abdel Bagi Ayii's court and militia systems in Khartoum had all the trappings of government, with military police and vehicles, jails – including in Wad Isein in Mayo – and an official court stamp recognised by the Khartoum state.[78] Ayii's court cracked down on youth gangs and antisocial behaviour in its suburb strongholds, sending men to arrest and detain people.[79] His armed authority was useful, if worrying to be too close to: as Lazarus Lual explained, 'you can go to a smaller [court] but then you think that it did not solve it well, then you can make an appeal to another higher one ... Until you went up to Ayii, and that's the worst one to see! [laughs].'[80]

Abdel Bagi's courts were not just useful for their coercive power. Abdel Bagi was widely recognised as a skilled arbitrator in particularly sensitive cases, even by his ostensible enemies: 'he used to settle complex interethnic cases, he tells it straight'.[81] Ayii knew the Sudan government system, had worked in courts in Abyei and Abiem, and with his extensive connections with other militia leaders and authorities in southern Darfur and Kordofan he could convene multi-ethnic negotiations – 'because if you're southern Sudanese or Darfurian, you feel the high court would favour Arabs'.[82] It was reported that Abdel Bagi Ayii could take on rape cases against non-Black Sudanese men, shifting the balance of power between displaced and marginalised

---

[76] Garang Diing Akol, in Maper Akot, 22 June 2013.
[77] Ngor Akol Jonkor, in Apada, 5 June 2013.
[78] Arou Piol Adam, in Apada village, 21 July 2013; Gabriel Deng Bulo and Marco Wiyu Deng, in Maper Akot, 22 June 2013; Dhieu Kuel, in Mayen Ulem, 4 July 2013.
[79] Madwok Diing, in Juba, 3 August 2013; Deng Macham, in Juba, 22 January 2017.
[80] Lazarus Lual, in Juba, 19 October 2013.
[81] Kuel Aguer Kuel, in Juba, 20 January 2017.
[82] Sadig Abdel Bagi, in Juba, 23 January 2017; Ngor Akol Jonkor, in Apada, 5 June 2013.

communities and their non-Black and Arab neighbours.[83] The ethnic make-up of militias was useful in inter-ethnic disputes; as Ngor Jonkor explained, 'if a person from Nuer is making something wrong, then you run to Paulino Matip; and if a Malwal [a Dinka section] makes something, then people run to Abdel Bagi'.[84] Khartoum's defensive locally and ethnically organised militias were not necessarily separate and hostile; in some respects, they had very similar politics. In the *dar es salaam* camp where Abdel Bagi had a compound, Stephen Ayaga – a Luo man and SPLA soldier who travelled to the south via Jongo in 1999 – explained that 'Luo, Dinka, Balanda – whatsoever, even some of Nuba people they were there with them – everyone, even Nuer they were there'.[85]

Running a militia, controlling roads southwards towards Meiram and Abiem, recruiting from desperate and angry displaced young men in Khartoum, and adjudicating and handing down punishments all meant that Abdel Bagi and his family could build a wartime business empire. The family had developed a commercial farm at Majak Ayii outside Meiram town in southern Kordofan – just across the Kordofan–Bahr el Ghazal border from Abiem – since the 1960s, marrying into local clans and over time building up a property portfolio of surveyed plots and houses in Meiram town itself.[86] These farms extended over 1989 to 1991, as the Sudan government paid off their armed proxies with farmland.[87] By the 1990s, Abdel Bagi's farms grew sorghum, okra, millet, *kerkade* (hibiscus) and gum arabic, trading to a Coca-Cola supplier for good profits.[88] The farms soaked up the desperate people who fled the raids and famines in 1986–88 and 1997–8, as well as SPLA soldiers who needed to work or wanted to leave the front lines.[89] Abdel Bagi integrated his Khartoum and Meiram interests by funnelling labour to the farms from his courts: 'if you have committed adultery and you have nothing to pay with, you

---

[83] Ngor Akol Jonkor, in Apada, 5 June 2013.
[84] Ngor Akol Jonkor, in Apada, 8 June 2013.
[85] Stephen Ayaga, in Aweil, 8 August 2013.
[86] Sadig Abdel Bagi, in Juba, 30 August 2017.
[87] African Rights, 'Food and Power in Sudan', 156–57; Malou Tong Tong, in Juba, 16 August 2017.
[88] Sadig Abdel Bagi, in Juba, 30 August 2017.
[89] Wol Akol Agany, in Amar-Jal, Madhol, 26 August 2017.

will be taken to the farm'.[90] Prisoners or guilty parties in Abdel Bagi's court cases could work off their sentences or fines through militia work or farming. As Lazarus remembers: 'he was having a *kerkade* farm in Meiram. So he takes you, you work there, and then after one month he will ask you if you want to turn military – saying I will pay the costs for your dowry.'[91]

This history is why Abdel Bagi has been such a tricky figure to discuss in South Sudan. Like many other people characterised as warlords in the region, he has worked within the realities of an exploitative and militarised postcolonial political economy, building systems that work for his people (and particularly for his family). Abdel Bagi's profiteering, his perpetuation of a brutal war, and his construction of armed authority on ethnic lines was all at odds with many people's emancipatory hopes for anti-racist futures and fundamental structural change in Sudan and the South. But at the same time, his parochial ethnic fiefdom and armed power were useful, not least for day-to-day survival and some men's personal ambitions, when there were very few other options. As Arou Piol put it:

So people feel angry – people felt angry indeed, especially those whom he oppressed, yeah. There was, uh – there was a division, especially like, in Meiram, all the Dinka communities who were there in Meiram were under Ayii, he's the one who colonised them *and* he's the one who recruited them also as soldiers.[92]

7.6 Military Work

The political economy and governance structures of the South Sudan Defence Forces were part of the realities of a militarised economy. Jobbing armed work was relatively common across Sudan since the precolonial years, and tens of thousands of southern men were working in the Sudan Armed Forces when the war started in 1983.[93] Working for the SAF was decent paid employment, and even militias

---

[90] Sadig Abdel Bagi, in Juba, 30 August 2017; Joseph Ukel Abango, in Juba, 1 November 2013.
[91] Lazarus Lual, in Juba, 19 October 2013.
[92] Arou Piol Adam, in Apada village, 21 July 2013.
[93] Ibrahim, 'Southern Sudanese Women Migrants'; following Marielle Debos, *Living by the Gun in Chad: Combatants, Impunity and State Formation* (Zed Books, 2016).

gave some chance of income, self-promotion, and self-respect, particularly if recruits bought into the brutal macho masculinities built during the conflict, and especially in comparison to men's other options in Sudan's embarrassingly menial and physically destructive labour market.[94] In the words of Michael, a Luo man and SAF soldier throughout the war,

> [Laughs] I joined the army just as work.... So there were very many of us. [My friends and I] just joined the army for the cash. Yeah. But we came by it in different places, one by one, and we met in the military training centre, in northern Atlabara. I think you know it, behind Khartoum. We were different, a large group from the Arabs, and Dinka and Nuba and Darfurians – so I spent six years in Juba, because I went two times, three years then the next three years. I went to Torit, from Torit to Kajo Keji; and Yei also.... You know, for me at that time as a soldier, they just take us to the operation, to the front line, and they don't explain what we are fighting for.[95]

Arou Piol had friends in militias fighting in the south:

> The sole thought of their families is – their son is bringing money home to the family. Because at that time, militias got a lot of money, because they were given 15 percent of the revenue. So they would get enough salary. Some people refused, like those who know what is happening. [But these people,] they're the kind of people who do not think.[96]

Some SAF soldiers managed to divorce their actions from their political support of the SPLM/A, like Dhieu's uncle Kuol, who served in the SAF for thirty-five years since the 1970s and who prided himself on his professionalism as a soldier. Kuol still supported the SPLA in principle, and helped fund men travelling via *jongo* to the training camps in Ethiopia. One of Kuol's sons joined the SPLA via *jongo*: 'Kuol told him that, please, I will die in the Arab army, so you go via Gedarif to *jongo* battalion, so that if we die here, you can live there, if you die there, then we can live here. He said that we are going to be divided, so let's divide ourselves.'[97]

---

[94] See Jok Madut Jok, 'War, Changing Ethics and the Position of Youth in South Sudan', in Jon Abbink, ed., *Vanguard or Vandals: Youth, Politics and Conflict in Africa* (Koninklijke Brill, 2005), 143–60; Kindersley and Majok, 'Monetized Livelihoods and Militarized Labour'.
[95] Juma Michael Atuko, in Maper Akot, 12 July 2013.
[96] Arou Piol Adam, in Apada village, 21 July 2013, on militia fighters.
[97] Dhieu Kuel, in Mayen Ulem, 4 July 2013.

7.6 Military Work

Choosing armed work at least gave men some kind of agency, in the face of coercive recruitment and conscription.[98] When the al-Bashir government's Islamist-fuelled militia the Popular Defence Forces was established in the early 1990s, evasion of the draft was common, but in April 1994 men who did not enrol were threatened with punishment.[99] By 1995 the draft was extended to all men between the ages of eighteen and thirty, and two years' service was compulsory by 1997 for all men who wanted to graduate from secondary school.[100] School certificates would be withheld until service was complete. And it was a chance at training and an income. As Arou said,

> [they] influenced them with – we shall provide you with salaries, which will be given to your family for you, you'll be trained as a soldier and you'll go to the front line. That was a trick done especially to the Black people's children, that they trick them that they are going to send them somewhere else, but then after they train them they send them back to the south to fight.[101]

By the early 2000s, this system drew displaced young men into the Sudan government's horrific war in Darfur. Dhieu Kuol, who was working as a court clerk by 2002 and trying to finish his secondary school certificate in evening classes, wanted to get his graduation certificate to take up his offer of a place at Nilein University. In order to get his certificate, Dhieu had to serve his time.

> I went to the military training camp, then we went to operation in Darfur, we recaptured so many towns, in 2002 to 2003. We fought there for six months. Yes, I will tell you about all what I have witnessed there, even the genocides. You hear about the genocide in Darfur. Yes, we made a genocide! I witnessed all this, we killed there.[102]

Dhieu's command worked to minimise political understanding of the war and nicknamed their enemy Tora Bora, after the mountainous area in Afghanistan where Osama bin Laden had his hideout.

---

[98] Much like back in the South; Joseph Tong Ngor, in Aweil, 16 June 2015. As in Tuttle's work, this confronting of the painful political context and wartime experience was a '[struggle] to gain control and to keep or regain the ability to make choices'. Tuttle, 'Life Is Prickly', 322.
[99] Lesch, *The Sudan*, 135–36; Rone, *Behind the Red Line*, 11, 13, 268–92.
[100] Riing Riing Lual, in Aweil, 3 September 2013; Lorins, 'Inheritance', 271, note 2; Lesch, *The Sudan*, 136.
[101] Arou Piol Adam, in Apada village, 21 July 2013.
[102] Dhieu Kuel, in Mayen Ulem, 4 July 2013.

That war in Darfur, we have committed genocide. You said okay, I have to do this for myself. And if you say I will not fight, they will say you belong to Abdul Wahid. If you don't want to fight, then you belong to the security – you will get a firing squad.'

He described his combination of guilt and horror at those six months, but emphasised that 'it was imposed on us that if you don't go and fight, you will not have your school certificate. So we went there and we fight! Because we have no alternative. You will not learn all these years, then you sit in zero at the end.'[103]

7.7 Conclusion

Over the late 1990s and early 2000s, militias built out of localised histories of conflict, competition, and ethnic community 'defence' grew their own systems of economic power and armed force across Sudan and in Khartoum. They drew on a wide pool of impoverished male workers within Sudan's by-then long-standing war economy. Their court judgments, economic systems, and militia work set out another logic of how political community could work in the aftermath of the war: of ethno-local authorities, made apparently independent through their armed power, working for the defence of their own community, in competition – but also in confederation – with each other. These militia systems shaped peoples' working lives and relationships, with the war and with each other.

These militias were brutal and generally despised. As editor Justin Bakta Logumolo wrote in the *Khartoum Monitor* in 2002,

these wolves are among us ... like cancer in the body of the Southerners spreading weakness, illness, suffering, servility, cowardice, flattery and subjection to the National Islamic Front government and tyrant who corrupts this country ... These wolves think that the NIF government is like paradise for them to shelter under it and they can do well. They expect the government to win a new country for their interests and positions.[104]

In the books, pamphlets, and songs of the previous three chapters, these people – together with the educated, middle-class people who

---

[103] Dhieu Kuel, in Mayen Ulem, 21 August 2013.
[104] Justin Bakta Logulomo, 'The Wolves in the Sudan Republic', *Khartoum Monitor*, 13 December 2002.

7.7 Conclusion

took up positions within the senior civil service and military – were all sell-outs. In Arou's terms, 'these are the dead-hearted people, and those who have been bribed by the Arabs, and those who do not know what will happen in the future'.[105] Akut Kuei's song 'Ciën këdië Kë Lëi' (I have no problem with foreigners) includes the lines

> I have no issue with foreigners
> It is between me and the Black person –
> The Black person who is making himself the Arab of the South.

However, this rhetorical, hard binary, essentially between freedom fighters and sell-outs, obscures both the economic realities of armed work during the war and more complicated histories of 'pro-government militias'. Studies of the SSDF generally characterise them as local groups primarily concerned with immediate self-defence, and politically in support of the separation of the South despite their practical dependence on funding from the Sudan government.[106] While this is a fair summary, it simplifies maybe more complicated political thinking within these militia groups. Sadig Abdel Bagi Ayii described his father:

> He was not really aiming at another future – he just wanted to help in the situation that he sees. Father had a good view of the southern Sudanese community. He said that, I can see it would be possible that South Sudan would be independent, but it would be difficult to rule ourselves – and all those people are sons of thieves [in the SPLA] who don't have a clear vision and fight amongst themselves. There are so many different civilisations that South Sudanese people are now coming from – it's going to be very hard to unite an ideology. So he was talking about this even before independence.[107]

Many people who had worked within Abdel Bagi or Paulino Matip's militias, or in the PDF and SAF, agreed with this conservative position. To them the revolution of a New Sudan was both unrealistic and destructive, but the state independence of the south was also a path to fragmentation. Instead, political community, security, and peace could be built from within regional ethnic structures, for another form of independence.[108] Even if this was not clearly articulated, what the

---

[105] Arou Piol Adam, in Apada village, 21 July 2013.
[106] John Young, 'The South Sudan Defence Forces', 15.
[107] Sadig Abdel Bagi, in Juba, 23 January 2017.
[108] Alina Sajed, 'Interrogating the Postcolonial: On the Limits of Freedom, Subalternity, and Hegemonic Knowledge', *International Studies Review* 20, no. 1 (2018): 155.

militia authorities built in Khartoum from the late 1990s was a demonstration of an alternative ethno-politics for an independent south. Their self-administered regional territories and armed industry, arbitrated on ethnic lines in parallel with other militia authorities, were their understanding of what liberation and independence could look like. These ideas were essentially summarised in the early 2000s in the concept of a South Sudanese 'nation of nationalities', a confederation of ethnic territories and representatives – probably as vague as the idea of a Black Sudanese 'New Sudan'.[109] The SSDF argued that their version of the future of a southern political community was a more realistic independence than any form of New Sudan.[110]

For the majority of poor, displaced people in Khartoum, the economic and political practicalities of survival also undermined more radical ideas of Black solidarity and of fundamental change to the violent state and inter-ethnic competition over power and resources. It was hard to imagine better futures.[111] Many people invested their energies in realistic projects, like neighbourhood chiefs and local government administrators making bargains for small reforms and protections. Compromise with militia leaders who were destroying one's villages at home was therefore necessary – as Dhieu said, 'some people are angry, unless [they] are educated to understand it'.[112] You 'cannot act like you are in Bilpam!'[113]

These were the depressing realities of work and life in Khartoum by the 2000s, after seventeen years of war, and even as the war shifted into peace negotiations after the 2002 Machakos Protocol. The conflict was not confined to a 'civil war arena' but was a basic structuring force, a banal reality, and a common source of employment.[114] The students organising Black activist events and singing SPLA songs, and

[109] Young, 'The South Sudan Defence Forces', 17; Arnold, 'The South Sudan Defence Force', 502.
[110] Arnold, 'The South Sudan Defence Force', 504.
[111] Dhieu Kuel, in Mayen Ulem, 21 August 2013. As veteran politician Peter Adwok Nyaba wrote, 'during those hard days, it was impossible to tell the truth from mere propaganda'. Nyaba, *Politics of Liberation*, 3.
[112] Dhieu Kuel, in Mayen Ulem, 21 August 2013.
[113] Bilpam village in Ethiopia was the original SPLA training camp in 1984, and is now the name of the South Sudan military headquarters in Juba. Ayii Bol, in Aweil, 16 August 2013.
[114] David M. Anderson and Øystein H. Rolandsen, 'Violence as Politics in Eastern Africa, 1940–1990: Legacy, Agency, Contingency', *Journal of Eastern African Studies* 8, no. 4 (2013): 546.

7.7 Conclusion

the evening schoolteachers reworking curriculums in solidarity with Nuba and Darfur people, were as integrated as everyone else into this impoverished economy where armed work and being part of the militia authorities were useful ways of making a living and organising a neighbourhood.[115] The rise of these southern militia authorities – thanks in part to the Sudan state – benefitted from a sprawling military job market that drew in impoverished and desperate young men. These military and capitalist realities were conservative and repressive forces, providing a measure of financial and practical security but also – as Mark Duffield observed in southern Darfur in 2001 – 'a guarded atmosphere of dependence and intimidation', setting limits to what could be spoken about, organised, and imagined within Khartoum.[116]

The ex-Khartoum residents I spoke with knew all this and made the same points. The war had built systems of exploitation, competition, and armed violence that had to be resolved before there could be any kind of peace – whether in the shape of independence in a militarised ethno-federalism, or the destruction of the old and the building of a new democratic nation.[117] As the Akut Kuei song 'Ka ye Bëny thëëth' (The spearmaster will regret his prophesy) said, the civil war was 'a disaster that will spare no one'.

---

[115] Riing Riing Lual, in Aweil, 3 September 2013; Arou Piol Adam, in Apada village, 21 July 2013; Anei Deng Akok, in Aweil, 13 August 2013; Dhieu Kuel, in Mayen Ulem, 21 August 2013; Michael Thiop Lang, in Aweil, 10 July 2013; Gabriel Deng Bulo and Marco Wiyu Deng, in Maper Akot, 22 June 2013.
[116] Duffield, 'Aid and Complicity', 96.
[117] Ambrose Sebit Pati, 'A kingdom Fighting against Itself Will Collapse (No Peace without Forgiveness)', *Khartoum Monitor*, 6 January 2003.

8 Return to the South, 2005–2011

After slow negotiations over two years, the SPLM/A and the Sudan government signed a peace deal on 9 January 2005 that ended a twenty-two-year civil war and left many questions open. The sudden death of SPLM/A leader Dr John Garang de Mabior in a helicopter crash on 30 July 2005 then precipitated a fundamental shift in Khartoum neighbourhoods and their possible futures and started a 'return home'.

This brief chapter surveys the events after Garang's death and reflects on the aftermath, via conversations with this book's protagonists. This book has a depressing trajectory: it was initially researched and written during a time of a loss of optimism and political freedom over 2011–13, as people rebuilt lives in the newly independent south and reflected on their histories and political philosophies. For most people, 2012 and 2013 involved the pressure of establishing personal security in grown-over rural spaces or fast-growing urban ones, navigating continued violence and new prejudices, military recruitment and economic empire-building by military and political interests locally and nationally, and then the start of a violent economic collapse encouraged by the government's shutdown of oil production in January 2012.[1] These pressures closed off messy but potentially radical ideas

---

[1] For summaries of this period, see Douglas H. Johnson, 'Briefing: The Crisis in South Sudan', *African Affairs* 113, no. 451 (2014): 300–309; Alex de Waal, 'When Kleptocracy Becomes Insolvent: Brute Causes of the Civil War in South Sudan', *African Affairs* 113, no. 452 (2014): 347–69; Øystein H. Rolandsen, 'Another Civil War in South Sudan: The Failure of Guerrilla Government?', *Journal of Eastern African Studies* 9, no. 1 (2015): 163–74. In late November 2013, with political tensions high in Juba, and while drinking tea in Hai Jabarona and talking to residents about the history of the neighbourhood name, I was detained by military police in Giada military headquarters.
My notebook full of Akut Kuei and Emmanuel Kembe lyrics and historical notes helped prove that I was a historian as my research permissions documents stated, and I left Juba a week before the civil war ignited in horrific violence in Juba on 15 December 2013.

8.1 Black Monday

The war has not ended. The day John was buried, everything has gone with him.[2]

The year 2005 was a fracture line in many people's personal histories.[3] Seven months after the Comprehensive Peace Agreement was signed, ending the civil war in the south but leaving many issues open, the SPLM/A leader Dr John Garang de Mabior died in a helicopter crash on 30 July. His death came soon after his joyfully emotional visit to Khartoum on 8 July, where he was greeted by hundreds of thousands of people, including many wearing and holding SPLM colours, before his inauguration as vice-president of Sudan the next day.[4] With John Garang's leadership, the options for a 'New Sudan' laid out in the CPA seemed briefly (if narrowly) achievable in those seven months. Twenty days after his triumphal visit to Khartoum, Garang's death was confirmed by radio early on Monday, 1 August.

People took to the streets in what has since been called Black Monday, initially in middle-class suburbs in central Khartoum including Soba, Haj Yousif, al Mamoura, and others, with unrest later spreading to the peripheries.[5] Both men and women began to burn cars and lash out at residents.[6] Lazarus remembers learning the news on the street:

---

[2] Nanne ep't Ende, interview with Philip Abbas Ghabush, 15 April 2006, Occasional Witness, www.occasionalwitness.com/Articles/20060704.htm.

[3] Abaker Thelatheen, in Apada, 8 June 2013; also Gabriel Deng Bulo and Marco Wiyu Deng, in Maper Akot, 22 June 2013.

[4] Josephine, in Maper Two, 26 June 2013; 'Ex-Rebel Leader Lands in Khartoum', BBC News, 7 August 2005.

[5] 'Khartoum Following the Death of Dr. John Garang', International Federation for Human Rights (FIDH), 4 August 2005; Arou Piol Adam, in Apada village, 22 July 2013.

[6] Michael Thiop Lang, in Aweil, 11 July 2013; the gendered point is supported by Khalid Mustafa Medani, 'Black Monday: The Political and Economic Dimensions of Sudan's Urban Riot', Middle East Research and Information Project, 9 August 2005. Lazarus remembered South Sudanese women making speeches inciting violence: Lazarus Lual, in Juba, 19 October 2013.

There were no vehicles – no pedestrians – it was empty, and I was like, is this Khartoum or somewhere else?! And as I kept on watching the silent street ... I heard the sound of people behind the building. SPLM Oyeee! For the first time in Khartoum, shouting like this. SPLM Oyeeee!... they told me – didn't you know that Garang is killed?! So they say – he's been killed – so when they said that, you get angry very fast. He's killed?! Who killed him?! So ... I joined the fight.[7]

As William Deng recalls: 'we were in Kalakla, where we burnt the vehicles and we killed so many people. We were fighting with stones.'[8]

By midday on that Monday, some of the army and police forces moved in to contain violence away from factories and major institutions, generally ignoring the poorest suburbs and allowing the violence to escalate there; other residents responded by forming vigilante groups.[9] By that Wednesday, soldiers and armed civilians were involved in retributive killings in many Darfuri and Southerner-majority neighbourhoods.[10] Eighty-four people were recorded killed by Thursday by the International Committee of the Red Cross, although many people put the count far higher; rumours that a southern militia leader had been killed briefly heightened the violence.[11] By the following week, the death toll was at more than 130 people.[12]

The riots emphasised the ambiguous lines of the Black community in Khartoum. One contemporary observer noted:

Despite reports to the contrary, the residents of Angola and Mandela are not exclusively southern Sudanese – and the rioters were not exclusively southern either. Their ranks included a large contingent from the war-torn western province of Darfur as well as the Nuba Mountains region in the east.[13]

---

[7] Lazarus Lual, in Juba, 19 October 2013.
[8] William Deng Aken, in Apada, 18 July 2013.
[9] Daniel, in Apada, 22 July 2013; 'With 84 Dead, Sudan Leaders Seek Calm', *New York Times*, 4 August 2005; Berridge, 'Nests of Criminals', 239–40.
[10] 'Deadly Violence Grips Sudan', *News24*, 3 August 2005; Medani, 'Black Monday'.
[11] 'With 84 Dead, Sudan Leaders Seek Calm'; Marco Majok Deng, in Khartoum Gedid, Kuajok, 28 August 2013; Dor Tartizio Buni, in Juba, 14 October 2013.
[12] Andrew England, 'Tensions Run High in Slums of Sudan after Death of Garang', *Financial Times*, 18 August 2005; Medani, 'Black Monday'.
[13] Medani, 'Black Monday'.

8.1 Black Monday

The rioters chose their targets also on roughly ethnic or racial lines: while people emphasised that 'the [Nuba and Darfur residents] were not attacked' by rioters, the riverain Sudanese Arab residents were 'going to be recognised', and vice versa.[14] As Garang Diing explained,

> the death of Dr John caused violence within the whole Black-skinned people in different areas of Khartoum, for like Darfurians, the Nuba Mountains, and especially southern Sudan. So, we're still thinking about Dr John because we hoped that he would become the leader for the whole Sudan, not only the south.[15]

From that Wednesday, the violence turned 'against any Black' – because 'it was not only South Sudanese, it was Nuba, it was Darfur, it was everybody brown, Black, against them'.[16] Police and vigilante violence from Wednesday included the murders of four of Tartizio's Nuba neighbours, who were shot by police while sitting together at a tea stall.[17] The Sudan government described Black Monday as an expression of 'grief and hysteria' but also as the work of an organised fifth column.[18] Rumours circulated among self-defined Arab Sudanese vigilante groups and police that southerners and Black Sudanese residents were planning a coup – reflecting racial anxieties over the potential outcomes of the CPA's new Sudan.[19]

Black Monday demonstrated the ambiguous Sudanese Black community and – at the same time – the practical powers of multi-ethnic militarised southern authorities in Khartoum. Paulino Matip, Abdel Baggi Ayii Akol, and other SSDF figures were apparently crucial in controlling the suburbs and stopping the fighting:

> They all came with their artilleries and patrolled around where the Dinka are, and the situation was cured by them.... When people were striking and Ayii Akol and Paulino Matip were helping people, even the Arabs knew that all the Black tribes are together that day. You know that time, before the

---

[14] Michael Thiop Lang, in Aweil, 11 July 2013; Medani, 'Black Monday'; Berridge, 'Nests of Criminals', 239.
[15] Garang Diing Akol, in Maper Akot, 22 June 2013.
[16] Lazarus Lual, in Juba, 19 October 2013.
[17] Dor Tartizio Buni, in Juba, 14 October 2013. [18] Medani, 'Black Monday'.
[19] Dor Tartizio Buni, in Juba, 14 October 2013.

crash of Dr John, people realised that Abdel Bagi and Paulino Matip are just looking for something to eat, but they might later come back to their people – as it happened.[20]

Many young men were arrested and detained for months, or otherwise disappeared.[21] Some of those who were released or were in hiding from police investigations joined Paulino Matip and Abdel Bagi's militias. This was part of the wider outcome of the post-Garang CPA period. Many unemployed or casually employed men were recruited to the SAF under the 2005 Joint Integrated Units agreement that fused SAF and SPLA units in a demonstration of Sudanese unity.[22] During 2005 and 2006, SSDF militias also recruited heavily. Their forces remained separate from the Joint Integrated Units of the SAF and SPLA until the Juba Declaration on 8 January 2006 brokered by Garang's successor and SPLA commander Salva Kiir Mayardit with the SSDF leaders. The declaration paved the way for SSDF soldiers to be integrated into the SPLA. The SSDF's leader Paulino Matip became deputy commander of the SPLA, and SSDF leaders recruited extensively to pad their militia numbers for financial and strategic benefit. Abdel Bagi grew his military training centre in Khartoum.[23] For recruits, this was a path to escape, potential pay and work, and joining the SPLA.[24] Abdel Bagi moved his forces to SPLA training grounds at Pariath and Wunrok; Paulino Matip moved his towards Malakal.[25] Because they consisted mainly of young men who had rioted on Black Monday, these forces were known among Khartoum residents as the Katip Ajer (Stone Battalion).[26]

---

[20] Garang Atak Rieu, in Mayen Ulem, 20 August 2013.
[21] Arou Piol Adam and friends in a group discussion, in Apada village, 22 July 2013; Dor Tartizio Buni, in Juba, 14 October 2013.
[22] 'Pendulum Swings: The Rise and Fall of Insurgent Militias in South Sudan', Small Arms Survey (2013).
[23] Gabriel Deng Bulo and Marco Wiyu Deng, in Maper Akot, 22 June 2013; also Arou Piol Adam, in Apada village, 22 July 2013.
[24] Arou Piol Adam and friends in a group discussion, in Apada village, 22 July 2013; Daniel, in Apada, 22 July 2013.
[25] Arou Piol Adam and friends in a group discussion, in Apada village, 22 July 2013.
[26] Lual Malong Yor, in Madhol, 26 August 2017; Arou Piol Adam and friends in a group discussion, in Apada village, 22 July 2013; Daniel, in Apada, 22 July 2013; William Deng Aken, in Apada, 18 July 2013; Arou Piol Adam, in Apada village, 21 July 2013.

Events in 2005 changed Khartoum suburbs. Social tensions combined with discussions of boundary commissions and repatriation of displaced people started to explicitly delineate the 'southern community'. As a non-southern resident of Kalakla told the *Financial Times* after the riots: 'Southerners should stay in the south and northerners should stay here.'[27] Rumours and conspiracy theories abounded, and practical relationships between local authorities, police, and chiefs became strained.[28] The new regional administration of the government of southern Sudan, the opening of SPLM party offices in Khartoum, and the convenient journalistic and political simplifications of north and south encouraged this distancing.

Garang's death fundamentally changed many people's hopes for the future. Deng, who was at that time a secondary school student in Nyala in Darfur, explained how his peers were 'hoping that Garang would make southerners regain their ultimate freedom in Sudan and be respected as citizens once again; and with his death, we feared more abuse in Darfur'.[29] Southern residents' discussions of self-determination and political change were funnelled into discussions of what could be achieved under the CPA and southern independence.[30] As Arop Madut Arop emphasised in a final note in his 2006 book: 'TO SOUTHERNERS: they should stop being vague about what they stand for. This is their last chance to have a state of their own.'[31]

8.2 Return and Reconstruction in the South

After 2005, relationships and prospects in Khartoum hardened quickly for specifically 'southern' residents. Growing questions over rights to land, houses, jobs, and pensions, as well as by 2007 the start of organised and internationally funded IDP returns programmes, encouraged hostility and increased policing in majority-Black suburbs. Garang's death finally meant that 'there's no way for us to stay

---

[27] England, 'Tensions Run High'.
[28] Abaker Thelatheen, in Apada, 8 June 2013.
[29] Deng Garang Ngong, in Juba, 24 September 2019.
[30] Mareike Schomerus and Lotje De Vries, 'Just Cause or Crisis in the Making? How Self-Determination Was Interpreted to Achieve an Independent South Sudan', in W. Zeller and J. Thomas, eds., *Secessionism in Africa* (Palgrave Macmillan, 2014), 23–24.
[31] Madut-Arop, *Sudan's Painful Road to Peace*, 414.

there ... That's how we lost the idea of staying there, and then we started mobilising ourselves, and started coming back to our motherland.'[32] Dor Tartizio was 'waiting on when the UN was going to collect us ... for me myself I decided – for me alone – so I took a vehicle to Kosti, from Kosti I came with the rivers'.[33]

Many chiefs and neighbourhood committees encouraged people to return, emphasising the need to organise land claims in old villages and be registered for the election and 2011 referendum on secession there. Many emphasised a lack of criminality or police violence in the south, and cordiality between new neighbours: 'we told the women and youth, in the South it is free for you to drink, not like here!'[34] A group of chiefs and committee members said they knew that even if they had to 'eat soil', it would be better to return to somewhere they had basic rights; they joked that 'we were donkeys in the North – we will be donkeys in the South',[35] still doing the donkeys' work. This idea was played with satirically by Micah Sowaka Mukhtar in a column for the *Khartoum Monitor* in 2010:

I hear that there are five million southerners in the north. If the authorities in the north let us secede, they are going to lose this manpower to build roads and houses. They will have no servants in their houses. Car washers will disappear. It will be difficult to find drivers to drive their business trucks and buses. There will be no watchmen to guard banks, restaurants, hotels, factories.... All the African traffic police will go to the south. All the Africans in the GoNU [Government of National Unity] will quit. All the African officers, including those in the armed forces, will go south. The Africans from the Nuba Mountains and those from Western Sudan living in the north will all move south, into the new Sudan. Khartoum will be empty without tenants to rent the deserted houses. There will be no mechanics to repair cars and trucks in the industrial areas. Yes, southerners in the North will only lose property. We came with nothing, but we are taking away the manpower with us.[36]

Repatriation was generally slow, and sometimes abortive. People split their families, with women and children heading south first while men

---

[32] Ahok Akec, in Maper chiefs' court, 13 April 2013.
[33] Dor Tartizio Buni, in Juba, 14 October 2013.
[34] Ngor Akol Jonkor, in Apada, 5 June 2013.
[35] Maper chiefs' court meeting, 29 June 2013.
[36] Micah Sowaka Mukhtar, 'Eye Opener: 24 Hours Dance', *Khartoum Monitor*, 24 August 2010.

stayed behind to sell houses, businesses, and cars, or keep earning cash incomes to fund setting up new homes in the south.[37] But over 2006 and 2007 this process was badly coordinated and poorly supported, and often significantly coercive on the part of both the Sudanese and southern Sudanese authorities; early returnees complained about this 'fake repatriation' as many of them returned to Khartoum when they failed to find land or support for reintegration back in southern villages.[38]

By 2008, though, huge numbers of families had begun the taxing and carefully managed process of moving back 'home', including many people who had never been to southern Sudan before. Numbers increased in 2010 in the run-up to the referendum in January 2011. What figures there are of people originating from southern Sudan remaining in Khartoum are calculated from a subtraction of these counted 'returnees' from an original estimate of about 1.7 million southern Khartoum residents.[39] SPLM offices in regional towns organised buses and (where possible) trains.[40] Abdel Bagi Ayii Akol is said to have organised some repatriation from Babanusa to Aweil because of local food shortages.[41] Political pressures to return intensified in Khartoum, including from politicians newly elected in 2010, organising their constituencies for a strong vote for secession.

As with the massive resettlements from 1986 to 1992, this was a period of intense disruption and rupture for those relocating their lives and families to often unfamiliar or strikingly changed areas. Court cases over unpaid or under-paid marriage bride wealth, child custody, and land rights boomed as people dug out paper records of decisions in Khartoum in southern courts. Single mothers with children organised to move with neighbours and friends, re-creating neighbourhoods in the International Organisation for Migration (IOM) 'returnee' villages and organising with elderly women returnees and residents to learn how to cut grass for thatch and build wattle houses in various styles, skills they had not been able to learn in Khartoum.[42]

---

[37] Maper chiefs' court meeting, 13 April 2013.
[38] 'The Poison of Electoralism', *Khartoum Monitor*, 1 August 2010; 'Is Life in Torit Really Normal?', *Khartoum Monitor*, 1 November 2002.
[39] Personal communication from anonymous Embassy staff, Juba, 2 October 2013.
[40] Santino Ayak, in Maper chiefs' court, 13 April 2013.
[41] Ayii Bol, in Aweil, 16 August 2013.   [42] Abuk Deng, in Apada, 5 June 2013.

The stress and complexity of this resettlement and re-establishment of social order has been documented in detail by a new wave of social anthropology.[43] It has also been articulated in South Sudanese contemporary discourse through discussions of social morality, stereotypes of the various 'returnee' communities from different parts of eastern Africa, and negotiations over rights to land. Previously slandered as *jellaba*, people who had lived in Khartoum during the war were called 'Khartoumers' and (in the late 2000s and early 2010s) often accused of being undereducated and too arrogant, deeply politically suspicious, conservatively dressed, over-serious, and snobbish by some who had lived in eastern Africa or stayed in southern Sudan during the wars.[44] Some ex-Khartoum residents tried to counter suspicions of their loyalties and political intentions by emphasising that they had also participated in the civil war, or at least were fighting a 'cold war' in Khartoum.[45] As a Nuer ex-politician and businessman said, with the weight of hindsight, 'of course not all of us were as good as to fight the revolution; and to the same degree, not everybody fought in the bush also was a revolutionary, you see. I was able to fight the lion in its own den'.[46]

For many people, the legal and political pressures during this transitional period demanded clear identifications that were not there. Many people were married across the 'south-north' line, and were forced to choose who would become a foreigner.[47] Many women from the Nuba Mountains, Darfur, and elsewhere who had married now–South Sudanese men moved to the south. Many other families – especially

---

[43] Tuttle, 'Life Is Prickly'; Meier, 'Returning to Northern Bahr El Ghazal'; Katarzyna Grabska, 'The Return of Displaced Nuer in Southern Sudan: Women Becoming Men?', *Development and Change* 44, no. 5 (2013): 1135–57; *Gender, Home & Identity*; Léonie Newhouse, 'South Sudan Oyee! A Political Economy of Refugee Return Migration to Chukudum, South Sudan', PhD dissertation, University of Washington (2012); Sara Pantuliano, 'Going Home: Land, Return and Reintegration in Southern Sudan and the Three Areas', in *Uncharted Territory: Land, Conflict and Humanitarian Action* (Practical Action Publishing, 2009), 153–70.

[44] James Garang, in Aweil, 15 June 2015.

[45] Peter Deng Akok, in Maper, 21 June 2013.

[46] Farouk Gatkuoth, in Juba, 30 October 2013; this is a common metaphor, used, for example, by Diing Chen Diing, in Aweil, 15 July 2013.

[47] In the words of writer Stella Gaitano: Enrico Ille, '"But They Can't Manage to Silence Us": Mahjoub Sharif's Prison Poem "A Homesick Sparrow" (1990) as Resistance to Political Confinement', *Middle East Topics & Arguments* 5 (2015): 125.

those that could afford to – split their investments and left some relatives, especially school-going children and those needing medical care, in Khartoum.

A marker of all these processes and complexities was the proliferation of neighbourhoods called Khartoum Gedid (New Khartoum) across southern Sudan in this period (from Godele in Juba to multiple settlements across Northern Bahr el Ghazal and Warrap). Although the name was fading away in most places by the 2010s, these neighbourhoods were mostly built by IOM-repatriated (or in the words of some residents, 'deported') returnees on land given by local and national government for resettlement. These neighbourhoods collected people returning with nowhere to go: 'everyone coming from Khartoum could ask where Khartoum people were settling, and they direct them here'.[48]

When I visited in 2013, older residents of Khartoum Gedid outside Gogrial wanted to shift the name to Mayen Gumel, the old name for the area; they were also trying to rename its sister site, the later-founded 'Khartoum Two' down the road, as War Ayat. A few elderly residents explained that they wanted to leave Khartoum behind and use the local language, avoiding political associations with Sudan and getting Khartoum 'out of the mind of the coming generation'.[49] But younger residents were arguing to keep the name, even though they knew they were 'already defeated' by the political priorities of the government and elders. In tea shops, young people who had spent their teenage years in Khartoum reminisced to me about how in Khartoum 'a job can just find you at home' and about the joys of electricity and air conditioning. They emphasised that even private schools were relatively easy to access, unlike the difficulty of getting good-quality education in the south, and how clinics in Gogrial relied on diagnosing all sicknesses as malaria. Several young men complained how they were told by locals that their lack of vernacular Dinka language skills meant they were like men wearing trousers but no underwear. The struggle over the name of the village was a touchstone for these wider conversations about class, wealth, social norms, personal safety, livelihoods, and aspirations, and what the future might or should look like. Both young men and women in those tea-shop discussions emphasised that New Khartoum was supposed to be an

---

[48] Lal Malou, in Khartoum Gedid, Kuajok, 27 August 2013.   [49] Ibid.

aspirational name, but 'now that we've formed this new Khartoum, we are worried that Khartoum will never come here'.[50]

8.3 South Sudan's Trajectories

By mid-2013 during the initial research for this book, events and discussions were going sour. In the same conversation with Dhieu detailed at the beginning of this book, he noted:

> The situation I'm witnessing now, I'm not happy with it.... I envisioned that the country was going to be liberated totally, and democracy was going to be practiced.... So when Kiir dismissed Machar [on 23 July 2013, when the president sacked his whole cabinet], and he appoints another person – it's the same person. What is the change there? We want a change when a man is brought to power and he does what we [the people] want ... we were hoping for a total change.[51]

Despite Dhieu's forthright complaints, during the 2013 research around Northern Bahr el Ghazal there were other dynamics that could not be openly discussed. Governor Paul Malong had been recruiting ad hoc militias at the SPLA Division 3 main training ground in Pantit since at least 2008, ostensibly in response to repeated clashes and continued tensions over the border region disputed with Sudan, commonly known as 'Mile 14'. These forces were locally described as defensive parts of the local SPLA, with a remit of *dut baai* (defend the homeland).[52] By early 2013, however, Malong had continued to recruit into these personal militias, at the same time as hosting a rally in Aweil at the end of July 2013 in support of President Salva Kiir Mayardit's dissolution of the national cabinet. These forces were increasingly tasked with *dut beny* (protect the boss). By December 2013 they were called the Mathiang Anyoor (Brown Caterpillar) and were deployed alongside Kiir's Tiger Battalion forces across Juba. These forces were responsible for extensive and horrific violence and

---

[50] Group of young people, in Khartoum Gedid, Kuajok, 27 August 2013.
[51] Simon Tisdall, 'South Sudan President Sacks Cabinet in Power Struggle', *The Guardian*, 25 July 2013; Dhieu Kuel, in Mayen Ulem, 21 August 2013.
[52] People have compared them to Sudan's old Popular Defence Forces: anonymous interviewee, 12 June 2015; although one former fighter, speaking to Radio Tamazuj, reportedly said 'they even aspired to march north to "annex Kosti"', much like Garang's speech: 'Generals Say Juba Massacres Done by Private Militia, not SPLA', *Radio Tamazuj*, 9 March 2015.

8.3 South Sudan's Trajectories

mass killings in Juba in December 2013 and across South Sudan, in Upper Nile, and Central Equatoria, in particular, over 2014–17.[53]

Recruitment continued after Malong's appointment as chief of staff of the SPLA in April 2014, fuelled by shock and anger across Northern Bahr el Ghazal at the mass murders of Dinka communities across Jonglei and Upper Nile during the ensuing civil war, with many people invoking the violent split in the SPLA in 1991 and the resulting ethnic divides as a direct comparator: 'they think that the old history has come back'.[54] Recruitment was also fuelled by an escalating economic crisis across South Sudan, with hyperinflation in mid-2015: for many young men around Aweil, the options were surviving floods and droughts on family farms, taking a seasonal or permanent return to waged labour in the north, or seeking out recruitment in the hope of finding work at checkpoints or as bodyguards for senior staff and politicians. In 2015, one elderly sub-chief described Northern Bahr el Ghazal to me as a 'dry wood forest' for collecting President Kiir's soldiers.[55]

Over the following years I heard about the Mathiang Anyoor's horrific abuses and sexual violence both from Aweil residents and from people who had suffered at their hands in Central Equatoria, in refugee camps in northern Uganda.[56] Several people I had met in Yei in early 2016 were killed a few months later when supposed 'counter-insurgency' by government forces, including poorly trained Mathiang Anyoor soldiers, escalated into direct clashes with local opposition fighters and brutal attacks on local populations. Arou Piol, the young Dinka-language teacher latterly unemployed in Apada at the end of 2013, disappeared as a new recruit in Upper Nile sometime in 2015, and his body was never returned.[57]

---

[53] Nicki Kindersley, 'Military Livelihoods and the Political Economy in South Sudan', in *Routledge Handbook of the Horn of Africa* (Routledge, 2022); Alan Boswell, 'Insecure Power and Violence: The Rise and Fall of Paul Malong and the Mathiang Anyoor', Small Arms Survey (2019).

[54] Apada chiefs' court meeting, 14 June 2015; anonymous interviewee, in Mayen Ulem, 12 June 2015; see Thomas, *South Sudan*, 281–85.

[55] Anonymous interviewee, in Mayen Ulem, 12 June 2015.

[56] Alan Boswell, 'Conflict and Crisis in South Sudan's Equatoria', USIP (2021); Kindersley and Rolandsen, 'Civil War on a Shoestring: Rebellion in South Sudan's Equatoria Region', *Civil Wars* 19, no. 3 (2017): 308–24.

[57] Other disappearances include Yor's brother: Yor, in Warawar, 13 December 2018.

The rebel forces arrayed against Kiir's government by mid-2014 – collectively called the SPLA in Opposition (SPLA-IO) – reformulated the SSPF. Led by former SSPF senior officers including David Yau Yau, its military forces fought to re-securitise many of the same areas the SSPF held against the SPLA during the late 1990s and early 2000s, building regional military governance and economic systems.[58] These resurgent former Khartoum-based military businessmen included the Ayii Akol family. The elderly Abdel Bagi Ayii Akol became a presidential advisor on border and traditional affairs to Salva Kiir in 2007, but after being shut out of the new cabinet in June 2010, Abdel Bagi announced an armed rebellion against Kiir, which ended with an amnesty in October 2011.[59] In the civil war during 2014, his son Agany – an SPLA general – commanded government forces fighting the IO in Bor and Upper Nile, but then defected to the IO in mid-2015, and re-defected to Peter Gatdet's factional South Sudan Liberation Army.[60] Throughout this, the Ayii Akol family, led in part by Agany's brother Hussein, built their own militia forces around the family's commercial farms in Meiram in southern Darfur; these forces were formed into the South Sudan Patriotic Movement/Army (SSPM/A) in 2015 when the family rejected the national peace agreement. As in past years and decades, the family militia recruited from young men heading north from the Aweil area, and attacked borderland areas, disrupting trade and farming.[61]

When the Sudan government brokered the 2018 agreement that led to a 'revitalised' peace process, the Ayii Akol SSPM/A joined the peace process as part of the South Sudan Opposition Alliance (SSOA) of localised rebel factions. Back within the government, the IO-affiliated SSPA reopened the training camp at Pantit for its forces.[62] With room

[58] John Young, 'A Fractious Rebellion: Inside the SPLM-IO', Small Arms Survey (2015).
[59] 'South Sudan Says None of Its Soldiers Joined Former Presidential Adviser', Sudan Tribune, 24 March 2011; 'Ex-Presidential Advisor Responds to Amnesty after Rebellion', Sudan Tribune, 2 October 2011.
[60] Agany then rejoined the SPLA in January 2019. 'A Renegade General Apologizes to Aweil Communities, Promises to Embrace Peace', United Nations Peacekeeping, 24 January 2019.
[61] 'S. Sudanese Army, Armed Men Clash in N. Bahr El Ghazal', Sudan Tribune, 27 April 2016.
[62] Nicki Kindersley and Joseph Diing Majok, 'Breaking Out of the Borderlands: Understanding Migrant Pathways from Northern Bahr El-Ghazal, South Sudan', Rift Valley Institute (2020) 22, note 64.

for five vice-presidents under the 'big tent'–style agreement, President Kiir and Sudan's sovereign council chair Abdel Fattah al-Burhan proposed the appointment of SSOA's representative Hussein Abdel Bagi as a vice-president of South Sudan. Vice-President Hussein Abdel Bagi also became chair of the South Sudan National Taskforce on COVID-19.[63]

President Kiir's government has gradually reworked its systems, using the brokerage of both peace agreements in 2015 and 2018, presidential decrees and appointments down to the county level, and – mainly outside urban areas – military and security forces paying their own salaries via armed business (e.g., the charcoal trading and the checkpoints industry).[64] Southern political systems from Khartoum have also been reformulated at more local levels. The now-late Deng Macham continued to organise the South Sudan Council of Chiefs, which mobilised people for pro-government demonstrations and until Macham's death acted as an intermediary and broker for chiefs to access ministerial and presidential offices.[65] By the early 2010s, also, interconnected multi-ethnic courts called Ashara Wilayat were re-established across Juba's peripheral and heavily militarised neighbourhoods, with many of the same organisers as in Khartoum. These courts retain the same logics as their Khartoum forebears, with men organising ethnic representation in inter-ethnic land and family disputes, and managing neighbourhood issues with local garrisons and resident soldiers via their personal connections. Many organisers are also powerful military-business figures themselves, like the Ashara Wilayat paramount chief organising in Juba's Hai Referendum, Mia Saba, and Moro Kurau neighbourhoods.[66] Some women, including Abuk Deng, took a chance on remarrying military officers; Abuk is

---

[63] 'The Vice President H.E Hussein Abdelbagi Office Corruption Blackens South Sudan Covid-19 Fight', *Juba Mirror*, 19 April 2021.
[64] Peer Schouten, Ken Matthysen, and Thomas Muller, 'Checkpoint Economy: The Political Economy of Checkpoints in South Sudan, Ten Years after Independence', Danish Institute for International Studies (2021); Jok Gai Anai and Nhial Tiitmamer, 'The Tragedy of the Unregulated: Why the Government Should Reform the Charcoal Sector', Sudd Institute (2022).
[65] Kuel Aguer Kuel, in Juba, 20 January 2017; group of elderly Dinka men, in Mia Saba, Juba, 20 October 2015.
[66] Group of elderly Dinka men, in Mia Saba, Juba, 20 October 2015; Ashara Wilayat court members, in Gumbo Shirikat, Juba, 13 October 2015.

now living in Juba, and her two children born in Khartoum are going to school. 'Every corner of life here is chaired by ex-soldiers.'[67]

8.4 The Hard Questions of the Future

If John Garang's death in 2005 was a moment of splintering, then the evolving civil war since 2018 to the present has broken down many people's projects for alternative futures. People have lost hope and trust, not just from the vicious impacts of conflicts but also from chronic economic stress, exploitative labour in towns and private farms, and increasingly unpredictable rains and droughts.[68] Many people moving to South Sudan after 2005's peace agreement invested in local government jobs and teaching, but the collapse of the South Sudanese pound (from about £3 to $1 in 2010, £420 to $1 in 2022, and £1,000 to $1 in 2023) has left salaries useless.[69] In Aweil many teachers had given up by 2015, in favour of fishing or working as handymen and cleaners at the UN base.[70] Across South Sudan many rural schools have collapsed or rely on the goodwill of volunteer student teachers. A series of droughts in Northern Bahr el Ghazal since 2015 have created food shortages and a famine in 2017. Economic stress has forced young people into towns to earn cash for school costs, medical care for relatives, and their own ambitions.[71] Young women in particular are stuck, with limited access to education and facing a growing labour burden of keeping food supplies and earning enough money to pay for basic living for families and children. As Raja reflected, 'I'm not free here. I keep thinking about so many things. I was really free in Khartoum, but since I came back here, I haven't found a chance to live.'[72]

Many young people and families have headed back to Darfur and Khartoum from Bahr el Ghazal, to Gambella in Ethiopia or Sudan from across Upper Nile, or into northern Uganda from Equatoria, and many say they are leaving for good.[73] Dhieu headed back to Darfur with his family after drought destroyed his farm and his teaching salary

---

[67] Dhieu Kuel, in Mayen Ulem, 12 June 2015.
[68] Joseph Tong Ngor, in Aweil, 16 June 2015. [69] Ibid. [70] Ibid.
[71] Diing et al., 'South Sudan: Youth, Violence and Livelihoods'; Kindersley and Majok, 'Monetized Livelihoods'; 'Breaking Out of the Borderlands'.
[72] Raja, in Apada, 3 September 2013.
[73] Abaker Thelatheen, in Apada, 21 August 2017.

8.4 The Hard Questions of the Future

became worthless; he was 'hoping to get changes here. But now we have got despair and desperation.'[74] Others, particularly older people, are still 'struggling to stay in our land' and hanging on to hope: 'we don't say that this area is bad, we are hoping it will be good'.[75]

In discussions reflecting on this book's project since 2015, many people have described their sense of a sharp narrowing of citizenship to a small elite who are building an 'inherited country', feeling that they are just 'human machinery' to the government apparatus.[76] Many – particularly teachers – see this as part of a conscious attempt to undermine and destroy public education systems and maintain poverty wages on military and political leaders' commercial farms and businesses, so that, in Dhieu's words, 'poor people can't reach them, like the sky and the ground'; these wealthy citizens themselves 'have exported their children' for education outside South Sudan. The remaining working majority, Dhieu explained, are seen as 'thorns for their fence'.[77]

The war's assertion of explicit tribal identifications and hierarchies and its propagation of violent prejudices and ideas of extermination have created a 'black hole among the South Sudanese community – I can name it as a social break'.[78] The dominant, zero-sum tribalist narrative of the civil war, in Dhieu's words, is 'creating a gravitational force that will pull you down'.[79] People from across Equatoria, Upper Nile, and Bahr el Ghazal discussed the ways that ethnic labels and suspicions can take over daily logics and relationships, even if you are consciously trying to challenge them, or if you are from a multi-ethnic family yourself; many people want to resist this way of approaching society, but are also defensive themselves, and frightened.[80] Many people whose work is detailed in this book note that this tribalism has been spread from the top and that the civil war is a 'political issue

---

[74] Dhieu Kuel, in Mayen Ulem, 12 June 2015.
[75] Ngor Akol Jonkor, in Apada, 5 June 2013.
[76] Dhieu Kuel, in Mayen Ulem, 12 June 2015. This is noted by Thomas, *South Sudan*, 23, 94–95.
[77] Dhieu Kuel, in Mayen Ulem, 12 June 2015.   [78] Ibid.
[79] Ibid. For example, there were a variety of mobilising ideas circulating in Aweil in mid-2015: that the Dinka would all be killed if the Nuer rebel Riek Machar took power, that the integrity of South Sudan demanded the eradication of rebel challengers to President Kiir, and, most arrogantly, the idea that as the Dinka are the national majority in South Sudan, they should not accept minority rule.
[80] AECOM staff member, in Aweil, 11 June 2015.

which has been preached in a tribal manner'.[81] During visits in 2015, 2017, and 2019, many people in Aweil expressed embarrassment, anger, and deep sadness about the propagation of ideas of Dinka supremacy, and argued themselves that Dinka government forces were perpetrating genocide against other ethnic groups. Dhieu recounted the proverb, 'If you want to dig a hole to bury your brother, make it large, because you will be in it tomorrow.' He went on:

It is not a matter of Dinka, Shilluk, Nuer, Bari, Zande. It is a matter of a bad man on a throne. We are not all children of Salva Kiir Mayardit. You tell them [in Juba] that there are still some Dinka brothers.[82]

---

[81] James Garang, in Aweil, 11 June 2015; anonymous interviewee, in Mayen Ulem, 12 June 2015.
[82] Dhieu Kuel, in Mayen Ulem, 12 June 2015.

Conclusion
Intellectual Histories for Other Possibilities

We are the tired ones
Born in the chaotic
Years of this nation
Suppressed in the
Corridors of darkness
With minds
Suffocated by gun smoke
We are the tired ones
Creative misfits
Intellectual outcasts everything they can't handle
We are the tired ones
Oppress our melodies
Erase our paintings
But you will never break our spirits.

Deng 'Forbes' Paul, 'The Tired Ones'[1]

This book is a history of other possibilities. It complicates overarching explanations of conflict and post-war reconstruction with the competing theories and histories made by refugees, urban workers, rural songwriters, tea-makers, and brewers.

This project has tried to give a small picture of the discussions that displaced people in Khartoum pursued over building some form of shared community, on imagined ethnic, racial, or shared political foundations, and for various ends: the creation and capture of a new southern state, the protection and continuity of more specifically local community, or for something more radical. Many people wanted a New Sudan of equity, anti-racism, and freedom, in one

---

[1] Performed in Juba, 2017.

form or other; many others who wanted a new breakaway South Sudan knew that secession alone would not be enough. The projects here maintain a relatively constant critique of exclusionary and violent state systems; of the middle and upper classes 'selling out' fundamental change in favour of their continued financial investments, cheap employees and an easy life; and, more widely, of modern capitalist greed and individualism. People of all ages and educational backgrounds sought, in various ways, to build societies that were not (or not only) based on racist and exploitative hierarchies and exclusionary nationalisms. All of this needed space, money, time, and security, and these – as well as political events well beyond their control – placed practical limits on creative work.

Documenting some of these lost alternatives opens up new intellectual space. First, for researchers of urban spaces, refugee lives, and civil wars, it emphasises that people living in impoverished, exhausting, expensive, and exploitative situations have extensive expertise in both the practical and the intellectual work of constructing better futures. Working-class intellectual history opens pathways to understanding how people have imagined and worked for safe, fair futures for myriad different political communities – not only in the heyday of decolonisation but also in the present.

Second, exploring these political projects challenges the currently dominant field of intellectual histories that generally struggle to include people who lack formal education or are less literate. This demands deeper histories of political thought written from the perspectives (and work) of people living at the sharp end of global systems of capitalism, migration, violent states, and societal change. In doing this, historians can explore what a 'global' intellectual history really looks like for the majority of people who are working with bits of ideas, images, and terminologies drawn as far as they could from global Black intellectual traditions but also from their own wider world of family conversations, local words, theories, and histories. In this book, no text, song, term, or undertaking is settled or finished, just like all intellectual projects.

And finally, these projects defy bleak current readings of South Sudan's post-independence politics. The 2010s have had a deadening effect on political analysis of South Sudan's state and future. The country is now commonly described in standard contemporary analysis as a less artful and more explicit version of the militarised neopatrimonial extractive and violent state of old Sudan.[2] It is now becoming hard to find any explanations of South Sudan's current crisis that do not implicitly or explicitly describe the state's collapse and renewed war as in some way predictable. These analyses also often infer a fundamental lack of political theory or imagination in this bleak world of greed and centralised power. This book tries to demonstrate that this is – of course – not true.

Instead, this book demands a much closer engagement with ideas of social and economic stratification and difference beyond reductive political ethnicities and the 'elite'. This requires a close engagement with histories of South Sudanese conversations over emergent economic classes, forms of wealth, leadership, and authority: crucial missing theory for political analyses that borrow their terms of reference from outside. This book is part of a wave of work that collectively demands recognition that South Sudanese people (of all social backgrounds) are engaged in sustained projects of political theory.[3] The recognition of this field of theory could unseat mainstream top-down analyses of South Sudan's civil wars that reduce political discourse to a bare competition for power, and could open up other possibilities for political futures that are imagined and organised well beyond the machinations of a handful of armed businessmen in the capital.

---

[2] De Waal, 'When Kleptocracy Becomes Insolvent'; 'South Sudan: The Perils of Payroll Peace', LSE Conflict Research Programme (2019); de Waal, 'A Political Marketplace Framework Analysis', LSE Conflict Research Programme (2019).

[3] For example, Jok Madut Jok, *Breaking Sudan: The Search for Peace* (Oneworld Publications, 2017); Zoe Cormack, 'The Spectacle of Death: Visibility and Concealment at an Unfinished Memorial in South Sudan', *Journal of Eastern African Studies* 11, no. 1 (2017): 115–32; Jedeit Jal Riek and Naomi Pendle, 'Speaking Truth to Power in South Sudan: Oral Histories of the Nuer Prophets', Rift Valley Institute (2018); Naomi Pendle, 'The "Nuer of Dinka Money" and the Demands of the Dead: Contesting the Moral Limits of Monetised Politics in South Sudan', *Conflict, Security & Development* 20, no. 5 (2020): 587–605; 'Contesting the Militarization of the Places Where They Met: The Landscapes of the Western Nuer and Dinka (South Sudan)', *Journal of Eastern African Studies* 11, no. 1 (2017): 64–85; Tounsel, *Chosen Peoples*; Julia Duany, Rebecca Lorins, and Edward Thomas, 'Education, Conflict, and Civicness in South Sudan: An Introduction', *South Sudan Studies Association* (2021): 24.

C.1 Reflections on South Sudan's Political Path

Every good citizen is pointing to the bad ones
You – who is selling your own people
You – who is involved in selling and killing your own people
You will pay a very high price,
Be careful, be careful,
Your ancestors will pay a very high price.

General Paulino, 'Jurlikam' (Our homeland)[4]

The memories this book is based on have been difficult to discuss with people through this period of unrolling conjuncture, in the words of Stuart Hall.[5] South Sudan's new civil war's violence, its bitter tribal rhetoric, and the immediate challenges of sustained economic collapse since 2013 place limits and rose tints on what can be remembered. But this crisis is also a moment of reflection on these old political projects and ideals.

Despite the work of poets, artists, songwriters, and activists to attempt to hold public space in recent years, it feels like there is currently very little room or purchase for a new South Sudan at the time of writing, and very little safety even for the types of intellectual projects detailed in this book. The lecturer, former aid worker, and briefly caretaker governor of Northern Bahr el Ghazal (who took up the post after Malong's promotion to SPLA chief of staff in 2014) Kuel Aguer Kuel, who spoke with me several times for this book, was until very recently a political prisoner in Juba, after he called for change with the People's Coalition for Civil Action in July 2021.[6] Diing, once the young student who had organised emergency care for those arriving in Khartoum railway station in 1988 (see Chapter 1), emphasised in 2015 that 'politics is meaningless now – they have taken our voices by force'.[7] And there is a lot to speak about. As a poem presented at an Ana Taban poetry slam night in Juba in 2017 said: 'If we the

---

[4] Written during the late 1990s or early 2000s.
[5] Stuart Hall, *The Hard Road to Renewal: Thatcherism and the Crisis of the Left* (Verso, 2021), 162.
[6] 'PCCA's Kuel Aguer Sick in Juba Prison, Daughter Says', *Radio Tamazuj*, 22 February 2022; Michael Daniel, 'Kuel Aguer Is Freed over Lack of Evidence', *Eye Radio*, 9 December 2022.
[7] Diing Chen Diing, in Aweil, 16 June 2015.

living cannot speak of things ourselves, how can we expect the dead to speak?'[8]

What is resistance when political organising and public speech are not possible, or appear pointless? This book demonstrates that small acts of rebellion like wearing a shorter skirt, or less 'rebellious' organising of adult education classes and photocopied pamphlet books, might not amount to revolution but are ways of thinking through it. These are attempts at praxis, ways of contemplating another future or sowing the seeds for it, even if that future is still unclear. This project has documented a tiny part of the extensive, practical, and emotional intellectual work people have been doing for generations, 'trying to answer the hard questions of our future.'[9] The rough idea of a New Sudan still has purchase, and people are trying to build one.

---

[8] Ana Taban poetry slam, in Juba, 19 November 2017.
[9] AECOM staff member, in Aweil, 11 June 2015. Echoed by Alfred Taban, in Juba, 16 October 2013.

Bibliography

Abbas Ghabboush, Philip. 'Growth of Black Political Consciousness in Northern Sudan'. *Africa Today* 20, no. 3 (1 January 1973): 29–43.
Abdalla, Muna A. 'Poverty and Inequality in Urban Sudan: Policies, Institutions and Governance'. PhD dissertation, African Studies Centre, 2008.
Abdelrahman, Babiker Abdalla. 'Internal Migration in the Sudan: A Study of the Socio-Economic Characteristics of Migrants in Khartoum'. PhD dissertation, University of Glasgow, 1979. http://encore.lib.gla.ac.uk/iii/encore/record/C__Rb1628982.
Abdinoor, Abdullahi S. 'Constructing Education in a Stateless Society: The Case of Somalia'. PhD dissertation, Ohio University, 2007. https://etd.ohiolink.edu/!etd.send_file?accession=ohiou1173755011&disposition=attachment.
Abdullahi Mohammed Abdel Hadi. 'The Impact of Urbanization on Crime and Delinquency'. In *Urbanization in the Sudan: Proceedings of the Seventeenth Annual Conference, Khartoum, 2nd–4th August, 1972*, edited by El-Sayed Bushra. Philosophical Society of the Sudan, 1972.
Abrahamsen, Rita. 'Internationalists, Sovereigntists, Nativists: Contending Visions of World Order in Pan-Africanism'. *Review of International Studies* 46, no. 1 (January 2020): 56–74. https://doi.org/10.1017/S0260210519000305.
Abu Sin, Mohad E., and H. R. J. Davies. *The Future of Sudan's Capital Region: A Study in Development and Change*. Khartoum University Press, 1991.
Abusharaf, Rogaia Mustafa. *Transforming Displaced Women in Sudan: Politics and the Body in a Squatter Settlement*. University of Chicago Press, 2009.
African Print Cultures: Newspapers and Their Publics in the Twentieth Century. University of Michigan Press, 2016.
African Rights. 'Food and Power in Sudan: A Critique of Humanitarianism'. African Rights, July 1997.
  Sudan's Invisible Citizens: The Policy of Abuse against Displaced People in the North. African Rights, 1995.
Ahmad, Adil Mustafa. 'The Neighbourhoods of Khartoum: Reflections on Their Functions, Forms and Future'. *Habitat International* 16, no. 4 (1992): 27–45. https://doi.org/10.1016/0197-3975(92)90052-Z.

Ahmed, Abdel Ghaffar M., and Mustafa Abdel Rahman. 'Small Urban Centres: Vanguards of Exploitation. Two Cases from Sudan'. *Africa* 49, Special Issue 3 (July 1979): 258–71. https://doi.org/10.2307/1159558.

Ahmed Mahmud, Ushari, and Suleyman Ali Baldo. 'The Dhein Massacre: Slavery in the Sudan'. Human Rights Abuses in the Sudan 1987. Sudan Relief and Rehabilitation Association, 1987.

Akol, Jacob J. *Burden of Nationality: Memoirs of an African Aidworker/Journalist, 1970s–1990s*. Paulines Publications Africa, 2006.

Akol, Lam. *Southern Sudan: Colonialism, Resistance, and Autonomy*. Red Sea Press, 2007.

Alexander, Leslie M., Brandon R. Byrd, and Russell Rickford. *Ideas in Unexpected Places: Reimagining Black Intellectual History*. Northwestern University Press, 2022.

Al-Gouni, Magdi. 'For Whom the Bells Toll: Kambo (18): Fifty Years of Solitude'. *Sudan Vision*, 9 March 2014. http://news.sudanvisiondaily.com/print.html?rsnpid=233109&copyType=1.

Anai, Jok Gai, and Nhial Tiitmamer. 'The Tragedy of the Unregulated: Why the Government Should Reform the Charcoal Sector'. The Sudd Institute, 26 April 2022. www.suddinstitute.org/publications/show/626953bc133ff.

Anderson, David M., and Øystein H. Rolandsen. 'Violence as Politics in Eastern Africa, 1940–1990: Legacy, Agency, Contingency'. *Journal of Eastern African Studies* 8, no. 4 (2 October 2014): 539–57. https://doi.org/10.1080/17531055.2014.949402.

Andrews, Kehinde. *Back to Black: Retelling Black Radicalism for the 21st Century*. Zed Books, 2018.

Aqra', 'Umar Muḥammad 'Abd al-Raḥmān, Mohamed Y. Shaddad, Sudanese Group for Assessment of Human Settlements, and International Institute for Environment and Development. *Housing Rentals in the Sudanese Capital: Popular Settlements, Phase II, 1986–1988*. Sudanese Group for Assessment of Human Settlements, 1988.

Arat-Koç, Sedef. 'New Whiteness(es), Beyond the Colour Line? Assessing the Contradictions and Complexities of "Whiteness" in the (Geo)Political Economy of Capitalist Globalism'. In *States of Race: Critical Race Feminism for the 21st Century*, edited by Thobani Razack Smith, 147–68. Between the Lines, 2010.

Arnold, Matthew B. 'The South Sudan Defence Force: Patriots, Collaborators or Spoilers?' *Journal of Modern African Studies* 45, no. 4 (1 December 2007): 489–516.

Babiker, Bushra El Tayed. *Khartoum: Past, Present and the Prospects for the Future*. Durham Middle East Papers 73. University of Durham, Centre for Middle Eastern and Islamic Studies, 2003.

Badiey, Naseem. *The State of Post-Conflict Reconstruction: Land, Urban Development and State-Building in Juba, Southern Sudan*. Boydell & Brewer, 2014.

Badri, Amna E. S., and Intisar I. A. Sadig. *Sudan between Peace and War: Internally Displaced Women in Khartoum and South and West Kordofan*. UNIFEM, 1998. www.africabib.org/rec.php?RID=W00067088.

Bakhit, A. H., and A. Johayna. 'Mubrooka: A Study in the Food System of a Squatter Settlement in Omdurman, Sudan'. *GeoJournal* 34, no. 3 (1 November 1994): 263–68. https://doi.org/10.1007/BF00813929.

Bakhit, Abdel Hamid. 'Availability, Affordability and Accessibility of Food in Khartoum'. *GeoJournal* 34, no. 3 (1994): 253–55.

Bakhit, Mohamed A. G. 'Negotiations of Power and Responsibilities in Khartoum Shantytowns'. In *Forging Two Nations: Insights on Sudan and South Sudan*, edited by Elke Grawert, 127–42.: OSSREA, 2014.

Bakta Logulomo, Justin. 'The Wolves in the Sudan Republic'. *Khartoum Monitor*, 13 December 2002.

Bannaga, Sharaf Eldin Ibrahim. *Peace and the Displaced in Sudan: The Khartoum Experience*. Swiss Federal Institute of Technology, 2002.

Barclay, Harold B. *Buurri al Lamaab: A Suburban Village in the Sudan*. Cornell Studies in Anthropology. Cornell University Press, 1964.

Baronnet, Bruno. 'Rebel Youth and Zapatista Autonomous Education'. *Latin American Perspectives* 35, no. 4 (7 January 2008): 112–24. https://doi.org/10.1177/0094582X08318982.

Bascom, Johnathan. *Losing Place: Refugee Populations and Rural Transformations in East Africa*. Refugee and Forced Migration Studies, v. 3. Berghahn Books, 1998.

Bayart, Jean-Francois. *The State in Africa: The Politics of the Belly*. Longman, 1993.

BBC News. 'Ex-Rebel Leader Lands in Khartoum'. 7 August 2005.

Becker, Felicitas, Salvatory S. Nyanto, James Giblin, Ann McDougall, Alexander Meckelburg, and Lotte Pelckmans. 'Researching the Aftermath of Slavery in Mainland East Africa: Methodological, Ethical, and Practical Challenges'. *Slavery & Abolition* 44, no. 1 (19 September 2022): 131–56. https://doi.org/10.1080/0144039X.2022.2121888.

Bellucci, Stefano, and Bill Freund. 'Introduction. Work across Africa: Labour Exploitation and Mobility in Southern, Eastern and Western Africa'. *Africa* 87, no. 1 (February 2017): 27–35. https://doi.org/10.1017/S000197201600067X.

Berman, Bruce J. 'Ethnicity, Patronage and the African State: The Politics of Uncivil Nationalism'. *African Affairs* 97, no. 388 (July 1998): 305–41.

Berridge, Willow. 'The Ambiguous Role of the Popular, Society and Public Order Police in Sudan, 1983–2011'. *Middle Eastern Studies* 49, no. 4 (2013): 528–46.

Civil Uprisings in Modern Sudan: The 'Khartoum Springs' of 1964 and 1985. Bloomsbury Publishing, 2015.

'"Nests of Criminals": Policing in the Peri-Urban Regions of Northern Sudan, 1964–1989'. *Journal of North African Studies* 17, no. 2 (1 March 2012): 239–55. https://doi.org/10.1080/13629387.2011.608574.

Bhagat, Ali. 'Governing Refugee Disposability: Neoliberalism and Survival in Nairobi'. *New Political Economy* 25, no. 3 (15 April 2020): 439–52. https://doi.org/10.1080/13563467.2019.1598963.

Bianchi, Claudia. 'Slurs and Appropriation: An Echoic Account'. *Journal of Pragmatics* 66 (May 2014): 35–44. https://doi.org/10.1016/j.pragma.2014.02.009.

Bjarnesen, Jesper, and Mats Utas. 'Introduction: Urban Kinship: The Micro-Politics of Proximity and Relatedness in African Cities'. *Africa* 88, no. S1 (March 2018): S1–S11. https://doi.org/10.1017/S0001972017001115.

Boadu, Gideon. 'Change and Continuity in Ghana's Intellectual History: From Late 19th Century to the Eras of Decolonisation and Independence'. *African Studies* 78, no. 4 (2 October 2019): 457–76. https://doi.org/10.1080/00020184.2018.1555309.

Boddy, Janice. *Wombs and Alien Spirits: Women, Men, and the Zar Cult in Northern Sudan*. University of Wisconsin Press, 1989.

Bonner, Raymond. 'A Reporter at Large: Famine'. *The New Yorker*, 13 March 1989. 71/8/61-76. Sudan Archives Durham.

Boswell, Alan. 'Conflict and Crisis in South Sudan's Equatoria'. Special Report, US Institute of Peace, April 2021.

'Insecure Power and Violence: The Rise and Fall of Paul Malong and the Mathiang Anyoor'. Briefing Paper, Human Security Baseline Assessment (HSBA) Small Arms Survey, October 2019.

Breidlid, Anders. 'Education in the Sudan: The Privileging of an Islamic Discourse'. *Compare: A Journal of Comparative and International Education* 35, no. 3 (1 September 2005): 247–63. https://doi.org/10.1080/03057920500212530.

'Sudanese Images of the Other: Education and Conflict in Sudan'. *Comparative Education Review* 54, no. 4 (2010): 555–79. https://doi.org/10.1086/653814.

'Sudanese Migrants in the Khartoum Area: Fighting for Educational Space'. *International Journal of Educational Development* 25, no. 3 (2005): 253–68.

Brennan, James R. 'Blood Enemies: Exploitation and Urban Citizenship in the Nationalist Political Thought of Tanzania, 1958–75'. *Journal of African History* 47, no. 3 (2006): 389–413.

Taifa: Making Nation and Race in Urban Tanzania. Ohio University Press, 2012.

Brubaker, Rogers. 'Ethnicity, Race, and Nationalism'. *Annual Review of Sociology* 35, no. 1 (2009): 21–42. https://doi.org/10.1146/annurev-soc-070308-115916.
Bushra, El-Sayed. *An Atlas of Khartoum Conurbation*. Khartoum University Press, 1976.
Byrd, Brandon R. 'The Rise of African American Intellectual History'. *Modern Intellectual History* 18, no. 3 (September 2021): 833–64. https://doi.org/10.1017/S1479244320000219.
Cabral, Estêvão, and Marilyn Martin-Jones. 'Writing the Resistance: Literacy in East Timor 1975–1999'. *International Journal of Bilingual Education and Bilingualism* 11, no. 2 (1 March 2008): 149–69. https://doi.org/10.2167/beb491.0.
Caddell, Martha. 'Private Schools as Battlefields: Contested Visions of Learning and Livelihood in Nepal'. *Compare: A Journal of Comparative and International Education* 36, no. 4 (1 December 2006): 463–79. https://doi.org/10.1080/03057920601024909.
Callaci, Emily. *Street Archives and City Life: Popular Intellectuals in Postcolonial Tanzania*. Duke University Press, 2017.
Cameron, Christopher. 'Haiti and the Black Intellectual Tradition, 1829–1934'. *Modern Intellectual History* 18, no. 4 (December 2021): 1190–99. https://doi.org/10.1017/S1479244320000281.
Christian, Michelle. 'A Global Critical Race and Racism Framework: Racial Entanglements and Deep and Malleable Whiteness'. *Sociology of Race and Ethnicity* 5, no. 2 (1 April 2019): 169–85. https://doi.org/10.1177/2332649218783220.
Christiansen, Christian Olaf, Mélanie Lindbjerg Guichon, and Sofía Mercader. 'Towards a Global Intellectual History of an Unequal World'. *Global Intellectual History* (10 June 2022): 1–17. https://doi.org/10.1080/23801883.2022.2062412.
Coben, Diana. *Radical Heroes: Gramsci, Freire and the Politics of Adult Education*. Routledge, 2013.
Cohen, Roberta, and Francis Mading Deng, eds. *The Forsaken People: Case Studies of the Internally Displaced*. Brookings Institution Press, 1998.
Conflict Research Programme. 'South Sudan: The Perils of Payroll Peace'. Memo, London School of Economics and Political Science, March 2019.
Cooper, Frederick. *On the African Waterfront: Urban Disorder and the Transformation of Work in Colonial Mombasa*. ACLS Humanities E-Book, 2014.
Copnall, James. *A Poisonous Thorn in Our Hearts: Sudan and South Sudan's Bitter and Incomplete Divorce*. Oxford University Press, 2014.
Cormack, Zoe. 'The Making and Re-making of Gogrial: Landscape, History and Memory in South Sudan'. Thesis, Durham University, 2014.

'The Spectacle of Death: Visibility and Concealment at an Unfinished Memorial in South Sudan'. *Journal of Eastern African Studies* 11, no. 1 (2 January 2017): 115–32. https://doi.org/10.1080/17531055.2017.1288410.

Daughtry, Carla N. 'Conflict and Community in Church-Based Refugee Havens in Cairo: The Quest for Space to Be Dinka'. *Arab Studies Journal* 14, no. 2 (2006): 39–59.

Davis, Mike. *Planet of Slums*. Verso, 2007.

Deng, Francis Mading. *Dinka Folktales: African Stories from the Sudan*. Africana, 1974.

The Dinka and Their Songs. Oxford Library of African Literature. Clarendon P, 1973.

Dynamics of Identification: A Basis for National Integration in the Sudan. Khartoum University Press, 1973.

War of Visions: Conflict of Identities in the Sudan. Brookings Institution, 1995.

Dia, Hamidou. 'From Field to Concept: The Example of Senegalese Multisited Villages'. *Journal of Intercultural Studies* 34, no. 5 (2013): 569–83.

Diing, Abraham, Bul Kunjok Majuch, Catherine Night, Chirrilo Madut Anei, Elizabeth Abuk, Elizabeth Nyibol Malou, James Gatkuoth Mut, et al. 'South Sudan: Youth, Violence and Livelihoods'. Rift Valley Institute, 2021.

Din, Mohamed El Awad Galal al-. 'The Nature and Causes of Labour Migration to the Khartoum Conurbation'. In *Urbanization and Urban Life in the Sudan*, edited by Valdo Pons, 425–48. Department of Sociology and Social Anthropology, University of Hull, 1980.

Dixon, Luke. 'Youth Theatre in the Displaced People's Camps of Khartoum'. In *African Theatre: Youth*, edited by Michael Etherton and Jane Plastow, 6:78–85. James Currey Publishers, 2006.

Duany, Julia, Rebecca Lorins, and Edward Thomas. 'Education, Conflict, and Civicness in South Sudan: An Introduction'. *South Sudan Studies Association*, February 2021, 24.

Duffield, Mark. 'Aid and Complicity: The Case of War-Displaced Southerners in the Northern Sudan'. *Journal of Modern African Studies* 40, no. 1 (1 March 2002): 83–104.

Dut, Lino Alëu Angïc. *Athör Käny* [History]. Khartoum, 2005.

Editor. 'A Kingdom Fighting against Itself Will Collapse (No Peace without Forgiveness)'. *Khartoum Monitor*, 6 January 2003.

El Gizouli, Magdi. 'South Sudanese Labour: Refill the "Kambo"'. *Sudan Tribune* (blog), 8 October 2012. www.sudantribune.com/spip.php?iframe&page=imprimable&id_article=44142.

Elias, Bedri Omer, and Hassan Yassin Bedawi. 'The Squatters Housing Problem: A Review of Government Policy and Solutions'. In *Urbanization in the Sudan: Proceedings of the Seventeenth Annual Conference, Khartoum, 2nd–4th August, 1972*, edited by El-Sayed Bushra, 213–21. Philosophical Society of the Sudan, 1972.

Elnur, Ibrahim. *Contested Sudan: The Political Economy of War and Reconstruction*. Durham Modern Middle East and Islamic World Series 14. Routledge, 2008.

Ende, Nanne op't. 'Interview with Philip Abbas Ghabush', 15 April 2006.

England, Andrew. 'Tensions Run High in Slums of Sudan after Death of Garang'. *Financial Times*, 18 August 2005.

Englund, Harri. 'Anti Anti-colonialism: Vernacular Press and Emergent Possibilities in Colonial Zambia'. *Comparative Studies in Society and History* 57, no. 1 (January 2015): 221–47. https://doi.org/10.1017/S0010417514000656.

Epstein, Andrew I. 'Maps of Desire: Refugee Children, Schooling, and Contemporary Dinka Pastoralism in South Sudan'. PhD dissertation, University of Wisconsin–Madison, 2012. http://search.proquest.com/docview/1024738921/abstract/46551306C88D402FPQ/23.

Evans-Pritchard, Edward Evan. 'A History of the Kingdom of Gbudwe'. *Zaire* 10, no. 5 (1956): 451–91.

Ewald, Janet J. *Soldiers, Traders, and Slaves: State Formation and Economic Transformation in the Greater Nile Valley, 1700–1885*. University of Wisconsin Press, 1990.

Falge, Christiane. 'The Effects of Nuer Transnational Churches on the Homeland Communities'. *Urban Anthropology and Studies of Cultural Systems and World Economic Development* 42, nos. 1–2 (2013): 171–205.

Faria, Caroline. 'Styling the Nation: Fear and Desire in the South Sudanese Beauty Trade'. *Transactions of the Institute of British Geographers* 39, no. 2 (April 2014): 318–30. https://doi.org/10.1111/tran.12027.

Farmer, Ashley D. 'Black Women's Internationalism: A New Frontier in Intellectual History'. *Modern Intellectual History* 19, no. 2 (June 2022): 625–37. https://doi.org/10.1017/S1479244321000081.

Feierman, Steven M. *Peasant Intellectuals: Anthropology and History in Tanzania*. University of Wisconsin Press, 1990.

FIDH [International Federation for Human Rights]. 'Khartoum Following the Death of Dr. John Garang'. 4 August 2005.

Fletcher, Robert. *Beyond Resistance: The Future of Freedom*. Nova Publishers, 2007.

Flint, Julie. 'Beyond "Janjaweed": Understanding the Militias of Darfur'. Small Arms Survey, 2009.

Fluehr-Lobban, Carolyn. 'Islamization in Sudan: A Critical Assessment'. *Middle East Journal* 44, no. 4 (1990): 610–23.

Fluehr-Lobban, Carolyn, and kharyssa rhodes, eds. *Race and Identity in the Nile Valley: Ancient and Modern Perspectives*. Red Sea Press, 2003.

Fourchard, Laurent. 'Undocumented Citizens and the Making of ID Documents in Nigeria: An Ethnography of the Politics of Suspicion in Jos'. *African Affairs* 120, no. 481 (1 October 2021): 511–41. https://doi.org/10.1093/afraf/adab022.

Frahm, Ole. 'Defining the Nation: National Identity in South Sudanese Media Discourse'. *Africa Spectrum* 47, no. 1 (2012): 21–49.

Franck, Alice, Barbara Casciarri, and Idris Salim El-Hassan. *In-Betweenness in Greater Khartoum: Spaces, Temporalities, and Identities from Separation to Revolution*. Berghahn Books, 2021. https://doi.org/10.2307/j.ctv2tsxjs8.

Freire, Paulo. *Literacy: Reading the Word & the World*. Routledge and Kegan Paul, 1987.

Garang, John. *The Genius of Dr. John Garang: Speeches on the War of Liberation*. Edited by PaanLuel Wël. CreateSpace Independent Publishing Platform, 2015.

Garuba, Harry. 'Race in Africa: Four Epigraphs and a Commentary'. *PMLA* 123, no. 5 (2008): 1640–48.

Geoffroy, Agnès de. 'Fleeing War and Relocating to the Urban Fringe – Issues and Actors: The Cases of Khartoum and Bogotá'. *International Review of the Red Cross* 91, no. 875 (September 2009): 509. https://doi.org/10.1017/S1816383109990361.

Getachew, Adom. 'Response to Forum on Worldmaking after Empire'. *Millennium* 48, no. 3 (1 June 2020): 382–92. https://doi.org/10.1177/0305829820936362.

Worldmaking after Empire: The Rise and Fall of Self-Determination. Princeton, NJ: Princeton University Press, 2019.

Gilbert, Juliet. 'Mobile Identities: Photography, Smartphones and Aspirations in Urban Nigeria'. *Africa* 89, no. 2 (May 2019): 246–65. https://doi.org/10.1017/S000197201900007X.

Glassman, Jonathon. *War of Words, War of Stones: Racial Thought and Violence in Colonial Zanzibar*. Indiana University Press, 2011.

Grabska, Katarzyna. 'In-Flux: (Re) Negotiations of Gender, Identity and "Home" in Post-War Southern Sudan'. University of Sussex, 2010. http://sro.sussex.ac.uk/2525/.

'The Return of Displaced Nuer in Southern Sudan: Women Becoming Men?' *Development and Change* 44, no. 5 (September 2013): 1135–57. https://doi.org/10.1111/dech.12051.

Green, Nile. 'The Waves of Heterotopia: Toward a Vernacular Intellectual History of the Indian Ocean'. *American Historical Review* 123, no. 3 (1 June 2018): 846–74. https://doi.org/10.1093/ahr/123.3.846.

Guarak, Mawut Achiecque Mach. *Integration and Fragmentation of the Sudan: An African Renaissance*. AuthorHouse, 2011.

Guichon, Mélanie Lindbjerg. '(Black) Neo-colonialism and Rootless African Elites: Tracing Conceptions of Global Inequality in the Writings of George Ayittey and Kwesi Kwaa Prah, 1980s–1990s'. *Intellectual History Review* 32, no. 4 (2 October 2022): 737–60. https://doi.org/10.1080/17496977.2021.1913390.

Deng, Wek. 'The Vice President H.E Hussein Abdelbagi Office Corruption Blackens South Sudan Covid-19 Fight', *Juba Mirror*, 19 April 2021. www.facebook.com/Official64tribespress/posts/the-vice-president-he-hussein-abdelbagi-office-corruption-blackens-south-sudan-c/815703525711066/.

Hale, Sondra. 'The Changing Ethnic Identity of Nubians in an Urban Milieu: Khartoum, Sudan'. PhD dissertation, University of Michigan, 1979.

'Nationalism, "Race", and Class: Sudan's Gender and Culture Agenda in the Twenty-First Century'. In *Race and Identity in the Nile Valley: Ancient and Modern Perspectives*, edited by Carolyn Fluehr-Lobban and kharyssa rhodes, 171–86. Red Sea Press, 2003.

'Nubians in the Urban Milieu: Greater Khartoum'. Paper presented at the 17th annual conference of the Philosophical Society of Sudan, 'Urbanization in the Sudan', 1972, https://discover.durham.ac.uk/discovery/fulldisplay?docid=alma991007789959707366&context=L&vid=44DUR_INST:VU1&lang=en&search_scope=MyInst_and_CI&adaptor=Local%20Search%20Engine&tab=Everything&query=any,contains,Nubians%20in%20the%20urban%20milieu:%20Greater%20Khartoum&offset=0.

Hall, Stuart. *The Hard Road to Renewal: Thatcherism and the Crisis of the Left*. Verso Books, 2021.

'Rethinking the Multicultural Question', a conversation with Nira Yuval-Davis, 'Racisms, Sexisms and Contemporary Politics of Belonging' conference, London, August 2004.

Hamdan, G. 'The Growth and Functional Structure of Khartoum'. *Geographical Review* 50, no. 1 (1960): 21. https://doi.org/10.2307/212333.

Hammond, John L. *Fighting to Learn: Popular Education and Guerrilla War in El Salvador*. Rutgers University Press, 1998.

Hammond, Laura C. *This Place Will Become Home: Refugee Repatriation to Ethiopia*. Cornell University Press, 2004.

Harengel, Peter, and Ayantunji Gbadamosi. '"Launching" a New Nation: The Unfolding Brand of South Sudan'. *Place Branding and Public Diplomacy* 10, no. 1 (February 2014): 35–54. https://doi.org/10.1057/pb.2013.12.

Harir, Sharif. *Racism in Islamic Disguise? Retreating Nationalism and Upsurging Ethnicity in Dar Fur, Sudan*. Centre for Development Studies, University of Bergen, 1993.

'Recycling the Past in the Sudan: An Overview of Political Decay'. In *Short-Cut to Decay: The Case of the Sudan*, edited by Sharif Harir and Terje Tvedt, 10–63. Nordiska Afrikainstitutet, 1994.

Harragin, Simon, and Chol Changath Chol. 'The Southern Sudan Vulnerability Study'. Save the Children Fund, 1999. www.alnap.org/resource/9969.aspx.

Hartman, Saidiya. 'Intimate History, Radical Narrative'. *Journal of African American History* 106, no. 1 (January 2021): 127–35. https://doi.org/10.1086/712019.

Hassaballa, Hassaballa Omer. 'Displacement and Migration as a Consequence of Development Policies in Sudan'. In *The Displacement Problem in the Sudan: Essays on the Crisis*, edited by Eltigani El Tahir Eltigani and Hatim Ameer Mahran, 34–50. Draft manuscript, 1991. Sudan Archives Durham, SAD.940/5/2.

Haumann, Mathew. *Travelling with Soldiers and Bishops: Stories of Struggling People in Sudan*. Paulines Publications Africa, 2004.

Henderson, K. D. D. *Sudan Republic*. Nations of the Modern World. Benn, 1965.

Henin, R. A. *Economic Development and Internal Migration in the Sudan*. [University of Khartoum?], 1960.

Herbert, Cassie. 'Precarious Projects: The Performative Structure of Reclamation'. *Language Sciences*, Slurs, 52 (November 2015): 131–38. https://doi.org/10.1016/j.langsci.2015.05.002.

Heredia, Marta Iñiguez de. 'The Conspicuous Absence of Class and Privilege in the Study of Resistance in Peacebuilding Contexts'. *International Peacekeeping* 25, no. 3 (2018): 325–48. https://doi.org/10.1080/13533312.2018.1449650.

Hodgkinson, Dan, and Luke Melchiorre. 'Introduction: Student Activism in an Era of Decolonization'. *Africa* 89, no. S1 (January 2019): S1–S14. https://doi.org/10.1017/S0001972018000888.

Holt, P. M., and M. W. Daly. *A History of the Sudan from the Coming of Islam to the Present Day*. 6th ed. Longman/Pearson, 2011.

hooks, bell. *Teaching Community: A Pedagogy of Hope*. Routledge, 2003.

Howe, Marvine. 'Promise of Regional Autonomy for Sudan Separatists Brings Mass Return to Southern Towns'. *The Times*, 1 January 1971.

Howell, J. 'Political Leadership and Organisation in the Southern Sudan'. PhD dissertation, University of Reading, 1978. http://ethos.bl.uk/OrderDetails.do?uin=uk.bl.ethos.483207.

Human Rights Watch Africa. *Children in Sudan: Slaves, Street Children and Child Soldiers*. Human Rights Watch, 1995.

Hunter, Emma. 'Dialogues between Past and Present in Intellectual Histories of Mid-Twentieth-Century Africa'. *Modern Intellectual History*, 22 June 2022, 1–9. https://doi.org/10.1017/S1479244322000233.

'Dutiful Subjects, Patriotic Citizens, and the Concept of "Good Citizenship" in Twentieth-Century Tanzania'. *Historical Journal* 56, no. 1 (March 2013): 257–77. https://doi.org/10.1017/S0018246X12000623.

Political Thought and the Public Sphere in Tanzania. Cambridge University Press, 2015.

Hunter, Emma, and Leslie James. 'Introduction: Colonial Public Spheres and the Worlds of Print'. *Itinerario* 44, no. 2 (August 2020): 227–42. https://doi.org/10.1017/S0165115320000248.

Hunter, Emma, Ismay Milford, Daniel Branch, and Gerard McCann. 'Another World? East Africa, Decolonisation, and the Global History of the Mid-Twentieth Century'. *Journal of African History* 62, no. 3 (2021): 394–410.

Hutchinson, Sharon Elaine. 'Food Itself Is Fighting with Us': A Comparative Analysis of the Impact of Sudan's Civil War on South Sudanese Civilian Populations Located in the North and the South'. In *Violence and Belonging: The Quest for Identity in Post-colonial Africa*, edited by Vigdis Broch-Due, 131–52. Routledge, 2005.

Nuer Dilemmas: Coping with Money, War, and the State. University of California Press, 1996.

Hutchinson, Sharon Elaine, and Jok Madut Jok. 'Gendered Violence and the Militarization of Ethnicity'. In *Postcolonial Subjectivities in Africa*, edited by R. Werbner, 84–108. Zed Books, 2002.

Ibrahim, F. N. 'The Conditions of the Southern Sudanese Women Migrants in Abu Siid Shanty Town, Omdurman, Sudan: A Case Study of Cultural Change'. *GeoJournal* 20, no. 3 (1 March 1990): 249–58. https://doi.org/10.1007/BF00642990.

'Hunger-Vulnerable Groups within the Metropolitan Food System of Khartoum'. *GeoJournal* 34, no. 3 (November 1994): 257–61.

'Migration and Identity Change in the Sudan'. *GeoJournal* 25, no. 1 (1 September 1991): 5–6. https://doi.org/10.1007/BF00179760.

'The Southern Sudanese Migration to Khartoum and the Resultant Conflicts'. *GeoJournal* 25, no. 1 (1 September 1991): 13–18. https://doi.org/10.1007/BF00179762.

Ibrahim, Salah El-Din El-Shazali. 'War Displacement: The Socio-cultural Dimension'. In *The Displacement Problem in the Sudan: Essays on the Crisis*, edited by Eltigani El Tahir Eltigani and Hatim Ameer Mahran, 51–68. Draft manuscript, 1991. Sudan Archives Durham, SAD.940/5/2.

Idris, Hélène Fatima. 'Modern Developments in the Dinka Language'. *Göteborg Africana Informal Series*, no. 3 (2004). www.kultur.gu.se/digitalAssets/1309/1309450_modern-developments-dinka.pdf.

Igga, Wani. *Southern Sudan: Battles Fought and the Secrecy of Diplomacy*. Roberts & Brothers General Printers, 2008.

Ille, Enrico. 'Brothers, Arrivals, Refugees: South Sudanese as Subjects of Naming and Reporting Practices in Sudan's Humanitarian Sector'. *Diaspora: A Journal of Transnational Studies* 22, no. 1 (March 2022): 11–32. https://doi.org/10.3138/diaspora.22.1.2022.12.17.

——— '"But They Can't Manage to Silence Us": Mahjoub Sharif's Prison Poem "A Homesick Sparrow" (1990) as Resistance to Political Confinement'. *Middle East – Topics & Arguments* 5 (3 November 2015): 117–30. https://doi.org/10.17192/meta.2015.5.3520.

Impey, Angela. 'The Poetics of Transitional Justice in Dinka Songs in South Sudan'. UNISCI Discussion Papers, no. 33 (2014): 57–77.

IOM [International Organisation for Migration]. 'Sustainable Reintegration of South Sudanese: Final Draft Strategy', March 2012.

——— 'Village Assessment Survey Report', 2013.

James, Wendy. *The Listening Ebony: Moral Knowledge, Religion, and Power among the Uduk of Sudan*. Oxford University Press, 1999.

——— 'Perceptions from an African Slaving Frontier'. In *Slavery and Other Forms of Unfree Labour*, edited by Léonie J. Archer, 130–41. Routledge, 1988, 130.

——— 'War and "Ethnic Visibility": The Uduk on the Sudan-Ethiopia Border'. In *Ethnicity & Conflict in the Horn of Africa*, edited by Katsuyoshi Fukui, 140–64. James Currey, 1994.

Jansen, Bram J. *Kakuma Refugee Camp: Humanitarian Urbanism in Kenya's Accidental City*. Zed Books, 2018.

——— 'The Refugee Camp as Warscape: Violent Cosmologies, "Rebelization," and Humanitarian Governance in Kakuma, Kenya'. *Humanity: An International Journal of Human Rights, Humanitarianism, and Development* 7, no. 3 (2016): 429–41. https://doi.org/10.1353/hum.2016.0024.

Johnson, Douglas H. 'Briefing: The Crisis in South Sudan'. *African Affairs* 113, no. 451 (4 January 2014): 300–309. https://doi.org/10.1093/afraf/adu020.

——— 'Judicial Regulation and Administrative Control: Customary Law and the Nuer, 1898–1954'. *Journal of African History* 27, no. 1 (1986): 59–78.

——— 'A New History for a New Nation: The Search for South Sudan's Usable Past'. Paper presented at the *9th International South Sudan and Sudan Studies Conference*. Bonn, Germany, 2012. www.bicc.de/fileadmin/Dateien/pdf/press/2012/Abstracts_9th_ISSC_01.pdf.

——— 'Recruitment and Entrapment in Private Slave Armies: The Structure of the Zarä'ib in the Southern Sudan'. *Slavery & Abolition* 13, no. 1 (1 April 1992): 162–73. https://doi.org/10.1080/01440399208575056.

——— *The Root Causes of Sudan's Civil Wars: Peace or Truce*. Revised ed. African Issues. Fountain Publishers, 2011.

——— 'The Structure of a Legacy: Military Slavery in Northeast Africa'. *Ethnohistory* 36, no. 1 (1989): 72–88.

'Sudanese Military Slavery from the Eighteenth to the Twentieth Century'. In *Slavery and Other Forms of Unfree Labour*, edited by Léonie J. Archer, 142–55. Routledge, 1988, 130.

Jok, Jok Madut. *Breaking Sudan: The Search for Peace*. Oneworld Publications, 2017.

'Diversity, Unity, and Nation Building in South Sudan'. US Institute of Peace, 2011.

'Militarism, Gender and Reproductive Suffering: The Case of Abortion in Western Dinka'. *Africa: Journal of the International African Institute* 69, no. 2 (1999): 194–212. https://doi.org/10.2307/1161022.

'Post-Independence Racial Realities'. In *Race and Identity in the Nile Valley: Ancient and Modern Perspectives*, edited by Carolyn Fluehr-Lobban and Kharyssa Rhodes, 187–206. Red Sea Press, 2003.

Sudan: Race, Religion and Violence. Oneworld, 2005.

'The Targeting of Civilians as a Military Tactic'. In *Coping with Torture: Images from Sudan*, edited by Ann Mosely Lesch and Osman A. Fadl, 21–29. Red Sea Press, 2004.

'War, Changing Ethics and the Position of Youth in South Sudan'. In *Vanguards or Vandals: Youth, Politics, and Conflict in Africa*, edited by Jon Abbink, 143–60. Koninklijke Brill, 2005.

War and Slavery in Sudan. Ethnography of Political Violence. University of Pennsylvania Press, 2001.

Juba in the Making. '"Boxing the Past"', 17 September 2018. https://jubainthemaking.com/boxing-the-past-the-south-sudan-national-archives-in-historical-perspective/.

Kameir, El-Wathig. 'Nuer Migrants in the Building Industry in Khartoum: A Case of the Concentration and Circulation of Labour'. Urbanisation and Urban Life in the Sudan. Department of Sociology and Social Anthropology, University of Hull, 1980, 449–85.

'Operationalizing the New Sudan Concept'. In *New Sudan in the Making? Essays on a Nation in Search of Itself*, edited by Francis Mading Deng, 447–51. Red Sea Press, 2010.

Kinaro, Joyce, Tag Elsir Mohamed Ali, Rhonda Schlangen, and Jessica Mack. 'Unsafe Abortion and Abortion Care in Khartoum, Sudan'. *Reproductive Health Matters* 17, no. 34 (1 November 2009): 71–77. https://doi.org/10.1016/S0968-8080(09)34476-6.

Kindersley, Nicki. 'Military Livelihoods and the Political Economy in South Sudan'. In *Routledge Handbook of the Horn of Africa*. Routledge, 2022.

'Politics, Power and Chiefship in Famine and War: A Study of the Former Northern Bahr El Ghazal State, South Sudan'. Rift Valley Institute, June 2018.

'Subject(s) to Control: Post-war Return Migration and State-Building in 1970s South Sudan'. *Journal of Eastern African Studies* 11, no. 2 (31 March 2017): 211–29. https://doi.org/10.1080/17531055.2017.1305678.

Kindersley, Nicki, and Joseph Diing Majok. 'Breaking Out of the Borderlands: Understanding Migrant Pathways from Northern Bahr El-Ghazal, South Sudan'. X-Border Local Research Network. Juba: Rift Valley Institute, November 2020.

'Monetized Livelihoods and Militarized Labour in South Sudan's Borderlands'. Rift Valley Institute, 2019.

Kindersley, Nicki, and Øystein H. Rolandsen. 'Civil War on a Shoestring: Rebellion in South Sudan's Equatoria Region'. *Civil Wars* 19, no. 3 (3 July 2017): 308–24. https://doi.org/10.1080/13698249.2017.1417073.

Kraft, Scott. 'Refugees from Sudan Civil War: Starving Boys Walk for Months to Relief Camps'. *Los Angeles Times*, 3 June 1988. http://articles.latimes.com/1988-06-03/news/mn-4653_1_refugee-camp.

Kuol Malith, Athian. 'Top 12 Famous South Sudanese Artists of All Time'. *PaanLuel Wël Media Ltd – South Sudan* (blog), 20 April 2018. https://paanluelwel.com/2018/04/20/top-12-famous-south-sudanese-artists-of-all-time/.

Kuyok, Kuyok Abol. *South Sudan: The Notable Firsts*. AuthorHouse, 2015.

Ladu Terso, Edward. 'Kwoto in Holland (Part One)'. *Khartoum Monitor*, 12 July 2003.

Laheij, Christian. 'Dangerous Neighbours: Sorcery, Conspicuous Exchange and Proximity among Urban Migrants in Northern Mozambique'. *Africa* 88, no. S1 (March 2018): S31–S50. https://doi.org/10.1017/S0001972017001139.

Lamoureaux, Siri. 'Message in a Mobile Risālah Fī Jawāl = Risaala Fi Jawaal: Mixed-Messages, Tales of Missing and Mobile Communities at the University of Khartoum'. Langaa Research and Publishing Common Initiative Group; African Studies Centre, 2011. http://search.ebscohost.com/login.aspx?direct=true&scope=site&db=nlebk&db=nlabk&AN=417122.

Lamphere, Louise. 'Migration, Assimilation and the Cultural Construction of Identity: Navajo Perspectives'. *Ethnic and Racial Studies* 30, no. 6 (November 2007): 1132–51. https://doi.org/10.1080/01419870701599556.

Larmer, Miles. 'Permanent Precarity: Capital and Labour in the Central African Copperbelt'. *Labor History* 58, no. 2 (15 March 2017): 170–84. https://doi.org/10.1080/0023656X.2017.1298712.

Leonardi, Cherry. *Dealing with Government in South Sudan: Histories of Chiefship, Community & State*. Boydell & Brewer, 2013.

"'Liberation" or Capture: Youth in between "Hakuma", and "home" during Civil War and Its Aftermath in Southern Sudan'. *African Affairs* 106, no. 424 (24 April 2007): 391–412. https://doi.org/10.1093/afraf/adm037.

'The Poison in the Ink Bottle: Poison Cases and the Moral Economy of Knowledge in 1930s Equatoria, Sudan'. *Journal of Eastern African Studies* 1, no. 1 (1 March 2007): 34–56. https://doi.org/10.1080/17531050701218825.

'South Sudanese Arabic and the Negotiation of the Local State, c. 1840–2011'. *Journal of African History* 54, no. 3 (November 2013): 351–72. https://doi.org/10.1017/S0021853713000741.

'Violence, Sacrifice and Chiefship in Central Equatoria, Southern Sudan'. *Africa* 77, no. 4 (November 2007): 535–58. https://doi.org/10.3366/afr.2007.77.4.535.

Leonardi, Cherry, Deborah Isser, Leben Moro, and Martina Santschi. 'The Politics of Customary Law Ascertainment in South Sudan'. *Journal of Legal Pluralism and Unofficial Law* 43, no. 63 (2011): 111–42.

Lesch, Ann Mosely. *The Sudan: Contested National Identities*. Indiana Series in Arab and Islamic Studies. James Currey, 1998.

Lesch, Ann Mosely, and Osman A. Fadl, eds. *Coping with Torture: Images from Sudan*. Red Sea Press, 2004.

Lienhardt, Godfrey. *Divinity and Experience: The Religion of the Dinka*. Oxford University Press, 1961.

Lonsdale, John, and Bruce J. Berman. *Unhappy Valley: Conflict in Kenya and Africa*. J. Currey, 1992.

Lorins, Rebecca M. 'Inheritance: Kinship and the Performance of Sudanese Identities'. PhD dissertation, University of Texas at Austin, 2007. http://search.proquest.com/docview/304811283/46551306C88D402FPQ/94.

Lukudu, David L. 'Seiko Five'. *Warscapes* (blog), 6 August 2013. www.warscapes.com/retrospectives/literary-sudans/seiko-five.

Lund, Christian. 'Twilight Institutions: Public Authority and Local Politics in Africa'. *Development and Change* 37, no. 4 (2006): 685–705.

Madut-Arop, Arop. *Sudan's Painful Road to Peace: A Full Story of the Founding and Development of SPLM/SPLA*. BookSurge, 2006.

Magnusson, Warren. *Politics of Urbanism: Seeing like a City*. Routledge, 2013.

Mahgoub Ahmed, Asia. 'Urbanisation and the Folk Verse of the Humr'. In *Urbanization and Urban Life in the Sudan*, edited by Valdo Pons. Department of Sociology and Social Anthropology, University of Hull, 1980.

Makor, Ajack. *African National Front (A.N.F.): 50 Years of Political Struggle by Sudanese University Students*. Leesberg Enterprises, 2010.

Malik, Saadia Izzeldin. 'Displacement as Discourse'. *Ìrìnkèrindò: A Journal of African Migration*, 2005. www.africamigration.com/archive_02/s_malik.pdf.

Malkki, Liisa H. *Purity and Exile: Violence, Memory, and National Cosmology among Hutu Refugees in Tanzania*. University of Chicago Press, 1995.

Malok, Elijah. *The Southern Sudan: Struggle for Liberty*. Kenway Publications, 2009.

Malwal, Bona. *Sudan and South Sudan: From One to Two*. Palgrave Macmillan, 2014.

Manoeli, Sebabatso. 'Narrative Battles: Competing Discourses and Diplomacies of Sudan's "Southern Problem", 1961–1991'. PhD dissertation, University of Oxford, 2017.

Marung, Steffi. 'Out of Empire into Socialist Modernity: Soviet-African (Dis) Connections and Global Intellectual Geographies'. *Comparative Studies of South Asia, Africa and the Middle East* 41, no. 1 (1 May 2021): 56–70. https://doi.org/10.1215/1089201X-8916939.

Masland, Tom. 'Khartoum Bursting with Refugee Slums'. *Chicago Tribune*, 30 September 1988. http://articles.chicagotribune.com/1988-09-30/news/8802030490_1_khartoum-north-and-omdurman-refugees-war-zone.

Matlon, Jordanna. '"Elsewhere": An Essay on Borderland Ethnography in the Informal African City'. *Ethnography* 16, no. 2 (23 January 2014): 145–65. https://doi.org/10.1177/1466138113513527.

Mawson, Andrew N. M. 'Il Murahaleen Raids on the Dinka, 1985–89'. *Disasters* 15, no. 2 (1 June 1991): 137–49. https://doi.org/10.1111/j.1467-7717.1991.tb00443.x.

Mazrui, Ali A. 'The Black Arabs in Comparative Perspective: The Political Sociology of Race Mixture'. In *The Southern Sudan: The Problem of National Integration*, edited by Dunstan M. Wai, 47–82. Frank Cass, 1973.

Mbembe, Achille. *Critique of Black Reason*. Duke University Press Books, 2017.

McGrath, Siobhán, Ben Rogaly, and Louise Waite. 'Unfreedom in Labour Relations: From a Politics of Rescue to a Politics of Solidarity?' *Globalizations* 19, no. 6 (18 August 2022): 911–21. https://doi.org/10.1080/14747731.2022.2095119.

McLoughlin, Peter F. M. 'The Sudan's Three Towns: A Demographic and Economic Profile of an African Urban Complex. Part I. Introduction and Demography'. *Economic Development and Cultural Change* 12, no. 1 (1963): 70–83.

Medani, Khalid Mustafa. 'Black Monday: The Political and Economic Dimensions of Sudan's Urban Riot'. Middle East Research and Information Project, 9 August 2005. www.merip.org/mero/mero080905.

Meier, Larissa Carol. 'Returning to Northern Bahr El Ghazal, South Sudan', 2013. http://lup.lub.lu.se/luur/download?func=downloadFile&recordOId=3798928&fileOId=3798940.
Milford, Ismay. 'Federation, Partnership, and the Chronologies of Space in 1950s East and Central Africa'. *Historical Journal* 63, no. 5 (December 2020): 1325–48. https://doi.org/10.1017/S0018246X19000712.
Miller, Catherine. 'Juba Arabic as a Way of Expressing a Southern Sudanese Identity in Khartoum'. In *Contemporary Arabic Dialects: Proceedings of the 4th Aida Meeting*, edited by A. Youssi, 114–22. Marrakesh, 2000.
Language Change and National Integration: Rural Migrants in Khartoum. Khartoum University Press, 1992.
'Language, Identities and Ideologies: A New Era for Sudan'. In *Proceedings of the 7th International Sudan Studies Conference 2006*, 2006.
'Southern Sudanese Arabic and the Churches'. *ROMANIA, Revue Roumaine de Linguistique* 3–4 (2010): 383–400.
Miller, Catherine, Enam Al-Wer, Dominique Caubet, and Janet C. E. Watson. *Arabic in the City: Issues in Dialect Contact and Language Variation*. Routledge, 2007.
Mondesire, Zachary. 'The Worldliness of South Sudan: Space, Home and Racial Meaning Making in Post Independence Juba'. PhD dissertation, UCLA, 2018.
Moorman, Marissa J. *Intonations: A Social History of Music and Nation in Luanda, Angola, from 1945 to Recent Times*. Ohio University Press, 2008.
Moro, Leben Nelson. 'Interethnic Relations in Exile: The Politics of Ethnicity among Sudanese Refugees in Uganda and Egypt'. *Journal of Refugee Studies* 17, no. 4 (12 January 2004): 420–36. https://doi.org/10.1093/jrs/17.4.420.
Motasim, Hanaa. 'Deeply Divided Societies: Charting Strategies of Resistance'. *Respect, Sudanese Journal for Human Rights, Culture and Issues of Cultural Diversity*, no. 8 (August 2008).
Moyn, Samuel, and Andrew Sartori, eds. *Global Intellectual History*. Columbia Studies in International and Global History. Columbia University Press, 2013. https://doi.org/10.7312/moyn16048.
Mugaddam, Abdel Rahim Hamid. 'Language Maintenance and Shift in Sudan: The Case of Migrant Ethnic Groups in Khartoum'. *International Journal of the Sociology of Language* 2006, no. 181 (2006): 123–36. https://doi.org/10.1515/IJSL.2006.056.
Mukhtar, Al-Baqir al-Afif. 'The Crisis of Identity in Northern Sudan: A Dilemma of a Black People with a White Culture'. Paper presented at the CODSRIA African Humanities Institute Tenured by the Program of African Studies at the Northwestern University, Evanston, IL, 2004.

Nahr, Dominic. 'Can Archivists Save the World's Newest Nation?' *National Geographic News*, 3 November 2016. http://news.nationalgeographic.com/2016/11/south-sudan-archives/.
New York Times. 'With 84 Dead, Sudan Leaders Seek Calm'. 4 August 2005.
Newell, Stephanie. 'Articulating Empire: Newspaper Readerships in Colonial West Africa'. *New Formations* 73, no. 73 (25 November 2011): 26–42. https://doi.org/10.3898/NEWF.73.02.2011.
Newell, Stephanie, and Onookome Okome, eds. *Popular Culture in Africa: The Episteme of the Everyday*. Routledge, 2014.
Newhouse, Léonie. 'South Sudan Oyee! A Political Economy of Refugee Return Migration to Chukudum, South Sudan'. PhD thesis, University of Washington, 2013. https://digital.lib.washington.edu/researchworks/handle/1773/22623.
 'Urban Attractions: Returnee Youth, Mobility and the Search for a Future in South Sudan's Regional Towns'. Research Paper, New Issues in Refugee Research. United Nations High Commissioner for Refugees (UNHCR), January 2012.
News24. 'Deadly Violence Grips Sudan'. News24, 3 August 2005.
Nikkel, Marc R. 'Aspects of Contemporary Religious Change among the Dinka'. *Journal of Religion in Africa* 22, no. 1 (1992): 78–94.
 Dinka Christianity: The Origins and Development of Christianity among the Dinka of Sudan with Special Reference to the Songs of Dinka Christians. Paulines Publications, 2001.
 'Jieng "Songs of Suffering" and the Nature of God'. *Anglican and Episcopal History* 71, no. 2 (2002): 223–40.
Norwegian Refugee Council. 'Profile of Internal Displacement: Sudan'. Global IDP Database. Norwegian Refugee Council, 25 March 2005.
Nyaba, Peter Adwok. *The Politics of Liberation in South Sudan: An Insider's View*. Fountain Publishers, 1997.
 South Sudan: The State We Aspire To. Centre for Advanced Studies of African Society (CASAS), 2011.
O'Fahey, Rex Seán. 'Islam and Ethnicity in the Sudan'. *Journal of Religion in Africa* 26, no. 3 (1996): 258–67.
Omanga, Duncan, and Kipkosgei Arap Buigutt. 'Marx in Campus: Print Cultures, Nationalism and Student Activism in the Late 1970s Kenya'. *Journal of Eastern African Studies* 11, no. 4 (2017): 571–89.
Pantuliano, Sara. 'Going Home: Land, Return and Reintegration in Southern Sudan and the Three Areas'. In *Uncharted Territory: Land, Conflict and Humanitarian Action*, edited by Sara Pantuliano, 153–70. Practical Action Publishing, 2009.
 'Responding to Protracted Crises: The Principled Model of NMPACT in Sudan'. In *Beyond Relief: Food Security in Protracted Crisis*, edited by

Luca Alinovi, Günter Hemrich, and Luca Russo, 25–63. Practical Action Publishing, 2008.

Pantuliano, Sara, Margaret Buchanan-Smith, Victoria Metcalfe, Sara Pavanello, and Ellen Martin. 'City Limits: Urbanisation and Vulnerability in Sudan: Synthesis Report'. Humanitarian Policy Group, January 2011. http://kms2.isn.ethz.ch/serviceengine/Files/ESDP/141173/ipublicationdocument_single document/f01e3eb9-789a-43fd-81f4-a1aaed5863e9/en/6518.pdf.

Parker, Michael. *Children of the Sun: Stories of the Christian Journey in Sudan*. Faith in Sudan, no. 9. Paulines Publications Africa, 2000.

Pendle, Naomi. 'Contesting the Militarization of the Places Where They Met: The Landscapes of the Western Nuer and Dinka (South Sudan)'. *Journal of Eastern African Studies* 11, no. 1 (2 January 2017): 64–85. https://doi.org/10.1080/17531055.2017.1288408.

―――. 'The "Nuer of Dinka Money" and the Demands of the Dead: Contesting the Moral Limits of Monetised Politics in South Sudan'. *Conflict, Security & Development* 20, no. 5 (2 September 2020): 587–605. https://doi.org/10.1080/14678802.2020.1820161.

Perlez, Jane. 'Sudanese Troops Burn Refugee Camp, Forcing Residents to a Desert Site'. *New York Times*, 4 November 1990. www.nytimes.com/1990/11/04/world/sudanese-troops-burn-refugee-camp-forcing-residents-to-a-desert-site.html.

Peterson, Derek R. *Creative Writing: Translation, Bookkeeping, and the Work of Imagination in Colonial Kenya*. Social History of Africa. Heinemann, 2004.

―――. *Ethnic Patriotism and the East African Revival: A History of Dissent, c. 1935–1972*. Cambridge University Press, 2012.

―――. 'The Intellectual Lives of Mau Mau Detainees'. *Journal of African History* 49, no. 1 (March 2008): 73–91. https://doi.org/10.1017/S0021853708003411.

―――. 'Vernacular Language and Political Imagination'. In *Tracing Language Movement in Africa*, edited by Ericka A. Albaugh and Kathryn M. de Luna. Oxford University Press, 2018.

Peterson, Derek R., and Giacomo Macola, eds. *Recasting the Past: History Writing and Political Work in Modern Africa*. Ohio University Press, 2009.

Pierre, Jemima. '"I Like Your Colour!" Skin Bleaching and Geographies of Race in Urban Ghana'. *Feminist Review* 90, no. 1 (2008): 9–29. https://doi.org/10.1057/fr.2008.36.

―――. *The Predicament of Blackness: Postcolonial Ghana and the Politics of Race*. University of Chicago Press, 2012.

―――. 'Race in Africa Today: A Commentary'. *Cultural Anthropology* 28, no. 3 (2013): 547–51.

'Slavery, Anthropological Knowledge, and the Racialization of Africans'. *Current Anthropology* 61, no. S22 (1 October 2020): S220–S231. https://doi.org/10.1086/709844.
Plageman, Nate. 'Recomposing the Colonial City: Music, Space, and Middle-Class City Building in Sekondi, Gold Coast c. 1900–1920'. *Interventions* 22, no. 8 (2019): 1013–31. https://doi.org/10.1080/1369801X.2019.1659173.
Poggo, S. *The First Sudanese Civil War: Africans, Arabs, and Israelis in the Southern Sudan, 1955–1972*. Palgrave Macmillan US, 2011.
Pons, Valdo, ed. *Urbanization and Urban Life in the Sudan*. Department of Sociology and Social Anthropology, University of Hull, 1980.
Powell, Eve M. Troutt. *A Different Shade of Colonialism: Egypt, Great Britain, and the Mastery of the Sudan*. University of California Press, 2003.
——— 'Tell This in My Memory: Stories of Enslavement from Egypt, Sudan, and the Ottoman Empire'. In *Tell This in My Memory*. Stanford University Press, 2012. https://doi.org/10.1515/9780804783750.
Pratten, David. 'The Politics of Protection: Perspectives on Vigilantism in Nigeria'. *Africa* 78, special issue no. 1 (February 2008): 1–15. https://doi.org/10.3366/E0001972008000028.
——— *Return to the Roots? Migration, Local Institutions and Development in Sudan*. Occasional Papers (University of Edinburgh, Centre of African Studies), no. 82. Centre of African Studies, Edinburgh University, 2000.
Prinsloo, Mastin, and Mignonne Breier. *The Social Uses of Literacy: Theory and Practice in Contemporary South Africa*. John Benjamins Publishing, 1996.
Prunier, Gérard. *Darfur: The Ambiguous Genocide*. Crises in World Politics. Hurst, 2005.
Pulitzer Center. 'Mission to Sudan: Thousands from the South Escape War, but Not Hardship, in Camps Near Capital; Fighting Forces Refugees to Live'. 6 February 2002.
Rabaka, Reiland. *Routledge Handbook of Pan-Africanism*. Routledge, 2020. https://doi.org/10.4324/9780429020193.
Radio Tamazuj. 'Generals Say Juba Massacres Done by Private Militia, Not SPLA'. 9 March 2015. https://radiotamazuj.org/en/article/generals-say-juba-massacres-done-private-militia-not-spla.
Ramba, Justin Ambago. 'The Kambo and Jongo Business in the Sudanese Relationships'. *South Sudan News Agency*, 12 October 2012. www.southsudannewsagency.com/health/articles?start=99.
Reed, Adolph L. *Class Notes: Posing as Politics and Other Thoughts on the American Scene*. New Press, 2000.
Rehfisch, F. 'Rotating Credit Associations in the Three Towns'. In *Urbanization and Urban Life in the Sudan*, edited by Valdo Pons,

689–706. Department of Sociology and Social Anthropology, University of Hull, 1980.

'A Study of Some Southern Migrants in Omdurman'. *Sudan Notes and Records* 43 (1 January 1962): 50–104.

'An Unrecorded Population Count of Omdurman'. *Sudan Notes and Records* 46 (1 January 1965): 33–39.

Riek, Jedeit Jal, and Naomi R. Pendle. 'Speaking Truth to Power in South Sudan: Oral Histories of the Nuer Prophets'. South Sudan Customary Authorities Project. Rift Valley Institute, 2018.

Rogge, John. 'Relocation and Repatriation of Displaced Persons in Sudan: A Report to the Minister of Relief and Displaced Persons Affairs'. University of Manitoba, 1990.

Too Many, Too Long: Sudan's Twenty-Year Refugee Dilemma. Rowman & Allanheld, 1985.

Rolandsen, Øystein H. 'Another Civil War in South Sudan: The Failure of Guerrilla Government?' *Journal of Eastern African Studies* 9, no. 1 (2 January 2015): 163–74. https://doi.org/10.1080/17531055.2014.993210.

Guerrilla Government: Political Changes in the Southern Sudan during the 1990s. Nordic Africa Institute, 2005.

'The Making of the Anya-Nya Insurgency in the Southern Sudan, 1961–64'. *Journal of Eastern African Studies* 5, no. 2 (2011): 211–32.

Rolandsen, Øystein H., and Nicki Kindersley. 'The Nasty War: Organised Violence during the Anya-Nya Insurgency in South Sudan, 1963–72'. *Journal of African History* 60, no. 1 (March 2019): 87–107. https://doi.org/10.1017/S0021853719000367.

Rone, Jemera. *Behind the Red Line: Political Repression in Sudan.* Human Rights Watch, 1996.

Rossi, Benedetta. 'Dependence, Unfreedom and Slavery in Africa: Towards an Integrated Analysis'. *Africa* 86, no. 3 (August 2016): 571–90. https://doi.org/10.1017/S0001972016000504.

Russo, Luca. 'Crisis and Food Security Profile: Sudan'. In *Beyond Relief: Food Security in Protracted Crises*, edited by Luca Alinovi, Günter Hemrich, and Luca Russo, 13–24. Practical Action Publishing, 2008.

Ryle, John, and Kwaja Yai Kuol. 'Displaced Southern Sudanese in Northern Sudan with Special Reference to Southern Darfur and Kordofan'. Save the Children Fund (UK), February 1989.

Sajed, Alina. 'Interrogating the Postcolonial: On the Limits of Freedom, Subalternity, and Hegemonic Knowledge'. *International Studies Review* 20, no. 1 (1 March 2018): 152–60. https://doi.org/10.1093/isr/vix068.

Sanderson, Lilian Passmore, and Neville Sanderson. *Education, Religion & Politics in Southern Sudan 1899–1964.* Sudan Studies Series, no. 4. Ithaca Press, 1981.

Schomerus, Mareike, and Tim Allen. 'Southern Sudan at Odds with Itself: Dynamics of Conflict and Predicaments of Peace', 2010. http://eprints.lse.ac.uk/28869/.
Schomerus, Mareike, and Lotje De Vries. 'Just Cause or Crisis in the Making? How Self-Determination Was Interpreted to Achieve an Independent South Sudan'. In *Secessionism in Africa*, edited by W. Zeller and J. Thomas. Palgrave Macmillan, 2014.
Schouten, Peer, Ken Matthysen, and Thomas Muller. 'Checkpoint Economy: The Political Economy of Checkpoints in South Sudan, Ten Years after Independence'. Danish Institute for International Studies (DIIS), December 2021.
Scott, James C. *The Art of Not Being Governed: An Anarchist History of Upland Southeast Asia*. Yale University Press, 2009.
Weapons of the Weak: Everyday Forms of Peasant Resistance. Yale University Press, 2008.
Seri-Hersch, Iris. 'Education in Colonial Sudan, 1900–1957'. In *Oxford Research Encyclopedia of African History*. Oxford University Press, 2017.
Shadid, Anthony. 'Lurking Insecurity: Squatters in Khartoum'. *Middle East Report*, no. 216 (2000): 6. https://doi.org/10.2307/1520206.
Shakry, Omnia El. 'Rethinking Arab Intellectual History: Epistemology, Historicism, Secularism'. *Modern Intellectual History* 18, no. 2 (June 2021): 547–72. https://doi.org/10.1017/S1479244319000337.
Sharkey, Heather J. 'Arab Identity and Ideology in Sudan: The Politics of Language, Ethnicity, and Race'. *African Affairs* 107, no. 426 (1 January 2008): 21–43. https://doi.org/10.1093/afraf/adm068.
'A Century in Print: Arabic Journalism and Nationalism in Sudan, 1899–1999'. *International Journal of Middle East Studies* 31, no. 4 (November 1999): 531–49. https://doi.org/10.1017/S0020743800057081.
Sikainga, Ahmad Alawad. *'City of Steel and Fire': A Social History of Atbara, Sudan's Railway Town, 1906–1984*. Social History of Africa. Heinemann, 2002.
Organized Labor and Social Change in Contemporary Sudan. Durham Middle East Papers 74. University of Durham, Centre for Middle Eastern and Islamic Studies, 2003.
'Slavery, Labour, and Ethnicity in Khartoum: 1898–1956'. Draft article, 1980. Justice Africa SAD.307/6/1-65. Sudan Archives Durham.
Slaves into Workers: Emancipation and Labor in Colonial Sudan. Modern Middle East Series (University of Texas at Austin, Center for Middle Eastern Studies), no. 18. University of Texas Press, 1996.
Simone, AbdouMaliq. *City Life from Jakarta to Dakar: Movements at the Crossroads*. Global Realities. Routledge, 2010.

'People as Infrastructure: Intersecting Fragments in Johannesburg'. *Public Culture* 16, no. 3 (2004): 407–29.

The Sixty One. 'Emmanuel Kembe Profile', 2009. http://old.thesixtyone.com/kembemusic/.

Small Arms Survey. 'Pendulum Swings: The Rise and Fall of Insurgent Militias in South Sudan'. Human Security Baseline Assessment (HSBA) Issue Brief for Sudan and South Sudan. Small Arms Survey, November 2013.

Smith, Tom W. 'Changing Racial Labels: From "Colored" to "Negro" to "Black" to "African American"'. *Public Opinion Quarterly* 56, no. 4 (21 December 1992): 496–514. https://doi.org/10.1086/269339.

Sommers, Marc. *Islands of Education: Schooling, Civil War and the Southern Sudanese (1983–2004)*. UNESCO, International Institute for Educational Planning, 2005.

'The South Sudan Defence Force (SSDF): A Challenge to the Sudan Peace Process'. Institute for Security Studies, 8 April 2004.

Sowaka Mukhtar, Micah. 'Eye Opener: 24 Hours Dance'. *Khartoum Monitor*, 24 August 2010.

Sudan News & Views. 'Row over the "New Sudan Brigade"'. 6 April 1995, no. 7. www.africa.upenn.edu/Newsletters/SNV7.html.

'Sudan: Refugees in Their Own Country: The Forced Relocation of Squatters and Displaced People from Khartoum'. Africa Watch, 10 July 1992.

Sudan Tribune. 'Ex-Presidential Advisor Responds to Amnesty after Rebellion'. 2 October 2011.

  'S. Sudanese Army, Armed Men Clash in N. Bahr El Ghazal'. 27 April 2016.

  'South Sudan Says None of Its Soldiers Joined Former Presidential Adviser'. 24 March 2011.

Sugarman, Jane C. 'Imagining the Homeland: Poetry, Songs, and the Discourses of Albanian Nationalism'. *Ethnomusicology* 43, no. 3 (1 October 1999): 419–58. https://doi.org/10.2307/852556.

Theodossopoulos, Dimitrios, and Elisabeth Kirtsoglou. *United in Discontent: Local Responses to Cosmopolitanism and Globalization*. Berghahn Books, 2010.

Thomas, Edward. 'Moving towards Markets: Cash, Commodification and Conflict in South Sudan'. X-Border Local Research Network. Juba: Rift Valley Institute, June 2019.

  'Patterns of Growth and Inequality in Sudan, 1977–2017'. Durham Middle East Papers, 25. Durham, 2017.

  South Sudan: A Slow Liberation. Zed Books, 2015.

Thompson, Daniel K., Kader Mohamoud, and Jemal Yusuf Mahamed. 'Geopolitical Boundaries and Urban Borderlands in an Ethiopian

Frontier City'. *Urban Geography*, 20 September 2021, 1–25. https://doi.org/10.1080/02723638.2021.1979285.
Tisdall, Simon. 'South Sudan President Sacks Cabinet in Power Struggle'. *The Guardian*, 24 July 2013. www.theguardian.com/world/2013/jul/24/south-sudan-salva-kiir-sacks-cabinet.
Tomaney, John. 'Parochialism: A Defence'. *Progress in Human Geography* 37, no. 5 (2013): 658–72.
Tombe Stephen, Enock. *In Hope & Despair: Serving the People, Church and Nation of South Sudan*. N.p., 2015.
Tounsel, Christopher. *Chosen Peoples: Christianity and Political Imagination in South Sudan*. Duke University Press, 2021.
——— 'Khartoum Goliath: SPLM/SPLA Update and Martial Theology during the Second Sudanese Civil War'. *Journal of Africana Religions* 4, no. 2 (2016): 129–53.
——— 'Race, Religion and Resistance: Revelations from the Juba Archive'. *Journal of Eastern African Studies* 11, no. 2 (2017). https://doi.org/10.1080/17531055.2017.1305672.
——— 'Two Sudans, Human Rights, and the Afterlives of St. Josephine Bakhita'. In *Christianity and Human Rights Reconsidered*, edited by Daniel Steinmet, 261–75. Cambridge University Press, 2022.
Trudell, Barbara. 'When "Prof" Speaks, Who Listens? The African Elite and the Use of African Languages for Education and Development in African Communities'. *Language and Education* 24, no. 4 (1 June 2010): 337–52. https://doi.org/10.1080/09500781003678688.
Tuttle, Brendan R. 'Life Is Prickly: Narrating History, Belonging, and Common Place in Bor, South Sudan'. PhD thesis, Temple University, 2013.
United Nations Peacekeeping. 'A Renegade General Apologizes to Aweil Communities, Promises to Embrace Peace', 24 January 2019. https://peacekeeping.un.org/en/renegade-general-apologizes-to-aweil-communities-promises-to-embrace-peace.
Vezzadini, Elena. *Lost Nationalism: Revolution, Memory and Anti-colonial Resistance in Sudan*. Boydell & Brewer, 2015.
——— 'The 1924 Revolution Hegemony, Resistance, and Nationalism in the Colonial Sudan'. PhD thesis, University of Bergen, 2008.
——— 'Setting the Scene of the Crime: The Colonial Archive, History, and Racialisation of the 1924 Revolution in Anglo-Egyptian Sudan'. *Canadian Journal of African Studies/Revue Canadienne Des Études Africaines* 49, no. 1 (2015): 67–93.
——— 'Spies, Secrets, and a Story Waiting to Be (Re)Told: Memories of the 1924 Revolution and the Racialization of Sudanese History'. *Northeast African Studies* 13, no. 2 (2013): 53–92. https://doi.org/10.1353/nas.2013.0013.

de Waal, Alex. 'A Political Marketplace Framework Analysis'. London School of Economics, Conflict Research Programme occasional paper no. 19, August 2019.

'When Kleptocracy Becomes Insolvent: Brute Causes of the Civil War in South Sudan'. *African Affairs* 113, no. 452 (7 January 2014): 347–69. https://doi.org/10.1093/afraf/adu028.

'Who Are the Darfurians? Arab and African Identities, Violence and External Engagement'. *African Affairs* 104, no. 415 (1 April 2005): 181–205. https://doi.org/10.1093/afraf/adi035.

Waters, Mary C., and Tomás R. Jiménez. 'Assessing Immigrant Assimilation: New Empirical and Theoretical Challenges'. *Annual Review of Sociology* 31, no. 1 (2005): 105–25. https://doi.org/10.1146/annurev.soc.29.010202.100026.

Werner, Roland, William Anderson, and Andrew C. Wheeler. *Day of Devastation, Day of Contentment: The History of the Sudanese Church across 2000 Years*. Paulines Publications Africa, 2000.

White, Luise. *Speaking with Vampires: Rumor and History in Colonial Africa*. University of California Press, 2000.

Willis, Justin. 'The Southern Problem: Representing Sudan's Southern Provinces to c. 1970'. *Journal of African History* 56, no. 2 (2015): 281–300.

Wol, Stephen Akot. 'Education of Displaced Southern Students and Pupils in Northern Sudan'. In *The Displacement Problem in the Sudan: Essays on the Crisis*, edited by Eltigani El Tahir Eltigani and Hatim Ameer Mahran, 69–76. Draft manuscript, 1991. Sudan Archive Durham, SAD.940/5/2.

Woldemikael, Tekle M. 'Southern Migrants in a Northern Sudanese City'. *Horn of Africa* 8, no. 1 (1985): 26–31.

Wöndu, Steven. *From Bush to Bush: Journey to Liberty in South Sudan*. African Books Collective, 2011.

Young, Alden. 'The Intellectual Origins of Sudan's "Decades of Solitude," 1989–2019'. *Capitalism: A Journal of History and Economics* 2, no. 1 (2021): 196–226. https://doi.org/10.1353/cap.2021.0007.

Transforming Sudan. Cambridge University Press, 2018.

Young, Alden, and Keren Weitzberg. 'Globalizing Racism and De-provincializing Muslim Africa'. *Modern Intellectual History* 19, no. 3 (September 2022): 912–33. https://doi.org/10.1017/S1479244321000196.

Young, John. 'A Fractious Rebellion: Inside the SPLM-IO'. Geneva, Small Arms Survey, September 2015. www.smallarmssurveysudan.org/fileadmin/docs/working-papers/HSBA-WP39-SPLM-IO.pdf.

'The South Sudan Defence Forces in the Wake of the Juba Declaration'. Human Security Baseline Assessment (HSBA) Working Paper 1. Geneva: Small Arms Survey, 2007.

Zambakari, Christopher. 'South Sudan and the Nation-Building Project: Lessons and Challenges'. *International Journal of African Renaissance Studies - Multi-, Inter- and Transdisciplinarity* 8, no. 1 (1 June 2013): 5–29. https://doi.org/10.1080/18186874.2013.834552.

Zeitlyn, David. 'Anthropology in and of the Archives: Possible Futures and Contingent Pasts. Archives as Anthropological Surrogates'. *Annual Review of Anthropology* 41, no. 1 (2012): 461–80. https://doi.org/10.1146/annurev-anthro-092611-145721.

Zeleke, Elleni Centime. *Ethiopia in Theory: Revolution and Knowledge Production, 1964–2016*. Brill, 2019.

Zink, Jesse. *Christianity and Catastrophe in South Sudan: Civil War, Migration, and the Rise of Dinka Anglicanism*. Baylor University Press, 2018.

'Lost Boys, Found Church: Dinka Refugees and Religious Change in Sudan's Second Civil War'. *Journal of Ecclesiastical History* 68, no. 2 (April 2017): 340–60. https://doi.org/10.1017/S0022046916000683.

Index

Abbas Ghabboush, Philip, 235
abduction, 31, 200, 203, 268, 275
African identity, 136, 147
African National Front (ANF), 27, 169, 187, 232, 235–36, 241, 246
aid agencies, 17, 31, 34–35, 39, 63, 67, 84–88
Akol, Lam, 233, 270
Akut Kuei, 1, 162, 167, 173–75, 178, 180, 185, 193–95, 198, 203, 207, 210, 212, 219, 224, 226, 230–31, 251–55, 259, 266, 285, 287–88
al-Bashir, Omar, 13, 58, 157, 171, 220, 258, 263–64, 268
alcohol, 55, 62, 93–94, 98, 100, 110, 114, 126, 143, 191
  beer-brewing, 44, 90, 98, 102, 123, 247, 258
al-Mahdi, Sadig, 58, 63, 66, 83, 232, 275
Al-Turabi, Hassan, 58
Anglican Church, 111. *See also* Church Missionary Society (CMS)
Anglo-Egyptian Condominium, 41, 205, 269
Anya Nya, 62, 71, 170, 187, 207, 238, 273–74
Anyanya Two, 116, 243, 270, 274
Arab identity, 59–60, 75, 80
  Arabization (*t'arib*), 59, 64, 74–78, 80
  and names, 79, 178
armed forces of Sudan, 241, 247
  Haras Watani, 273, 276
  Joint Integrated Units, 292
  Popular Defence Forces (PDF), 84, 90–91, 220, 283, 285
  recruitment into, 43, 84, 90–91, 167, 263, 265–66, 277, 292
  Sudan Armed Forces (SAF), 84, 167, 220, 250, 263, 274–75, 281

arts movements, 154–55, 181, 198. *See also* Akut Kuei; Kwoto; Shabaab Club
theatre, 146, 153–54, 156
Ashara Wilayat, 107–8, 268–70, 272, 278, 301
Aweil Youth Union, 17, 33–34, 52, 60, 103, 109–10, 132, 138, 145
Ayii Akol, Abdel Bagi, 27, 107, 269–70, 272–79, 281, 285, 292, 295, 300
Ayii Akol, Hussein Abdel Bagi, 300–1

Bakhita, Saint, 119, 127
Black Monday, 289, 291–92
Blackness, 9, 11–12, 34, 43, 50, 58, 118–20, 204, 206, 217, 221–22, 290
  beauty, 129–31
  global Black cultures, 10, 100, 125, 127, 131, 213
bride wealth, 62, 106, 124, 126, 139, 226, 277, 281, 295

Cairo, 7, 34, 137, 153, 232
Catholic Archdiocese of Khartoum, 95, 112, 114, 149, 160, 169
  St Vincent de Paul, 150
cattle, 36, 48, 51, 56, 62, 81, 106, 159, 198, 204, 208, 221, 255
  raiding, 30, 259, 275
Christianity, 113, 127, 152, 158–59, 163, 202
  Bible translation, 147, 151–52, 174
  catechists, 112, 152, 170, 180
  conversions to, 75, 111–13
Church Missionary Society (CMS), 158
churches, 111, 150
  and education, 14, 46, 111, 187
  space, 3, 14, 111–14, 150–51, 155, 158, 174, 181, 234–35, 249, 263

336

Index 337

civilising project (*mashru al-hadari*), 58, 73, 75, 77–78
class, 109, 164, 188
  divides, 64, 82, 92, 115, 165–66, 231, 247–51, 303
  sell-outs, 223–24, 263, 285, 306
Communist party, 13, 172, 186, 218, 230, 232–33, 236
Comprehensive Peace Agreement (CPA), 28, 100, 269, 289, 291–93

Darfur, and Darfuri identity, 80, 120, 216, 220–22, 290
Deng Nhial, William, 30, 63, 195, 197, 206–8, 218, 254
Dinka Cultural Society, 1, 47, 73, 79, 89, 99, 120, 130, 147, 151–52, 173, 175, 180, 185, 189, 204, 222, 251

Ed-Daein massacre (1987), 173, 203
education, 5, 13–14, 26, 45, 81, 142, 168, 197, 238. *See also* University of Juba; University of Khartoum
  Catholic schools, 159, 161–62
  Comboni Ground, 54–55, 114, 142, 154, 159, 234, 237, 241, 251
  funding for, 1, 110, 150–51, 160, 162, 166, 168, 174
  higher education, 3, 90, 110, 157, 161, 167, 169–70, 177, 181, 187, 198, 231–32, 234–35, 242, 246–48, 261, 283
  independent and night schools, 3, 81, 109–10, 112, 114, 145, 150, 157, 160, 162, 236
  secondary schools, 46, 159–61, 167
elections, 233, 273, 275, 294
Ethiopia, 17, 31, 138, 240, 257–59, 261, 282, 286, 302
ethnicity, 11–12, 97, 211, 213–14, 220, 281
  and language, 98, 190
  and social organisation, 50, 52, 97, 99, 101, 191, 286
  and tribalism, 50, 98, 116, 212, 280, 304

famine, 16, 24, 29, 31, 33, 35–36, 44, 61, 109, 202, 205, 221, 225, 274, 277, 280, 302–3

gangs, 96, 99–100, 103–4, 126, 138–39, 212, 279
  vigilantism, 96, 103, 290–91
Garang de Mabior, John, 13, 28, 60, 148, 172, 190, 192, 203, 217, 219, 222, 225, 237, 241, 250, 259, 288–91, 293
Gatdet, Peter, 300
gender, 122
  clothing and styling, 126–27, 129, 132
  gender norms, 96, 125, 132, 135, 140, 205
  sex and pregnancy, 100, 121, 127, 135, 139–40, 191, 278–80
  women's work, 46–47, 123, 125, 136, 236

Islam, 79
  conversion to, 64, 79–80, 117, 260, 273
  Islamization (*hidayah*), 59, 75–78, 82, 91

Juba, 24, 36, 39, 46, 104, 168, 194, 203, 232, 240, 282, 297–98, 301, 304, 308
Juba Arabic, 56, 131, 136, 149–50
Juba Declaration (2006), 292

kasha, 72–73, 75, 124, 143, 150, 157
Katip (or Diin) Ajer, 242–43, 292
Kembe, Emmanuel, 153, 175, 209, 288
Kenya, 17, 176
Khartoum Agreement (1997), 264, 271
Khartoum urban authorities, 61–62, 74, 78, 85, 91, 103, 265
  Popular Committees (*lejna shaabiya*), 64, 79, 85, 88, 265
Kiir Mayardit, Salva, 274, 292, 298–301, 304
Kongor Arop, George, 69
Kuanyin Bol, Kerubino, 27, 203, 216, 243–44, 270–71
Kwoto, 146, 154–56, 174, 180, 201

labour, 9, 27, 41–44, 46, 53, 59, 72, 82–84, 87, 276–77, 281, 287
  and abduction, 31
  forced, 30–32, 84, 107

labour (cont.)
  and identification with tribes, 42, 49
  jongo, 116, 176, 231, 243, 251, 253, 256–60, 280, 282
  and paid work in Khartoum, 18, 36, 40, 46–47, 51, 63, 83, 267
Lagu, Joseph, 71–72
land and neighbourhoods, 53, 59, 62, 73, 94, 116, 208, 293
  bulldozing and demolition, 59, 64, 66–74, 84, 93–94, 103, 166
  negotiations, demarcation and registration, 54, 69–71
  returnees, 68, 288, 294–97
language, 190, 297
  Arabic language, 149
  education, 134, 147–48, 153, 253
  and naming of places, 25, 54–57, 297
  and orthography, 149, 151, 174
  Summer Institute for Linguistics, 147, 151–52, 167

Macham, Deng, 244, 269, 301
Machar Teny, Riek, 244, 270–72, 298, 303
Malcolm X, 127, 194
Mandela, Nelson, 8, 55, 127, 204, 213
marriage, 6, 51, 80, 101, 105–6, 118, 124, 126, 129, 136, 139, 205, 212, 226, 270, 295
  divorce, 105, 135–36, 139
  and ethnicity, 126, 139
Matip, Paulino, 27, 107, 244, 263, 270–72, 276–77, 279–80, 285, 291–92
Mboro, Clement, 63
mental health crises, 36, 93, 95, 98–99, 113, 177, 192
  and suicide, 36
militias, 19, 27, 98, 107, 138, 231, 264, 270, 272, 276, 285, 291. *See also* Southern Sudan Defence Forces (SSDF)
  Mathiang Anyoor, 298–99
  murahaleen, 1, 29–30, 275
  Peace Forces, 277
money, 106, 126, 225–26
  and debt, 105–7
  and savings, 108, 112

music, 153–54
  cassette tapes, 4, 14, 24, 149, 173, 178–79, 186, 195, 227, 252, 255–56
  and songs, 16, 23, 156, 175–76, 183–84, 206, 216, 251

National Action Movement, 232
National Congress Party (NCP), 83, 85, 101, 171, 235, 269
National Democratic Alliance, 27, 77, 83, 230, 234, 236, 240–41, 245, 259, 261, 271
National Islamic Front (NIF), 58, 63–64, 66, 75, 83, 171, 284
National Salvation Front (NSF) (al-Ingaz), 58, 63
New Khartoum, 20, 28, 297
New Sudan, 13, 60, 173, 188, 192, 217, 236, 245, 271, 285, 289, 305
Nimeiri, Gaffar, 58, 71, 73–74, 153, 218, 232–33
Nuba Mountains, 23, 25, 29, 45, 49, 51, 53, 111, 115, 120, 139, 154, 158, 169, 205, 216, 218, 221, 233, 236–37, 246, 259, 290, 294, 296

oil, 226, 278, 288
Operation Lifeline Sudan, 87–88
Ottoman empire, 40, 269

Paulino Mesaka, General, 136, 149, 153–54, 174, 180, 193, 209, 255, 308
peace villages (*dar es salaams*), 57, 67–69, 79, 87, 123, 157, 250, 267, 280
Philip Abbas Ghabboush, 112, 169, 205, 233
policing, 64, 78, 90–91, 103–4, 107, 146, 163, 265, 278–79
  detention and torture, 89, 91–92, 98, 102, 124, 170, 237, 239, 243–44, 246–47, 250, 256, 265, 281, 292
  national security services, 64, 101, 188, 240, 246, 260, 263
Popular Defence Forces (PDF), 84, 90–91, 220, 283, 285
publishing, 21, 152, 171–72, 174, 179, 181, 183, 186, 188–90
  fax machines, 7, 14, 239
  of history, 171–72, 202–5, 220

Khartoum Monitor, 173, 189, 239, 284, 294
newspapers, 18
self-publishing, 22, 27, 171, 178, 184, 189, 237–38
The Vigilant, 186

race and racism, 52, 60, 62, 72, 80, 82, 100, 291
  language and labels, 43–44, 50, 73
  skin colour and bleaching, 129–30, 136, 178, 191, 213
radio, 14, 21, 149, 153–54, 162, 187–88, 240, 289
  SPLA Radio, 18, 138, 148–49, 177, 188, 240
Relief and Rehabilitation Commission (RRC), 63, 85–86

secession, 1, 28, 232, 236–37, 245, 261, 265, 285, 294–95, 306
Shabaab Club, 153
slavery, 9, 31, 43, 89, 94, 197, 204–6, 215, 221, 275
  history of, 9, 12, 16, 40–45, 49, 55, 61, 70, 72, 114, 119, 149, 172, 187, 203–4
social life, 51, 100, 110, 112, 114, 118, 126
  clubs, 51, 108, 110–11, 114, 153, 158, 161, 165, 240
  dances, 3, 51, 108, 117, 122, 132, 135, 143, 150, 154–55, 163, 169, 174, 186, 252
Southern Sudan Defence Forces (SSDF), 271, 277, 285–86, 291–92
Southern Sudan Liberation Movement/Front, 232
SPLM/A, 1, 16, 18, 27–28, 30–31, 60, 89, 95, 114, 124, 148, 153, 163, 167, 170, 176, 181, 187–88, 203, 216–17, 221, 231, 236–38, 240–46, 250–52, 254, 256–62, 264–65, 270–71, 274, 277, 279–80, 282, 285–86, 288–89, 292, 298–300, 308
  1991 split, 98, 169, 217, 236, 270, 299
  battalions, 242, 250–51, 260, 282, 292, 298
  manifesto, 13, 172, 217, 238
  New Sudan Brigade, 27, 232, 259
St Vincent de Paul, 150
Sudan African National Union (SANU), 48, 63, 145, 206, 218, 233
Sudan Armed Forces (SAF), 84, 167, 220, 250, 263, 274–75, 281
Sudan Council of Churches, 67, 88, 235, 241, 244, 249, 265
SudanAid, 33, 35, 38, 53

teachers, 13, 81, 90, 109, 134, 143–45, 154, 157–58, 160, 162–65, 167, 169–72, 180–81, 188, 198, 235, 237–41, 244, 246–47, 249, 252
  of history, 163–64, 171–72, 202, 233
  of southern languages, 147–52, 163, 252
  women, 168
traditional authorities, chiefs, 34, 38–39, 101, 105, 108, 138
  and arbitration, 102–5, 264, 267–69, 278–79
  creation of, 38–39
  networks of, 38, 101, 107, 268, 301
  South Sudan Council of Chiefs, 301

Union of Southern African Parties (USAP), 166, 233, 235, 238, 241, 245, 271
University of Juba, 143, 160, 170, 244, 248
University of Khartoum, 165–67, 186–87, 240
urban ethnic associations, 33–34, 40, 50, 52, 101, 109, 138. *See also* Aweil Youth Union
  funding of, 248

Zubeir Wako, Gabriel, 114

African Studies Series

1 *City Politics: A Study of Leopoldville, 1962–63*, J. S. La Fontaine
2 *Studies in Rural Capitalism in West Africa*, Polly Hill
3 *Land Policy in Buganda*, Henry W. West
4 *The Nigerian Military: A Sociological Analysis of Authority and Revolt, 1960–67*, Robin Luckham
5 *The Ghanaian Factory Worker: Industrial Man in Africa*, Margaret Peil
6 *Labour in the South African Gold Mines*, Francis Wilson
7 *The Price of Liberty: Personality and Politics in Colonial Nigeria*, Kenneth W. J. Post and George D. Jenkins
8 *Subsistence to Commercial Farming in Present-Day Buganda: An Economic and Anthropological Survey*, Audrey I. Richards, Fort Sturrock, and Jean M. Fortt (eds)
9 *Dependence and Opportunity: Political Change in Ahafo*, John Dunn and A. F. Robertson
10 *African Railwaymen: Solidarity and Opposition in an East African Labour Force*, R. D. Grillo
11 *Islam and Tribal Art in West Africa*, René A. Bravmann
12 *Modern and Traditional Elites in the Politics of Lagos*, P. D. Cole
13 *Asante in the Nineteenth Century: The Structure and Evaluation of a Political Order*, Ivor Wilks
14 *Culture, Tradition and Society in the West African Novel*, Emmanuel Obiechina
15 *Saints and Politicians*, Donal B. Cruise O'Brien
16 *The Lions of Dagbon: Political Change in Northern Ghana*, Martin Staniland
17 *Politics of Decolonization: Kenya Europeans and the Land Issue 1960–1965*, Gary B. Wasserman
18 *Muslim Brotherhoods in the Nineteenth-Century Africa*, B. G. Martin
19 *Warfare in the Sokoto Caliphate: Historical and Sociological Perspectives*, Joseph P. Smaldone
20 *Liberia and Sierra Leone: An Essay in Comparative Politics*, Christopher Clapham
21 *Adam Kok's Griquas: A Study in the Development of Stratification in South Africa*, Robert Ross
22 *Class, Power and Ideology in Ghana: The Railwaymen of Sekondi*, Richard Jeffries
23 *West African States: Failure and Promise*, John Dunn (ed)

24 *Afrikaaners of the Kalahari: White Minority in a Black State*, Margo Russell and Martin Russell
25 *A Modern History of Tanganyika*, John Iliffe
26 *A History of African Christianity 1950–1975*, Adrian Hastings
27 *Slaves, Peasants and Capitalists in Southern Angola, 1840–1926*, W. G. Clarence-Smith
28 *The Hidden Hippopotamus: Reappraised in African History: The Early Colonial Experience in Western Zambia*, Gywn Prins
29 *Families Divided: The Impact of Migrant Labour in Lesotho*, Colin Murray
30 *Slavery, Colonialism and Economic Growth in Dahomey, 1640–1960*, Patrick Manning
31 *Kings, Commoners and Concessionaries: The Evolution of Dissolution of the Nineteenth-Century Swazi State*, Philip Bonner
32 *Oral Poetry and Somali Nationalism: The Case of Sayid Mahammad 'Abdille Hasan*, Said S. Samatar
33 *The Political Economy of Pondoland 1860–1930*, William Beinart
34 *Volkskapitalisme: Class, Capitals and Ideology in the Development of Afrikaner Nationalism, 1934–1948*, Dan O'Meara
35 *The Settler Economies: Studies in the Economic History of Kenya and Rhodesia 1900–1963*, Paul Mosely
36 *Transformations in Slavery: A History of Slavery in Africa*, 1st edition, Paul Lovejoy
37 *Amilcar Cabral: Revolutionary Leadership and People's War*, Patrick Chabal
38 *Essays on the Political Economy of Rural Africa*, Robert H. Bates
39 *Ijeshas and Nigerians: The Incorporation of a Yoruba Kingdom, 1890s–1970s*, J. D. Y. Peel
40 *Black People and the South African War, 1899–1902*, Peter Warwick
41 *A History of Niger 1850–1960*, Finn Fuglestad
42 *Industrialisation and Trade Union Organization in South Africa, 1924–1955*, Stephen Ellis
43 *The Rising of the Red Shawls: A Revolt in Madagascar 1895–1899*, Stephen Ellis
44 *Slavery in Dutch South Africa*, Nigel Worden
45 *Law, Custom and Social Order: The Colonial Experience in Malawi and Zambia*, Martin Chanock
46 *Salt of the Desert Sun: A History of Salt Production and Trade in the Central Sudan*, Paul E. Lovejoy

47 *Marrying Well: Marriage, Status and Social Change among the Educated Elite in Colonial Lagos*, Kristin Mann
48 *Language and Colonial Power: The Appropriation of Swahili in the Former Belgian Congo, 1880–1938*, Johannes Fabian
49 *The Shell Money of the Slave Trade*, Jan Hogendorn and Marion Johnson
50 *Political Domination in Africa*, Patrick Chabal
51 *The Southern Marches of Imperial Ethiopia: Essays in History and Social Anthropology*, Donald Donham and Wendy James
52 *Islam and Urban Labor in Northern Nigeria: The Making of a Muslim Working Class*, Paul M. Lubeck
53 *Horn and Crescent: Cultural Change and Traditional Islam on the East African Coast, 800–1900*, Randall L. Pouwels
54 *Capital and Labour on the Kimberley Diamond Fields, 1871–1890*, Robert Vicat Turrell
55 *National and Class Conflict in the Horn of Africa*, John Markakis
56 *Democracy and Prebendal Politics in Nigeria: The Rise and Fall of the Second Republic*, Richard A. Joseph
57 *Entrepreneurs and Parasites: The Struggle for Indigenous Capitalism in Zaire*, Janet MacGaffey
58 *The African Poor: A History*, John Iliffe
59 *Palm Oil and Protest: An Economic History of the Ngwa Region, South-Eastern Nigeria, 1800–1980*, Susan M. Martin
60 *France and Islam in West Africa, 1860–1960*, Christopher Harrison
61 *Transformation and Continuity in Revolutionary Ethiopia*, Christopher Clapham
62 *Prelude to the Mahdiyya: Peasants and Traders in the Shendi Region, 1821–1885*, Anders Bjorkelo
63 *Wa and the Wala: Islam and Polity in Northwestern Ghana*, Ivor Wilks
64 *H. C. Bankole-Bright and Politics in Colonial Sierra Leone, 1919–1958*, Akintola Wyse
65 *Contemporary West African States*, Donal Cruise O'Brien, John Dunn, and Richard Rathbone (eds)
66 *The Oromo of Ethiopia: A History, 1570–1860*, Mohammed Hassen
67 *Slavery and African Life: Occidental, Oriental, and African Slave Trades*, Patrick Manning
68 *Abraham Esau's War: A Black South African War in the Cape, 1899–1902*, Bill Nasson

69 *The Politics of Harmony: Land Dispute Strategies in Swaziland*, Laurel L. Rose
70 *Zimbabwe's Guerrilla War: Peasant Voices*, Norma J. Kriger
71 *Ethiopia: Power and Protest: Peasant Revolts in the Twentieth-Century*, Gebru Tareke
72 *White Supremacy and Black Resistance in Pre-Industrial South Africa: The Making of the Colonial Order in the Eastern Cape, 1770–1865*, Clifton C. Crais
73 *The Elusive Granary: Herder, Farmer, and State in Northern Kenya*, Peter D. Little
74 *The Kanyok of Zaire: An Institutional and Ideological History to 1895*, John C. Yoder
75 *Pragmatism in the Age of Jihad: The Precolonial State of Bundu*, Michael A. Gomez
76 *Slow Death for Slavery: The Course of Abolition in Northern Nigeria, 1897–1936*, Paul E. Lovejoy and Jan S. Hogendorn
77 *West African Slavery and Atlantic Commerce: The Senegal River Valley, 1700–1860*, James F. Searing
78 *A South African Kingdom: The Pursuit of Security in the Nineteenth-Century Lesotho*, Elizabeth A. Elredge
79 *State and Society in Pre-colonial Asante*, T. C. McCaskie
80 *Islamic Society and State Power in Senegal: Disciples and Citizens in Fatick*, Leonardo A. Villalon
81 *Ethnic Pride and Racial Prejudice in Victorian Cape Town: Group Identity and Social Practice*, Vivian Bickford-Smith
82 *The Eritrean Struggle for Independence: Domination, Resistance and Nationalism, 1941–1993*, Ruth Iyob
83 *Corruption and State Politics in Sierra Leone*, William Reno
84 *The Culture of Politics in Modern Kenya*, Angelique Haugerud
85 *Africans: The History of a Continent*, 1st edition, John Iliffe
86 *From Slave Trade to 'Legitimate' Commerce: The Commercial Transition in Nineteenth-Century West Africa*, Robin Law (ed)
87 *Leisure and Society in Colonial Brazzaville*, Phyllis Martin
88 *Kingship and State: The Buganda Dynasty*, Christopher Wrigley
89 *Decolonialization and African Life: The Labour Question in French and British Africa*, Frederick Cooper
90 *Misreading the African Landscape: Society and Ecology in an African Forest-Savannah Mosaic*, James Fairhead and Melissa Leach
91 *Peasant Revolution in Ethiopia: The Tigray People's Liberation Front, 1975–1991*, John Young
92 *Senegambia and the Atlantic Slave Trade*, Boubacar Barry

93 *Commerce and Economic Change in West Africa: The Oil Trade in the Nineteenth Century*, Martin Lynn
94 *Slavery and French Colonial Rule in West Africa: Senegal, Guinea and Mali*, Martin A. Klein
95 *East African Doctors: A History of the Modern Profession*, John Iliffe
96 *Middlemen of the Cameroons Rivers: The Duala and Their Hinterland, c. 1600–1960*, Ralph Derrick, Ralph A. Austen, and Jonathan Derrick
97 *Masters and Servants on the Cape Eastern Frontier, 1760–1803*, Susan Newton-King
98 *Status and Respectability in the Cape Colony, 1750–1870: A Tragedy of Manners*, Robert Ross
99 *Slaves, Freedmen and Indentured Laborers in Colonial Mauritius*, Richard B. Allen
100 *Transformations in Slavery: A History of Slavery in Africa*, 2nd edition, Paul E. Lovejoy
101 *The Peasant Cotton Revolution in West Africa: Cote d'Ivoire, 1880–1995*, Thomas J. Bassett
102 *Re-imagining Rwanda: Conflict, Survival and Disinformation in the Late Twentieth Century*, Johan Pottier
103 *The Politics of Evil: Magic, State Power and the Political Imagination in South Africa*, Clifton Crais
104 *Transforming Mozambique: The Politics of Privatization, 1975–2000*, M. Anne Pitcher
105 *Guerrilla Veterans in Post-War Zimbabwe: Symbolic and Violent Politics, 1980–1987*, Norma J. Kriger
106 *An Economic History of Imperial Madagascar, 1750–1895: The Rise and Fall of an Island Empire*, Gwyn Campbell
107 *Honour in African History*, John Iliffe
108 *Africans: A History of a Continent*, 2nd edition, John Iliffe
109 *Guns, Race, and Power in Colonial South Africa*, William Kelleher Storey
110 *Islam and Social Change in French West Africa: History of an Emancipatory Community*, Sean Hanretta
111 *Defeating Mau Mau, Creating Kenya: Counterinsurgency, Civil War and Decolonization*, Daniel Branch
112 *Christianity and Genocide in Rwanda*, Timothy Longman
113 *From Africa to Brazil: Culture, Identity, and an African Slave Trade, 1600–1830*, Walter Hawthorne
114 *Africa in the Time of Cholera: A History of Pandemics from 1817 to the Present*, Myron Echenberg

115 *A History of Race in Muslim West Africa, 1600–1960*, Bruce S. Hall
116 *Witchcraft and Colonial Rule in Kenya, 1900–1955*, Katherine Luongo
117 *Transformations in Slavery: A History of Slavery in Africa*, 3rd edition, Paul E. Lovejoy
118 *The Rise of the Trans-Atlantic Slave Trade in Western Africa, 1300–1589*, Toby Green
119 *Party Politics and Economic Reform in Africa's Democracies*, M. Anne Pitcher
120 *Smugglers and Saints of the Sahara: Regional Connectivity in the Twentieth Century*, Judith Scheele
121 *Cross-Cultural Exchange in the Atlantic World: Angola and Brazil during the Era of the Slave Trade*, Roquinaldo Ferreira
122 *Ethnic Patriotism and the East African Revival*, Derek Peterson
123 *Black Morocco: A History of Slavery and Islam*, Chouki El Hamel
124 *An African Slaving Port and the Atlantic World: Benguela and Its Hinterland*, Mariana Candido
125 *Making Citizens in Africa: Ethnicity, Gender, and National Identity in Ethiopia*, Lahra Smith
126 *Slavery and Emancipation in Islamic East Africa: From Honor to Respectability*, Elisabeth McMahon
127 *A History of African Motherhood: The Case of Uganda, 700–1900*, Rhiannon Stephens
128 *The Borders of Race in Colonial South Africa: The Kat River Settlement, 1829–1856*, Robert Ross
129 *From Empires to NGOs in the West African Sahel: The Road to Nongovernmentality*, Gregory Mann
130 *Dictators and Democracy in African Development: The Political Economy of Good Governance in Nigeria*, A. Carl LeVan
131 *Water, Civilization and Power in Sudan: The Political Economy of Military-Islamist State Building*, Harry Verhoeven
132 *The Fruits of Freedom in British Togoland: Literacy, Politics and Nationalism, 1914–2014*, Kate Skinner
133 *Political Thought and the Public Sphere in Tanzania: Freedom, Democracy and Citizenship in the Era of Decolonization*, Emma Hunter
134 *Political Identity and Conflict in Central Angola, 1975–2002*, Justin Pearce
135 *From Slavery to Aid: Politics, Labour, and Ecology in the Nigerian Sahel, 1800–2000*, Benedetta Rossi

136 *National Liberation in Postcolonial Southern Africa: A Historical Ethnography of SWAPO's Exile Camps*, Christian A. Williams
137 *Africans: A History of a Continent*, 3rd edition, John Iliffe
138 *Colonial Buganda and the End of Empire: Political Thought and Historical Imagination in Africa*, Jonathon L. Earle
139 *The Struggle over State Power in Zimbabwe: Law and Politics since 1950*, George Karekwaivanane
140 *Transforming Sudan: Decolonisation, Economic Development and State Formation*, Alden Young
141 *Colonizing Consent: Rape and Governance in South Africa's Eastern Cape*, Elizabeth Thornberry
142 *The Value of Disorder: Autonomy, Prosperity and Plunder in the Chadian Sahara*, Julien Brachet and Judith Scheele
143 *The Politics of Poverty: Policy-Making and Development in Rural Tanzania*, Felicitas Becker
144 *Boundaries, Communities, and State-Making in West Africa: The Centrality of the Margins*, Paul Nugent
145 *Politics and Violence in Burundi: The Language of Truth in an Emerging State*, Aidan Russell
146 *Power and the Presidency in Kenya: The Jomo Kenyatta Years*, Anaïs Angelo
147 *East Africa after Liberation: Conflict, Security and the State since the 1980s*, Jonathan Fisher
148 *Sultan, Caliph, and the Renewer of the Faith: Ahmad Lobbo, the Tārīkh al-fattāsh and the Making of an Islamic State in West Africa*, Mauro Nobili
149 *Shaping the African Savannah: From Capitalist Frontier to Arid Eden in Namibia*, Michael Bollig
150 *France's Wars in Chad: Military Intervention and Decolonization in Africa*, Nathaniel K. Powell
151 *Islam, Ethnicity, and Conflict in Ethiopia: The Bale Insurgency, 1963–1970*, Terje Østebø
152 *The Path to Genocide in Rwanda: Security, Opportunity, and Authority in an Ethnocratic State*, Omar Shahabudin McDoom
153 *Development, (Dual) Citizenship and Its Discontents in Africa: The Political Economy of Belonging to Liberia*, Robtel Neajai Pailey
154 *Salafism and Political Order in Africa*, Sebastian Elischer
155 *Performing Power in Zimbabwe: Politics, Law and the Courts since 2000*, Susanne Verheul

156 *Revolutionary State-Making in Dar es Salaam: African Liberation and the Global Cold War, 1961–1974*, George Roberts
157 *Race and Diplomacy in Zimbabwe: The Cold War and Decolonization, 1960–1984*, Timothy Lewis Scarnecchia
158 *Conflicts of Colonialism: The Rule of Law, French Soudan, and Faama Mademba Sèye*, Richard L. Roberts
159 *Invoking the Invisible in the Sahara: Islam, Spiritual Mediation, and Social Change*, Erin Pettigrew
160 *Wealth, Land, and Property in Angola: A History of Dispossession, Slavery and Inequality*, Mariana P. Candido
161 *Trajectories of Authoritarianism in Rwanda: Elusive Control before the Genocide*, Marie-Eve Desrosiers
162 *Plunder for Profit: A Socio-environmental History of Tobacco Farming in Southern Rhodesia and Zimbabwe*, Elijah Doro
163 *Navigating Local Transitional Justice: Agency at Work in Post-Conflict Sierra Leone*, Laura S. Martin
164 *Arming Black Consciousness: The Azanian Black Nationalist Tradition and South Africa's Armed Struggle*, Toivo Tukongeni Paul Wilson Asheeke
165 *Child Slavery and Guardianship in Colonial Senegal*, Bernard Moitt
166 *African Military Politics in the Sahel: Regional Organizations and International Politics*, Katharina P.W. Döring
167 *Black Soldiers in the Rhodesian Army: Colonialism, Professionalism, and Race*, M. T. Howard
168 *Ethiopia's 'Developmental State': Political Order and Distributive Crisis*, Tom Lavers
169 *Money, Value and the State: Sovereignty and Citizenship in East Africa*, Kevin Donovan
170 *New Sudans: Wartime Intellectual Histories in Khartoum*, Nicki Kindersley
171 *Smugglers, Speculators, and the City in the Ethiopia-Somalia Borderlands*, Daniel K. Thompson